THE DAY AFTER
TOMORROW

THE DAY AFTER
TOMORROW

A Handbook on the Future of Economic Policy in the Developing World

OTAVIANO CANUTO

AND

MARCELO GIUGALE

Editors

THE WORLD BANK
Washington, D.C.

1818 H Street NW
Washington DC 20433
Telephone: 202-473-1000
Internet: www.worldbank.org

ISBN: 978-0-8213-8498-5
eISBN: 978-0-8213-8546-3
DOI: 10.1596/978-0-8213-8498-5

Library of Congress Cataloging-in-Publication Data
The day after tomorrow : a handbook on the future of economic policy in the developing world / Otaviano Canuto and Marcelo Giugale, editors.
    p. cm.
  Includes bibliographical references and index.
  ISBN 978-0-8213-8498-5 — ISBN 978-0-8213-8546-3 (electronic)
  1. Developing countries—Economic policy. 2. Poverty—Developing countries. 3. Developing countries—Foreign economic relations. I. Canuto, Otaviano. II. Giugale, Marcelo.
  HC59.7.D344 2010
  338.9009172'4—dc22

                                       2010033308

Cover art: Michael S. Geller, *Je Suis Ailleurs/I Am Elsewhere*, 2010, oil on canvas, 48" × 60"
Cover design: Drew Fasick
Photo credit: Dave Scavone

Contents

Boxes

Figures

Tables

Preface

The global financial crisis of 2008–09 changed not only the global economic order, but also the way we think about that order. Principles and practices that were once accepted wisdom are now in doubt or discredited. New and fundamental questions have opened. And the search for answers has barely begun.

For the countries of the developing world, this conceptual uncertainty is particularly uncomfortable—through a combination of good policies and good luck, they had begun to achieve real progress. Will all that now be derailed? What does the new horizon hold for them? Can they find new policy ideas that will turn the shock of the crisis into a final run toward "developed" status? How does the future look when seen from various geographic regions?

These are the kind of questions that we asked a group of our colleagues at the World Bank during the summer of 2010. This book is an unfiltered collection of their views. As seasoned practitioners in the leading development institution, they have a unique perspective from which to visualize—we would dare say "to sense"—what may be coming. Some of them look at the big picture of the role that the developing world is about to play and the way it will play that role. Others walk us through the conceptual links around specific issues that will affect that world—say, the likely evolution of macrofinancial regulation. And others take us to continents and countries, teach us about their realities, and tell us how life will differ in the coming years. Put together, they paint a picture of reasoned optimism.

Why?

Because developing countries as a whole face an unprecedented opportunity. Most have shown to themselves that, with good management, prosperity is possible and need not be the privilege of their elites. These countries are integrating with each other and catching up technologically with advanced economies. Many have natural resources that will remain in high demand. And all are now heard more loudly, their relevance embedded in the fabric of the G-20 and in the improved governance of multilaterals.

Does this situation mean the endgame for the fight against poverty? Will we soon erase the word "developing" from our technical lingo? Probably not—at least not for a while. But it is a time to step up the pace of development. To go for that endgame. To see nations in East and South Asia and Latin America become global icons. To fulfill the long-delayed promise of the Middle East. To help reform where reform is needed—as in Eastern Europe. And, yes, to see Africa finally take off.

In brief, it is a time to debate, decide, do, and deliver. This book is a contribution to that process. It does not seek agreements, propose universal recipes, or invent new paradigms. It just looks forward and describes for us what it sees.

Otaviano Canuto
Vice President and Head
Poverty Reduction and Economic Management Network
The World Bank

Marcelo Giugale
Director
Poverty Reduction and Economic Management
   for Latin America and the Caribbean
The World Bank

Summer 2010

Acknowledgments

This volume is the result of a team effort. More to the point, it is the result of the passion and professionalism of a group of colleagues who agreed to lend their time and talent to a collective adventure in thinking. They worked on this book while attending to their busy day jobs—that is, they gave us their personal time. They cut no corners, skipped no idea, and shied away from no debate so they could ensure that their views and positions were clear, substantiated, and honest. They were a development community at its best.

So, we have many people to thank.

First, we thank the authors, each of whom took us on an intellectual journey from the issues and countries on which they worked to the way they saw those issues and countries transforming in the future. We are indebted to them not only for the quality of their contributions, but also for their agreement in letting us bring them together, for the comments they provided on each other's chapters, and for the patient way they dealt with our never-ending questions.

Second, we are grateful to the colleagues who helped us move from a pile of unsynchronized drafts to this neatly produced book: Diane Stamm, our outstanding language editor, who made the writings of mostly non-native English speakers read impeccably well; Michael S. Geller, our production manager who was responsible for, among other tasks, the amazing visuals of the book; Riccardo Trezzi, who set a new, world-class standard in the craft of researching in real time (more frequently than not, that time meant late nights and long weekends); Cristina Palarca, our task programmer who ensured that the many components of the process happened at the right time and in the right way; and Janet Piller, who helped us allocate and maximize our resources.

To all of them, our sincere gratitude.

Otaviano Canuto
Vice President and Head
Poverty Reduction and Economic Management Network
The World Bank

Marcelo Giugale
Director
Poverty Reduction and Economic Management for
Latin America and the Caribbean
The World Bank

Summer 2010

Abbreviations

ASEAN	Association of Southeast Asian Nations
BRIC	Brazil, the Russian Federation, India, and China
CAB	current account balance
CCT	conditional cash transfer
CIC	China Investment Corporation
DRC	Democratic Republic of Congo
DSAs	debt sustainability analyses
ECA	Europe and Central Asia
EPA	export promotion agencies
EPZ	export processing zone
EU	European Union
FDI	foreign direct investment
GAFI	General Authority for Investment (the Arab Republic of Egypt)
GCC	Gulf Cooperation Council
GDP	gross domestic product
GHI	Global Hunger Index
HICs	high-income countries
HOI	Human Opportunity Index
ICT	information and communication technologies
IMF	International Monetary Fund
IT	information technology
LAC	Latin America and the Caribbean
LDCs	least developed countries
LICs	low-income countries
LMICs	Low- and middle-income countries
MENA	Middle East and North Africa

MFN	most favored nation
MICs	middle-income countries
MNC	multinational corporation
NRF	Natural Resource Fund
OECD	Organisation for Economic Co-operation and Development
PPP	purchasing power parity
R&D	research and development
SEM	société d'economie mixte local
SEZ	special economic zone
SMEs	small and medium enterprises
SNG	subnational government
SPV	special-purpose vehicle
SWF	sovereign wealth fund
TFP	total factor productivity
TK	traditional knowledge
UAE	United Arab Emirates
UMICs	upper-middle-income countries

Synthesis

Otaviano Canuto and Marcelo Giugale

Introduction and Main Messages

Development economists are paid to look into the future. They ask not not only how things work today, but also how a new policy, program, or project would make them work tomorrow. They view the world and history as a learning process—past and present are just inputs into thinking about what's coming. It is that appetite for a vision of the future that led us to invite some 40 development economists, most of them from the World Bank's Poverty Reduction and Economic Management Network— an epicenter of the profession—to tell us what they see on the horizon of their technical disciplines and of their geographic areas of specialization. We did not want their forecasts—those could quickly become outdated, or prove embarrassingly wrong. Rather, we asked them to visualize how key economic policy issues will be dealt with over the next three, four, or five years and which countries will be dealing with what issues.

The timing could not be better. The 2008–09 global financial crisis shook the ground under the conventional wisdom that had been held as true for decades. From what the role of governments should be in markets to which countries will be the engines of the world's economy, from what people need to leave poverty to what businesses need to stay competitive,

1

it is all up for reexamination. The disconcerting but exciting search for a new intellectual compact has just begun.

So we set our authors free. They wrote under their own names, independently of their institutional affiliation. We imposed no conceptual framework or limits. Their views were taken "as is," whether we agreed with them or not. And we allowed writers to speak before we started our search for a common agenda—the equivalent of composing a musical score by first listening to each member of the orchestra play.

This synthesis provides an account of what we heard. It is not meant to be comprehensive. Instead, it picks from each chapter what is new, what is likely to change, and what will be different in the future. Four take-home messages emerge:

1. While the rich world puts its house in order, and macroeconomics and finance get to a new consensus, developing countries will become a (perhaps, "the") growth engine for the world. Faster technological learning and more South-South integration will fuel that engine.

2. Governments in developing countries will be better—they may even begin to earn the trust of their people.

3. A new, smarter generation of social policy will bring the end of poverty within reach, but inequality is another matter.

4. Staying with sensible policies, many regions of the developing world will break out of their "developing" status and will graduate into something akin to "newly developed." Africa will eventually join that group. Others, like Eastern Europe, will have a legacy of problems to fix beforehand.

Markets: New Engines, New Ideas

Most developed countries came out of the 2008–09 crisis in bad shape. They are burdened with exploding debts; face massive fiscal adjustments (or solvency crises of unimaginable consequences if they do not adjust); and can expect a slow, medium-term recovery at best. Their consumers will be retrenching, worried by the loss of wealth (think houses and stocks), lack of jobs, and stricter lenders. Will this heavy slog drag down the developing world too? Not necessarily. More likely, emerging economies will become a pulling force for advanced ones—they will become a new engine of global growth.

The short-term economic cycles of developing countries have for decades been, and will continue to be, correlated with those in the G-7. There has been no "decoupling" of cycles. However, long-term growth trends did separate (decouple), almost 20 years ago. In the mid-1990s, developing nations began to grow at their own, much faster pace.[1] Part of this had to do with technological convergence ("catching up" is relatively easy). But mostly it was due to better policies.

This superior performance will go on. In fact, it is projected that, as a group, the size of the developing countries' economies will surpass that of their developed peers by 2015. How could that happen while the rich world remains stagnant? Because there are several autonomous sources of growth that emerging markets can still tap, as long as they adhere to sensible policies. First, they have room for more leverage in the balance sheets of their public and private sectors. In other words, they will not need to postpone investment for lack of finance (greenfield infrastructure comes to mind). Second, the expansion of the middle classes will permanently raise the level of domestic demand. Third, technological learning and catch-up may speed up, as the cost and risk of transferring knowledge continues to fall. Fourth, trade integration will accelerate with the emergence of production networks that cross borders, and with it, there will be further reallocation of resources (human or otherwise) to higher-productivity activities. Finally, commodity prices will stay high, and commodity revenues will be better managed. The result will be a faster transformation of natural wealth into increases in (or less loss of) productivity. Let us elaborate on the last three sources of autonomous growth (learning, integration, and commodities), because they pose the most direct policy challenges.

If You Want to Grow, Learn

A less developed country is "less developed" not only because it lacks inputs (labor, capital), but also because it uses them less efficiently. In fact, inputs are estimated to account for less than half of the differences in per capita income across nations. The rest is due to the inability to adopt and adapt better technologies to raise productivity. As an engine of growth, the potential of technological learning is huge—and largely untapped. Four global trends have begun to unlock that potential and are bound to continue. First, the vertical decomposition of production across frontiers allows less advanced countries to insert themselves in supply chains by specializing in single, simpler tasks first. Second, the expansion of "South-South" trade (since 1990, at twice the speed of global trade) increases the availability of technologies that have been tested and adapted to developing-country settings. Third, information and communication technology gets ever cheaper and more widely embraced. Fourth, as the middle class grows in emerging economies, local technological adaptations begin to break even (India's US$2,000 Nano car is a good example).

It all looks promising. But, left by themselves, markets may not generate enough learning. Producers tend not to share profitable ideas, and financiers tend not to finance ideas they do not understand. There is room for public policy. What can developing countries do, and what are they likely to do, to spur technological learning? While each country's reality is different, successful strategies have several common features. They focus on the incentives firms face—competition, taxes, labor laws, corporate governance. They invest in management and worker skills alike. They make sure information spreads quickly to all. They provide public funding where necessary, especially to finance experimentation. They involve all actors, big and small, formal or informal, rich and poor. They are part of an attempt at integration—at benefiting from globalization, not just surviving it. And they constantly benchmark, monitor, evaluate, and adjust.

A Different Kind of Trade

Over the past three decades, global trade grew almost twice as fast as global gross domestic product (GDP). This massive process of commercial integration was made possible by technological revolutions in transport (containerized shipping) and communications technologies and by a dramatic decline in import tariffs. This allowed many developing countries to implement export-led growth strategies that lifted hundreds of millions out of poverty. Some succeeded in sought-after manufacture markets and, more recently, even in services.

But the 2008–09 crisis showed the volatile side of integration. In two years, the volume of world trade fell by a third. International production networks carried country-to-country contagion at staggering speed. Naturally, calls for government intervention have multiplied.

The question is: what kind of intervention will that be? The probability of going back to preglobalization, import-substituting industrial policy is not high, but is not negligible either—concern for unemployment may still trigger protectionism. More likely, public policy will, in most countries, take an "enlightened path" that uses the power of the state to make markets work. This will still involve the traditional prescriptions of sound macroeconomic fundamentals, qualified human capital, and efficient institutions. It will also involve renewed effort at the less glamorous art of facilitating trade, that is, at reducing the cost of moving goods (more competition in logistics markets, faster border agencies), helping exporters survive (stable finance; maintenance of standards, certifications, and licenses), linking export processing zones with local clusters (more flexible zone rules), and enhancing the practical value of export promotion (dissemination of best practices and commercial intelligence).

Strategically, the enlightened path (call it "export-led growth 2.0") will be defined by two new, powerful trends in global trade. First, South-South integration. With the United States, the eurozone, and Japan forced to "rebalance" their saving-consumption mix in favor of the former, commerce among developing countries will play a much larger role. More advanced emerging markets will account for a larger share of the demand for lower-income countries' exports. A multipolar pattern of global growth will emerge. In fact, the crisis has only accelerated a decline in the relative importance of rich-country demand that had started almost two decades before. This does not mean that South-South trade will be easy. Consumers in developing countries care more about price than quality or variety. Import tariffs are higher (by several multiples) compared to Organisation for Economic Co-operation and Development (OECD) countries. And investment climates are worse.

Second, the new trade strategies will put a higher premium on diversification—not only of partners, but also of products—as an insurance against volatility. Expect more trade agreements, and more mutual surveillance, among developing countries. And expect innovation to be the new code word for success in trade. The quest for new brands and new niches will dominate the second generation of internal reforms (from incentives for research and development to tertiary education) that can make export-led growth models viable.

Will exchange rate policy be an effective, even common, instrument in the new multipolar, diversification-driven trade framework? Unlikely. The proliferation of production chains, where import content is critical for exports, will not sit well with artificially high exchange rates. For most countries, the cost of managed undervaluation in terms of reserve accumulation and inflationary pressures will prove unbearable. And the uncertainty associated with large exchange rate misalignments will slow export-oriented investments.

In sum, the crisis will not usher in the end of globalization. On the contrary, there will be more integration. But this time, it will take place mostly in the developing world and will be led by those that have more ideas, not necessarily more resources.

Commodities: That Uncomfortable Feeling of Wealth

Over the next five years, commodity prices will be the external variable to watch for developing countries, perhaps more than interest rates. Those prices will stay high until at least 2015, before supply responses and lower relative demand by a burgeoning global middle-class moderate them. And while commodity dependence has been declining for decades, many a developing country's exports and fiscal revenues will remain dominated by natural resources. Is this postcrisis, continuing bonanza good news? The literature on whether commodity wealth is a "curse" is as vast as it is ambivalent. What is certain from empirical evidence is that good policies and good governance are necessary, but not sufficient, conditions for natural riches (especially oil and minerals) to turn into development, that is, necessary to solve the five main problems associated with those riches:

- Dutch Disease (noncommodity exports become less competitive)
- Price volatility (which complicates investment decisions)
- Overborrowing (lenders are laxer with governments that expect to collect lots of cash)
- Sustainability (how much of the natural wealth to preserve for future generations)
- Corruption (the larger the rent, the more voracious the rent-seeking).

But what are those "good" policies and "good" governance? Will the developing world succeed now where it mostly failed in the past? This time, the odds are in favor of better development outcomes out of high commodity prices. With important differences across countries, democratization has, on average, enhanced citizens' demand for transparency and has improved institutional checks and balances. In parallel, natural resource funds have become more common, and the technology to administer them has improved. Public investment processes, from identification to evaluation, are better than before. Fiscal policy in general is more robust, backed by more rules, better coordination with other agencies of the state (notably, central banks), and a gradual penetration of techniques for results-based management. Monetary anchors are stronger (scores of countries follow, and meet, inflation targets). And while we are still far away from a general acceptance of the prudent "permanent income rule" (that is, from spending only the annuity value of our natural wealth), there is a general sense among policy makers and voters that consumption binges financed by commodity revenues tend to end in tears.

Meanwhile, Policy Wisdom Catches Up with Reality

While autonomous sources fuel growth in the developing world, and help it turn into a global engine, the search for a new consensus around economic policy will continue. The 2008–09 crisis opened the door to a different kind of thinking in international macroeconomics—and closed it on some of the previous orthodoxy. Some now see a bit of inflation (perhaps as high as 5 percent per year) as desirable for countries that pursue inflation targets, because it would allow more space to reduce nominal interest rates when an economy falls in recession. In fact, what to target (consumer, producer, asset, housing, or other prices) is in question. Regulatory parameters and practice in the financial sector have proved to be more critical for real growth than we previously thought, whether through systemic risk, overlending, costly bailouts, or other channels. Floating exchange rate regimes are falling out of favor, since "managed" ones proved to be better at controlling inflation and reducing sudden, unnecessary fluctuations. Controls on the movement of capital across boundaries have become an acceptable tool (they were heretical), almost a price to pay for policy success. Multilateral surveillance is in the cards, initially through the G-20, since the actions of hard-hit, overindebted rich countries cause volatility in many an emerging market. Fiscal policy advice is bifurcated—between a short-term need for sustained stimulus and a medium-term need for consolidation, and between massive deficits in the developed world and the accumulation of surpluses into sovereign funds in the developing one. From all this, a new paradigm is likely to rise. The profession is in flux.

Nowhere is that flux clearer than in finance. There is broad agreement that inadequate prudential regulation of finance was the main cause (albeit not the only cause) of the global crisis. There is much less agreement on what to do about it. In particular, massive systemic risk was allowed to accumulate on the balance sheet of unregulated institutions and off the balance sheet of regulated ones. Their failure could, and did, bring down the whole system. This has sparked a flurry of reform proposals.

Some of the proposals are focused on the relationship across financial agents—on how one agent's fate is correlated with others'. The core idea is "to tax" (literally or through various forms of capital requirements) institutions that can jeopardize the system, not just because they are "too big" but because they are also "too interconnected". The assumption is that regulation will now reach all agents—the "regulatory perimeter" will expand. In practice, regulators may not have enough information to impose that "tax". So, various proxies for an institution's contribution to systemic risk have been put forward—sheer size of its balance sheet, degree of leverage, maturity mismatches, and so on. All of them are yet to be tested by experience.

Other reform proposals emphasize time, that is, how financial risk changes over the economic cycle. When the economy booms, there is less perceived risk, asset prices rise, and it is easier to borrow. When the economy turns, the opposite happens, perhaps more abruptly. What kind of macroprudential regulations can automatically moderate lending in the upswing and ease it during downturns? Two candidates stand out—procyclical capital requirements and procyclical bank provisioning. Only the latter has actually been deployed (in Spain and, more recently, in Colombia and Peru). But the jury is still out on its impact.

Whether reforms are geared toward interconnectedness or timing, there is another potential reason to render their result uncertain at best: lack of international coordination. If countries (developed and developing) adopt different regulatory standards, then money, risk, and bubbles will shift to jurisdictions that are less strict or less capable of enforcement. With regulatory wisdom under construction, is there anything macroeconomics can do in the meantime to help financial stability? Possibly. Monetary policy could target asset prices, not just inflation or output gaps, although it may end up promoting inconsistent objectives, or serving none very well. Fiscal policy can help too, especially if it can inject resources in the economy automatically and rapidly during recessions, and if it can avoid giving tax incentives to borrowing (to mortgages, for example). And external financing decisions will also have a bearing on the stability of domestic financial markets—the risk of sudden exchange rate fluctuations will be lower when foreign debts are smaller and reserves are larger.

The bottom line is that the search for financial stability, through regulatory or macroeconomic policy, is just beginning. This is putting developing countries in a bind. Should they wait for new global standards to emerge, or should they tailor their own regulatory strategies? A prime example of that dilemma is happening in Latin America. The region pursued financial stability and financial development through a mix of "getting the macro right" (low inflation, low deficits, low debt), heavy-handed oversight (initially inspired in the 1988 Basel Accord but with oversized capital and liquidity requirements), and entry of reputable foreign banks. The mix did not deliver much in terms of financial development—the depth and reach of, and access to, intermediation remained limited. But it proved resilient. Latin America's financial system suffered little, if at all, during the global crisis.

This raises many questions. One is about innovation: should Latin American supervisors continue to keep a tight leash on new products, especially those that most agents do not understand ("collective cognition failure")? Another is whether to regulate by type of institution (separate regulators for banks and nonbanks, for example) or by type of function (say, credit, whoever gives it). A third relates to financial globalization itself: should foreign banks' local operations be ring-fenced? Fourth, what role should state-owned banks play? For all their weaknesses, they were a useful mechanism to inject liquidity at a time of turmoil. Fifth, would regional regulators have the data to apply countercyclical prudential norms? Sixth, if the world decides to use taxes to handle systemic risk, should Latin America follow, knowing the many problems with the region's tax system? These are just some of the issues that an actual geographic group of developing countries—a group that did well, mind you—will have to face while "the center" comes up with a new international standard—if it ever does.

Governments: Earning the Trust

There is no evidence that the crisis changed citizens' trust in the state, in either direction. Well before the crisis, that trust was already in long-term decline among advanced countries and was stuck at a very low level among developing ones. And while markets may have lost their shine, governments did not pick up the credit. Data, of course, are limited, and definitions are problematic. But there are good indications that not all institutions of the state are distrusted equally or everywhere: people in rich countries look up to their armed forces and down on political parties; in Latin America, they trust basically nobody; and in very poor places where clientelism takes the space of institutions, they tend to trust the incumbent to deliver privileges. This matters for public policy. Distrustful citizens minimize their relationship with the state—they work in informality, opt out of public education, dodge taxes, settle disputes by their own hand, and stay out of politics. Reforms and, more generally, the emergence of a national strategic vision become much more difficult.

Can "trust in government" be restored or, where it never existed, created? Yes, but the levers of trust vary across stages of development. In OECD countries, the marginal need is for more accountability. There, the state has achieved an adequate level of service provision, even a constant flow of improvement in service quality. But citizens have gotten used to it. They are now more impressed by values in public life—probity, commitment, and responsibility. In contrast, performance seems the missing key to trust in developing countries. Tangible, communicable results are what their voters look for and what they reward (Brazilian governors are pioneers in this). Where clientelism is the tradition, a track record of both accountability and performance is necessary before people risk abandoning the incumbent and begin to rely on institutions.

Of course, all trust building has common elements—performing well in some services raises trust more than in others (health provision has higher returns than market regulation, for example); expectations are ratcheted up (what you achieved yesterday becomes today's baseline); confidence can be quickly squandered (any suspicion of gaming evaluations is a trustbuster); and a sense of generational betterment gathers support (we appreciate a state that opens opportunities for our children).

But in the postcrisis world, what will be the most effective trust builders for governments of developing countries? Primarily, four: manage professionally, spend wisely, borrow little, and account well for your assets.

Fiscal Quality

Most advanced countries face a postcrisis period in which fiscal adjustment will be the norm. They need more revenues and less expenditure. Their priority is quantity. In contrast, developing countries came in and out of the crisis with relatively strong fiscal positions and see a horizon of solvency, especially those that export commodities. This gives them an opportunity to improve the functioning of fiscal policy—their priority is quality. There are several reasons to believe that many of them will seize the opportunity.

First, fiscal policy may start leaning more "against the wind," that is, may become more countercyclical. This is not just because of the proliferation of "medium-term budget frameworks", "fiscal rules", and "fiscal responsibility laws", many of which were in place before the crisis. There are also the political rewards that accrued to leaders that had previously accumulated funds and could spend them at the outset of the global recession. Imitation is likely.

Second, independent fiscal agencies will be more common. They will increasingly become the credible, neutral parties that monitor compliance with fiscal norms, cost out initiatives, evaluate impact, and validate forecasts—credit rating agencies do some of this, but lost credibility during the crisis.

Third, more commodity revenue will flow into sovereign wealth funds. Their value will not be only financial; they will also foster a culture of transparency and professionalism in other areas of the treasury. One of those areas will be the management of the state's nonfinancial assets. Why insist on transparency in, say, an oil-driven wealth fund if the state-owned oil company operates in secrecy?

Fourth, more governments will adopt performance-based management, initially through results-based budgeting. The technology to define, measure, and disseminate standards has improved. So it is easier to hold governments accountable, especially at the subnational level where governors and mayors are in closer contact with their constituents. And fifth, the process of decentralizing fiscal decision making down to states and municipalities is mutating into "devolution" from the state to the citizen. The logistical mechanisms to transfer cash directly to the poor (from debit cards to cell phones) are now in place in many developing (and developed) countries. It is just a matter of time before those mechanisms will be used for other public services and for all social strata. This kind of state-citizen relationship will improve the quality of fiscal outlays—better targeting, smarter design, less duplication, and more progressivity.

Public Expenditure: Spring Cleaning

On average, the hope that countries would respond to the crisis through increases in public expenditure that would both sustain aggregate demand in the short run and, at the same time, contribute to long-term growth proved too optimistic. Things may turn out better in the postcrisis. Worries about fiscal sustainability may facilitate a "spring-cleaning," that is, a push for sharper targeting, more effective budget institutions, and lower costs in delivering public services. Old-fashioned, across-the-board cuts and freezes are unlikely—most governments have learned to replace the ax with the scalpel. Even in 2009, growth in all-important social spending among developing nations slowed but did not stall (from above 5 percent per year to just under 2 percent), and it is expected to return to its previous trend in about three years.[2]

More important, the 10 early lessons of 2009 are being heeded in the design of public expenditure plans. First, policy responses must be tailored to country circumstances (from fiscal space and initial debt levels to monitoring capacity and political maturity). Second, the risk of a double-dip global recession cannot be assumed away. Third, medium-term budgetary frameworks help anchor expectations. Fourth, actual service delivery is still the key to credibility. Fifth, ministries of finance need neutral and professional project evaluation capacity. Sixth, line ministries need implementation capacity. Seventh, public-private partnerships in infrastructure are very useful, but there should be no rush into long-term obligations. Eighth, electorates love to know how money is being spent (see the popularity of expenditure-tracking Web sites in the United States and Brazil). Ninth, a large-enough crisis will bend any fiscal rule, and rightly so. And, tenth, it cannot be assumed that donor funding will not be cut.

Debt Management Will Get Tougher

The crisis brought respect to public debt managers in developing countries. Over the previous decades, they had lightened debt burdens both by arranging outright repayments and by engineering better terms for the remaining liabilities (lower interest rates, longer maturities, more local currency). Their offices became more professional, more independent, and more transparent—not unlike most central banks. All this proved handy, almost visionary, when the world's financial markets entered a tailspin. But for all their new craftiness, those debt managers had been operating in a favorable global landscape—growth, prudent policies, financial innovation, and, for low-income countries, plenty of debt relief.

That placid landscape has drastically changed and is now mined with new risks that will put debt management capacity to the test. The recovery in the G-7 may falter or keep growth minimal for years. The fiscal adjustment necessary among advanced economies to bring their debts down to sustainable levels may prove politically impossible. So a sovereign debt crisis among them cannot be assumed away. Financial regulation is, as mentioned earlier, in flux and may get Balkanized if each country follows its own, uncoordinated path toward financial reregulation. In the medium term, international interest rates have only one way to go—up. Developing countries are seeing their currencies appreciate—in some cases, out of speculative capital movements across borders. Plenty of contingent liabilities have been incurred by the state to inject capital into banks, soothe depositors, back corporate obligations, or guarantee returns on private infrastructure investments. If debt managers in developing countries can successfully navigate these uncharted waters, they will deserve much more than respect.

To make matters worse, the debt management capacity that developing countries have built over the past decade has jurisdiction and control over the liabilities of the central (federal) government only. But much of the growth in public indebtedness is taking place at the subnational level (states, provinces, municipalities), where capacity and transparency are at best limited. By now, about a third of all public debt in, for example, Brazil is owed by subnationals. The numbers are not small (30 percent of GDP in India, to name one case). The borrowing is driven by the decentralization of public services (and, implicitly, of political power), the speed of urbanization, and, until the 2008–09 crisis, the competitive pressure on lenders to find new clients. What are the main risks? First is the fact that sovereign credit ratings cap subsovereign ones, and any turbulence in the macroeconomic fundamentals of the country as a whole derails subnational financing plans, no matter how well thought out. Second is the precariousness of ex ante regulatory frameworks for subnational borrowing (who decides who is allowed to borrow how much) and of ex-post mechanisms for resolving insolvencies (how a province or a city goes through bankruptcy). Third is the growing volume of contingent liabilities that subnationals carry, from the special-purpose vehicles so popular among China's local authorities that want to finance infrastructure, to the pension promises made to local civil servants in Brazil. The standards for disclosure and the accounting rules for these kinds of contingencies vary widely in quality—when they are followed at all. And, fourth, the level of competition in subnational lending still leaves a lot to be desired. Usually a municipal bank or equivalent dominates, keeping borrowing costs unnecessarily high and borrowing options unnecessarily narrow.

Asset Management: The Time of Sovereign Wealth Funds

Two global factors will increase the size and number of sovereign wealth funds. On the one hand, interest rates in the G-7 will stay low for a while. Seeking higher returns, capital will flow into promising developing countries. Those countries' central banks will accumulate foreign currency reserves and will try to invest them in something more profitable than the traditional U.S. Treasury Bills. On the other hand, in resource-rich economies, the combination of higher commodity prices and more fiscal discipline will drive cash accumulation in governments' books. It is estimated that, by 2017, sovereign wealth funds might hold assets worth US$17 trillion (roughly the size of the U.S. economy), of which up to US$5 trillion (five times Mexico's economy) could be invested in emerging markets. And that is before any geostrategic consideration—like securing priority access to energy.

Will all this be a repeat of the 1980s recycling of oil money into a debt crisis? Probably not. Much of the new investment flow will be South-South and will go into long-term positions: China buying African assets is a prime example. Recipient nations have stronger fundamentals, including a lot less debt. Monitoring and reporting techniques have improved. And, being part of the balance sheet of the state, the funds and their operations enter into the scrutiny of creditworthiness calculations. This does not mean that sovereign capital flows will be riskless for the recipients—their purchases (sales) can cause price bubbles (busts) if the local financial market is small; politically motivated sudden repatriations are not unthinkable; and many subcontract part of their portfolio to highly leveraged hedge funds. But they will become a major source of external financing.

People: The Beginning of the End of Poverty

The world is beginning to win the war against poverty. Over the past 30 years, the proportion of people living on US$1.25 a day or less fell by half—to less than a quarter. The trend is also clear when using each country's own definition of poverty. Hunger, a bottom-line indicator of progress, is falling too. The 2008–09 crisis pushed some 60 million people into poverty, but it is unlikely to have much permanent impact on the downward direction in global poverty counts. Of course, differences across regions are significant—in China, 400 million people are no longer poor, while in Sub-Saharan Africa, about half the population still is. And inequality remains a tall and diverging order—it is contracting slowly from high levels in places like Brazil and rising rapidly from low levels in others like China. But having fewer poor people makes it easier to deal with inequality.

More fundamentally, there is now a budding consensus on what reduces poverty: it is the combination of fast and sustained growth (more jobs), stable consumer prices (no inflation), and targeted redistribution (subsidies only to the poor). If these are going in the right direction, where should poverty fighters focus next? On better jobs (productivity), more human opportunity (equity), lower risk (social protection), less discrimination (gender), and easier cross-border help (remittances).

A Job, a Chance, and a Hedge

Labor income is the main source of revenue for poor households. It is so important that, in the least developed countries, poverty is higher among the employed—unemployment is a luxury people cannot afford. So their only way out of poverty is through earning more from their work. What matters to reduce poverty is not just jobs, but also how productive that employment is. This points toward a more efficient allocation of resources in the economy as a whole and to the broad agenda of reforms that make an economy more competitive. It also points toward something much closer to the individual: skills, both cognitive (say, critical thinking or communication ability) and noncognitive (say, attitude toward newness or sense of responsibility).

At the same time, it is now possible to measure how important personal circumstances—like skin color, birthplace, or gender—are in a child's probability of accessing the services—like education, clean water, or the Internet—necessary to succeed in life. That measure, called the Human Opportunity Index (Molinas and others 2010), opened the door for social policy to focus on giving everybody not just the same rewards, but also the same chances—not just on equality, but also on equity. A few countries, mostly in Latin America, now evaluate existing social programs, and design new ones, with equality of opportunity in mind. Others will follow.

Crises, new and old, have shown how fragile social progress is. A few quarters of recession, a sudden inflationary spike, or a natural disaster occur, and poverty counts skyrocket—and stay sky-high for years. The technology to protect the middle class from slipping into poverty, and the poor from sinking even deeper, is still rudimentary in the developing world. Unemployment benefits, when they exist at all, cover only formal workers, who usually are a minority. Public works programs are not very useful when the problem is not unemployment

but a sudden contraction in real wages. And direct transfers are difficult to expand in a hurry without endangering the quality of their
targeting.

Treat Women Fairly

The 2008–09 crisis, and the spikes in international food and fuel prices
that preceded it, also highlighted the crude economic consequence of
gender inequality—it slows growth when you need it the most. Women
saw the crisis hit hard the sectors where they are disproportionately represented (informal self-employment, assembly-line manufacturing
exports, and high-value agricultural exports). They responded by seeking further participation in the labor market, formal or informal. And in
general, when governments reacted, they focused on the right short-term
priorities, like attaching child-care facilities to public works programs,
channeling through mothers all direct cash transfers to households,
expanding nutritional supplementation for infants, and reaching female
farmers with production inputs.

But the true impact will likely be felt for, and by, a generation, since
it is estimated that a 1 percent drop in per capita GDP raises infant
mortality by twice as much for girls as for boys. In fact, the future priorities of gender policy will be defined by demographic dynamics.
Countries still facing demographic "explosions" (mostly in Sub-Saharan
Africa) will continue to prioritize maternal health and family planning
services, especially among teenage mothers, who are about a hundred
times more likely to die during childbirth than their Western European
peers. Two-thirds of developing countries are, instead, in demographic
transition, with large working-age populations relative to children and
the elderly. Here, the gender priority is in women's effective participation in the labor markets, primarily through skill formation and support to entrepreneurship. A smaller, but growing, group of countries
(all of them in Eastern Europe) are experiencing demographic "implo-
sions," with rapidly aging populations. This has exposed the dearth of,
and the need for, social security for women, a legacy of comparatively
lower labor market participation, higher informality, and smaller salaries. Finally, two dozen countries are trapped by armed conflicts or
by chronic diseases (like HIV/AIDS) in an "hourglass" demography:
they are depleted of working-age adults. While wars affect men much

more than women, three-quarters of HIV-positive, young African adults (age 15–24) are female.

Poor-to-poor Transfers

Past financial collapses and natural disasters in individual, migrant-sending countries had been shown to increase the remittances those migrants wire home—to help the family in trouble or to buy local assets on the cheap. But how remittances would react to a global crisis was unknown. The answer came in 2009: they are resilient, even countercyclical. Overall, remittances to developing countries fell by just 6 percent, to some US$300 billion, and are projected to grow again, albeit more slowly. That relative stability is a blessing: for many recipient economies, remittances are the largest source of foreign currency—larger than any export, private financing, or official aid. As such, they even feature high in sovereign credit ratings (Bangladesh, the Philippines).

What kept remittances going? For starters, a global crisis, one that affected all countries, caused little change in the stock of migrants abroad (why return if things are bad everywhere?). Not even financial incentives convinced migrants to leave the Czech Republic, Japan, or Spain. Charity played a part too: remittances are usually a small part of the migrant's income at destination, so he or she can afford to send extra cash to help relatives cope with the downturn. Exchange rate movements in favor of the U.S. dollar made investing in assets at the countries of origin cheaper; this "sale effect" was patent in, for example, Ethiopia, India, and Pakistan. Tightening borders to shield native workers from competition made migrants less willing to leave (it is more difficult to come back) and their remittances more stable. And those that did leave took their accumulated savings with them, making the total flow of remittances even bigger.

If remittances are so large and so stable, is there anything governments can do to leverage them into faster economic development? Yes, plenty. First and foremost, there is too little competition and transparency in remittance markets, where transfer fees tend to be unrelated to cost (usually, and unjustifiably, a fixed percentage of the value remitted). Subsidizing banks' marketing (Pakistan), mobile money-transfer technology (Kenya), or settlement systems (the Philippines) is worth an experiment. Funding investment projects with "diaspora bonds," that is, securities that are targeted to migrants who may feel more comfortable with local regulatory standards, has proven useful (El Salvador). Bilateral efforts to establish guest-worker programs (for example, between Europe and India) have served well both origin and destination countries—and have taken some of the political pressure out of immigration debates.

Developing Regions: The Path to "Newly Developed"

How does the new horizon of markets, governments, and people translate in each geographic region of the developing world? How will it impact their challenges—and their opportunities? It is difficult to draw a single conclusion. Their initial conditions are just too different—from physical endowments and human capital to cultural preference and political systems. Still, a sense of optimism is in order. While the remaining risks are large—a sovereign default in an advanced economy or a "bubble-like" explosion in a large emerging-market exporter—the fundamentals are solid. Developing countries have, on average, done their homework and are likely to stay with sensible policies. More fundamentally, their citizens' feeling of prosperity will make it increasingly implausible for leaders to radically change course—close their economies to the world, abuse the public treasury, jeopardize investment flows. The opposite is more likely. That will mean a new development stage (and status) for regions like East Asia, Latin America, South Asia, and, soon, Africa. The Middle East and North Africa will get a new opportunity to take off. Things will for a while be more complicated for Eastern Europe (its legacy problems need to be solved first) and for small states (their size will not make it easier to adjust to the new global reality).

Africa: Takeoff Time

In the decade up to 2007, Africa gave us a glimpse of what it is capable of. Growth was fast and sustained. Poverty fell by almost 10 percentage points (when measured at US$1.25 or less per person per day). Median inflation was halved. High commodity prices and more foreign aid, private capital flows, and remittances all played a part in that performance. But the ingredient that made the difference, the one that was not present in previous booms, was better economic management. Sure, too many African countries remain trapped in conflict, which makes prosperity impossible. But most were beginning to trace a promising development path. In came the global crisis, with its destruction of export demand, capital flows, remittances, and prospects for further aid. Growth stayed positive, but slowed to a trickle. This had an immediate human cost—it is estimated that for each percentage point of growth lost, the region sees 30,000 additional children die before their first birthday. By and large, governments responded as well as they could—lowering taxes, enlarging safety nets, spending some of the windfall that they had saved. The questions now are: Can Africa return to its previous path when the world recovers? Can it make that path even more promising?

Yes, it can. But it will have to show more than good macroeconomics and address the four structural challenges that still tie it down. First, its massive infrastructure gaps. The needs are so large (some US$50 billion per year) that no single government can afford them. The challenge is how to attract the private sector to take more long-term "Africa risk." Second, its difficult demographics. For some countries, this means reigning in still-explosive fertility rates. For others, it means employing the bulge of youth (some 10 million per year) that is beginning to arrive at the labor market. Third, the quality of its state institutions. Public services, from education and health to sanitation and security, have rarely been up to par or commensurate with the resources they absorb. And fourth, making the case for, and the most of, additional foreign aid. In a postcrisis world where traditional donor countries face huge budget problems themselves, keeping past promises of larger assistance (like the Gleneagles commitment) will not be easy. Ironically, the chances that aid could help Africa transform itself have never been higher.

East Asia and Pacific: A "New Normal"

The countries of East Asia are leading the world out of its economic and financial crisis and may well become the new engine of global growth. Their response to the crisis was swift and effective, based on large fiscal and monetary stimuli. Their postcrisis macrofundamentals are strong—low inflation, low debt, and low fiscal deficits. Growth is returning to its trademark high path, especially in all-important China. But the region is about to face "a new normal," one in which the growth in the United States, Japan, and the eurozone will be slow or nonexistent. This will shrink East Asia's export markets and may increase the cost of its financing.

How should East Asia respond to that new normal? Can it complete its exemplary march toward development? Yes, but only if it tackles its pending agenda of structural reforms. That agenda varies significantly across countries. China needs "rebalancing": its capital-intensive, industry-led, export-oriented model does not create enough jobs, consumes too much energy, is environmentally unsustainable, and depends on an external demand that may remain weak for years. That model now needs to be complemented by the expansion of domestic consumption and by a larger role for the service sector, something that points to public investment in health and education and to the removal of distortions in the pricing of capital, energy, and land. For the middle-income countries of East Asia (Indonesia, Malaysia, the Philippines, and Thailand), the challenge is to move up the value chain; they still lack the necessary physical and human capital to break into knowledge- and innovation-based markets. In turn, trade facilitation is the key for the low-income economies of East Asia (Cambodia, the Lao People's Democratic Republic, and Vietnam) to break into the production networks of the region; they are in the right neighborhood and ought to make the most of it. The Pacific Islands will continue to face the problems associated with small scale; their hope is in new telecommunication technologies, subregional integration, and better aid coordination. Nor have the commodity exporters of the region (Mongolia, Papua New Guinea, and Timor Leste) benefited from revenue stabilization techniques; adopting, and respecting, medium-term fiscal frameworks is a priority for them.

Despite the many differences across its countries, East Asia does have a common regional agenda around two issues: its own economic integration and its adaptation to and mitigation of climate change. The former calls for better logistics, lowering of mutual investment barriers, liberalization of trade in services, more fluid coordination in financial market regulation, and intraregional labor migration. The latter could be well served by directing a part of the region's impressive investment levels toward greener technologies.

Eastern Europe and Central Asia: Dealing With a Heavy Legacy

Following the fall of the Berlin Wall, Eastern Europe and Central Asia (ECA) experienced two decades of rapid growth, rising living standards, middle-class expansion, institutional development, and integration into the European Union (de jure or de facto). But the global crisis hit ECA hard—harder than any other region in the world—and reversed many of its earlier achievements. It also unmasked a critical weakness behind the region's success: its unsustainable dependence on foreign savings. ECA was living beyond its means, and the abundance of external financing had allowed it to indulge in public and private expenditures that it could not afford. Further, much of the public expenditure was achieving little and inequitable results.

This lays bare the policy agenda going forward, an agenda that is relevant to virtually all countries in the region in spite of their many natural, economic, and scale differences. First, the region will need to recover, and eventually accelerate, growth with fewer resources—in other words, through increases in productivity. This calls for more efficiency in the use of public resources (fiscal consolidation), a better investment climate (tax, customs, and regulatory reform), a consolidated financial industry (especially, domestic banking), an enhanced energy and transport infrastructure, and a constant search for new market niches through innovation. Second, focalization and accountability will be required to improve the efficiency, quality, and fairness of social services (health, education, social security). This could not come too soon, for ECA's population is rapidly aging, and the viability of its production capacity is being challenged by the imperatives of climate change (notably, the central-planning legacy of high energy consumption).

Latin America: A New Maturity

The global financial crisis had a mild impact on Latin America, especially when compared with past experience. This time, there were no debt defaults, bank runs, collapsing currencies, inflationary spikes, capital flight, or bursts of emigration. Growth came to a standstill and poverty increased (by some 8 million people), but there was no economic or social meltdown. Efforts over the previous decade at better macroeconomic management and smarter social programs paid off. Perhaps more important, the crisis and the recovery opened the possibility of a new level of quality in the region's policies, the possibility of a new maturity in how Latin America seeks development.

First, independent fiscal agencies will, in various forms, become common. Countercyclical fiscal policy—the simple idea of saving in good times to spend more in bad ones—was tested in the region for the first time during the crisis (in Chile) and proved to be politically very popular. This will foster imitation. Much as, 10 years ago, Latin America left behind its history of high inflation by giving control of money creation to independent central banks, the idea of neutral oversight of fiscal expenditures cannot be too far behind. This will complement well the various forms of fiscal rules, frameworks, and pacts with which Latin American countries have been experimenting. And it will come in handy if commodity revenues continue to flow apace and lead to the emergence of sovereign wealth funds.

Second, success in trade will depend less on new free trade agreements than on new products. With rich-country partners expected to remain stagnant and local currencies already traveling on a long-term trend of appreciation, additional commercial penetration will have to come from new brands—that is, from innovation. The problem is that few regional countries provide environments where innovation can happen, ranging from intellectual property rights that are protected to universities that talk to businesses.

Third, having sailed through the crisis unharmed, Latin American financial sectors will see reform at both ends of the technical spectrum. On one side, the international regulatory wisdom will shift toward more (and, hopefully, better) oversight by the state over matters like systemic risk, countercyclical bank provisioning, and nonbank intermediaries. How much of that will the region adopt, adapt, or avoid? On the other side, political pressure will reach a tipping point to raise competitive pressure in, and widen access to, financial services for the poor.

Fourth, the focus of social policy will begin to shift from equality toward equity. This will be facilitated by two new technologies that were discussed before: (a) the individualized relationship between the state and the poor that was built in 13 countries of the region to make conditional cash transfer programs possible; and (b) the emergence of the Human Opportunity Index, a statistical tool that measures how personal circumstances affect the chances children have in life.

Fifth, new technologies will also spur a new contract between Latin Americans and their state. Management by results will become more common, as people demand of their governments, whether national or local, the best performance standards that they see elsewhere—from education to security. Monitoring and evaluation techniques will be in high demand. In a gradual but visible transformation, the individualized mechanisms to transfer resources mentioned above will push the decentralization of state functions—a process that gained unstoppable momentum over the past two decades—to its natural consequence: devolution. There will be fewer intermediaries between the makers of public policy and those that are supposed to benefit from it.

Middle East and North Africa: One More Chance

The countries of the Middle East and North Africa (MENA) felt the crisis in different ways. Those in the Gulf Cooperation Council were hit on three fronts: lower oil prices, a credit freeze, and the bursting of the real estate bubble. Less integrated into global financial markets, the developing oil exporters suffered mostly from the sudden loss of value of their main export. And the oil importers saw a collapse in trade (especially with Europe), a contraction in remittances, and a cooling of foreign direct investment. All this exacerbated the region's chronic unemployment problem. It is not easy to see how MENA will create the 40 million new jobs it needs over the next decade, just to keep up with its young demographics.

The solution to that fundamental problem, and the key to unlocking MENA's enormous potential, has not changed much with the crisis (and varies very little across countries): the door has to open for a new generation of private entrepreneurs to emerge and for women to join economic life. There has been no lack of reforms in the business environment over the past decade (the Arab Republic of Egypt led the way). But private investment did not respond—it lingers at half the level of East Asia—and manufacturing productivity did not improve—it stayed at half the level of Turkey. Why? Because many of the reforms were captured by unreformed institutions that favor connected, incumbent firms. The benefit of newcomers bringing state-of-the-art management, technological innovation, and the sheer energy to imagine brands and open markets did not materialize. Real competition has not started.

More critical, the region is yet to use the talent of its women. Ironically, they are more likely to attend university than men. But, on average, only one in four joins the labor force—much less the political leadership. Some progress has been made, notably in reducing fertility rates. However, at the current speed, the challenge of building a vibrant economy that can stand up to world standards will go unmet.

South Asia: An Opportunity to Transform

South Asia withstood the crisis better than any other area of the world and was the first to return to its growth path. The problem is that that path is not fast enough or inclusive enough to deal with the 1 billion people that subsist in the region on less than US$2 a day—the largest concentration of the world's poor. This defines a very specific policy agenda, one that attends to medium-term macroeconomic needs while it transforms the fundamental tenants by which South Asian societies live.

On the first front, high fiscal deficits and high public debt leave little fiscal space to spend on priority social programs and critical infrastructure gaps. This is hardly surprising, since tax collection is dismal (India aside, the tax burden hovers at around 10 percent of GDP) and much of what is collected is spent on untargeted subsidies (to oil, electricity, fertilizers, food, and many other things) or unproductive purposes (military expenditures or pay raises to the civil service). This puts a premium on attracting ("crowding-in") the private sector to fund infrastructure, something that is fortunately beginning to happen (Bangladesh, Bhutan, India, Pakistan). But more fiscal discipline should also help deal with another looming threat—settling on a higher inflation rate than before the crisis (around 10 percent). That would make poverty reduction even more difficult.

Beyond better macroeconomics, a deeper transformation is at stake. South Asians are demanding better and cleaner governments—governments that can deliver results—not just because corruption and inefficiency are slowing private initiative, but also because better governance is necessary to seize the four opportunities ("the four dividends," if you will) that the region faces. First is ending the violent conflicts for which this part of the world stands out. A "peace dividend" in the form of a 2-to-3-percentage-point increase in the rate of long-term growth is possible. Second, there could be a "demographic dividend" in the changing shape of the population pyramid: 150 million new workers will have to be incorporated into the labor force over the coming decade. This will be no easy task, because half of today's population is illiterate. Third, an "urbanization dividend" lies behind the fact that South Asia is very densely populated, but very scantly urbanized. Economies of scale and of agglomeration wait to be exploited. Fourth is an "integration dividend." The region is embracing the global trade rebalancing with gusto. China has overtaken the United States as India's largest trading partner, and South-South trade now dominates exports from Bangladesh, Pakistan, and Sri Lanka. Further, the new destinations are boosting manufacturing, a sector that was relatively dormant.

In Conclusion

While some regions will do better than others, and some technical areas will be clearer than others, there is no question that the horizon of economic policy for developing countries is promising—risky, yes, but promising. The rebalancing of global growth toward, at the very least, a multiplicity of engines will give the developing world a new relevance. It will validate the many sensible policy positions that, on the whole, sheltered that world from the 2008–09 crisis. And it will give a new sense that governments can do good things, notably eliminate poverty.

There is, however, a humbling lesson behind that optimistic horizon— the large gap between what we think we know and what we actually know. Before the crisis, our "grip" on macroeconomic and financial policy was almost a certainty. Advanced economies could do no wrong. Government action was bad until proven otherwise. Attachment to a rich, western market was all we needed to be rich and western. Those and many other certitudes proved to be subprime truths. So this book, and the many readings on the future that it contains, should be kept in perspective.

Notes

1. The decoupling in trends is observed even when unusually fast-growing economies, like China and India, are taken out of the data sample.
2. Eastern Europe may be the exception.
3. See Molinas and others 2010.

Reference

Molinas, J., R. Paes de Barro, J. Saavedra, and M. Giugale. 2010. *Do Our Children Have a Chance? The 2010 Human Opportunity Report for Latin America and the Caribbean.* Washington, DC: World Bank.

Part I
Markets

Recoupling or Switchover? Developing Countries in the Global Economy

Otaviano Canuto

Developing countries as a whole had been growing faster than advanced economies for several years prior to the 2008–09 economic crisis. As the signs of increasing financial fragility and impending economic slow-down in major advanced economies became clear in 2007 and the first three quarters of 2008, much was said about a possible "decoupling" of emerging markets. This was quickly followed by talk of a downward "reverse coupling," when these and other developing economies were also impacted by the near collapse of finance and international trade during the last quarter of 2008 and in early 2009.

More recently, however, developing countries as a group have been recovering faster than advanced economies while also maintaining the positive growth premium that emerged prior to the crisis. Indeed, growth in developing countries is projected by the World Bank to reach 6.1 percent in 2010, 5.9 percent in 2011, and 6.1 percent in 2012, while corresponding figures are 2.3 percent, 2.4 percent, and 2.6 percent for high-income countries. Almost half of global gross domestic product (GDP) growth is currently coming from developing countries.

In this environment, two questions arise: Will developing economies experience a renewed downward "recoupling" as a result of a low-growth scenario in advanced economies? Or, on the contrary, could developing countries "switch over" to become locomotives in the global economy, providing a countervailing force against an otherwise slowing train? This chapter discusses the factors pushing in these two opposite directions.

Cyclical Coupling and Trend Decoupling

As figure 1.1 shows, there has long been a close correlation between economic cycles in advanced and developing economies. Developing-country growth fell sharply in 2009 through several channels: declining exports to developed countries, steep falls in private capital inflows, and domestic financial freeze as a form of contagion. So there has been no decoupling in the cyclical component of developing country growth.

On the other hand, looking only at global aggregates may obscure an emerging story about *trend decoupling* between advanced and developing countries. More recently, since the early 2000s, the cyclical synchrony has been combined with systematically higher growth rates in developing economies relative to advanced economies. As the exercise of trend-cycle decomposition depicted in figure 1.2 reveals, before the mid-1990s the trend growth in developing countries was close to that in advanced countries. Since then, it has become substantially higher: a "cyclical coupling" has arguably continued, as in the past, but together with some trend decoupling in underlying rates of growth.

Figure 1.1 World Output Growth

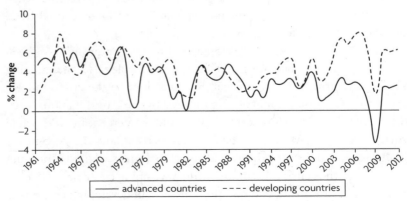

Source: World Bank, World Development Indicators and Development and Economics interim forecasts, April 2010.

Figure 1.2 Trends and Cycles: Potential and Cyclical GDP Growth

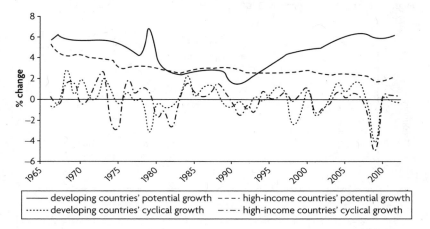

Source: World Bank, DEC prospects group.

The improved growth performance in developing countries is not just a reflection of strong performance by the two largest developing countries, China and India. Figure 1.3 shows the frequency distributions of individual country growth rates in 2009, the expected trough of the crisis. Median growth in developing countries was substantially higher (2.13 percent) than in advanced economies (−3.72 percent). And a much larger proportion of developing countries has continued to enjoy positive growth than among advanced or high-income countries.

Most of the developing countries situated at the right-side tail of the corresponding distribution benefited from better macroeconomic, structural, and other policies adopted over the past two decades. They had the capacity to resort to fiscal, monetary, and financial counter-cyclical policies, and to use foreign exchange reserves and exchange rate fluctuations as elements of their responses to the 2008–09 shock (Lin and Canuto 2010). On the opposite side of the distribution are those countries that had combined overborrowing and asset price "bubbles" with shaky domestic growth foundations, as in several Eastern European and Central Asian countries. There, one can also find cases in which trade and financial integration led to severe impacts, such as Mexico and several Central American and Caribbean countries. In any case, one

Figure 1.3 Frequency Distribution of GDP Growth in Developing Countries and High-Income OECD Countries, 2009

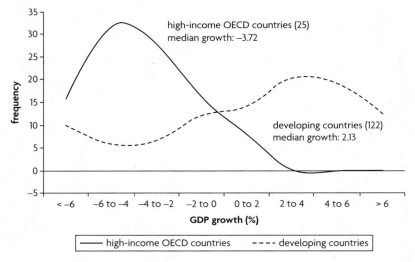

Source: World Bank data and staff estimates.
Note: OECD = Organisation for Economic Co-operation and Development.

may associate the overall high performance of developing countries as a whole before and during the crisis to an improvement of quality of economic policies in the previous decade or so.

Not Good: Growth Prospects in Advanced Economies

High-income countries are facing strong headwinds in the wake of the crisis—not to mention new unexpected shocks such as the one derived from the Greek crisis, which erupted at the end of 2009. It is still an open question whether the promptness and strength of recovery in private absorption (consumption and investment) will be sufficient to render unnecessary the current life support provided by aggressive monetary and fiscal policies, before their unwinding becomes inevitable. If postwar recessions in Organisation for Economic Co-operation and Development (OECD) countries serve as a template, the switchover from public to private sectors will not be automatic, since recessions associated with credit crunches, house price busts, or equity price busts tend to be both deeper and longer than normal. In fact, very few OECD recessions in the postwar period—4 out of 122—have occurred with a combination of a credit crunch, a housing bust, and an equity bust. The 2008–09 crisis entailed all three in a severe form (Claessens, Kose, and Terrones 2008).

Several factors point to a reduction of both actual and potential growth in the medium term.

First, sooner or later fiscal consolidation will become a major issue among advanced economies once—or even before—recovery is fully established. Many advanced economies entered the crisis with weak structural fiscal positions, and these have been eroded further, not only by anticrisis measures, but also by underlying spending pressures. Structural primary deficits in advanced countries are expected to have worsened by 4 percentage points of GDP between 2007 and 2010.

Even with the reversal of temporary anticrisis measures, public debt in advanced G-20 economies[1] is expected to reach 118 percent of GDP by 2014 (figure 1.4). According to the International Monetary Fund (IMF), "simply letting the stimulus expire would still leave the government debt of many advanced countries on an explosive path" (IMF 2009:21). Stabilizing debt at postcrisis levels will also not be enough because it will reduce the ability of fiscal policy to deal with future shocks and will push postcrisis real interest rates much higher.

On average, according to the IMF, bringing government debt-to-GDP ratios in advanced G-20 economies to a prudent level below 60 percent by 2030 would require steadily raising the structural primary balance from a deficit of 5.3 percent of GDP in 2010 to a surplus of 4 percent of GDP in 2020—a 9.3-percentage-point swing in one decade—and keeping it at that level for the following decade. Those are large, politically difficult adjustments to make.

Thus, even if one considers that different features of national fiscal packages will have corresponding different consequences in terms of long-term growth drivers, some future fiscal contraction negatively affecting the private sector will be the price paid for the role of fiscal stimulus in rescuing advanced economies from the brink of the abyss during the crisis. And even if monetary policy maintains its current accommodative stances for some time, managing to sustain basic short-term interest rates at low levels, the yield curve on public debt may still steepen.

Figure 1.4 General Government Debt, Real and Projected

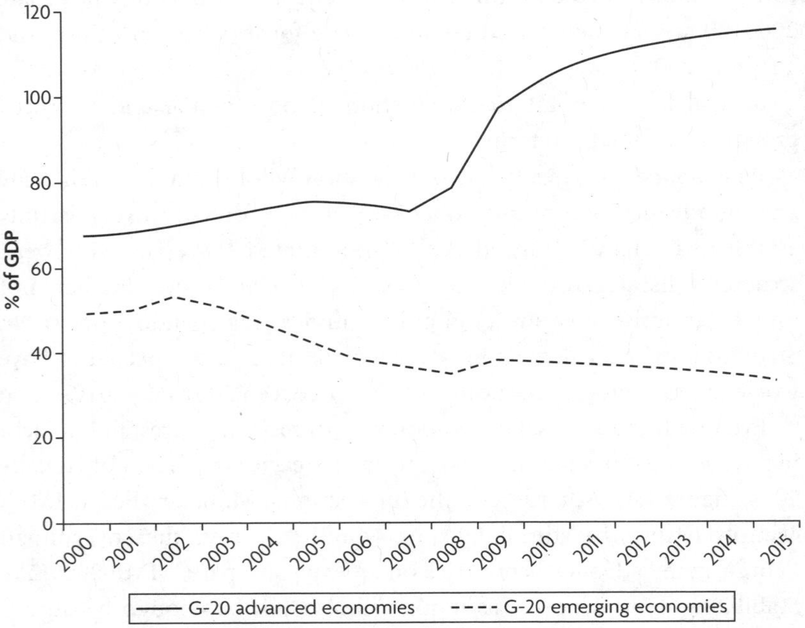

Source: World Bank calculations based on International Monetary Fund data.

Second, the process of U.S. households' balance-sheet deleveraging and adjustment is far from complete. Consumption spending growth is likely to remain weak, wobbly, or both in the absence of large renewed hikes in asset prices. In the past, strong U.S. consumer spending was buttressed by rising housing prices, allowing rising household debt and reduced personal savings (figure 1.5). Lower savings were reflected in a rising U.S. current account deficit and in export demand for the rest of the world. Now, as housing and other household asset prices have fallen substantially, deeply indebted households are unlikely to undertake a new spending spree anytime soon. Rebuilding household balance sheets will be a lengthy process.

A third aspect to weigh against a return to a high-growth path is the likely jobless nature of the current recovery in many high-income countries. The recent evolution of unemployment in advanced economies can only partially be attributed to Okun's Law—relationships between output fluctuations and unemployment. Were these relationships to

Figure 1.5 United States: Personal Savings Rate and Current Account Balance, 1960–2009

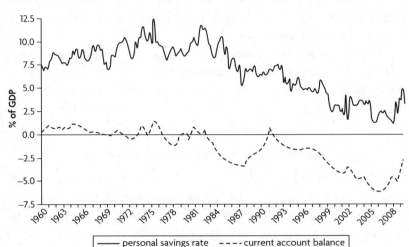

Source: U.S. Bureau of Economic Analysis.

prevail, the current GDP recovery would bode well in terms of a positive feedback loop with labor markets. However, slow-to-reverse shocks—a financial crisis combined with a housing price bust, and cross-sector differentiated job creation and destruction—have been in play, and continued macroeconomic uncertainty is also countering employment growth (IMF 2010a, chapter 3). The share of temporary workers has been on the rise in most advanced economies for years, reflecting institutional changes in labor markets. Recent crisis-related increases in temporary employment will tend to have a limited effect on enhancing expenditures while uncertainty regarding macroeconomic and sectoral prospects remains high.

Fourth, proposals for the reregulation of the financial sector point to higher costs of financial intermediation. After all, the general purpose is to curb the unbridled "endogenous liquidity factories" and excessive leverage that led to widespread asset bubbles in the run-up to the economic crisis (Canuto 2009). Regardless of the long-run payoffs of such moves, access to long-term finance—including for research and development and for venture-capital funding—could stay harder to obtain and costlier compared to prior to the crisis, no matter how accommodative monetary policies remain. New bouts of pressure on bank balance sheets are also likely as new sources of financial stress emerge, such as corporate restructurings (Dubai, the United Arab Emirates), sovereign debt stress (Southern Europe), and so on.

Therefore, it is not by chance that most analysts expect the crisis—and the response to it—to leave advanced economies with a long-term legacy of lower growth, both in potential output and in aggregate domestic demand.

Recoupling or Switchover? Switchover

Three questions follow from the previous sections: (a) how sustainable is the "trend decoupling" exhibited by developing countries; (b) how high can both actual and potential growth rates remain in developing countries, if advanced economies face headwinds; and (c) to what extent can high-growth performance by developing countries provide a positive feedback loop for advanced economies, helping to avoid a situation where, even though developing countries continue to grow faster than their advanced peers, both do so at relatively low rates?

Figure 1.6, on the growth interdependence between the two groups of economies, provides a simplified illustration of possible outcomes. Channels for growth interdependence may be interpreted here as trade and corresponding investment prospects and as factor incomes abroad (return on foreign assets, remittances). The steepness of the lines for advanced countries (AC) reflects the precrisis smaller weight of developing countries (DC) in the former's performance, whereas the greater sensitivity of DC to variations in AC growth rates is expressed in the slopes of the corresponding lines. The legacy of the crisis on AC is exemplified by the shift from AC_0 to AC_1. The adverse impact of slower advanced-country growth on developing countries—which we call the negative "recoupling" of developing countries—is reflected in a global move from point A to point B. However, if new "autonomous" sources of trend growth in DC can be tapped and DC_0 shifts to DC_1, then the global economy can settle at point C. Here, not only can developing countries escape from the negative recoupling, but there can also be a "switchover," where developing countries become the global growth locomotives and partially rescue advanced economies.

Figure 1.6 Recoupling and Switchover

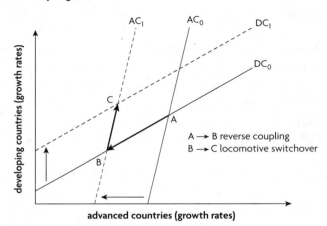

Source: Author.

The weight of developing countries as a whole in the global economy has been rising steadily since 2000, and the continuation of that trajectory comes out in most GDP projections. In terms of levels, the size of G-7 countries[2] at market prices is still 60 percent of GDP, and the major potential new poles of growth (China, India, and Brazil) might count for no more than 30 percent. As time passes, however, the absolute size of the two groups of countries may reverse positions. IMF forecasts for global GDP at purchasing-power-parity-adjusted exchange rates indicate that developing countries as a group will bypass advanced economies before 2015. Although developing countries in Asia have the lead in that dynamic, rising shares in global GDP are also a feature of other regions. What will make the developing world run, if developed nations walk? What will be the autonomous sources of growth?[3]

Autonomous Sources of Growth in Developing Countries and their Challenges

Scope for Higher Degrees of Leverage in Private and Public Balance Sheets

The fast recovery in many large emerging markets has reflected the good shape and sustainability of their national balance sheets. The 2008–09 financial frenzy in many developed economies did not lead to a serious deterioration of local financial conditions in emerging markets as a whole (with several well-known exceptions, especially in Eastern Europe). This suggests that the boom in most emerging markets prior to the crisis was not very dependent on the "bubbly" financial conditions in developed countries. Furthermore, the availability of some fiscal space, and large foreign exchange reserves and scope for monetary relaxation, were fundamental for the implementation of policy responses to the financial and trade crunches of late 2008 and early 2009 (Lin and Canuto 2010).

The IMF in its *World Economic Outlook: Sustaining the Recovery, October 2009* (2009b) calculates an index of financial market stress covering foreign exchange, sovereign debt, the banking sector, and equity markets in emerging markets. After adjustment for the higher level of stress in advanced economies during the 2008–09 crisis, the IMF found that emerging market financial stress rose much less than in previous episodes, and financial market resilience was observed in most emerging market countries.

What explains the greater resilience in most emerging financial markets? Three factors may be highlighted:

- Improved macro conditions in emerging economies, including better fiscal positions and higher foreign reserves
- Declining foreign currency exposure among borrowers
- In many cases, low levels of financial leverage in corporate and household balance sheets.

Looking forward, there is a wide range of greenfield investment opportunities in developing economies that may benefit from higher financial leverage by both the public and the private sectors. Infrastructure provides an obvious example. Given its relative scarcity, social marginal returns as measured in terms of total factor productivity tend to be high in projects that address the many existing bottlenecks. If projects are well designed, the partial monetary capture of those returns by either public- or private-sector entities may well constitute feasible vehicles for asset creation and finance.

Nonetheless, potential pitfalls or obstacles will have to be faced, including the following:

- Public sector management capacities and appropriate governance mechanisms must be in place to guarantee the use of adequate criteria in project choices and design, and to avoid misappropriation of returns. While this principle applies to public sector operations in general, the long-term and risky nature of infrastructure investments puts an especially high premium on following it.

- There are limits beyond which increasing leverage on developing-country balance sheets will also lead to increased financial fragility, particularly if ad hoc unconventional measures adopted as part of the response to the crisis are not unwound.
- The incoming flood of sovereign debt issues by fiscally strapped advanced economies may crowd out corresponding issues by developing countries. This is one of the mechanisms through which "backward recoupling" powers may bite.
- Higher overall costs of finance in advanced countries will also imply increased financial costs for developing countries, in both the public and the private sectors. Estimates presented by the World Bank suggest that U.S. base interest rates that are 100 basis points higher than precrisis levels, combined with the spreads prevailing in October 2009, would lead to a transitional impact of –0.7 percent on potential GDP growth (World Bank 2010).
- The mix of solid growth in many developing economies—and ensuing upward pressure on domestic interest rates—with prolonged monetary laxity in advanced economies is likely to remain for some time. This may cause another surge in private capital flows to emerging markets with a profile potentially conducive to fostering asset market bubbles rather than to building greenfield assets. The pathway toward funding long-maturing investment projects may then become problematic, with increased volatility and overvaluation of existing assets.

However, careful economic management should help address at least some of those "backward recoupling risks", allowing countries to reach a higher potential growth plateau through infrastructure and corporate investment leverage.

Convergence Gap and Nonrival Use of Existing Technologies

A twofold feature of technologies in general is worth remembering (Nelson and Winter 1982; Canuto 1995). Notwithstanding the fact that any specific technology application requires some tacit and idiosyncratic component of knowledge, and some degree of embodiment in hardware or blueprints, there is usually some degree of transferability and possible replication. By the same token, the use of that transferable technology is nonrival, that is, one application does not preclude others.

With some country and sector exceptions, most developing countries face a technological convergence gap relative to the frontier level of knowledge in advanced economies. There is thus a wide scope for technological learning and catching up, with corresponding positive impacts on local productivity. Unexploited latecomer advantages are an avenue for local productivity improvements via technology transfer and adaptation that remains open and wide even if the advance of technology frontiers slows in high-income countries (Rodrik 2009). The possibilities for technology transfer among developing countries, while still in the preliminary stages, may further facilitate such technological diffusion.

The obstacles to more rapid technology diffusion are many: (a) information asymmetries and uncertainties plaguing investments in technology that are common in advanced economies often appear more intensively in developing countries; (b) complementary factors such as reliable infrastructure, access to finance, and a formally educated labor force are sometimes not available; (c) institutional factors that negatively affect the investment climate tend to harm investments in technology even more; and (d) institutional barriers to competition curb the selection process that would operate in favor of good technology performers.

On the other hand, global changes in recent years have been making technological transfer easier than before, including "increased international trade in goods and services, FDI [foreign direct investment], Intellectual Property and technology licensing flows ... increases in data storage and transmission capabilities, fall in costs and uptake of information and communication technologies" (Canuto, Dutz, and Reis 2010).

Again, the balance in favor of high potential growth will tip depending on domestic policy action. In this case, the removal of the barriers to creative technological absorption and diffusion mentioned above will be of the essence.

Trade and Structural Change as Vents for Surplus Labor

The extraordinary growth performance of some Asian economies (and China in particular), like some other past experiences of long periods of growth in the developing world, cannot be fully understood without taking into account that to a large extent they expressed a peculiar process of structural change (at least at the start of the process): the dislocation of large contingents of low-skilled workers from stagnant and low-productivity activities to others whose value at world prices is significantly higher and where there also exists a wide scope for productivity increases.[4] These workers moved from occupations in which their physical and monetary marginal productivity was close to zero, as in production for subsistence in many rural areas, to light-manufacturing production with much higher market value, a move generally accomplished without the need for major increases in worker skills. This is the move depicted in the pioneer work by Lewis (1954) and Fei and Ranis (1964) in their stylized model of transition from traditional surplus-labor rural economies to modern industrial ones. More recently, Rodrik (2009) refers to a dislocation from the production of "traditional, primary products" to "nontraditional tradable activities."

This kind of structural change is not a linear, smooth, or automatic process. Even at its "light" stages, industrialization is "lumpy" in products, space, and time (UNIDO 2009): minimum scales and scope of production, agglomeration gains, and minimum thresholds of competitiveness are needed to start operating. Furthermore, some basic market institutions must be functioning. As Rodrik (2009:6–7) puts it, there tend to be "various market failures and externalities associated with modern activities, such as learning spillovers and coordination failures," and "institutional weaknesses that are felt more intensively in tradable activities, such as poor protection of property rights and weak contract enforcement. . . . In both cases, industrial activity and investment are underprovided in market equilibrium."

But rising international trade and the technological changes already mentioned in this chapter have made such structural change easier. Among technology trends, "a trend towards the standardization, modularization, and codification of technologies, especially in the electronics and auto industries [and in some services, we add; see Ghani and Kharas (2010)] make it easier to deverticalize and offshore production" (Yusuf 2010). With the fragmentation of production and trade in tasks and the decreasing costs of transport and communication, the "lumpiness" barriers become relatively easier to surmount. Local market size becomes less of a constraint on requisites of scale and scope, while learning spillovers and coordination needs may be found through integration in cross-border networks of production. Local institutional requirements remain, however.

To take additional steps up the ladder of technological sophistication, moving on beyond early "easy" production of tradables, an economy has to increasingly develop some capabilities that transcend particular existing lines of production at a given moment in time. This requires the ability to learn, master, and adapt technologies in a creative way; to manage complex processes of design, production, marketing, and so forth. Again, recent trade and technology trends have been favorable to latecomers from a cost-competitiveness standpoint, as long as domestic complementary factors, observed in the section on technology convergence, are in place.

Will a less exuberant pace of domestic absorption in advanced markets in coming years weaken trade as a source of technological transformation for export-oriented countries? Will it unwind hitherto successful export-led growth models? Will it make it impossible for newcomers to undergo structural change and grow by exploiting trade-cum-technology windows of opportunity?

The following are important to note:

(a) The export-led, high-growth experience has been limited in terms of both geographic and sector coverage (Yusuf 2010). There are many developing countries yet to benefit from trade and technology transfer as a vent for surplus labor. And such a labor surplus may also be found in current contingents of low-paid informal urban workers.

(b) The present level of imbalances is relatively recent—a phenomenon of the 2000s. Yet developing countries were able to pursue export-oriented strategies previously with relatively limited global imbalances. In other words, export-led growth does not necessarily mean current-account-surplus-led growth. This suggests that in the longer term, countries could continue to pursue balanced outward-oriented strategies with strong growth in both exports and imports, availing themselves of trade as a means to overcome lumpiness in scale and scope.

(c) The magnitude of the contribution of the recent great current account deficits should not be oversold. It was to some extent the counterpart of very high oil prices.

(d) Most developing-country exports are so small that there should be plenty of room for them to expand despite broad global rebalancing shifts and less exuberant absorption in OECD countries. China and just seven other developing countries comprise 85 percent of all developing-country exports. The exports of these eight countries are equivalent to 15 percent of all OECD imports. By contrast, another 130 developing countries comprise only 15 percent of developing-country exports, equivalent to just 2.5 percent of OECD imports. The typical country in this group could increase its exports by 40 percent if it could capture another 0.01 percent of OECD import market share.

(e) It is true that China as a major component of the OECD deficits acted as a peculiar channel for the transmission of growth. China's huge trade surplus made feasible its high-growth combination of high investment-to-GDP and low consumption-to-GDP ratios. Given China's size, its high growth generated considerable stimulus to regional manufacturing neighbors and to commodity exporters. But in principle, such a role as growth pole can be maintained without gigantic trade surpluses. If domestic absorption rises faster than output in developing countries as a whole, especially in China, and South-South trade is further opened and maintains its rising trend of recent years (Canuto, Haddad, and Hanson 2010) (figure 1.7), a new round of export-oriented growth via structural change can be envisioned.[5]

Social Trickle Down of Growth

After World War II, Europe and Japan sustained a long growth cycle through a process of technological and mass consumption catching up with the U.S. frontier. From the 1990s onward, however, as observed before, many developing countries achieved high growth through a combination of innovations in production technology (including finance) and globalization. The time may now have come for better matching of increases in production and consumption within developing countries.

Figure 1.7 Rising South-South Trade: Toward an Export-Led Growth v2.0?

a. Share of developing country markets in developing country exports

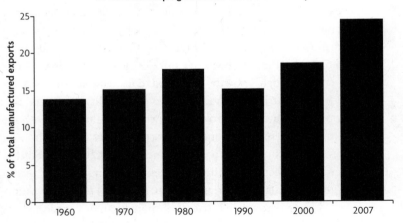

b. Intra-developing countries' manufactured exports

Source: Canuto, Haddad, and Hanson 2010.

That rebalancing in itself could become a powerful tool to hasten poverty reduction.

This is not to be confused with pursuing isolationism through higher local integration per se. Channels for international trade and investment need to be kept wide and open. But programs of investment in human capital, poverty reduction, and social inclusion in developing countries can stimulate local consumption and investment, producing positive feedback loops of sustainable global growth.

The argument for building effective networks of social protections should not be underestimated by a relatively strong growth performance among developing countries as a whole. First and foremost, negative shocks have the greatest effect on the poorest and most vulnerable; by definition, they live on smaller margins and have weaker safety nets to draw on. But there are also efficiency reasons that justify protection. Even short-lived crises may have devastating long-term implications for growth. The way households cope with crisis, the effects on workers' long-term abilities, and the impact on firm creation and firm destruction dynamics are all examples. Households may be forced to make choices that stave off the crisis over the short term but that have negative long-term consequences on human capital, individual earnings potential, and economywide competitiveness. They may be obliged to take children out of school, spend less on health care, and reduce caloric consumption.

Concluding Remarks

The bird's-eye view taken in this chapter leads to the conclusion that, yes, there is scope for a switchover where developing countries as a whole take on a greater role as global locomotive and move global growth forward, offsetting forces toward a negative recoupling deriving from less buoyancy in advanced countries. Nevertheless, comprehensive efforts in terms of domestic policies and reforms will be fundamental to accomplish that mission.

Notes

1. Members of the G-20 are Argentina, Australia, Brazil, Canada, China, France, Germany, India, Indonesia, Italy, Japan, Mexico, the Republic of Korea, the Russian Federation, Saudi Arabia, South Africa, Turkey, the United Kingdom, the United States, and the European Union.
2. The G-7 countries are Canada, France, Germany, Italy, Japan, the United Kingdom, and the United States.
3. Though not explored here, the discrepancy in population growth will be one factor contributing to divergent potential growth between developed and

developing countries. Almost half of the population of the developing world is under 24 years of age compared to one-third of the population of industrial countries. However, some emerging markets (China, the Russian Federation) will face aging similar to, if not worse than, developed countries.

4. It is important to frame the question in terms of value, since it is not appropriate to rank physical productivities as "high" or "low" across different types of products (say, rice versus shoes).

5. An important dimension not discussed here is what the likely implications would be of such a rebalancing in global demand, in terms of types of products and production processes. Resource-based commodities are addressed in chapter 5.

Bibliography

Brahmbhatt, M., and C. Otaviano. 2010. "Natural Resources and Development Strategies after the Crisis." *Economic Premise* Note 1, February, World Bank, Washington, DC. http://www.worldbank.org/economicpremise.

Brahmbhatt, M., C. Otaviano, and E. Vostroknutova. 2010. "Dealing with Dutch Disease." *Economic Premise* Note 16, June, World Bank, Washington, DC. http://www.worldbank.org/economicpremise.

Canuto, O. 1995. "Competition and Endogenous Technological Change: An Evolutionary Model." *Revista Brasileira de Economia* 49 (1): 21–33.

———. 2008. "Three Tiers of Commodity Price Drivers." April 21. http://www.roubini.com/author/otaviano_canuto.

———. 2009. "The Developing World in a Post-Bubble Economy." April 9. http://www.roubini.com/author/otaviano_canuto.

Canuto, O., M. A. Dutz, and J. Guilherme Reis. 2010. "Technological Learning: Climbing a Tall Ladder." *Economic Premise* Note Series, Poverty Reduction and Economic Management Network. World Bank, Washington, DC.

Canuto, O., M. Haddad, and G. Hanson. 2010. "Export-led Growth v2.0." *Economic Premise* Note 3, March, World Bank, Washington, DC. http://www.worldbank.org/economicpremise.

Claessens, S., M. A. Kose, and M. Terrones. 2008. "What Happens during Recessions, Crunches, and Busts?" IMF Working Paper 08/274, December. International Monetary Fund, Washington, DC.

Fei, G., and G. Ranis. 1964. *Development of the Labor Surplus Economy: Theory and Policy.* Homewood, IL: Richard D. Irwin.

Ghani, E., and H. Kharas. 2010. "The Service Revolution." *Economic Premise* Note 14, May, World Bank, Washington, DC.

IMF (International Monetary Fund). 2009a. "The State of Public Finances Cross-Country Fiscal Monitor: November 2009." Staff Position Note SPN/09/25, November 3, IMF, Washington, DC.

————. 2009b. *World Economic Outlook: Sustaining the Recovery, October 2009.* Washington, DC: IMF.

————. 2010a. *World Economic Outlook.* Washington, DC: IMF. April. http://www .imf.org/external/pubs/ft/wed/2010/01/index.htm.

————. 2010b. "IMF Fiscal Monitor." IMF, Washington, DC. May. http://www.imf .org/external/pubs/ft/fm/2010/fm1001.pdf.

Lewis, W. A. 1954. "Economic Development with Unlimited Supplies of Labor." *Manchester School* 22 (2): 139–90.

Lin, J., and O. Canuto, eds. 2010. "The Global Crisis and Medium-Term Growth Prospects for Developing Countries." World Bank, Washington, DC.

Nelson, R., and S. Winter. 1982. *An Evolutionary Theory of Economic Change.* Cambridge, MA: Belknap Press of Harvard University Press.

Rodrik, D. 2009. "Growth after the Crisis." Working Paper 65, Commission on Growth and Development, World Bank, Washington, DC.

UNIDO (United Nations Industrial Development Organization). 2009. *Industrial Development Report.* Vienna: UNIDO.

World Bank. 2010. *Global Economic Prospects 2010: Crisis, Finance, and Growth.* Washington, DC: World Bank. June. http://www.worldbank.org.

Yusuf, S. 2010. "The Past and Future of Export-led Growth." http://blogs.worldbank .org/growth/past-and-future-export-led-growth, February 24.

2

Technological Learning: Climbing a Tall Ladder

Otaviano Canuto, Mark A. Dutz,
and José Guilherme Reis

Innovation is defined as new ways to solve problems by combining technology (an improvement in product, process, marketing, or organization) with transformational entrepreneurship (activity typically involving commercialization of technologies via formal firms but also including value generation by informal, not-for-profit, and governmental entities). It is a major driver of economic growth and productivity. Innovation ranges from incremental new-to-the-firm adoption and adaptation of existing technologies to radical new-to-the-world creation and commercialization of disruptive products and processes.

Innovation is always accompanied by technological learning, which also requires investment. Traditionally, there has been too much focus on the creation of new high-tech products and not enough focus on the power of innovation to increase growth and jobs through technological learning and the adaptation of existing technologies across all products and sectors—agriculture; manufacturing; and services, including education, health, and infrastructure services.

Technological learning and innovation can lead to lower costs for existing and new (or higher-quality) products, enhancing productivity and thereby competitiveness and inclusive growth.[1] A key fact of development is that differences in measured inputs explain less than half of the enormous differences in per capita national income (Caselli 2005; Jones and Romer 2010). Less-developed economies are less developed not only because they have less physical and human capital per worker than developed economies, but more important, also because they use their inputs less efficiently. Among other reasons, they do so because they are not learning sufficiently from existing better technologies and are not adequately improving prevailing production practices.

Do markets lead to a socially desirable level of technological learning and innovation? In contrast to investment in tangible capital, the decision to invest in technological learning and innovation involves spillovers. Ideas are nonrival in use, meaning that ideas leak across people and firms in a way that tangible capital and other products do not: ideas can be used by any number of people simultaneously without depletion or congestion. If ideas are productive, there are gains to society from sharing them globally as soon as they are discovered somewhere, provided that the costs of diffusing and using them are not prohibitive.[2] But markets on their own do not operate effectively with ideas, since a single price cannot allocate an idea to its most efficient uses (which would be at a marginal cost close to zero) and simultaneously provide appropriate incentives to invent and commercialize the idea in the first place. Ideas are therefore undersupplied by private markets relative to socially desirable outcomes, absent appropriate forms of public intervention. In addition to such technological externalities, investments in ideas typically involve demonstration externalities, with a positive impact of mavericks on later adopters and society at large, especially if prevailing norms favor unproductive rent extraction over productive entrepreneurship. Investments in learning and innovation also involve higher risk and asymmetries between what the firm does and what the financier can gauge, leading to funding gaps.

Given these key gaps between private and social returns, there is a strong case for appropriate public policy support. Sensible policy design requires careful attention to the characteristics of each locality. Particular policies are often necessary but not sufficient to have impact, given that complementary soft infrastructure may be missing, including appropriate competition, trade, investment, and technology policies;

rule-of-law-based policy certainty; educational, financial, legal, and other institutions; and required local capabilities.

So what are the most important determinants of innovation? Key determinants of innovation, or levers for innovation policy, can be organized into four main areas:

- Incentives for productive entrepreneurship (rule of law, sufficiently generous rewards that allow entrepreneurs to grow without fear of expropriation, sufficient competition pressures to prevent deviation from efficient innovation actions)
- Skills (including research and development [R&D] support for the building of absorptive capacity within enterprises,[3] the responsiveness of management and worker training to changes in market demands, technical assistance to facilitate long-term collaboration for education and research between business associations and universities, and scholarships to study abroad)
- Information (including openness to foreign trade, foreign direct investment [FDI], technology licensing, and global talent flows, specific programs to encourage multinational corporations [MNCs] to increase domestic spillovers by transferring learning to local workers and managers, and widespread access to the Internet)
- Finance (including the availability of a mix of public and private financial instruments and institutional delivery mechanisms) (see Trajtenberg 2009).[4]

This chapter focuses on technological learning and its potential to become an even more important determinant of growth through its impact on innovation, as the stock of ideas expands and is better diffused across and within countries. The chapter begins by reviewing global trends, which make a policy focus on technological learning and innovation more important than ever before; briefly explores how the recent global financial crisis may affect these trends; and concludes by outlining several implications of these trends for innovation policy moving forward. The main message is that developing countries should prioritize diffusion, technological learning, and the adaptation of more efficient existing technologies for productivity upgrading and for the sustainable generation of more and better jobs.

What Has Changed in Recent Years?

Four recent trends in the world economy are (a) the increasing global knowledge flows and accompanying global decomposition of production, (b) the increasing South-South trade, (c) the increased uptake of information and communication technologies (ICT), and (d) the continued growth in emerging economies. All of these trends have important implications for technological learning and innovation.

In recent decades, there has been a substantial increase in international trade in goods and services, FDI, intellectual property and technology licensing flows, and talent flows. The volume of world trade increased 27-fold between 1950 and 2006, three times more than the growth in global gross domestic product (GDP). Trade has grown twice as fast as GDP since 1990. Even more striking, the global value of stocks of FDI rose sixfold between 1990 and 2006, substantially faster than the growth in trade, which increased "only" 3.5 times over the same period. Importantly, these flows have been accompanied by a continuing trend of global decomposition of production, leading to an increasing spatially fragmented production and stage specialization. Vertical trade in developing countries increased from 8 percent in 1985 to around 33 percent in 2005 (figure 2. 1). Eastern Europe and East Asia have shown dramatic

Figure 2.1 Regional Trends in Vertical Specialization as a Percentage of Exports, 1985–2005

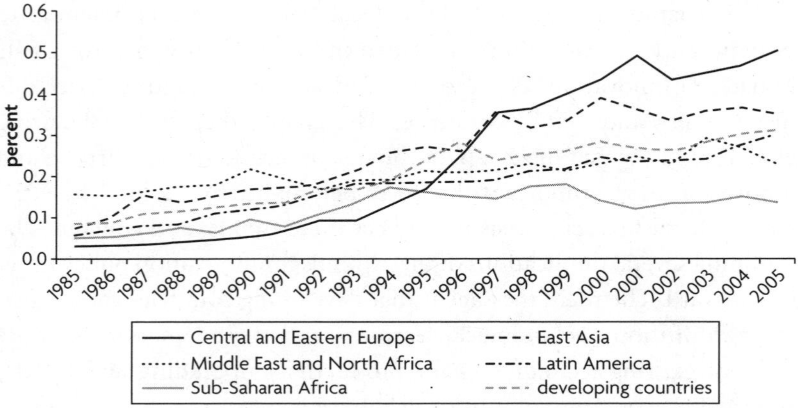

Source: Authors' calculations using United Nations Commodities Trade Statistics database (UN Comtrade).

increases in vertical trade in the 1990s, whereas Sub-Saharan Africa has shown weak integration through international production chains. A global company today imports and exports parts to different countries— international trade within MNCs is estimated to account for around one-third of all international transactions—and in 2000, over 46 percent of U.S. imports were intra-firm (Corcos and others 2009; Bernard and others 2010).

With global decomposition of production, there are now more opportunities for technological learning and innovation from enterprises inserting themselves into global supply chains.[5] Getting started by undertaking a single task is far less daunting than breaking into the global market for an entire product. Potentially, trade in tasks could be a lifeline for countries yet to industrialize because manufacturing can start with specialization in tasks most suited to the skills available. And there is no evidence that task-based production is less technologically sophisticated than production of final products.[6] Recent evidence for an "emerging 8" grouping of developing countries (Argentina, Brazil, China, Hungary, India, Mexico, the Russian Federation, and South Africa) suggests an upswing in available measures of innovation, especially for China, followed by India and Brazil (see figures 2.2 and 2.3).

Figure 2.2 Number of Annual Patents Granted in the United States, 1996–2009

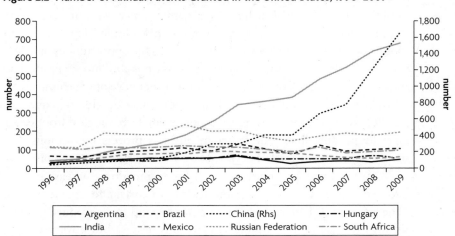

Source: U.S. Patent and Trademark Office, http://www.uspto.gov/web/offices/ac/ido/oeip/taf/reports.htm#by_geog.
Note: Rhs = right-hand side.

Figure 2.3 Total Number of Scientific and Technical Journal Articles, 1995–2005

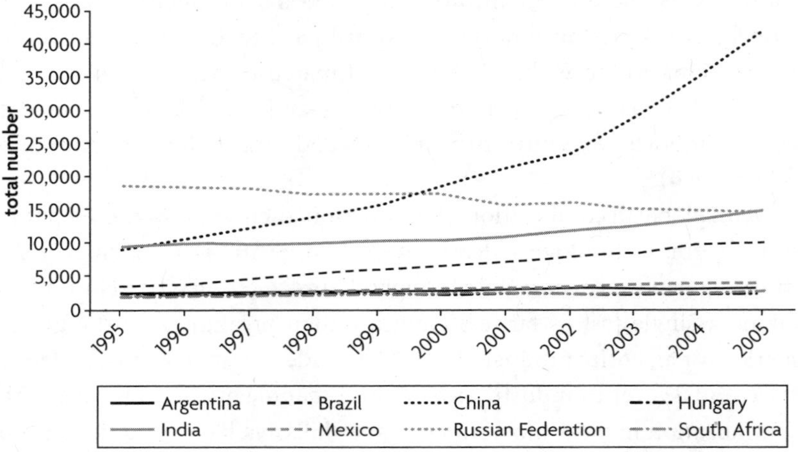

Source: World Bank, World Development Indicators database.

A second related trend has been a change in the direction of trade. The average annual growth rate in South-South trade since 1990 is almost twice that of total world trade; developing countries' trade with each other is now 39 percent of their total trade. In addition, low- and middle-income countries have increased their participation in bilateral trade relations, and the average value of such relations has been increasing in recent years (see Haddad and Hoekman in chapter 3 of this volume). This increase in South-South trade and knowledge flows raises the opportunities of learning by developing country enterprises from possibly more appropriate technologies adapted to local conditions in other developing countries. In particular, the technological challenges for many developing countries reside less in pushing outward the labor-saving technological frontier for specific product lines, but rather in business process innovations that deliver an adequate level of performance at a much lower price point.

A third important trend has been the tremendous increase in data storage and transmission capabilities, fall in costs, and uptake of ICT. The effect of ICT on economies goes far beyond their production. The innovative use of ICT by individuals, businesses, and government— and the untapped potential for the diffusion, technological learning, and use of ideas that mobile phones and fixed and mobile broadband provide—makes a far bigger impact on economies. As a signal of just how productive ICT is viewed by firms, information-processing equipment (hardware, software, communications, and related equipment) today accounts for well over half of all business investment in equipment in the United States.[7] And empirical evidence has been mounting that economywide productivity growth has been driven by innovations in both products and processes in the industries that are the most intensive users of ICT (Jorgenson, Ho, and Stiroh 2008), based on technological learning that builds organizational capital, including complementary investments in new business process skills and management practices.[8] One implication is that for enterprises in developing countries to exploit new ICT-enabled innovations more effectively, they will need to learn and adopt complementary "people management" practices, including decentralized decision making, high-powered rewards, and flexible work rules, in addition to investing more in ICT.

A final important trend has been the continued income growth in emerging economies, including but not limited to the more technologically advanced emerging economies such as Brazil, China, India, and Russia. This process, which showed resilience to the recent economic crisis, has led to a significant reduction in poverty levels; to the gradual emergence of a large new middle class in many developing countries;[9] and to the creation of an attractive market, provided firms are able to explore its scale. The recent growth of developing economies is associated with a long-term trend rather than with cyclical fluctuations, suggesting a sustainable process (Hanson 2010). An implication of this trend is that selected enterprises have started new and disruptive forms of innovation in low-income economies in general, and in China and India in particular (Kaplinsky and others 2010). This new approach to innovation, also called "frugal," "constraint-based," or "reverse" innovation (*The Economist* 2010), is premised on the reality of growing technological capabilities in a number of developing economies, in the significant incentives provided by large and rapidly growing (albeit low-income) local consumer markets, and in low labor costs. The continued growth in emerging economies has opened the opportunity for developing countries to "piggyfrog," a combination of piggybacking on foreign technologies by imitating them combined with leapfrogging by adapting these technologies through lower-cost solutions. Examples include Tata Motors'

US$2,200 Nano car aimed at India's lower-middle class, with low-cost engineering adaptations such as one windshield wiper, tubeless tires, and a two-cyliner engine with top speed of 65 miles per hour (105 kilometers per hour), and Tata Consulting Services' US$24 Swach (Hindi for "clean") water filter targeted at rural households with no electricity or running water, with adaptations such as use of one of the country's most common waste products, ash from rice milling, to filter out bacteria.

The Crisis and its Impacts

The recent global financial crisis added some new elements to these trends. Technological learning and innovation could be adversely affected through lower R&D spending, loss of human capital from longer spells of unemployment, lower appetite for risk, and weaker international diffusion of technologies. On balance, however, the impact of the crisis on technological learning in developing countries is not clear and could actually spur such learning.

Innovation could be negatively affected, especially in developed economies, as some of the enabling conditions have deteriorated. Macroeconomic imbalances, with high fiscal deficits, do not work in favor of both private and public investments in innovation. This is important, because the decisions of firms to invest in innovative activities are sensitive to financial frictions (Ayyagari, Demirgüç-Kunt, and Maksimovic 2007; Gorodnichenko and Schnitzer 2010). The current trend toward more regulation, leaving less space for innovative financing, may have an impact on innovation and, hence, on productivity growth.[10] However, as inefficient firms go out of business, new opportunities emerge for learning, innovation, and leapfrogging.

Trade may also continue to suffer. The crisis brought the most remarkable trade contraction since the Great Depression. Between the last quarter of 2007 and the second quarter of 2009, world merchandise imports fell by no less than 36 percent. A recovery is under way, but the risks of protectionist measures still exist. So far, protectionism remains muted. Some trade-restrictive measures were adopted, but full-scale escalation of protectionism has largely been averted. The coverage of trade-restrictive policies (new import restrictions and trade remedy initiations) has been limited to about 0.4 percent of world imports. But "murky protectionism" that is more difficult to quantify and categorize—including state emergency interventions and "buy local" requirements—remains pervasive. In addition, potentially higher future oil prices and policies to curb greenhouse gas emissions may lead to more regionalized trade flows, dampening the global diffusion of ideas.

Finally, the tightening of financial conditions may affect the ability of firms to finance FDI. While it is unlikely that FDI will be as constrained as debt flows over the medium term, FDI flows to developing countries—an important source of technology transfer with potentially large spill-over effects—are nonetheless expected to be sharply lower in the next few years than in the period of accelerated growth in the past decade (World Bank 2010). Nonetheless, developing countries may end up benefitting from increased inflows of capital, provided the management of the recovery in capital flows is done in ways that effectively channel them to productive investments, in which case they could present a major boon to these countries.

Implications: Options for an Innovation Policy Agenda

Changes in the global landscape and recent trends can have huge consequences for developing countries, both posing challenges and presenting new opportunities. With no intention to be exhaustive, in this final section we explore innovation policy options for developing countries in selected areas linked to technological learning.

First, and perhaps most important, the productivity upgrading potential provided by the huge precrisis increased flows of products, finance, and ideas makes a policy focus on technological learning imperative for developing countries. Even if the advance of the global technological frontier slows in the face of developed countries' temporary lower investments in cutting-edge technologies, developing countries still have huge unrealized benefits from catching up to the frontier (Canuto 2009). Developing countries should therefore prioritize diffusion, technological learning, and adaptation of existing technologies. All developing countries have more to gain in terms of growth and improved living standards from the adoption of technologies that already exist in the world than from riskier and costlier invention and commercialization of new technologies. In many developing countries, a thick clump of unproductive companies in each industry continues to operate far behind the industry's vanguard, even if one considers that economies of scale may explain part of these differences. In India, for example, a leading group in each industry—across 2,300 companies spanning makers of drugs, foods, car parts, and textiles, as well as metal-bashers and garment weavers in 16 states—was about five times as productive as the average firm (Dutz 2007). In Brazil, the disparity in productivity between leading and subsistence firms was even higher, a factor of 10 on average for several sectors (Rodríguez, Dahlman, and Salmi 2008).

Second, and related, policy makers need to better understand the binding constraints to technological learning and innovation facing businesses in their specific country settings. With all investment resources more limited postcrisis, sufficient investments in technological learning will not be forthcoming without focused policies addressing the underlying causes of perceived low returns to technological learning. Why do some business environments allow a large number of low-productivity enterprises to survive without workers and managers either learning and adapting existing ideas from best-practice firms or implementing new profit-enhancing ideas of their own, and how important is this lack of technological learning? In an attempt to address this question, Bloom and others (2010) have undertaken a randomized experiment on large Indian textile plants by giving treatment firms extensive consulting services to upgrade prevailing management technologies as a way to explore whether technological learning and adaptation of cutting-edge management practices have a causal impact on productivity. They find huge effects on productivity and profitability. The natural follow-on question is why profitable technological learning and innovation did not take place without the external intervention.

Not surprisingly, a range of interacting constraints underlie these and related manifestations of insufficient technological learning and innovation, including the following:

- Inadequate incentives for productive entrepreneurship (limited product-market competition; lack of rule of law leading to insufficient decision-making delegation; outsider consultants being unwelcome due to the breaking of tax, labor, and safety laws; and underreporting of profits)

- Insufficient management and worker skills (access and quality issues related to basic education, vocational, firm-based, and management training)
- Lack of information (insufficient use of ICT, little contact with knowledge intermediaries such as MNCs, and no benchmarking)
- Inadequate finance (even for larger firms, impeding of borrowing for management training or consultant advice and stifling of new entry and competition due to insufficient access).

This line of work suggests the need for better measures of different types of technological learning and innovation (the huge differences in levels of learning of management technologies across firms were not appreciated until they were actually measured) and for careful subsequent empirical analyses to pinpoint the binding constraints in different environments—and how they depend on complementary soft infrastructure, including competition, trade, investment, and technology policies; educational, financial, legal, and other institutions; and required local capabilities.

Finally, given the adverse impact of the crisis on the most vulnerable people, it is important to explore how technological learning and innovation can better help meet the needs of the poor. There are at least four distinct areas of policy intervention. For inclusive growth, the likely most important policy area is to foster a business-enabling environment that creates productive employment opportunities for the poor, through the generation of more and better jobs by transformational entrepreneurs. Here, to impact the productivity of enterprises across all sectors of the economy, innovation policy should seek to incentivize local spillovers rather than external leakages and to develop the absorptive capacity of enterprises.

A second policy area is the promotion of appropriate technological learning by grassroots entrepreneurs. These are typically farmers, artisans, and subsistence entrepreneurs who may have little or no formal education and who devise new solutions at the individual or collective level largely through improvisation and experimentation. The power of the Internet in diffusing productive information and spurring technological learning in rural areas is illustrated by the impact of the gradual introduction of Internet kiosks (called e-Choupals, from the Hindi for "village gathering place") in the Indian state of Madhya Pradesh, starting in late 2000. The kiosks display prices, along with agricultural information and weather forecasts, plus the purchase price that the sponsoring company is prepared to pay directly. In addition to cutting into vested interests by eliminating middlemen and providing price transparency, the kiosks increased the cultivation of crops and raised farmer profits.[11] Thus, policies that can help establish sustainable business models to spread the Internet in the poorest parts of the world can have significant impact on local innovation and livelihoods.

Registries and databases are a novel set of mechanisms which, among other things, can promote traditional knowledge (TK). The Indian Ministry of Science and Technology established the National Innovation Foundation in 2000 to provide institutional support for scaling up grassroots innovations. It does so by helping to manage a national register of innovations, including the HoneyBee Network database on grassroots innovations and TK practices. The database includes over 140,000 new or undocumented products and processes such as plant varieties, general machinery, farm implements, energy devices, livestock management, herbal remedies, and related ideas (Dutz 2007). This approach has not yet benefited from proper impact evaluation. The protection of TK and its commercialization stand to benefit from further analysis, including how to share rents from sales of products derived from collectively owned TK that is not already in the public domain, building on the experience of a variety of national and subnational experiments.

A third policy area is the support of incremental adaptation of existing technologies across the range of informal and formal micro and small enterprises in developing countries. These enterprises are often in traditional clusters and are typically characterized by limited deployment of capital and by low technical and managerial capabilities. Their main challenge is usually not commercializing new technologies but upgrading quality and productivity by reverse engineering existing technologies. Though policy makers typically understand the constraints to knowledge diffusion, learning, and innovation in these contexts, it would be helpful if they understood what structural changes need to be made to overcome these obstacles, including how to most effectively provide basic skills upgrading and to increase access to information about both existing technologies and the broader potential demand for the products of micro and small enterprises.

A fourth area of policy intervention is how to effectively spur technological learning efforts by larger formal enterprises for the poor—including the development of private products for underserved "bottom-of-the-pyramid" consumers and the development of new global technologies for public goods of high value to developing countries (such as medicines for neglected diseases or seeds and fertilizers for local soil and climate conditions). To promote technological learning in these areas, public policy may need to tilt incentives facing universities and local and global private firms toward the creation and commercialization of products that directly meet the needs of the poor, including via an appropriate mix of more favorable matching grants for early-stage technology development, tax subsidies, advance market commitments, prizes, patent pools, and open source approaches (Dutta, Dutz, and Orszag 2010). A related policy issue facing governments is to carefully allocate their public funding for basic and applied research, and to calibrate the incentives facing local researchers, so that there is a balance between following the priorities set by the global science and technology frontier (priorities that are generally driven by the interests and needs of developed countries) and addressing local needs.[12]

Notes

1. Benhabib and Spiegel (2005) generalize the Nelson-Phelps catch-up model of technology diffusion, and find empirical support for the notion that human capital plays a positive role in the determination of productivity growth rates through its influence on the rate of catch-up, as a facilitator of technology diffusion and innovation. The direct performance of human capital on its own is less robust.
2. Jones and Romer (2010) insightfully claim that the powerful incentives to connect as many people as possible into trading networks that make ideas more widely available is the deep explanation underlying globalization.
3. Griffith, Redding, and Van Reenen (2004) find empirical support in a panel of industries across 12 countries for the two faces of R&D—the notion that R&D, in addition to stimulating the generation of new technologies, also enhances a firm's learning or absorptive capacity, improving the firm's ability to adopt existing technologies and allowing firms to more easily understand and assimilate the discoveries of others (tacit knowledge).
4. See also Dutz (2007) for a similar broad definition of innovation and a description of the four areas that provide key levers for innovation policy, namely

incentives (for diffusion and adoption of existing technologies and for creation and commercialization of new technologies), supporting skills, information, and finance. See Banerjee and Duflo (2005) for a more detailed discussion of many of these constraints.

5. Based on firm-level data from 27 emerging market economies, Gorodnichenko, Svejnar, and Terrell (2010) provide empirical support for the view that developing countries benefit (by increasing domestic firms' innovation activities) from globalization through the vertical transfer of capabilities from foreign to domestic firms (through supplying of MNCs, as well as exporting and importing, across manufacturing and service sectors).

6. See Breznitz and Murphree (2010) for examples of the rapid global decomposition of production, driven by specialization and capability building, and economies of scale and scope.

7. See Brynjolfsson and Saunders (2010), in particular, table 2.3.

8. Bloom, Sadun, and Van Reenen (forthcoming) document how learning to make better use of ICT is linked to innovations in how employees work, including decentralized decision making (to allow employees to experiment), promotion and higher-powered rewards (to encourage efficient exploitation of private knowledge), flexible work rules (to allow employees to take on new roles), and firing (to remove underperformers). Such complementary management practices allowed U.S. firms to exploit ICT-enabled innovations, and their absence in Europe explains why the United Kingdom and mainland European countries did not follow the U.S. ICT-led productivity acceleration after 1995.

9. Official statistics understate consumer spending in emerging markets, in part due to continued poor statistical coverage of spending on services. Asia, for example, is now the biggest market for many services, accounting for 43 percent of all mobile phones and for two-thirds of the increase in world demand for energy services since 2000.

10. Productivity is currently estimated to grow at rates well below those observed recently in the United States and Europe, given the serious macroeconomic imbalances and the procyclicality of productivity (Feldstein 2010).

11. Cultivation of soybeans increased by an average of 19 percent in districts with kiosks, and farmers' profits increased by 33 percent (Goyal forthcoming). By buying some produce directly, the sponsoring company (ITC Limited, an Indian company that is one of the largest buyers of soybeans) reduced its costs, which paid for the kiosks.

12. Given the important research incentives engendered by the inclusion of journals in globally recognized citation indexes, Xue (2008) argues that certain trends in global science threaten local innovation in developing countries. He highlights the need to reexamine the governance of global science to ensure that international norms and standards are more accommodating to the needs of developing countries and to include appropriate journals in local languages from developing countries that address local research priorities.

Bibliography

Ayyagari, M., A. Demirgüç-Kunt, and V. Maksimovic. 2007. "Firm Innovation in Emerging Markets: The Roles of Governance and Finance." Policy Research Working Paper 4157, World Bank, Washington, DC.

Banerjee, A., and E. Duflo. 2005. "Growth Theory through the Lens of Development Economics." In *Handbook of Economic Growth*, vol. 1A, ed. P. Aghion and S. Durlauf, 473–552. Amsterdam: North Holland.

Benhabib, J., and M. Spiegel. 2005. "Human Capital and Technology Diffusion." In *Handbook of Economic Growth*, vol. 1A, ed. P. Aghion and S. Durlauf, 935–66. North Holland: Elsevier.

Bernard, A. B., J. B. Jensen, S. J. Redding, and P. K. Schott. 2010. "Intra-Firm Trade and Product Contractibility." Working Paper 15881, National Bureau of Economic Research, Cambridge, MA.

Bloom, N., B. Eifert, A. Mahajan, D. McKenzie, and J. Roberts. 2010. "Does Management Matter? Evidence from India." Stanford, CA: Stanford University.

Bloom, N., R. Sadun, and J. Van Reenen. Forthcoming. "Americans Do IT Better: U.S. Multinationals and the Productivity Miracle." *American Economic Review.*

Breznitz, D., and M. Murphree. 2010. *Run of the Red Queen: Government, Innovation, Globalization, and Economic Growth in China.* New Haven: Yale University Press.

Brynjolfsson, E., and A. Saunders. 2010. *Wired for Innovation: How Information Technology Is Reshaping the Economy.* Cambridge, MA: MIT Press.

Canuto, O. 2009. "Decoupling, Reverse Coupling, and All That Jazz." September 1. http://blogs.worldbank.org/growth.

Caselli, F. 2005. "Accounting for Cross-Country Income Differences." In *Handbook of Economic Growth*, vol. 1A, ed. P. Aghion and S. Durlauf, 679–741. Amsterdam: North Holland.

Corcos, G., D. M. Irac, G. Mion, and T. Verdier. 2009. "The Determinants of Intra-Firm Trade." Discussion Paper 7530, Centre for Economic Policy Research, London.

Dutta, A., M. A. Dutz, and J. M. Orszag. 2010. "Intellectual Property and Innovation: Unresolved Issues Regarding the Value of Patent Protection for Economic Development." Unpublished. World Bank, Washington, DC.

Dutz, M. A. 2007. *Unleashing India's Innovation: Toward Sustainable and Inclusive Growth.* Washington, DC: World Bank.

Economist. 2010. "The World Turned Upside Down: A Special Report on Innovation in Emerging Markets." 395 (8678), April 17.

Feldstein, M. 2010. "America's Growth in the Decade Ahead." Project Syndicate, Cambridge. http://www.project-syndicate.org/commentary/feldstein19/English. January 25, 2010.

Gorodnichenko, Y., and M. Schnitzer. 2010. "Financial Constraints and Innovation: Why Poor Countries Don't Catch Up." Working Paper 15792, National Bureau of Economic Research, Cambridge, MA.

Gorodnichenko, Y., J. Svejnar, and K. Terrell. 2010. "Globalization and Innovation in Emerging Markets." *American Economic Journal: Macroeconomics* 2 (2): 194–226.

Goyal, A. Forthcoming. "Information, Direct Access to Farmers, and Rural Market Performance in Central India." *American Economic Journal: Applied Economics*.

Griffith, R., S. Redding, and J. Van Reenen. 2004. "Mapping the Two Faces of R&D: Productivity Growth in a Panel of OECD Countries." *Review of Economics and Statistics* 86 (4): 883–95.

Hanson, G. 2010. "Sources of Export Growth in Developing Countries." San Diego: University of California–San Diego. Unpublished.

Jones, C. I., and P. M. Romer. 2010. "The New Kaldor Facts: Ideas, Institutions, Population, and Human Capital." *American Economic Journal: Macroeconomics* 2 (1): 224–45.

Jorgenson, D., M. Ho, and K. Stiroh. 2008. "A Retrospective Look at the U.S. Productivity Growth Resurgence." *Journal of Economic Perspectives* 22 (1): 3–24.

Kaplinsky, R., J. Chataway, N. Clark, R. Hanlin, D. Kale, L. Muraguri, T. Papaioannou, P. Robbins, and W. Wamae. 2010. "Below the Radar: What Does Innovation in Emerging Economies Have to Offer other Low Income Economies?" Working Paper Series 2010-020, United Nations University, Maastricht, The Netherlands.

Lin, J., and O. Canuto, eds. 2010. "The Global Crisis and Medium-Term Growth Prospects for Developing Countries." World Bank, Washington, DC.

Pitigala, Nihal. 2009. "Global Economic Crisis and Vertical Specialization in Developing Countries." PREM Note 133, World Bank, Washington, DC.

Rodríguez, A., C. Dahlman, and J. Salmi. 2008. *Knowledge and Innovation for Competitiveness in Brazil.* World Bank Institute Development Studies. Washington, DC: World Bank.

Trajtenberg, M. 2009. "Innovation Policy for Development: An Overview." In *The New Economics of Technology Policy*, ed. D. Foray. Cheltenham, UK: Edward Elgar Publishing.

World Bank. 2010. *Global Economic Prospects 2010: Crisis, Finance, and Growth.* Washington, DC: World Bank.

———. 2010. *World Development Indicators 2010.* Washington, DC: World Bank. http://publications.worldbank.org/ecommerce/catalog/product?item_id=9585416.

World Bank and OECD (Organisation for Economic Co-operation and Development). 2009. *Innovation and Growth.* Paris: OECD.

Xue, L. 2008. "China: The Prizes and Pitfalls of Progress." *Nature* 454: 398–401.

3

Trading Places: International Integration after the Crisis

Mona E. Haddad and Bernard Hoekman

The global financial crisis is stimulating a broad reassessment of economic integration policies in developed and developing countries alike. The crisis was associated with the "Great Trade Collapse"—the sharpest synchronized decline in international trade flows since the Great Depression (Baldwin 2009). The collapse—a whopping 36 percent fall in world merchandise imports between the fourth quarter of 2007 and the second quarter of 2009—followed a long period of steady expansion of global trade and direct investment flows. This growth was supported by a steady movement toward opening markets. Apart from pockets of protection in agriculture and in certain labor-intensive parts of certain sectors (for example, clothing), high-income countries at the start of the crisis had very low rates of protection. Many developing countries had also been dismantling trade barriers unilaterally or in the context of trade agreements.

The sharp and deep collapse in trade that occurred was primarily a reflection of the splintering of global value chains. As demand for final goods dried up following the credit shock and collapse in confidence in the

We are grateful to Ana Cusolito and Cosimo Pancaro for their excellent background analytical work.

second half of 2008—especially for durables and investment goods—so did demand for intermediate inputs and components and the associated transport and logistics services. The rapid recovery in trade flows that was observed between the second quarters of 2009 and 2010 is the counterpart to the collapse—because of the international nature of production chains, as demand for final products recovered so did demand for parts, components, and the associated assembly tasks. Uncertainty remains, however, about whether, in the medium term, the structure of production and specialization that had emerged before the crisis will be sustained.

Specifically, the crisis and its aftermath call into question whether development and growth strategies that are premised on deep integration into the world economy—the so-called export-led growth model—remain appropriate. For example, Klein and Cukier (2009:11) claim that "the era of export-led growth is over in its current form." Outward-oriented or export-led growth strategies are being reassessed for two main reasons. The first is because of the speed with which the trading system transmitted simultaneous negative shocks in major markets to the rest of the world—thus contradicting extreme versions of the "decoupling" thesis and making outward orientation seem a riskier proposition. Di Giovanni and Levchenko (2009a) show that sectors that are more open to international trade are more volatile, and that as trade is accompanied by increased specialization, more openness increases aggregate volatility. Offsetting this is that sectors that are more open to trade are less correlated with the rest of the economy. This reduces overall volatility but not enough to offset the impact of the other factors.[1]

Second, successful export-led growth strategies are often associated with large trade surpluses, foreign exchange reserves, and an undervalued currency (or "financial mercantilism"; see, for example, Aizenman and Lee 2008). The flipside of these trade surpluses has been large deficits in some of the main importing markets such as the United States and in many (less successful) developing countries. The prospect of continued (cheap) financing of these deficits will decline in the postcrisis period, and political pressures to restrict the continued export growth of surplus countries can be expected to remain high.

Some degree of global rebalancing is surely going to take place in the medium term. This process might limit the capacity of newly developing countries to rely on overseas demand, but it also offers low-income countries an opportunity to expand trade with the more advanced emerging markets. Integration remains a key dimension of any development strategy. However, because the postcrisis period will most likely be characterized by a world with multiple growth poles and lower global growth than in the precrisis decade, developing countries will benefit from greater diversification across products and markets. A clear lesson of the crisis is that openness brings with it the risk of volatility and the associated human and economic costs. Diversification will help reduce such volatility.

A remarkable feature of the policy responses to the crisis was the limited recourse to overt protectionism in an effort to shelter domestic firms. The last time the world economy went through a global downturn, following the second oil price shock and the winding down of inflation at the end of the 1970s, there was a widespread resort to "voluntary" export restraints and quantitative restrictions for products such as cars, textiles, and steel. Nontariff barriers came to apply to over one-third of all developing country exports in the early 1980s (Nogues, Olechowski, and Winters 1986), on top of average tariffs that were significantly higher than they are today. So far, this response has largely been avoided in the current downturn (Evenett 2009; WTO 2009).

One reason for the limited use of protectionist instruments is the globalization of production: countries that are a part of a specific production chain do not have an incentive to raise the cost of the imports that they process for reexport. Aside from changing political economic incentives to use trade policy, the crisis also revealed that international disciplines matter: the rules of the game that are embodied in trade agreements—both the World Trade Organization and regional arrangements such as the European Union (EU), the North American Free Trade Agreement (NAFTA), and so forth—constrained recourse to protectionism. The fact that the institutions that make up the global trading system proved to be robust illustrates the importance of further strengthening the trade regime.

Conclusion of the Doha Round will limit the ability of governments to increase tariffs or agricultural subsidies in the future and reaffirm the international community's commitment to keep cross-border trade and investment flowing (Hoekman, Martin, and Mattoo 2010). As important, it will open the way to launch international efforts to limit the possible negative spillovers associated with national policies and policy responses to external shocks. Although trade policy is likely to feature less prominently in the toolbox of governments, other instruments—such as the exchange rate or specific types of industrial (sectoral) policy—continue to have an important role to play. These are appropriate instruments for governments to use in the pursuit of growth and development goals, but they also can have beggar-thy-neighbor features and generate international tensions. Addressing these tensions—which are in part the consequence of successful pursuit of export-led growth—in a cooperative manner is important both to prevent recourse to unilateral retaliation by trading partners and to allow those countries that are most in need of effective proactive policies to use them without fear of negative reactions from the rest of the world.

The trade agenda moving forward does not center on stepping back from integration into the world economy. Instead, the focus should be on finding ways to maximize the benefits from trade and foreign direct investment while reducing the vulnerabilities that come with greater openness. Four broad policy implications flow from this assessment:

- *Focus more on South-South trade.* Higher growth in many middle-income developing countries (Brazil, the Russian Federation, India, and China [BRIC], and so forth) provides an opportunity (incentive) for more South-South trade. This will reduce exposure to possible prolonged slow-growth markets in Europe, Japan, and the United States. A policy implication is a greater focus on reduction of barriers to such trade, which are higher than for South-North trade.
- *Promote greater diversification.* More South-South trade will expand the number of markets developing countries trade with. Also, expanding the number of products they export—including services—can reduce output growth volatility.
- *Acknowledge that sustained export growth and successful diversification require supportive policies.* These include a competitive exchange rate and policies that support the ability of firms to operate on international markets.
- *Expand international cooperation* at both the global and the regional levels. Such expansion will help to manage the tensions that will arise as the result of both the rebalancing of the world economy ("the rise of

the rest") and, more specifically, the use of policies that may have negative repercussions for other countries. Continued efforts are needed to agree to rules of the game that extend beyond the narrow ambit of trade policy.

Increasing South-South Trade

Trade levels began to recover starting in the third quarter of 2009, and world trade is predicted to grow by some 10 percent in 2010. A feature of the trade expansion is that it has been driven in part by restocking (which is of a one-time nature) and by the monetary and fiscal stimuli put in place by the major economies (Freund 2009). High debt and deficit levels in many Organisation for Economic Co-operation and Development (OECD) countries will continue to be drags on growth, and thus consumption, for a substantial length of time. Thus, developing countries may not be able to rely on developed countries to fuel their export-led growth, as rapidly industrializing countries, such as China in the 1990s and the Asian Tigers before it, were able to do. Over the medium term, the development of "export-led growth v2.0," in which South-South trade plays a more important role, will be essential (Canuto, Haddad, and Hanson 2010).

Northern markets are still important, but low- and middle-income countries (LMICs) are increasingly a source of import demand and varied products. The import share of BRIC countries doubled from 6 percent to 12 percent during 1996–2008 (figure 3.1). Other LMICs increased their share from 13 percent to 16 percent. In relative terms, the importance of the high-income countries (HICs) as a direct source of import demand is decreasing, from a total share of 81 percent in 1992 to 72 percent in 2008. South-South trade increased at both the extensive and the intensive margins. Exports of LMICs to BRIC countries rose from 7 percent of the total in 2000 to 12 percent in 2008. By contrast, exports of LMICs to HICs decreased during the same period, from some 80 percent to 69 percent. The average value of a transaction from LMICs to BRIC countries increased 444 percent during 1996–2008, while that from LMICs to HICs increased only 180 percent. However, more trade among developing countries is not an exact substitute for trade with developed countries. For consumers in developing countries,

Figure 3.1 Developing Countries Account for an Increasing Share of World Trade

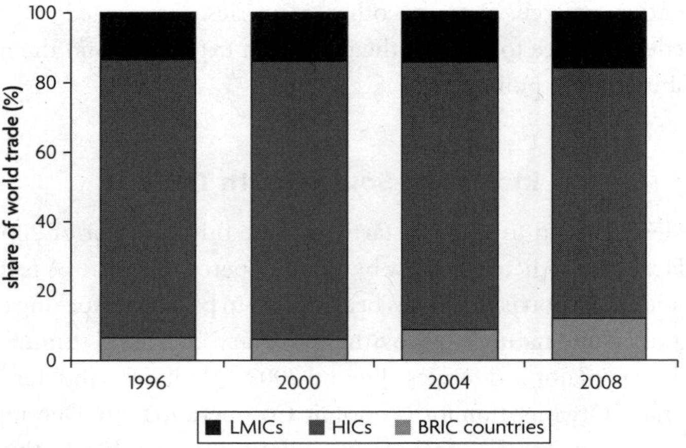

Source: United Nations Commodity Trade Statistics database (UN Comtrade).
Note: LMICs = low- and middle-income countries, HICs = high-income countries.

price is a more important consideration than quality or variety (Kaplinsky and others 2009). Moreover, Southern countries still export substantially fewer varieties than high-income or even middle-income countries (figure 3.2).

The recent growth in South-South trade has been driven by three factors: growth of emerging economies, reduction of trade policy barriers, and, more generally, improvements in the investment climate. Rapid growth of gross domestic product (GDP) is behind a significant proportion of growth in import demand in low- and middle-income countries, and particularly in the BRIC countries (figure 3.3, based on gravity-model-based decomposition of trade growth). These effects exceed the combined contribution of GDP growth in the United States and the EU. Effective stimulus packages in the major Southern economies complemented actions taken by OECD countries to support demand. China has led the way on this front. The rapid return to relatively high growth in Brazil, China, and India has been an important stabilizing factor for global trade.

Reductions in the average level and the dispersion of border protection have also been a significant force behind South-South trade.[2] The average tariffs imposed by BRIC countries decreased 44 percent during 1996–2008. Tariffs in LMICs experienced negative growth rates of 31 percent during

Figure 3.2 Southern Countries Still Export Fewer Varieties Than Northern Countries

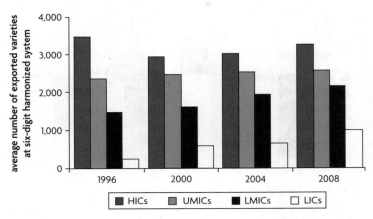

Source: UN Comtrade.
Note: LICs = low-income countries, UMICs = upper-middle-income countries, LMICs = low- and middle-income countries, HICs = high-income countries..

Figure 3.3 LMIC GDP Growth Helps Drive LIC Export Growth, 2000–08

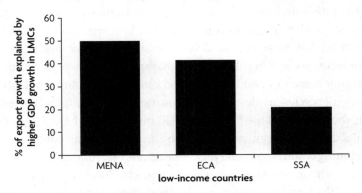

Source: UN Comtrade; World Integrated Trade Solution (WITS).
Note: MENA = Middle East and North Africa, ECA = Europe and Central Asia, SSA = Sub-Saharan Africa.

the same period. As noted, although there have been a variety of measures imposed to restrict trade during the crisis, in the aggregate these have not been significant (Evenett 2009; WTO 2009). However, the trend in the average level of tariffs in HICs has been up—although the movements reflected in figure 3.4 are exaggerated because the base in HICs is very low (the average is less than 5 percent).

Figure 3.4 Tariffs' Drastic Drop in Developing Countries Since 2000

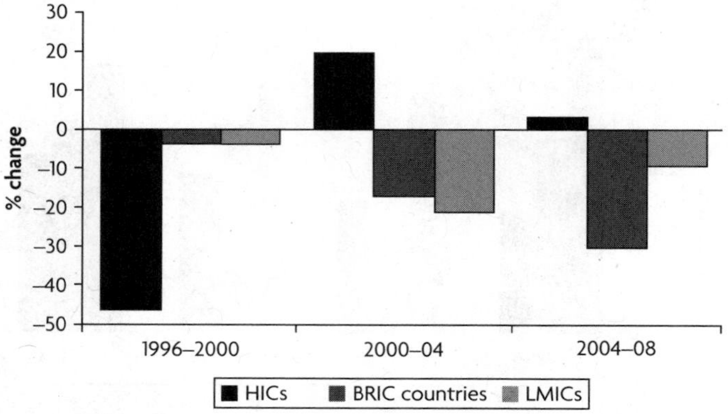

Source: UN Comtrade; World Integrated Trade Solution (WITS).

Reducing Volatility from Openness

Globalization and openness increase cross-border economic interdependence and may lead to convergence of business cycle fluctuations. The crisis has generated a debate on international business cycle co-movements as a result of the remarkable growth performance of emerging countries and the increased intensity of South-South trade. Economic cycles in developing countries remain closely correlated with those in developed countries (Brahmbhatt and Da Silva 2009). While there has been no decoupling in the cyclical component of developing country growth (Kose, Prasad, and Terrones 2003), a decoupling in underlying trend rates of growth may have occurred after the 2000s—the trend rate of growth in developing countries was closer to that in developed countries before the early 2000s; since then, trend growth in developing countries has become substantially higher than in the advanced world.

Supporters of the "trend decoupling" hypothesis argue that there are three reasons to believe that it is possible to sustain the trend decoupling (Canuto 2009). First, the recent fast recovery in many large emerging markets has reflected the strength and sustainability of their national balance sheets. Second, even if the advance of the technological frontier slows in developed countries, developing countries still have a wide scope for technological learning and catching up, given the existing "convergence gap" (Rodrik 2009). Third, the structural dependence of developing countries on exports to developed countries as an outlet for their increasing GDP levels may have been somewhat overstated.

Although the decoupling of LMICs from HICs protects the South against demand shocks in the North, the outward-oriented strategy can still make the economies of developing countries more volatile. Greater openness to trade typically increases vulnerability to product-specific and country-specific shocks from overseas. Transmission of terms-of-trade volatility to output and growth rises as export earnings become a more important source of national income. However, a second mechanism works in the opposite direction. As a country's export sector starts to operate more closely in tune with overseas market conditions, it necessarily becomes less strongly correlated with home market conditions. Because demand shocks at home and overseas are only imperfectly correlated, this force tends to reduce overall volatility of output.

Diversification can operate as insurance against volatility. Outward orientation means that a country is more likely to export more products to more markets. Diversification offers a way of buying the benefits of openness while managing the downside risks. It can take the form of breaking into new products or new markets. A higher degree of export concentration implies a greater impact of an idiosyncratic price shock on the country's terms of trade, inducing greater fluctuations in a country's growth process. Furthermore, a higher level of product diversification weakens the link between openness and growth volatility (Haddad, Lim, and Saborowski 2010). Geographic diversification also plays a role in reducing volatility. Countries whose main export markets are volatile are more likely to import volatility from their trading partners and be exposed to external fluctuations. Thus, if there is low correlation between the fluctuations in different partner countries, geographic diversification reduces the exposure of countries to external shocks. Yet, the relationship between exposure to shocks and geographic diversification is nonlinear, with the beneficial effect of diversification becoming smaller the more diversified a country is (Bacchetta and others 2009).

The exports of developing countries have become more diversified over time, driven in part by South-South trade. The export diversification index based on the Herfindahl-Hirschman Index of concentration shows an improvement of around 10 percent for low-income countries between 1997 and 2007. South-South trade has driven much of this diversification. China's import share of capital equipment and its consumption goods imports from low- and middle-income countries nearly tripled between 2000 and 2008. Low-income countries are increasingly filling the apparel niche previously occupied by middle-income countries; they are shifting away from raw textiles like cotton toward simple manufactured clothing. Higher-middle-income country demand for petroleum, iron, and steel is also helping low-income countries diversify away from their traditional reliance on food exports to Northern markets.

With export product and market diversification acting as effective stabilizers, developing-country policy makers should emphasize measures that help broaden their countries' economic base and expand the range of exportable products. A comprehensive array of policies can help a country's exporters achieve this goal (see also Reis and Farole, in chapter 4 of this volume). This array spans four broad areas: facilitating the costly search process for exporters by alleviating information externalities (export promotion agencies) or setting tax incentives for firms to engage in the costly trial and error process of exporting; getting the incentive structure right to reduce or eliminate policy-induced bias against exports in relative prices; lowering the costs of trade-related services, including telecommunications, ports, transport, and customs administration; and instituting proactive interventions by governments, including notably export promotion and standards (Newfarmer, Shaw, and Walkenhorst 2009). Producer services are an important part of the equation (Francois and Hoekman forthcoming).

The idea is to shift the attention from interventions that distort prices (such as trade policies) to interventions that deal directly with other problems that keep trade low (Harrison and Rodríguez-Clare 2010). Thus, instead of reducing tariffs and increasing export subsidies, programs and grants that help improve market logistics can be more effective. This includes measures that increase the efficiency of the clearance process (that is, speed, simplicity, and predictability of formalities) by border control agencies including customs; improve the quality of trade- and transport-related infrastructure (for example, ports, railroads,

roads, information technology); and enhance the competence and quality of logistics services providers (for example, transport operators and customs brokers).

Policies to Promote Trade: A Competitive Real Exchange Rate

Real exchange rate undervaluation has often been used by developing countries to boost their exports. A policy of managed real depreciation was an important factor determining the success of the Asian export-led growth model (Rodrik 2008). While export-led growth strategies as such are politically relatively uncontroversial, the same cannot be said for a policy of managed real exchange rate depreciation, as recent debates illustrate (Evenett 2010).

The empirical evidence shows that real exchange rate variations can affect growth outcomes. Hausmann, Pritchett, and Rodrik (2005) analyze more than 80 episodes of growth acceleration between 1957 and 1992, which last for at least eight years, and encompass acceleration in growth of at least 2 percentage points. They find that faster economic growth is significantly associated with real exchange rate depreciation. Easterly (2005) finds a negative correlation between real exchange rate overvaluation and per capita growth rates. Johnson, Ostry, and Subramanian (2007) show that real overvaluation hampers the export sector and leads to a fall in economic growth.

Rodrik (2008) argues that real undervaluation promotes economic growth, increases the profitability of the tradable sector, and leads to the expansion of the latter's share in domestic value added. He contends that the tradable sector in developing countries suffers from institutional weaknesses and market failures more than the nontradable sector. A real exchange rate undervaluation can then work as a second-best policy to compensate for the negative effects of these distortions by enhancing the sector's profitability, thus promoting investment that expands capacity to be closer to what is optimal, and by increasing economic growth.

The real exchange rate can be used as a policy tool since in most developing countries it is largely determined by economic policies rather than market-driven factors. The real exchange rate depends on the balance between savings and investment and expenditures and income. Policies that produce higher savings with respect to investment can lead to real exchange rate depreciation. Governments have a variety of policy instruments to achieve a competitive real exchange rate, including moderate fiscal consolidation in the presence of low private absorption, controls on capital inflows and liberalization of capital outflows, targeted intervention on foreign exchange markets, and anti-inflationary policies such as price and wage moderation. However, undervaluation has not had a significant impact on growth and exports, except for some low-income countries (figure 3.5).

A stable real exchange rate is critical for sustained growth. Large mis-alignments of the real exchange rate from its equilibrium can hamper economic growth, as can real exchange rate variability (Eichengreen 2008). Aguirre and Calderón (2005) show that both large real exchange rate overvaluation *and* large real exchange rate undervaluation (devaluations) reduce growth. Bleany and Greenaway (2001) find that exchange rate instability negatively affects investment in Sub-Saharan African

Figure 3.5 Positive Impact of Undervaluation on Export and GDP Growth for Low-Income Countries, 1950–2004

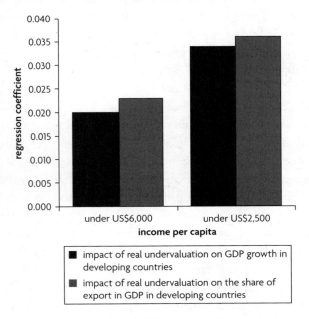

Source: Data for 187 countries based on Penn World Tables.

countries. Bosworth, Collins, and Chen (1995) provide evidence that, in a large sample of industrial and developing countries, real exchange rate volatility hampers economic growth, reducing productivity growth. Aghion and others (2006) replicate this result but also show that the negative effect of real exchange rate volatility on economic growth shrinks in countries with a higher level of financial development.

An export-led growth strategy paired with managed undervaluation is likely to incur costs if the real exchange rate is kept too low for too long. It may cause an excessive accumulation of low-yielding foreign reserves, which is inefficient and may imply an adjustment pattern characterized by high and destabilizing inflation. From a global perspective, current account surpluses in a large number of developing countries would have to be matched by deficits in the industrialized world. One result of the crisis is that large-deficit countries such as the United States may be neither prepared to run nor capable of running ever larger deficits to absorb an increase in the exports of developing countries. Instead, a reduction in consumption spending in deficit countries is likely and a global rebalancing almost inevitable. While this is a critical issue for large players such as China, it is likely to be less significant for most developing countries. For these countries, the challenge is to diversify across more markets—including the BRIC countries. Maintaining a competitive real exchange rate is a key precondition for beginning to expand market shares in these countries. Appreciation of currencies of large middle-income countries will benefit low-income exporters.

The use of the exchange rate as a policy instrument to boost exports and growth would be ineffective if many developing countries were to employ it, due to competition among them. It would also hurt both domestic consumption and export-oriented industries with high import content. Thus, undervaluation should be considered only for small countries at an early stage of development, with stagnant export growth and a need to enter more resources into the tradable sector (Freund and Pierola 2009).

Deepening International Cooperation

The real exchange rate is a key determinant of the ability of firms to be able to compete on export markets. But many other policies also play an important role, including elaborating and implementing trade agreements that enhance access to markets and creating economic zones, programs that signal the existence of potential partners and help to screen associates that can be trusted from a quality and credit perspective, investments in infrastructure and trade corridors, trade support and investment promotion institutions, financial support and tax incentives to promote quality upgrading, and so forth. Greater product and market diversification needs to be supported by a comprehensive array of policies to help a country's exporters upgrade existing products, break into new geographic markets, and launch and consolidate new lines of business abroad.

Trade agreements can be an important tool to support better access to markets—especially other developing country markets, given that barriers to trade are still substantially higher in the South than in OECD countries (by a factor of 2, 3, or more). They can also be an important instrument to help governments manage proactive policies that aim to offset market and government failures that create a bias against investment in tradable activities. Joint surveillance of the effects of policies, their incidence, and effectiveness can be a source of valuable information and accountability. Agreements can be structured to increase the credibility of exit strategies—helping to ensure that support does not become a source of rents and to keep in place activities that are not viable. Finally, and most important, trade agreements offer a mechanism through which the potential negative externalities that are created by national policies can be addressed in a cooperative manner.

Looking Forward

In our view, the crisis has not in any way weakened the case for international integration to be a core component of development strategies. What it has illustrated is that a globalized world economy can generate very severe volatility. This calls for social policies and countercyclical policy instruments, but does not imply that countries should in the future devote less effort to integrate further into the world economy and seek to expand the tradable sector of the economy—both goods and services. Diversification across markets and products can help reduce output volatility, especially volatility that is due to idiosyncratic shocks that are specific to a sector or source of demand. The type of highly synchronized global credit crisis that the world has just gone through is likely to be a very infrequent occurrence.

An important consequence of the crisis is that the differential growth performance between high-income and emerging-market economies that was already evident will be strengthened. One result is that South-South trade will continue to expand, in the process helping to diversify trade patterns. From a policy perspective, a multipolar world calls for efforts by developing countries to reduce the barriers to trade they impose on each other. Initiatives that can make a difference include the extension of duty-free and quota-free access for least-developed-country exporters by all G-20 members;[3] further reductions of tariffs and non-tariff barriers on a nondiscriminatory basis on products in which poorer developing countries have a comparative advantage; and a concerted effort to cooperate on a regional basis to lower real trade costs created by poor trade and transport-related infrastructure, inefficient logistics services, and border management.

Notes

1. Di Giovanni and Levchenko (2009b) extend the analysis to the more disaggregated firm as opposed to sector level and show that country size matters importantly—trade increases aggregate volatility much more (by a factor of 10) in a small economy like Belgium than in a large economy like the United States.
2. For example, between 1991 and 1995, Brazil's tariffs fell from an average of 29 percent to zero percent. During that period, Argentina's exports to Brazil quadrupled while its exports to the rest of the world increased only 60 percent (Bustos 2010).
3. Members of the G-20 are Argentina, Australia, Brazil, Canada, China, France, Germany, India, Indonesia, Italy, Japan, the Republic of Korea, Mexico, the Russian Federation, Saudi Arabia, South Africa, Turkey, the United Kingdom, the United States, and the European Union.

Bibliography

Aghion, P., P. Bacchetta, R. Ranciere, and K. Rogoff. 2006. "Exchange Rate Volatility and Productivity Growth: The Role of Financial Development." *Journal of Monetary Economics* 56: 494–513.

Aguirre, A., and C. Calderón. 2005. "Real Exchange Rate Misalignments and Economic Performance." Working Paper 315, Central Bank of Chile, Santiago.

Aizenman, J., and J. Lee. 2008. "Financial versus Monetary Mercantilism: Long-run View of Large International Reserves Hoarding." *World Economy* 31 (5): 593–611.

Bacchetta, M., M. Jansen, C. Lennon, and R. Piermartini. 2009. "Exposure to External Shocks and the Geographical Diversification of Exports." In *Breaking into New*

Markets: Emerging Lessons for Export Diversification, ed. R. Newfarmer, W. Shaw, and P. Walkenhorst, 81–100. Washington, DC: World Bank.

Baldwin, R., ed. 2009. *The Great Trade Collapse: Causes, Consequences and Prospects.* London: Centre for Economic Policy Research.

Berg, A., and Y. Miao. 2010. "The Real Exchange Rate and Growth Revisited: The Washington Consensus Strikes Back?" IMF Working Paper 58, International Monetary Fund, Washington, DC.

Bleaney, M., and D. Greenaway. 2001. "The Impact of Terms of Trade and Real Exchange Rate Volatility on Investment and Growth in Sub-Saharan Africa." *Journal of Development Economics* 65: 491–500.

Bosworth, B., S. Collins, and Y. Chen. 1995. "Accounting for Differences in Economic Growth." Unpublished manuscript, Brookings Institution, Washington, DC.

Bouët, A., D. Laborde, E. Dienesch, and K. Elliott. 2010. "The Costs and Benefits of Duty-Free, Quota-Free Market Access for Poor Countries: Who and What Matters?" Working Paper 206, Center for Global Development, Washington, DC.

Brahmbhatt, M., and L. P. Da Silva. 2009. "The Global Financial Crisis: Comparisons with the Great Depression and Scenarios for Recovery." PREM Note 141, World Bank, Washington, DC.

Bustos, P. Forthcoming. "Trade Liberalization, Exports and Technology Upgrading: Evidence on the Impact of MERCOSUR on Argentinean Firms." *American Economic Review.*

Canuto, O. 2009. "Decoupling, Reverse Coupling, and All That Jazz." September 1. http://blogs.Worldbank.org/growth.

Canuto, O., M. Haddad, and G. Hanson. 2010. "Export-led Growth v2.0." *Economic Premise* Note 3, March, World Bank, Washington, DC.

Di Giovanni, J., and A. A. Levchenko. 2009a. "Trade Openness and Volatility." *Review of Economics and Statistics* 91 (3): 558–85.

———. 2009b. "International Trade and Aggregate Fluctuations in Granular Economies." RSIE Discussion Paper 585, Research Seminar in International Economics, University of Michigan.

Easterly, W. 2005. "National Policies and Economic Growth: A Reappraisal." In *Handbook of Economic Growth*, ed. P. Aghion and S. Durlauf, 1015–59. Amsterdam: North Holland.

Eichengreen, B. 2008. "The Real Exchange Rate and Economic Growth." Working Paper 4, Commission on Growth and Development, World Bank, Washington, DC.

Evenett, S., ed. 2009. *Broken Promises: Global Trade Alert.* London: Centre for Economic Policy Research.

———, ed. 2010. *The US-Sino Currency Dispute: New Insights from Economics, Politics and Law.* London: Centre for Economic Policy Research.

Francois, J., and B. Hoekman. Forthcoming. "Services Trade and Policy." *Journal of Economic Literature.*

Freund, C. 2009. "The Trade Response to Global Downturns: Historical Evidence." Policy Research Working Paper 5015, World Bank, Washington, DC.

Freund, C., and D. Pierola. 2009. "Exports Surges. The Power of a Competitive Currency." Policy Research Working Paper 4750, World Bank, Washington, DC.

Haddad, M., J. J. Lim, and C. Saborowski. 2010. "Trade Openness Reduces Growth Volatility When Countries Are Well Diversified." Policy Research Working Paper 5222, World Bank, Washington, D.C.

Harrison, A., and A. Rodríguez-Clare. 2010. "Trade, Foreign Investment, and Industrial Policy for Developing Countries." In *Handbook of Development Economics*, ed. D. Rodrik and M. Rosenzweig, vol. 5, chapter 63, 4039–214. Amsterdam: Elsevier.

Hausmann R., L. Pritchett, and D. Rodrik. 2005. "Growth Accelerations." *Journal of Economic Growth* 10: 303–29.

Hoekman, B., W. Martin, and A. Mattoo. 2010. "Conclude Doha: It Matters!" *World Trade Review* 9 (3): 505–30.

Johnson, S., J. D. Ostry, and A. Subramanian. 2007. "The Prospects for Sustained Growth in Africa: Benchmarking the Constraints." IMF Working Paper 52, International Monetary Fund, Washington, DC.

Kaplinsky, R., and M. Farooki. 2010. "What Happens in Global Value Chains When the Market Shifts from the North to the South?" Policy Research Working Paper No. 5205, World Bank, Washington, DC.

Klein, B., and K. Cukier. 2009. "Tamed Tigers, Distressed Dragon: How Export-Led Growth Derailed Asia's Economies." *Foreign Affairs* 88 (4): 8–16. Poverty Reduction and Economic Management Network.

Klinger, B., and D. Lederman. 2009. "Diversification, Innovation, and Imitation of the Global Technological Frontier." In *Breaking into New Markets: Emerging Lessons for Export Diversification*, ed. R. Newfarmer, W. Shaw, and P. Walkenhorst, 101–10. Washington, DC: World Bank.

Kose, M. A., E. S. Prasad, and M. E. Terrones. 2003. "Financial Integration and Macroeconomic Volatility." *IMF Staff Papers* 50: 119–41.

Newfarmer, R., W. Shaw, and P. Walkenhorst, eds. 2009. *Breaking into New Markets: Emerging Lessons for Export Diversification*. Washington, DC: World Bank.

Nogués, J., A. Olechowski, and L. A. Winters. 1986. "The Extent of Non-Tariff Barriers to Industrialized Countries' Imports." *World Bank Economic Review* 1: 181–99.

Rodrik, D. 2008. "The Real Exchange Rate and Economic Growth." *Brookings Papers on Economic Activities* (2): 365–412.

———. 2009. "Growth after the Crisis." Discussion Paper 7480, Centre for Economic Policy Research, London.

World Bank. 2010. *Global Economic Prospects 2010: Crisis, Finance, and Growth*. Washington, DC: World Bank.

WTO (World Trade Organization). 2009. "Report to the TPRB from the Director-General on the Financial and Economic Crisis and Trade Related Developments." World Trade Organization, Geneva.

4

Exports and the Competitiveness Agenda: Policies to Support the Private Sector

José Guilherme Reis and
Thomas Farole

Since most developing countries abandoned wholesale import substitution models in the 1980s in favor of export-led growth, the pace of global trade integration has been nothing short of extraordinary. Indeed, trade has arguably been the most important driver of global growth, convergence, and poverty alleviation over the past quarter century. During 1983–2008, global trade grew 85 percent faster than gross domestic product (GDP). Developing countries in particular have benefited—annual exports from low- and middle-income countries grew 14 percent annually since 1990 compared to only 8 percent for high-income countries. China and East Asia's rise is intrinsically linked to their export-led growth policies, which contributed to a rapid economic diversification and a shift in trade from commodities to manufactured products. The share of manufactured products in total exports of low- and middle-income countries rose dramatically from only 15 percent in 1970 to 57 percent by 2008, a level approaching the share in high-income countries (72 percent).

This rapid period of export growth from developing countries has been enabled by two critical structural changes in global trade: (a) the vertical and spatial fragmentation of manufacturing into highly integrated global production networks, and (b) the rise of services trade.

Both of these in turn were made possible by major technological revolutions supported by multilateral trade policy reforms and broad liberalizations in domestic trade and investment environments in both developed and developing countries. Average tariffs in high-income countries declined dramatically since the 1960s. In the United States, for example, average most favored nation (MFN) applied tariffs more than halved to reach around 10 percent by 1990 (figure 4.1); they have since more than halved again. Yet the major response from developing countries only took off from the late 1980s. At this point, major technological advances, particularly in transport (containerized shipping) and communications technologies, dramatically lowered the cost of shipping intermediate goods and of managing complex production networks. The highly integrated network of trade in East Asia, anchored in China, has enabled the benefits of trade to spill over, supporting growth rates approaching double digits in many countries in the region over the past decade.

A second major area of growth potential for developing countries that has been made possible by rapidly expanding trade is in the area of services. Many of the same trends driving the offshoring of manufacturing

Figure 4.1 Relationship between Market Access and Trade Growth from Developing Countries

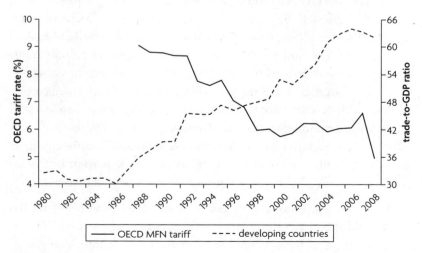

Source: Authors' calculations.
Note: OECD = Organisation for Economic Co-operation and Development.

have contributed to the globalization of services. Specifically, this includes dramatic changes in the so-called 3Ts—technology, transportability, and tradability—of many services activities, which allow powerful forces of comparative advantage to play out. In South Asia, for example, the services sector accounted for more than 50 percent of the growth in regional GDP between 1980–85 and 2000–07 (Ghani 2010). And while significant barriers remain in the trade policy environment, growth in services trade has benefited from substantial liberalization in many markets, particularly on investment openness (Gootiz and Matoo 2009).

At the heart of the developments in both global production networks and services offshoring has been the rapid and innovative private sector response to exogenous change; trade liberalization and technological advances facilitated organizational and managerial innovations by multinational corporations (MNCs), initially from high-income countries, that seized the opportunity to take advantage of locational sources of comparative advantage at each stage of the production chain. This would not have been possible, however, without an equally strong supply response from the private sector in developing countries. Indeed, the reforms in Asia (by China, India, Vietnam, and others) to establish a more competitive environment for the private sector were crucial to facilitating the conditions that allowed these integrated trade networks to develop.

The Crisis and the End of an Era

The global economic crisis came crashing into the middle of this long-running export-led growth party during 2008 and 2009. As the financial crisis drained liquidity from the market and risk was dramatically recalibrated, the financial shock quickly affected demand and then reverberated rapidly through these now closely integrated global supply chains. Between the last quarter of 2007 and the second quarter of 2009, global trade contracted by 36 percent (see Haddad and Hoekman, in chapter 3 of this volume). Governments around the world moved relatively rapidly to head off the crisis, flooding the markets with liquidity, supporting trade finance, and investing in massive stimulus packages to boost demand. And although for a period there was a fear that creeping protectionism might undermine the recovery, governments for the most part managed to forego the temptation to engage in populist trade wars on a large-scale basis; however, since employment recovery is likely to lag significantly behind trade and output recovery, at least in high-income economies, the risk of protectionism may remain on the agenda for some time (Gregory and others 2010).

The open, integrated economies of East Asia, which benefited most from export-led growth and global production networks, were among the first to emerge from the crisis and appear to be moving quickly back to robust growth. As the recovery strengthens in 2010, however, the longer-term impacts of the crisis on the policy environment around trade and growth are becoming more apparent. Indeed, the crisis has led to some serious rethinking of some of the conventional wisdom around the growth agenda—the most important result of which is the likelihood that governments will play a much more activist role in the coming years. This is due to three principle reasons.

First, the crisis has shaken faith in markets and discredited laissez-faire approaches that rely simply on trade policy liberalization. Instead, governments and local markets have been "rediscovered." In this sense, the demand for activist government is likely to go well beyond financial markets and regulation and will impact the policy environment in which trade and industrial strategies are designed.

Second, the crisis highlighted the critical importance of *diversification* (of sectors, products, and trading partners) in reducing the risks of growth volatility. The recent era of globalization contributed to substantial specialization of many economies. While this was predicted by trade theory, what was perhaps unexpected was the degree of vertical specialization that emerged through task-based trade in global production networks. As the next era emerges, diversification will be at the top of the policy agenda in most developing countries. This will create further demand for government activism.

Finally, despite the dramatic rise of East Asia and India in recent years, their success in export-led growth may be more the exception than the rule in developing countries. Many developing countries have failed to benefit from the opportunities afforded by liberalized trade over the past quarter century. Even with the benefits of preferential market access, few exporters from low-income countries are in a position to compete in international markets due to poor productivity, high trade costs, and the inability to benefit from internal and external scale economies. Indeed, the realization of this gap has contributed to the emergence of the "aid for trade" agenda in recent years. This approach aims to go beyond the simple focus on eliminating policy barriers imposed on goods as they cross borders (for example, tariffs, quantitative restrictions, and foreign exchange controls) and engage with the more complex set of competitiveness challenges that restrict the supply response from the private sector.

The Coming Era of Government Activism: Old Industrial Policy or a New Competitiveness Agenda?

The demand for a more activist approach raises the risk of going back to old-style industrial policy that is associated with the import-substitution era. One risk here is that the heavy hand of government—in picking winners, in managing unrealistic exchange rates, and in attempting to derive demand through import substitution—will distort the market and undermine private sector competitiveness in the long term.[1] As shown in Rodríguez-Clare (2005), even in the presence of externalities and clustering, distorting prices policies such as import tariffs, export subsidies, and other tax breaks and fiscal incentives are likely to reduce welfare. Further, such demand for protection—which would inevitably emerge through traditional industrial policies—could eventually undermine the gains made in trade liberalization over recent decades.

On the other hand, greater active government commitment to growth policy also opens up the possibility of countries adopting a more comprehensive, competitiveness-based approach to exports and growth. As Klinger (2010) points out, firm productivity is determined in large part by public inputs to firm production and the good functioning of the markets in which they operate. Thus, government can play a valuable role—indeed, its role is critical—in overcoming market failures, particularly with regard to information externalities and to collective action and coordination challenges. If acting effectively, government can create the conditions that allow the private sector to respond to market opportunities. While there is still a debate on the role of government intervention and about the nature and usefulness of industrial policy, there is a consensus today that the identification of a set of microeconomic interventions from governments, without distorting relative prices, can lead to significant improvements in coordination among actors and private sector development. As discussed in Rodríguez-Clare (2005), Harrison and Rodríguez-Clare (2009), and Klinger (2010), these interventions can include both policies to induce discovery, as per Hausmann and Rodrik (2002), and policies to promote the benefits of agglomeration (inspired by the seminal work from Porter [1990]). The mix of these two sets of policies should vary across countries according to their stage of development (Rodríguez-Clare 2005).[2]

The "enlightened path" above would result in a deepening of the competitiveness agenda and a strengthening of government's role in supporting the private sector by unlocking the constraints that discourage private sector innovation, investments, and export diversification, while also facilitating the adjustment capacity of the economy. What might this path look like? Much of it would be familiar; for example, it would recognize the fundamental role of human capital, sound macroeconomic foundations, and basic institutions—like property rights, the rule of law, and effective regulation—as the basis for long-term competitiveness. But it would carry on beyond these basic foundations to address the *microeconomic environment*, which shapes individual firms' capacities and incentives on a daily basis, by also addressing market and information failures, providing public goods, and improving coordination and the diffusion of knowledge and best practices. The competitiveness policy framework might be described as being based on the following three pillars:

- *Aligning macro-incentives:* For example, removing economic biases arising from tariff and nontariff barriers, real exchange rate misalignment, and distortive tax regime; ensuring overall fiscal health of the economy, efficient labor market operation, product and factor market conditions, property rights protection, effective regulation, and ease of firm entry and exit.
- *Reducing trade-related costs:* For example, improving backbone services and inputs such as energy, telecommunications, finance, and other services inputs; improving capacity and coordination of government agencies at the border, international transit arrangements, regional and multilateral agreements, and policy reforms that ensure more competitive markets for services (international transport, logistics, and others) that facilitate trade transactions.

- *Proactive policies for overcoming government and market failures:* For example, promoting technology creation and adaptation, developing product standards and certifications, providing trade finance, supporting industry clusters, facilitating special economic zones and other spatial developments, and ensuring coordination of economic actors and links and spillovers to the local economy.

Many of the issues on the agenda within this broad framework of competitiveness are not new; indeed, governments have always played an important role in addressing some of these. However, with the growing postcrisis emphasis on more proactive policies, several issues are likely to emerge as priorities within the competitiveness agenda. These are discussed briefly in the coming sections and include *targeting transport and trade facilitation to reduce the cost of bringing goods to market; retooling export promotion to support improved export survival; using special economic zones and clusters to facilitate externalities;* and *strengthening competition policy and institutions to support adjustment.*

Targeting Transport and Trade Facilitation to Reduce the Costs of Bringing Goods to Market

Labor costs and productivity are critical determinants of competitiveness, but these stop at the factory or farm gate. For exporters in many developing countries, comparative advantage is eroded step-by-step across the miles between production and markets. Distance alone will, in many sectors, determine the potential to compete in international markets. But more controllable factors, such as transport and communications infrastructure, border-related processes, and local logistics markets, will play a critical role in shaping exporters' competitiveness through their impact on cost, time, and supply chain reliability. Data from the World Bank's *Logistics Performance Index 2010* (Arvis and others 2010) show a clear relationship between logistics performance and exports (see figure 4.2). Empirical literature tracing the effect of transport and trade facilitation constraints on trade flows, while limited by the difficulties of properly measuring these barriers (Pagés 2010), shows unequivocal impacts of time and costs on developing country exports and, particularly, perishable agricultural products

Figure 4.2 Relationship between Logistics Performance and Exports

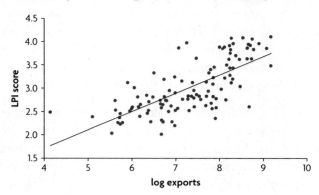

Sources: Arvis and others 2010; United Nations Commodity Trade Statistics database (UN Comtrade)
  (US$ exports, 2008).
Note: LPI = *Logistics Performance Index.*

(Djankov, Freund, and Pham 2006) and on the composition of trade
(Li and Wilson 2009).

Taking up the competitiveness agenda, governments will play an increasingly active role in trying to overcome transport, trade facilitation, and
logistics constraints. This will start by putting in place the hard and soft
infrastructure to facilitate goods movement. But it will also involve more
active efforts to identify and develop transport corridors, to improve coordination across border clearance agencies (both internally and in concert
with trading partners), to strengthen competition in local logistics markets,
and to work with the private sector to overcome coordination failures in
export logistics and facilitate greater scale and predictability.

In addition, given that many developing countries' exports of services are a key element of their trade diversification strategy, an expanded
trade facilitation agenda must also contemplate telecommunication
and connectivity, because maintaining and upgrading both the quantity
and the quality of communication infrastructure is crucial for ensuring
the possibility of engaging in trade in services.

Retooling Export Promotion to Support
Improved Export Survival

Government support for export promotion is based on the significant
information externalities and coordination failures that affect the private

sector with respect to export markets. Export promotion agencies (EPAs) have a long history in both high-income and developing economies. Although EPAs have often been criticized, recent research (Lederman, Olarreaga, and Payton 2009) shows they have generally had a positive impact on export performance in developing countries. Yet, in light of the changing trade dynamics discussed in this chapter and the increasingly risky and competitive conditions in export markets, there is likely to be a need for EPAs to shift from their traditional focus on finding new export market opportunities to supporting new and existing exporters to increase survival rates in export markets, particularly during the first few years after beginning to export. Indeed, as illustrated in figure 4.3, survival rates in developing countries can be dramatically lower than in high-income countries as a result of many additional barriers to competitiveness they face (Brenton, Pierola, and von Uexkull 2009).

Addressing the agenda of export sustainability will require governments to address a much wider set of issues that have an impact on export competitiveness. Some of these will be particularly relevant for certain sectors that offer high opportunities for developing-country exporters. For example, competing in high-value (usually perishable) agricultural exports may require support to ensure standards and certification requirements are met on an industrywide level to facilitate market access for new exporters. In the services sector, which suffers from

Figure 4.3 Ten-Year Survival Rate of Export Relationships: Pakistan and Germany

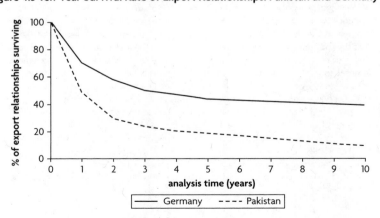

Source: Calculated based on data from UN Comtrade (sourced via World Integrated Trade Solution, World Bank).

notorious information asymmetries, collective action on licensing and accreditation may be necessary to enable competitiveness. Across virtually all sectors, access to trade finance (see box 4.1) is critical to enable exporters to enter and sustain participation in international markets. All of this is likely to imply significant institutional changes in the approach of EPAs, in particular, taking on a greater coordination role and working more closely with other public and private sector actors.

Using Special Economic Zones and Clusters to Facilitate Externalities

Because task-based trade and investment patterns have become ingrained in the global production system and the sources of competition are highly globalized, developing countries are likely to face significant challenges in

---

Box 4.1 Financing Trade in a Postcrisis World

By providing liquidity and security to facilitate the movement of goods and services, trade finance lies at the heart of the global trading system. Indeed, as Auboin (2009) notes, trade finance—upon which some 80 to 90 percent of world trade relies—has become ever more critical as global supply chains have increasingly integrated in recent years. During the recent global crisis, the availability of trade finance was seen to have been substantially reduced, particularly for small and medium enterprises and in developing countries. This acted as a further constraint to trade and became yet another source of contagion that reverberated down supply chains to exacerbate and prolong the crisis.

Although governments and multilateral institutions responded aggressively to stave off the trade finance "gap"—involving the provision of up to US$250 billion in support—evidence from past crises indicates that trade finance may continue to be a problem. For example, in a study of the Asian financial crisis, Love, Preve, and Sarria-Allende (2007) find that the total amount of credit provided collapses in the aftermath of a crisis and continues to contract for several years. This is because credit is generally a complement rather than an alternative to bank credit. When firms are constrained in their access to bank credit, they tend to reduce the amount of trade credit they extend in the supply chain; when they are flush with bank credit, they extend more trade credit.

This highlights the potential vulnerability of trade finance in a postcrisis world. If banks continue to limit lending (exacerbated by regulatory requirements like Basel II), the integrated nature of global production networks means these credit constraints are likely to amplify across supply chains. Proactive responses by governments to promote not only the provision of trade finance, but also wider credit facilities, particularly for small and medium enterprises, will be critical to supporting the competitiveness of the export sector.

Source: Authors.

developing new sources of competitiveness and upgrading their position in value chains. Addressing the challenge of upgrading in developing countries will require facilitating better links between foreign direct investment (the source of potential spillovers) and the domestic private sector. This will require a greater emphasis on human capital upgrading (in terms of both core education and vocational training). Beyond that, however, there is an important role for governments to facilitate spillovers by promoting collaboration between local producers and foreign buyers and overcoming gaps in coordination among the local private sector and institutions. In this regard, governments are likely to put greater emphasis on spatial industrial policies in the years ahead.

One such policy instrument that has been used in many developing countries is special economic zones (SEZs), most commonly export processing zones (EPZs). Traditionally, these have focused primarily on attracting foreign direct investment by establishing a more competitive investment environment than would be available in the domestic market. Such SEZs played a valuable role in catalyzing industrialization and trade integration, particularly in East Asia. However, the traditional EPZ model that has been implemented in most countries[3]—reliant on low wages, trade preferences, and substantial fiscal incentives—paid too little attention to facilitating dynamic links with the local private sector. As such, this model is unlikely to be effective as a tool for growth and development in the new era. Indeed, for many developing countries, it is more likely to facilitate lock-in to a "low road" development path. A more innovative approach to using spatial industrial policy will be part of the new agenda of supporting industrial upgrading in developing countries. This will involve the use of more flexible, integrated zones that combine cluster-based development models with a host of policies designed to facilitate links between foreign investors and the local private sector. This will ensure that the high-quality investment environment on offer in SEZs is also available to the local private sector and will facilitate knowledge and technology spillovers.

As a complement to these spatial policies, governments will increasingly aim to support the development of public-private institutions that promote public goods (for example, training, joint research, certification, and market information) linked directly to local clusters. Indeed, such development of local "institutional thickness" (Amin and Thrift 1994), involving cooperation and knowledge sharing among government agencies, universities, training institutions, and business organizations establishes a governance framework that is perhaps ideally suited to the new competitiveness agenda.

Strengthening Competition Policy and Institutions to Support Adjustment

Central to the aims of the trade policies discussed in this chapter is facilitating and managing the dynamic process of economic adjustment that is inherent in capturing the benefits of trade. This requires redeploying resources (capital, labor, institutions) to higher-value activities. The ability of economies to adapt to a changing environment depends on their degree of flexibility, not only at the more conventional macroeconomic level, but also at the microeconomic level. The foundations of long-run adjustment are, of course, human capital and innovation.[4] But beyond this agenda (and, indeed, intrinsicly linked to it), governments will increasingly focus— as part of their trade and industrial policy—on competition and other policies to promote firm entry and exit and on building and sustaining of dense networks of high-quality and flexible economic institutions.

An effective competition regime is a vital complement to trade liberalization in promoting economic efficiency, development, and growth. Indeed, anticompetitive market distortions inside borders may be partially responsible for the fact that a significant part of the trade liberalization gains of the 1990s did not flow to consumers (Singham 2007). Yet competition, while generally acknowledged as an important element of the growth agenda, has been frequently relegated to a kind of second- or third-priority level. And industrial policies that engage in building "national champions" are frequently at odds with competition policy, which contributes to their long-run welfare deficits. Competition policy plays a critical role in facilitating entry and exit (in both product and factor markets), which Aghion and Howitt (2006) show to be the primary channel through which economic adjustment processes occur in a Schumpeterian growth paradigm.[5]

Finally, delivering on the competitiveness agenda will rely on the existence of effective institutions, including those of the state, the private sector, and civil society. Acemoglu, Johnson, and Robinson (2005) argue that institutions—the "rules of the game" in a society (North 1991)—are the fundamental, "deep determinants" of economic growth and development differences across countries, since they ultimately shape incentives for innovation and entrepreneurship and set the main constraints for societies to adapt. Indeed, the fundamental role of institutions in a society—to facilitate cooperation and collective action among individual (economic) agents—is to address the market and coordination failures that are the basis for the "new" competitiveness agenda discussed in this chapter. But institutions are endogenous, and so can also act as barriers to adjustment by blocking reform (Aghion, Alesina, and Trebbi 2002; Acemoglu and Robinson 2006). And weak institutions may have a negative influence on the provision of public goods and on the development and delivery of policies aimed at improving skills or innovation capacity or other potential sources of growth. Therefore, building networks of dense, flexible, and reform-minded institutions that bring together the public and private sectors will be one of the primary challenges in the long-term agenda of competitiveness.

Notes

1. Noland and Pack (2003) survey a series of studies showing that, contrary to popular belief, industrial policy in East Asia was not successful in supporting high-growth sectors. The sectors that received the most support in terms of subsidies, tax breaks, and protection were not the ones that later showed the highest growth in Japan; the Republic of Korea; and Taiwan, China. This provides further support for valid skepticism regarding policies that attempt to "pick winners."
2. Imbs and Wacziarg (2003) show that growth is first associated with export diversification and later with increasing concentration.
3. Many of the successful East Asian countries, most notably the Republic of Korea and Malaysia, actually implemented much more dynamic SEZ models, with an explicit focus on facilitating spillovers.
4. See Glaeser (2003, 2008) for an ample discussion of the role of human capital in the recovery and adaptation of cities to external shocks and, in particular, how it helped Boston reinvent itself.
5. According to the Schumpeterian growth paradigm, innovation is driven by entrepreneurial investments that are themselves motivated by the prospect of monopoly rents. In addition, new technologies drive out old technologies (the process of creative destruction).

References

Acemoglu, D., S. Johnson, and J. A. Robinson. 2005. "Institutions as a Fundamental Cause of Long-Run Growth." In *The Handbook of Economic Growth*, ed. P. Aghion and S. Durlauf, 385–472. Amsterdam: North Holland.

Acemoglu, D., and J. Robinson. 2006. "De Facto Political Power and Institutional Persistence." *American Economic Review* 96 (2): 325–30.

Aghion, P., A. Alesina, and F. Trebbi. 2002. "Endogenous Political Institutions." CEPR Discussion Paper 3473, Centre for Economic Policy Research, London.

Aghion, P., and P. Howitt. 2006. "Appropriate Growth: A Unifying Framework." *Journal of the European Economic Association* 4 (2–3): 269–314.

Amin, A., and N. Thrift. 1994. *Globalization, Institutions and Regional Development in Europe.* Oxford, UK: Oxford University Press.

Arvis, J. F., M. A. Mustra, L. Ojala, B. Shepherd, and D. Saslavsky. *Connecting to Compete: Logistics Performance Index 2010.* Washington, DC: World Bank.

Auboin, M. 2009. *Boosting the Availability of Trade Finance in the Current Crisis: Background Analysis for a Substantial G20 Package.* London: Centre for Economic Policy Research.

Brenton, P., M. Pierola, and E. von Uexkull. 2009. "The Life and Death of Trade Flows: Understanding the Survival Rates of Developing-Country Exporters." In *Breaking into Markets: Emerging Lessons for Export Diversification*, ed. R. Newfarmer, W. Shaw, and P. Walkenhorst, 127–44. Washington, DC: World Bank.

Djankov, S., C. Freund, and C. Pham. 2006. *Trading on Time.* Washington, DC: World Bank.

Ghani, E. 2010. *The Services Revolution in South Asia.* New Delhi: Oxford University Press.

Glaeser, E. 2003. "Reinventing Boston: 1640–2003." Working Paper 10166, National Bureau of Economic Research, Cambridge, MA.

———. 2008. "The Economic Approach to Cities." Discussion Paper 2149, Harvard Institute of Economic Research, Cambridge, MA.

Gootiz, B., and A. Matoo. 2009. "Services in Doha: What's on the Table?" Policy Research Working Paper 4903, World Bank, Washington, DC.

Gregory, R., C. Henn, B. McDonald, and M. Saito. 2010. "Trade and the Crisis: Protect or Recover." IMF Staff Position Note SPN/10/07, International Monetary Fund, Washington, DC.

Harrison, A., and A. Rodríguez-Clare. 2009. "Trade, Foreign Investment, and Industrial Policy for Developing Countries." NBER Working Paper 15261, National Bureau of Economic Research, Cambridge, MA.

Hausmann, R., and D. Rodrik. 2002. "Economic Development as Self-Discovery." CEPR Discussion Paper 3356, Centre for Economic Policy Research, London.

Imbs, J., and R. Wacziarg. 2003. "Stages of Diversification." *American Economic Review* 93 (1): 63–86.

Klinger, B. 2010. "(New) Export Competitiveness." Center for International Development, Harvard University, Cambridge, MA.

Lederman, D., M. Olarreaga, and L. Payton. 2009. *Export Promotion Agencies Revisited.* Policy Research Working Paper 5125, World·Bank, Washington, DC.

Li, Y., and J. Wilson. 2009. *Trade Facilitation and Expanding the Benefits of Trade: Evidence from Firm Leval Data.* Asia-Pacific Research and Training Network on Trade (ARTNeT), an initiative of the United Nations Economic and Social Commission for Asia and the Pacific (UNESCAP) and the International Development Research Center (IDRC), Canada.

Love, I., A. Preve, and V. Sarria-Allende. 2007. "Trade Credit and Bank Credit: Evidence from Recent Financial Crises." *Journal of Financial Economics* 83 (2): 453–69.

Noland, M., and H. Pack. 2003. *Industrial Policy in an Era of Globalization.* Washington, DC: Institute for International Economics.

North, D. C. 1991. "Institutions." *Journal of Economic Perspectives* 5 (1): 97–112.

Pagés, C., ed. 2010. *The Age of Productivity: Transforming Economies from the Bottom Up.* New York: Palgrave MacMillan.

Porter, M. 1990. *The Competitive Advantage of Nations.* New York: Free Press.

Rodríguez-Clare, A. 2005. "Coordination Failures, Clusters, and Microeconomic Interventions." *Economía* 6 (1): 1–42.

Rodrik, D. 2007. "Industrial Development: Some Stylized Facts and Policy Directions." In *Industrial Development for the 21st Century: Sustainable Development Perspectives,* Department of Economic and Social Affairs, 7–28. New York: United Nations.

Romalis, J. 2007. "Market Access, Openness, and Growth." NBER Working Paper 13048, National Bureau of Economic Research, Cambridge, MA.

Singham, S. 2007. *A General Theory of Trade and Competition: Trade Liberalization and Competitive Markets.* London: Cameron May.

UN Comtrade (United Nations Commodity Trade Statistics Database). http://comtrade.un.org/.

5

Natural Resources and Development Strategy after the Crisis

Milan Brahmbhatt, Otaviano Canuto,
and Ekaterina Vostroknutova

Recent events have rekindled interest in the role of primary commodities in development. Was the boom in commodity prices from around 2003 through 2008 just a cyclical event, or does it suggest that prices have entered a period of secular strength, driven by factors such as demand in big, fast-growing developing countries like China? It is notable that, while commodity prices fell sharply from their peak in 2008 with the onset of the global recession, they generally remained much higher than previous recession lows, often as high as in 2005–07, a period of robust world growth. Furthermore, prices rebounded smartly during 2009 (figures 5.1 and 5.2).

If a period of sustained commodity strength is imminent, what are the implications for development policies? Development economists have long debated the problems associated with the traditionally high specialization in production and export of primary commodities of most developing countries. Many argue that dependence on primary commodities has proved to be a poisoned chalice or curse for development, which, given

The authors would like to thank Manu Sharma for his excellent research assistance.

Figure 5.1 Commodity Price Indexes, January 2000 to July 2009

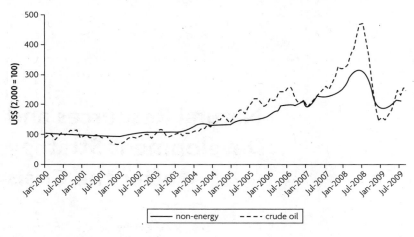

Source: World Bank data and staff estimates.

Figure 5.2 Commodity Price Indexes, January 2000 to August 2009

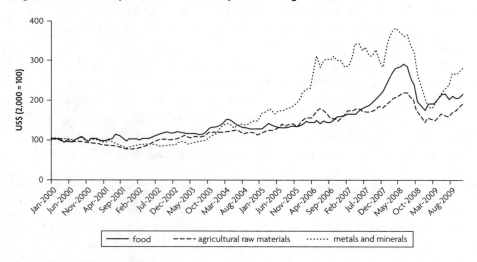

Source: World Bank data and staff estimates.

this view, necessarily entails structural change and rapid industrialization. Others, however, suggest that sustained high commodity prices could reduce the relevance of an industrialization-focused development strategy for commodity-dependent, low-income countries (LICs) (see *Oxford*

Analytica International 2009). In this chapter, we briefly review four questions: How dependent are developing countries on primary commodity exports? What is the outlook for primary commodity prices? Is there a natural resource "curse" (or blessing)? What policies can help poor countries best manage commodity resources for long-run development?

How Dependent Are Developing Countries on Primary Commodity Exports?

If we view developing countries as a single aggregate, then only about 40 percent of their merchandise exports were primary commodities by value during 2005–07, down from around 50 percent in the early 1990s. This aggregate measure can be misleading, however, because it is dominated by a few big economies like China that are almost entirely exporters of manufactures.

A different picture emerges if we take a *simple average* across developing countries (that is, giving each country an equal weight). Commodities still composed a little over 60 percent of the merchandise exports of the average developing country in the middle part of this decade, although this was down from over 90 percent in the late 1960s.

Looking at the *median*, half of developing countries still have commodity export dependence of over 70 percent. Among LICs, commodity export dependence averages around 75 percent. Viewed by region, Africa, Latin America and the Caribbean, and the Middle East and North Africa are the most commodity dependent, while South Asia, East Asia, and Europe and Central Asia are the least (figure 5.3). So, although declining, commodity or natural resource dependence remains a fact of life for a majority of developing countries.

What Is the Outlook for Primary Commodity Prices?

In the 1950s, the famous Prebisch-Singer thesis argued that real primary commodity prices (for example, relative to manufactures prices) displayed a long-run *declining* trend. Faced with a resulting steady decline in their terms of trade, developing countries should foster industrialization, following, according to the thinking of the time, an import substitution strategy. During the commodity price spike of the 1970s, on the

Figure 5.3 Developing Countries: Commodity Exports Share, 2003–07

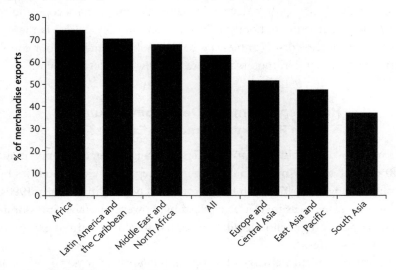

Source: World Bank, World Development Indicators database.
Note: Simple averages for country groups.

other hand, many analysts argued that permanent natural resource scarcity would result in steadily *rising* real commodity prices.

Based on econometric study of long time series, the present consensus appears to be that real commodity prices do not display any permanent trend or drift over time. Figure 5.4 shows the Grilli and Yang time series of real non-energy commodity prices (updated by other researchers) for 1900–2008 (Grilli and Yang 1988; Pfaffenzeller, Newbold, and Rayner 2007). The series is a weighted index of the nominal prices of 24 non-energy commodities, divided by an index of the unit values of manufactured goods exported from developed to developing countries. Figure 5.4 suggests a definite downward trend, and this appears to be confirmed by regression of the log of the Grilli-Yang series on a deterministic time trend (modeling the error process as a first-order AR1 process) over the period 1900–2008, which yields an estimate that real commodity prices fall on average by 0.5 percent per year, apparently confirming the Prebisch-Singer hypothesis.

However, it is now well understood that attempts to assess long-term trends on the basis of visual inspection and simple time series models can be misleading, especially if the series in question are so-called unit root processes. In this case, processes without any deterministic trend

Figure 5.4 Real Non-energy Commodity Prices, 1900–2015

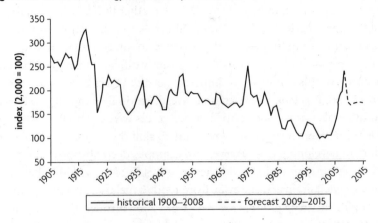

Sources: Grilli and Yang 1988; Pfaffenzeller, Newbold, and Rayner 2007. World Bank estimates 2004–08; and
forecasts 2009–15.
Note: Deflated by unit value of manufactured exports.

can yield apparently significant but actually spurious regression results. Cuddington, Ludema, and Jayasuriya (2007) carefully survey econometric studies of the Grilli-Yang series through 1998. Their overall conclusion is that, although there is clear evidence of a structural break in 1921, it is not possible to reject the unit root hypothesis for real commodity prices. There is also no evidence of drift, either positive or negative. We find essentially the same results for the Grilli-Yang series during 1900–2008.

Thus, on the basis of statistical properties alone, we have little reason to expect real commodity prices to trend either up or down in the long term. It is a feature of unit root processes, however, that series with this property are highly correlated over time. So it is quite possible for commodity prices to move significantly lower or higher for substantial periods even in the absence of a long-term trend or drift, such as the long period of unusually low prices from the mid-1980s through the 1990s. Again, on the basis of statistical properties alone, one would not be surprised to see a sustained period of high prices following the low prices of the 1980s and 1990s.

Are there plausible fundamental economic factors to support such an outlook? The price of commodities relative to the price of manufactures can be usefully analyzed in terms of supply and demand—that is, the supply of commodities *relative to* the supply of manufactures, and the demand for primary commodities *relative to* the demand for manufactures.

On the supply side, if long-term productivity growth in agriculture and minerals is less than in manufacturing, then other things being equal, one would expect agricultural and mineral prices to rise relative to those of manufactures. But there is little evidence to suggest that productivity growth in commodities sectors is significantly different from that in manufactures, so this is unlikely to influence relative prices either way (World Bank 2009). It is true, however, that investment in new capacity in energy and minerals was cut substantially when prices were low in the 1980s and 1990s and is recovering only slowly due to skill shortages, technical difficulties in developing new reserves (for example, deep offshore), and political uncertainty in regions with new reserves. Biofuel subsidies have also helped switch grain acreage away from food to fuel use, providing a major reason for the steep grain price hikes from 2005 through the early part of 2008. Over the longer term, though, one would expect a more copious supply response, as skill shortages and technical difficulties are overcome and new reserves and acreage are brought into production.

Relative demand for commodities could also rise in the medium term to the extent that world growth after the financial crisis is more dependent on developing countries and demand in these countries is more commodity intensive than elsewhere. In the longer term, however, production processes in developing countries will continue to become more efficient in terms of raw material consumption, approaching developed country levels, while relative final demand for commodities like food will continue to decline due to low-income elasticity relative to things like services. Evidence suggests that real commodity prices are affected by monetary conditions (Frankel 2008). Since commodities are traded in flexible price markets, their prices tend to overshoot in response to monetary changes relative to general manufactures and services prices, which adjust more sluggishly. Commodity prices will tend to be high when real interest rates are low and monetary conditions lax, as at present, since inventory carrying costs are low and there is more incentive to leave depletable natural resources in the ground. In the longer term, however, general price levels and real interest rates can be expected to rise, removing the overshooting in real commodity prices.

So both supply and demand factors could support the present, relatively high level of real commodity prices in the medium term, although these factors will tend to dissipate in the longer term. Current World Bank

forecasts are consistent with this scenario, projecting only a gradual easing in real commodity prices from existing levels by 2015. Forecast real
prices in this period are in fact squarely in the range that prevailed from
the 1920s through the early 1980s (figure 5.4). If correct, this means that
commodity exporters are likely to face a more benign medium-term price
environment than in the 1980s and 1990s.

Is There a Natural Resource "Curse" or Blessing?

The short answer is "no," or rather, "it depends." A survey of the large and
rapidly growing empirical research in this area suggests that, in the words
of a recent World Bank report, natural resources are "neither curse nor
destiny" (Lederman and Maloney 2007). Studies of the relationship
between natural resource abundance and growth have, however, often
tended to generate disparate and sometimes contradictory results. The
influential study by Sachs and Warner (1995) is representative of results
that find that natural resource abundance has a strong *negative* impact on
growth. Lederman and Maloney (2007), on the other hand, challenge the
Sachs and Warner findings on measurement and econometric grounds
and find natural resource abundance to have a *positive* effect on growth.

A recent effort to reconcile such apparently disparate research findings (Collier and Goderis 2007) observes that, first, negative long-term
growth effects are mostly related to oil and minerals—concentrated
"point source" resources that can easily become the object of rent-seeking
and redistributive struggles (including armed conflict). On the other
hand, there is little evidence of negative growth effects related to high
prices for agricultural commodities, which are generally more open to
competitive entry. Second, high oil and mineral prices mostly have a
negative impact on long-term growth in exporting countries *with bad
governance.* They have a significant *positive* impact on growth in exporting countries with good governance. This finding suggests that continued high commodity prices in the next few years could provide valuable
resources to accelerate economic and social development in commodity-
exporting countries with good policies and governance.

There are several considerations to keep in mind when evaluating the
ways in which natural resource abundance *can* lead to worse economic
performance, especially under conditions of poor governance.

First, because of political economy reasons, countries with weak governance are more likely to adopt poor economic policies to manage commodity booms, contributing to significant misallocation and mismanagement of resources. For example, politicians may expand public spending and employment excessively and too rapidly, with the aim of increasing their patronage networks and improving their chances of staying in power, while resources shift out of productive activity into unproductive rent-seeking activity. (Mehlum, Moene, and Torvik 2006; Robinson, Torvik, and Verdier 2006.) Poor fiscal policy indeed appears to be at the heart of economic mismanagement in the wake of natural resource booms. Studying natural resource boom episodes in the 1970s and 1980s, Gelb and Associates (1988:139) concluded that "the most important recommendation to emerge from this study is that spending levels should have been adjusted to sharp rises in income levels more cautiously than they actually were."[1]

Second, natural resource booms create complicated problems in macroeconomic management that are challenging even in economies with good governance and capable institutions, and much more so in economies without these advantages. One of these issues is the so-called Dutch Disease effect, which refers to the change in the structure of production of the economy that is predicted to occur in the wake of a favorable shock such as a large natural resource discovery or a rise in the international price of an exportable commodity that is perceived to be permanent. Such structural changes are expected to include, in particular, a contraction or stagnation of other (non-natural-resource) tradable sectors of the economy, such as manufacturing, and to be accompanied by an appreciation of the country's real exchange rate.

How do such structural changes occur? When studying Dutch Disease, the economy is typically modeled as consisting of three sectors: the natural resource sector, the non-resource tradable sector (usually understood as agriculture and manufacturing), and the nontradables sector (including nontradable services and construction), as in Corden and Neary (1982). The prices for both the natural resource and the non-natural-resource tradables sectors are set in the world market, while those in the nontradables sector are set in the domestic economy. The real exchange rate is defined as the price of nontradables relative to the price of tradables.

There are generally two types of effects leading to Dutch Disease and real exchange rate appreciation:

- The *spending effect*, where increased domestic income from the booming natural resource sector generates higher spending on domestic goods (as well as imports), leading to higher prices and output in the nontradables sector. Wages in the economy also tend to rise, squeezing profits in sectors of the economy that are internationally tradable but that are not based on natural resources, such as manufacturing, where prices are largely fixed at international levels. With increased inflation in nontradables prices, there is an appreciation of the real exchange rate and an output contraction in non-resource-tradables sectors like manufacturing.[2]
- The *resource movement effect*, which takes place when a boom in the natural resource sector attracts capital and labor from other parts of the economy, tending to reduce output in the rest of the economy. In particular, reduced output in the nontradables sector causes the price of nontradables to rise relative to those of tradables, whose prices are set in the world market. This effect is less likely in low-income economies, where most inputs used in the natural resource "enclave" are imported from abroad.

Both effects result in a fall in the output share of non-natural-resource tradables relative to nontradables and in a real exchange rate appreciation, that is, a rise in the price of nontradables relative to that of tradables.

Empirical evidence on the size of Dutch Disease effects has tended to be mixed, but recently, Ismail (2010) presented strong evidence on the impact of oil price shocks, using detailed disaggregated sectoral data for manufacturing and allowing for the possibility that the extent of Dutch Disease will depend on the capital intensity of the manufacturing sector and the economy's openness to capital flows. Ismail finds that, in general, a 10 percent increase in an oil windfall is associated with a 3.4 percent fall in value added across manufacturing sectors. Such effects are larger in economies that are more open to capital flows and in relatively less-capital-intensive manufacturing sectors, consistent with the theoretical model developed in the study. One of the measurement issues with Dutch Disease is the difficulty in finding the counterfactual size of the tradables sector, that is, how large the tradables sector would have been in the absence of natural resources. We use the Chenery and Syrquin (1975) norms approach to estimate a norm for the size of the tradable sector (manufacturing and agriculture) for all countries over time, after controlling for factors such as per capita income, population, and a time trend. Figure 5.5 shows the difference between the actual size of the tradable sector (as defined) and the Chenery-Syrquin norm for both resource-rich and non-resource-rich countries. For the purpose of this figure, resource-rich countries are defined as those in which the resource sector produces more than 30 percent of gross domestic product (GDP). On average, the tradables sector in such countries is lower than the norm by around 15 percent of GDP.

Is the change in economic structure that comprises Dutch Disease a concern for development and welfare? After all, an increase in national wealth associated with a natural resource discovery or a permanent improvement in the terms of trade is, on the face of it, a positive development, allowing higher incomes and consumption of both nontradables and tradables (the latter in part through increased purchasing power over imports). Rents from mineral resources can provide resources for

Figure 5.5 A Measure of Dutch Disease: Difference between Actual and Normative Size of the Tradable Sector, 1975–2005

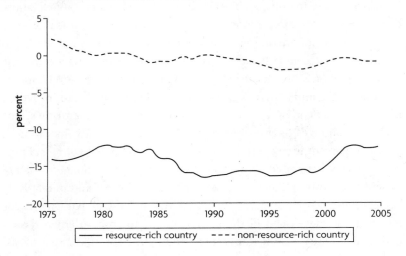

Source: Authors' calculations based on Chenery and Syrquin 1975.

investment in public goods and other development expenditures that would otherwise have been unaffordable. Analyzing the historical development of several European countries and the United States, Gelb and Associates (1988:33) conclude that "there is evidence that, at least in some cases, high-rent activities... have provided an important stimulus to growth," a point also confirmed in the historical review by Lederman and Maloney (2008). Dutch Disease effects are of concern, however, if one believes that sectors like manufacturing have some special characteristics that stimulate higher overall long-term growth, for example, increasing returns to scale, learning by doing, or abundant positive technological spillovers. Evidence that manufacturing possesses these special characteristics is mixed, but there is fairly robust evidence for the proposition of a negative relation between real exchange rate overvaluation and growth. Perhaps among the most carefully designed and well known of these studies is that of Aguirre and Calderón (2005). Others include Razin and Collins (1999); Prasad, Rajan, and Subramanian (2006); and Williamson (2008).

Other macroeconomic management problems related to natural resources are the result of the volatility of primary commodity prices. Volatility in natural resource revenues can drive volatility in government spending and real exchange rates, with the resulting uncertainty damaging investment and growth. Another related way in which commodity price volatility may affect growth is by fostering overborrowing. High commodity prices in the 1970s encouraged many resource-abundant countries to borrow heavily from abroad to finance large investment projects and high public consumption. When prices plunged in the 1980s, these countries were left with balance-of-payments crises and unsustainable external debt levels. Again, it is critical to note that the actual extent of Dutch Disease effects, volatility, and overborrowing will depend to a large extent on policies—for example, on the extent to which cautious fiscal policies are able to moderate aggregate demand pressures, smooth volatility in government revenues, and curb external overborrowing.

Finally, in addition to problems of short-term economic management, natural-resource-abundant countries also face important longer-term questions about the optimal pace at which to deplete their resources today and the amount to save for the welfare of future generations.[3] An important metric here is whether the country's economic strategy is *sustainable*,

Figure 5.6 Natural Resource Depletion and Net Savings Rates, 2007

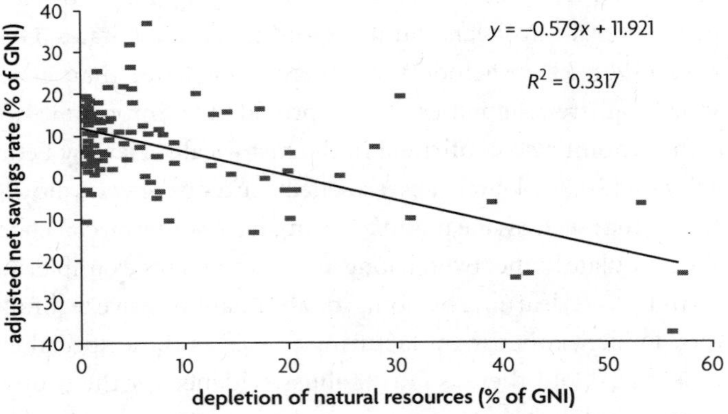

Source: World Bank, World Development Indicators database.
Note: GNI = gross national income.

meaning one that transfers sufficient capital to future generations to allow them to achieve at least the same level of welfare as current generations. From this perspective, natural resources can be viewed as part of a country's overall capital stock, alongside its physical capital stock (such as existing machinery and buildings) and intangible capital (including human capital, social capital, and other factors such as the quality of its institutions). To increase its overall capital stock, a country's investment in its physical, human, and other capital must be larger than the depreciation of that capital, including the depletion of its natural resources. This measure of countries' *adjusted net savings rates* is shown on the vertical axis of figure 5.6. The horizontal axis shows countries' annual depletion of their natural resources (principally oil and minerals, together with a measure of forest depletion). The figure suggests that countries with high rates of natural resource depletion are often on unsustainable development paths: they are not saving enough to cover the depletion, resulting in negative adjusted net savings rates.

What Policies Can Help Poor Countries Best Manage Commodity Resources for Development?

First, given the evidence that issues of governance are at the root of economic problems associated with natural resource abundance, efforts to enhance transparency and strengthen checks and balances concerning all aspects of natural resource extraction and use are clearly vital. Those aspects include the terms of contracts with companies engaged in resource extraction or operation, ongoing monitoring of operations, and the collection and use of government taxes and other revenues from natural resources. Broad global efforts like the Extractive Industries Transparency Initiative can play a part, as, at the domestic level, can anti-corruption reforms, measures to improve transparency and scrutiny by civil society and media, procurement reforms, strengthening of formal audit, parliamentary scrutiny, and so on. Equitable sharing of benefits across regions, ethnic groups, and so forth can also help reduce the danger of civil strife over resources.

An institutional innovation that has attracted much recent attention is the use of a separate (extra-budgetary) Natural Resource Fund (NRF) to facilitate good management of revenues. Experience suggests that the establishment of such funds can help buttress the right policy mix but that, by themselves, they are no substitute for sound overall fiscal and economic management. While NRFs are sometimes created to protect resource revenue from political pressure and potential waste and corruption, and this argument has its merits, an NRF of itself will not prevent such waste and abuse unless it is part of a broader effort to strengthen governance and integrate the fund within an overall fiscal policy framework. Chile's Economic and Social Stabilization Fund (which replaced its Copper Stabilization Fund in 2007) provides an example of a well-managed NRF that meets these conditions, one that we return to below.

Second, in addition to governance issues, attention also needs to be paid to the actual substance of economic policy decisions about the allocation of natural resource revenues between consumption and savings of various kinds. These decisions will help determine how well the country is able to handle the macromanagement problems associated with natural resource abundance, such as Dutch Disease and commodity price volatility, and the impact of natural resources on the country's longer-term growth and poverty reduction efforts. Figure 5.7 provides a schematic of basic choices open to the government, for example, whether to return revenues to private citizens (via tax cuts, transfers, or an equal "citizens' dividend," which will then be reflected in private consumption and investment) or to retain resource revenues in public hands, which

Figure 5.7 Government Choices in Allocating Resource Revenues

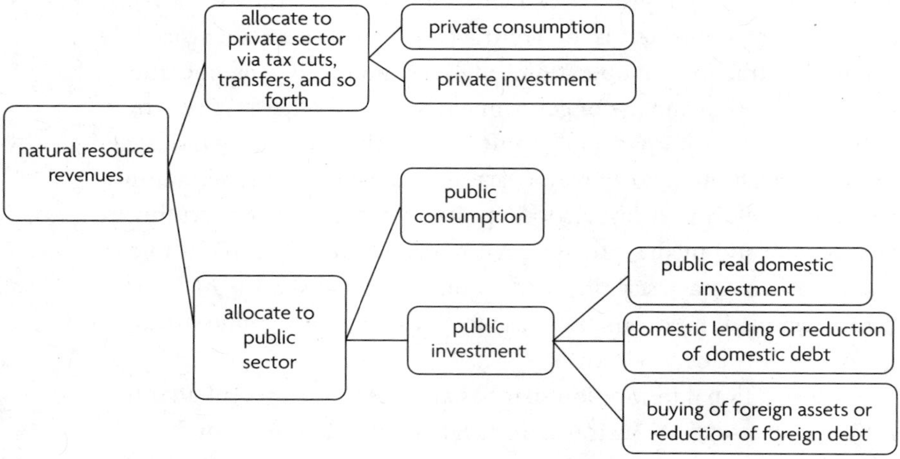

Source: Authors' preparation.

then need to be allocated between public consumption and various kinds of public investment (or net asset accumulation). The potential advantages from a direct transfer or dividend to citizens should not be overlooked. It allows an immediate increase in consumption utility for the poor and provides them with resources to overcome liquidity constraints and undertake their own potentially high-return microinvestments. Such transfers or dividends also give citizens a stake in the country's natural wealth and an incentive to demand and monitor good governance of the resources. Concerns about the macro impacts of direct transfers to citizens can in principle be addressed through offsetting fiscal policy, for example, through reductions in public spending.

At a very general level, these decisions need to be guided by a comparison of the government's social discount rate (which measures the value it puts on consumption today compared to consumption at later dates) with the rates of return available on various kinds of investment, for example, the return on foreign assets, the return from reduction of foreign debt (not generally the same thing in developing countries), and returns to domestic public and private investments. A commonly used benchmark for fiscal policy in a natural-resource-rich economy is the *permanent income rule*. Under this rule, the country should save all resource revenues over and above a certain permanently sustainable increase in the level of consumption, which is equal to the annuity value of the country's natural resource wealth.[4] In practice, the rule often leads to a recommendation to establish a Natural Resource or Sovereign Wealth Fund that invests in foreign assets, the returns from which can support spending on the government's non-natural-resource fiscal budget.

The permanent income approach addresses several of the key issues associated with natural resource fiscal management. It is by definition a sustainable policy in that it converts a temporary, exhaustible stock of natural resources into a stock of financial assets that generates a permanent income stream. Since the policy calls for saving a substantial proportion of natural resource revenues, it reduces the pressure of rising domestic demand that leads to real exchange rate appreciation and Dutch Disease effects. By smoothing expenditures, the policy also moderates the problems caused by volatility in natural prices and revenues. Experience during the 2008–09 global financial crisis showed how a well-managed NRF or Sovereign Wealth Fund based on permanent income ideas can assist countercyclical macrostabilization policies. During the boom period before the crisis, when copper prices were extremely high, Chile's Economic and Social Stabilization Fund saved a high proportion of the surge in revenues, reaching savings of 12 percent of GDP at the end of 2008, even after paying down public debt. During the crisis, Chile was then able to undertake robust increases in countercyclical spending and even to provide resources to finance reconstruction in the wake of the devastating, magnitude 8.8 earthquake of February 2010.

There is nevertheless something anomalous about viewing the permanent income rule as a long-term development strategy, with poor capital-scarce countries financing investments in rich countries through sovereign wealth funds. Several analysts have argued that the permanent income rule is optimal only under special circumstances that do not apply to most developing countries; essentially, these conditions are the ability to freely borrow and lend at the world rate of interest, which would result in foreign and domestic rates of return becoming aligned (Collier and Venables 2008; Van der Ploeg and Venables 2009). Most developing countries, however, are characterized by restricted access to world capital markets, capital scarcity, and potentially high rates of return on domestic investment, especially if the government is able to efficiently supply scarce public infrastructure and to improve the investment climate to raise returns on private investment. Under these circumstances, a more optimal strategy would be to devote a larger portion of resource revenues to high-return public domestic investments, leading to higher growth and, ultimately, a higher value of consumption than under the permanent income strategy.

Evidently, much of the success of a strategy oriented more toward domestic investment will depend on how efficiently public investment funds can be allocated and managed to achieve high returns in practice. So, third, reforms to strengthen public investment management, cost-benefit analysis, monitoring and evaluation, and budget processes and institutions provide another crucial element of a successful natural-resource-based development strategy. To the extent that it will take time to develop a pipeline of good projects and to strengthen public investment management capacity, it may be prudent for the country to initially continue to invest most of its revenues in foreign assets, but to then increase the proportion invested domestically, in line with domestic absorptive capacity.

We conclude that booming commodity revenues raise difficult challenges that, if not adequately addressed, can harm long-term development. However, with good policies, governance, and management, such revenues can also be a valuable platform from which to accelerate overall economic and social development.

Notes

1. A stronger version of the political economy channel argues that natural resource booms can even lead to a worsening of governance, for example, a "voracity effect" as political actors race to seize and spend natural resource revenues before others do, provoking more intense political, bureaucratic, and even violent conflicts for control of natural resource revenues (Tornell and Lane 1999). The evidence for this hypothesis is mixed.
2. This is the so-called spending effect cause of Dutch Disease. A so-called resource-movement effect can also cause Dutch Disease when the boom in the natural resource sector attracts labor and capital away from other parts of the economy.
3. Heal (1996) discusses alternative interpretations of sustainability.
4. The permanent income approach to fiscal policy in natural-resource-abundant economies is studied in more detail in Van Wijnbergen (2008); Davis, Ossowsky, and Fidelinom (2003); and Barnett and Ossowski (2002).

References

Aguirre, A., and C. Calderón. 2005. "Real Exchange Rate Misalignments and Economic Performance." Central Bank of Chile Economic Research Division. Santiago. April.

Barnett, S., and R. Ossowski. 2002. "Operational Aspects of Fiscal Policy in Oil-Producing Countries." IMF Working Paper WP/02/177, International Monetary Fund, Washington, DC.

Chenery, H., and M. Syrquin. 1975. *Patterns of Development, 1950–1970.* London: Oxford University Press.

Collier, P., and B. Goderis. 2007. "Commodity Prices, Growth and the Natural Resources Curse: Reconciling a Conundrum." Working Paper 276, Centre for the Study of African Economies, Oxford.

Collier, P., and A. Venables. 2008. "Managing Resource Revenues: Lessons for Low Income Countries." Paper for the Africa Economic Research Consortium 2008 Annual Conference, Nairobi, September 15–17.

Corden, W. M., and P. J. Neary. 1982. "Booming Sector and Deindustrialization in a Small Open Economy." *Economic Journal* 92 (December): 825–48.

Cuddington, J. T., R. Ludema, and S. A. Jayasuriya. 2007. "Prebisch-Singer Redux." In *Natural Resources: Neither Curse Nor Destiny*, ed. D. Lederman and W. F. Maloney. Washington, DC: World Bank; and Stanford, CA: Stanford University Press.

Davis, J. M., R. Ossowsky, and A. Fidelinom, eds. 2003. *Fiscal Policy Formulation and Implementation in Oil-Producing Countries.* Washington, DC: International Monetary Fund.

Frankel, J. 2008. "The Effect of Monetary Policy on Real Commodity Prices." In *Asset Prices and Monetary Policy*, ed. J. Campbell. Chicago: University of Chicago Press.

Gelb, A., and Associates. 1988. *Oil Windfalls: Blessing or Curse?* Washington, DC: World Bank; and New York: Oxford University Press.

Grilli, E. R., and M. C. Yang. 1988. "Primary Commodity Prices, Manufactured Goods Prices, and the Terms of Trade of Developing Countries: What the Long Run Shows." *World Bank Economic Review* 2 (1): 1–47.

Heal, G. 1996. "Interpreting Sustainability." Paine Webber Working Paper Series in Money, Economics, and Finance PW-95-24, Columbia Business School, New York.

Ismail, K. 2010. "The Structural Manifestation of the 'Dutch Disease': The Case of Oil Exporting Countries." IMF Working Paper 10/103, International Monetary Fund, Washington, DC.

Lederman, D., and W. F. Maloney, eds. 2007. *Natural Resources: Neither Curse nor Destiny.* Washington, DC: World Bank; and Stanford, CA: Stanford University Press.

———. 2008. "In Search of the Missing Resource Curse." Policy Research Working Paper WPS 4766, World Bank, Washington, DC.

Mehlum, H., K. Moene, and R. Torvik. 2006. "Institutions and the Resource Curse." *Economic Journal* 116 (508): 1–20.

Oxford Analytica International. 2009. "Commodities Force Re-think on Growth." August 18.

Pfaffenzeller, S., P. Newbold, and A. Rayner. 2007. "A Short Note on Updating the Grilli and Yang Commodity Price Index." *World Bank Economic Review* 21 (1): 151–63.

Prasad, E., R. Rajan, and A. Subramanian. 2006. "Foreign Capital and Economic Growth." Paper presented at a Federal Reserve Bank of Kansas City Conference, Jackson Hole, WY, August 25.

Razin, O., and S. M. Collins. 1999. "Real-Exchange-Rate Misalignments and Growth." In *The Economics of Globalization: Policy Perspectives from Public Economics*, ed. A. Razin and E. Sadka. Cambridge, U.K.: Cambridge University Press.

Robinson, J. A., R. Torvik, and T. Verdier. 2006. "Political Foundations of the Resource Curse." *Journal of Development Economics* 79 (2): 447–68.

Rodrik, D. 2007. "The Real Exchange Rate and Economic Growth: Theory and Evidence." John F. Kennedy School of Government, Harvard University, Cambridge, MA.

Sachs, J. D., and A. M. Warner. 1995. "Natural Resource Abundance and Economic Growth." NBER Working Paper 5398, National Bureau of Economic Research, Cambridge, MA.

Tornell, A., and P. R. Lane. 1999. "The Voracity Effect." *American Economic Review* 89 (1): 22–46.

Van Der Ploeg, F., and A. Venables. 2009. "Harnessing Windfall Revenues: Optimal Policies for Resource-Rich Developing Economies." Working Paper 2571, CESifo Group, Munich, Germany.

Van Wijnbergen, S. 2008. "The Permanent Income Approach in Practice." Unpublished paper, PREM Network, World Bank, Washington, DC.

Williamson, J. 2008. "Exchange Rate Economics." Working Paper 2, Commission on Growth and Development, Washington, DC.

World Bank. 2009. Global Economic Prospects *2009: Commodities at the Crossroads*. Washington, DC: World Bank.

6

The Times, They Are "A-changin": A New Look at International Economic and Financial Policy

Jeff Chelsky

For those immersed in discussions of international economic and financial policy, these are interesting times. The unexpected breadth and severity of the 2008–09 crisis has cast doubt on many of our earlier assumptions about how markets work and has drawn unprecedented attention to interconnections and channels of transmission that previously gave policy makers little cause for a second glance. Much of the conventional wisdom about these issues is being revisited, with credible academics and serious commentators discussing ideas that, until very recently, had been considered almost radical by mainstream economists, a phenomenon that has led Martin Wolf of the *Financial Times* to suggest that "from the inconceivable to the habitual has taken a year" (Wolf 2009).

In response to recent events, macroeconomists have been rushing to address gaps in their intellectual toolkit. Joseph Stiglitz, former chief economist of the World Bank, and others have argued that, prior to the crisis, few macroeconomists looked at—and fewer understood—the links between the associated regulatory issues and monetary policy. Stiglitz has also pointed to a failure to appreciate the implications for macroeconomic stability of microeconomic factors such as asymmetric information and the incentives faced by individual agents (as evident in problems with executive compensation schemes and incentives for accounting firms and rating agencies) as a key oversight (Stiglitz 2010:19–49). Macroeconomists, including within the International Monetary Fund (IMF), are now scrambling to enhance their financial sector expertise to assess financial sector impacts on the real economy and to better map the transmission channels of macrofinancial instability. At the same time, efforts are underway to improve understanding of potential international spillovers from financial and other shocks and policies, responding, albeit with a lag, to recognized weaknesses in analyzing economic policy links identified earlier.[1] The G-20's[2] Mutual Assessment Process is a clear acknowledgment by senior policy makers of policy interdependence and the need to improve economic policy consistency.

An excellent illustration of the rethinking underway is a recent and particularly refreshing paper prepared by IMF staff, under the direction of Economic Counselor Olivier Blanchard, that presents an insightful discussion of the lessons from the financial crisis for macro policy practitioners.[3] In "Rethinking Macroeconomic Policy," Blanchard, Dell'Ariccia, and Mauro (2010) go beyond perfect hindsight and ask three questions essential to avoiding a repeat of the blindsiding as the financial crisis hit and then deepened, beyond expectations: "What did we think we knew before the crisis?" "What did we learn from the crisis?" and taking into account those lessons, "What are the implications for the design of future policy?"

In their frank reflection on recent experience, the authors question elements of conventional wisdom such as the beliefs that monetary policy should have one target (inflation) and one instrument (the policy rate), that policy makers should target inflation not higher than 2 percent, that monetary policy should not concern itself with asset price bubbles, that financial regulation stands apart from monetary policy, and that advanced economies are immune to the problems faced by the financial sectors in emerging market economies. Not all the lessons they derive are new; some appear to simply have been forgotten, like the importance of building fiscal space in good times to permit more aggressive use of countercyclical fiscal policy in bad times.

William White, chairman of the Economic and Development Review Committee of the Organisation for Economic Co-operation and Development (OECD) and former Head of the Monetary and Economic Department of the Bank for International Settlements, has also sought to reevaluate the conventional wisdom that dominated the economist profession and led so many to miss the signs of the impending crisis. In his article "Modern Macroeconomics Is on the Wrong Track" (White 2009), he notes that in many markets in the recent crisis, expectations were based simply on the extrapolation of past events, which demonstrated the inadequacy of models based on the assumption of rational expectations, not least because of a lack of clarity on what it exactly means to be "rational." More broadly, he considered that the crisis provided evidence that "many of the simplifying assumptions underpinning much of modern macroeconomics were not useful in explaining real world developments" (White 2009:15).

Similar "revolutionary" ideas have been advanced on the subject of capital controls and their potential use in managing capital inflow surges (Ostry and others 2010). Here, the IMF's thinking on the value of capital controls appears to take a leap forward, with staff concluding (albeit tentatively) that

> . . . if the economy is operating near potential, if the level of reserves is adequate, if the exchange rate is not undervalued, and if the flows are likely to be transitory, then use of capital controls—in addition to both prudential and macroeconomic policy—is justified as part of the policy toolkit to manage inflows. (p. 5)

Even this highly qualified statement is a far cry from the balance of opinion on the IMF Executive Board just 10 years ago, when only "several directors pointed to the possible usefulness of capital controls, including temporary capital controls in certain circumstances" (IMF 1999:2).[4] This change in view has, in fact, been an evolutionary one. The IMF actively encouraged capital account liberalization throughout the early 1990s, emphasizing "the benefits to developing countries of greater access to international capital flows . . . pay[ing] comparatively less attention to the potential risks of capital flow volatility" (IMF 2005:3). Following the Asia crisis, IMF staff became quite conservative in promoting capital account liberalization.[5] Since that time, the more positive experiences with capital controls of Chile, Malaysia, and, more recently, China and India have gained increasing recognition.

Now, when faced with the challenge of managing capital inflows, the IMF appears willing to go beyond its more traditional calls for fiscal tightening and exchange rate flexibility. IMF staff are more confidently prepared to be explicit in advising on the design of capital controls, preferring, for example, temporary, price-based controls on capital inflows rather than more permanent administrative ones. Earlier fears that detailed advice on designing capital controls to minimize their costs and associated distortions would be interpreted as condoning the use of controls appear to be waning. In fact, in the context of recent discussions of the IMF's evolving surveillance mandate, it was suggested that the IMF "could also foster collaboration among members in the design and implementation of capital controls when they become necessary, ensuring that negative spillovers are avoided (imagine discriminatory provisions) and that broader goals are taken into account (imagine if concerted action were needed to slow down the withdrawal of foreign bank lines in a regional crisis)" (IMF 2010a:7). Similar views were expressed in the April 2010 *Global Financial Stability Report*, which argued that when other policy responses are not sufficient to address temporary capital inflow surges, "capital controls may have a role in complementing the policy toolkit" (IMF 2010b:135). The significance of this evolution has not gone unnoticed. Dani Rodrik (2010), for example, with only some degree of hyperbole, has called the IMF staff's views a "stunning reversal" and "the end of an era in finance."

The crisis has also changed the way the IMF approaches its core business—bilateral surveillance. While the IMF has paid considerable attention to the risks associated with volatile capital flows since the Asia crisis, the focus of the analysis was on what emerging market economies should do to cope with volatility (IMF 2005). A new chapter may have begun in the IMF's surveillance dialogue, sparked by the impact on emerging markets of a global financial crisis originating in some advanced economies. In the context of recent discussions on the IMF's mandate, IMF management has called for new procedures "to consider the systemic effects of country policies beyond the coverage possible in bilateral surveillance . . . [which] rarely touches on the systemic effects of country policies" (IMF 2010a:1–3). This was motivated by a sense that the crisis has changed attitudes to addressing the spillover effects of individual country policies, including tensions emanating from country-level developments. The context within which this issue is gaining traction includes the desire to discuss the impact of high levels of liquidity emanating from recession-affected advanced economies on the level and volatility of capital flows into emerging market countries.

Also noteworthy is recent work coming out of the IMF on exchange rate regimes. As Ghosh and Ostry (2009) note, there has been significant evolution in views on the "preferred" exchange rate regime, from a preference for "corner solutions" (that is, hard pegs or floating rates) in the late 1990s giving way (in the wake of the collapse of Argentina's Currency Board) to a clear preference for floating regimes in the mid-2000s. In the wake of more recent experience, the authors have now concluded that pegged exchange rates *are* associated with the "best inflation performance" among developing and emerging market countries (albeit with caveats for undervalued pegs) and are also associated with less volatile real exchange rates and greater trade openness. That these findings were not uncovered previously, IMF staff attribute to the fact that their recent analysis was based on an assessment of both de facto and de jure exchange rate regimes, rather than de facto regimes alone (as was the case with earlier analysis). They also find that "intermediate" regimes are associated with better growth performance for those developing and emerging market economies that do not float freely.

That much of this rethinking is emanating from an institution that for much of its history was seen as a bastion of conservative economic thought is itself noteworthy.[6] That several of these conclusions have been attacked by practitioners in some quarters as heresy is also not surprising given the significant investment many policy makers, particularly in some central banks, had in the precrisis paradigm. Indeed, among the many disciples and devotees of inflation targeting, for example, debates had long ago shifted from consideration of targeting low inflation of between 1 and 3 percent to serious consideration of price *level* targeting, even in the face of well-acknowledged shortcomings in consumer price indexes themselves. It is likely that many will look back on earlier discussions of such refinements as of limited use in a world of chastened policy makers.

Which brings us to a point made in Blanchard, Dell'Ariccia, and Mauro (2010) that has received somewhat less attention than the controversial suggestion that 4 percent inflation may be an appropriate target. On a number of occasions, the authors point to differences between the rhetoric of policy makers and their actual conduct. They note, for example:

> Few central banks, if any, cared only about inflation. Most of them practiced "flexible inflation targeting," the return of inflation to a stable target, not right away, but over some horizon. Most of them allowed for shifts in headline inflation, such as those caused by rising oil prices, provided inflation expectations remained well anchored. And many of them paid attention to asset process (house prices, stock prices, exchange rates) beyond their effects on inflation and showed concern about external sustainability and the risks associated with balance sheet effects. But they did this with some unease, and often with strong public denial (p. 4).

The authors also note that many of the more theological points of view "were more closely held in academia: policymakers were often more pragmatic" (Blanchard, Dell'Ariccia, and Mauro 2010:3). A similar point was made by William White, who has argued that "there is very little evidence that these modern academic theories had much impact on the way most central bankers used policy instruments" (White 2009:16). This phenomenon is what Mankiw has described as "the substantial disconnect between the science and engineering of macroeconomics" (Mankiw 2006:30). To describe it as cognitive dissonance may be going too far, but it is indicative of an implicit awareness among many practitioners of the limits to their understanding and methodology, perhaps even an acknowledgment that economics is more of a "social science" than many in the profession have previously acknowledged to themselves or were prepared to acknowledge "outside the family."

The reopening of some policy debates may prove to be a mixed blessing. Take again, for example, the suggestion by Blanchard, Dell'Ariccia, and Mauro (2010) that monetary policy should target inflation above 2 percent—say 4 percent—to ensure that sufficient room is available to use monetary policy when large shocks occur. On one hand, the rethinking of the conventional wisdom is a welcome development. On the other hand, its timing is problematic. With large fiscal burdens having been taken on by many (if not most) advanced economies, there is a significant risk that a shift upward in inflation targets could be misinterpreted as part of a strategy to address high debt levels through higher inflation. This would be disastrous in that it could trigger a wage-price spiral, as implied by IMF First Deputy Managing Director John Lipsky in a speech to the China Development Forum, where he notes that "a moderate increase in inflation would have only a limited impact on real debt burdens, while accelerating inflation would impose major economic costs and create significant risks to a sustained expansion" (Lipsky 2010).

It is worth noting that questioning aspects of conventional wisdom is not new; concern with macrofinancial links, for example, has been around for some time. (White goes as far back as Irving Fisher, who in 1933 expressed concern with "successive stages of lending with ever easier credit conditions.") But the past year has witnessed unprecedented attention to alternative perspectives and new ways of looking at old problems. What explains the timing of the new openness? First, the severity and unexpectedness of the crisis has made it possible for issues and ideas that would have been considered radical just a few years ago to be discussed in the mainstream, including among policy makers and practitioners. Second, the world, aided by the crisis, has reached a geopolitical tipping point, where near-term economic prospects in many advanced economies remain dim (and indeed, some face full-on crises), while major emerging markets have shown their potential to be important engines of global growth. It is this phenomenon that has underpinned the ascendency of the G-20 and the waning of the G-7,[7] and this is resonating heavily in policy circles where no country or country grouping can any longer claim the "high ground" in economic management. We are finding that, more than ever, we all have something to learn from one another. We can see this in the increasing frequency with which we speak of "South-South" learning and find ourselves paying increasing attention to ideas that had previously been abandoned by advanced economies, sometimes more out of dogma than experience.

So what lies ahead? Once the froth settles, will we find ourselves with a new conventional wisdom and restored confidence in our understanding of economic relationships grounded in new findings about the central role of the financial sector to macroeconomic stability and a greater role for government? Probably. Will we lose sight of what were previously considered central factors determining macroeconomic stability, including exchange rate regimes and inflation? Probably not, given that these earlier concerns were well grounded in experiences too numerous to mention.

Once "normal" global economic conditions return, will we also witness a return of complacency about economic relationships and threats to stability? Possibly. On one hand, the renewed pragmatism and flexibility that we have seen in the economic policy response to the crisis should help in the retention of an intellectual openness that recent history lacked. And a clear consensus has formed in the mainstream concerning the limitations of markets alone to deliver efficient and stable solutions. Related to this is an enhanced comfort with the place of government in market regulation. On the other hand, we thought we had learned many of these recent lessons from previous crises, including those of the late 1990s. The resilience of many emerging markets in the wake of the 2008–09 crisis suggests that many emerging markets did learn these lessons. Perhaps we failed to realize that advanced economies had similar weaknesses and needed to absorb many of the same lessons. The long road ahead of fiscal consolidation in advanced countries will most likely preoccupy the thinking of economic policy makers for some time to come, and this will no doubt serve as a reminder to advanced economies that their level of development does not assure stability.

We will no doubt come again to the point at which we believe we understand the prerequisites for economic stability and will assert them with confidence. And it is with equal certainty that the next crisis will come from some place at the periphery of, or just beyond, our field of vision. In any event, that this crisis has reopened so many basic policy questions cannot but extend our perspective. It may be premature to declare the death of dogma and theology among economic policy makers, but it is unlikely that they will be as willing to act on faith when it comes to financial market policy. We can only hope that our new-found pragmatism has a half life that extends well into the eventual recovery and beyond.

Notes

1. See, for example, IMF (2006).
2. Members of the G-20 are Argentina, Australia, Brazil, Canada, China, France, Germany, India, Indonesia, Italy, Japan, the Republic of Korea, Mexico, the Russian

Federation, Saudi Arabia, South Africa, Turkey, the United Kingdom, the United States, and the European Union.

3. Much of this chapter deals with views emanating from the IMF. This is more out of convenience than because the IMF has "gotten it wrong" more often than others within the economics profession. In fact, to their credit, the IMF has produced a significant amount of excellent material in the wake of the crisis questioning many of its own priors. This reevaluation has been facilitated by the introduction of a new publication vehicle—"Staff Position Notes"—an ingenious communications vehicle that has unbridled IMF staff members and allowed them to advance ideas without requiring their vetting by an often intellectually more conservative Executive Board.

4. While "several" is not one of the qualifiers formally defined by the IMF (see http://www.imf.org/external/np/sec/misc/qualifiers.htm), it can reasonably be understood to be more than two but fewer than "many," which the IMF defines to be at least 10 of the 24 Executive Directors.

5. See, for example, Abdelal (2007:196–212), which contains an extensive description of IMF advice on capital account liberalization in emerging market economies, including those acceding to the European Union and OECD.

6. Although it should be noted that much of the rethinking has come in the form of "Staff Position Notes" rather than Executive Board–endorsed analysis.

7. Members of the G-7 are Canada, France, Germany, Italy, Japan, the United Kingdom, and the United States.

References

Abdelal, R. 2007. "The Rebirth of Doubt." In *Capital Rules: The Construction of Global Finance*, 196–212. Cambridge, MA: Harvard University Press.

Blanchard, O., G. Dell'Ariccia, and P. Mauro. 2010. "Rethinking Macroeconomic Policy." IMF Staff Position Note SPN/10/03, International Monetary Fund, Washington, DC.

Fisher, I. 1933. "The Debt-Deflation Theory of Great Depressions." *Econometrica* 1 (4): 337–57.

Ghosh, A., and J. Ostry. 2009. "Choosing an Exchange Rate Regime." *Finance and Development* 46 (4): 38–40.

IMF (International Monetary Fund). 1999. "Summing Up by the Acting Chairman of Countries' Experiences with the Use of Controls on Capital Movements and Issues in Their Orderly Liberalization." BUFF/99/45, Meeting of the IMF Executive Board, Washington, DC, April 6.

———. 2005. *The IMF's Approach to Capital Account Liberalization*. Independent Evaluation Office. Washington, DC: International Monetary Fund.

———. 2006. "Multilateral Surveillance: Evaluation Report." Independent Evaluation Office, International Monetary Fund, Washington, DC.

————. 2010a. "The Fund's Mandate—An Overview." January 22. Washington, DC. http://www.imf.org/external/np/pp/eng/2010/012210a.pdf.

————. 2010b. "Global Liquidity Expansion: Effects on 'Receiving' Economies and Policy Response Options." In *Global Financial Stability Report, April 2010*, 119–51. Washington, DC: International Monetary Fund.

Lipsky, J. 2010. "Fiscal Policy Challenges in the Post-Crisis World." Speech by John Lipsky, First Deputy Managing Director, International Monetary Fund, to the China Development Forum, March 21. http://www.imf.org/external/np/speeches/2010/032110.htm.

Mankiw, N. G. 2006. "The Macroeconomist as Scientist and Engineer." *Journal of Economic Perspectives* 20 (4): 30.

Ostry, O., A. Ghosh, K. Habermeier, M. Chamon, M. Qureshi, and D. Reinhardt. 2010. "Capital Inflows: The Role of Controls." IMF Staff Position Note SPN/10/04, International Monetary Fund, Washington, DC.

Rodrik, D. 2010. "The End of An Era in Finance." Project Syndicate. March 11. http://www.project-syndicate.org/commentary/rodrik41/English.

Stiglitz, J. 2010. "The Financial Crisis of 2007–8 and Its Macroeconomic Consequences." In *Time for a Visible Hand: Lessons from the 2008 World Financial Crisis*, ed. S. Griffith-Jones, J. A. Ocampo, and J. Stiglitz, 19–49. New York: Oxford University Press.

White, W. 2009. "Modern Macroeconomics Is on the Wrong Track." *Finance and Development* 46 (4): 15–19.

Wolf, M. 2009. "Seeds of Its Own Destruction." In *The Future of Capitalism. Financial Times,* supplement, March 9.

7

Macroprudential Policies in the Wake of the Global Financial Crisis

Luis Servén

The debate about the global financial crisis of 2008–09 has identified a variety of causes, including large global imbalances, low world interest rates, and loose monetary policy in advanced countries. In truth, there is little consensus on the relative roles of each of these factors in triggering the crisis. In contrast, there is broad agreement that inadequate prudential regulation of the financial system was one of the main forces—or, in the view of many qualified observers, the key force—behind the worldwide financial meltdown. The regulatory framework allowed a massive buildup of systemic risk in the shadow banking system, that is, on the balance sheets of unregulated intermediaries and off the balance sheets of regulated ones. It provided incentives for procyclical risk taking that fueled a vicious circle of asset bubbles and expanding credit, whose unraveling brought the global financial system to its knees. It failed to take account of the huge systemic risks triggered by the undercapitalization of large and complex institutions.

Hence, one of the key policy lessons from the crisis is the need for a radical reconsideration of prudential regulation that puts at center stage systemic risk. This chapter updates the status of the prudential reform debate, the main reform proposals, and their analytical underpinnings.

However, regulatory reform alone is unlikely to make boom-bust financial cycles a thing of the past. As the chapter explains, other policy tools—
monetary, fiscal, and financial—may have to play a major role to contain
the buildup of systemic risk.

Making Sense of Macroprudential Regulation

The starting point for the reconsideration of prudential policies is the
realization, brought about by the global financial crisis, that existing prudential regulation focuses too much on the management of the risk of the
individual financial institution and too little on systemic risk. Systemic
risk is a negative externality that each financial firm imposes on the system, and it arises primarily from the fact that the social cost of failure (or
undercapitalization) of individual financial institutions exceeds the private cost to the institutions themselves. In contrast with microprudential
regulation, which focuses on the resilience of individual institutions to
exogenous risks, the basic concern of macroprudential regulation is the
management of endogenous systemwide risk.

The key issue is that ensuring the stability of individual institutions
does not ensure system stability. Actions that enhance the stability of
individual institutions may weaken systemwide stability, owing to externalities and spillovers across institutions.[1] For example, an institution
that cuts lending to reduce its exposure may weaken other institutions
in need of funding, forcing them to cut their own lending (Allen and
Gale 2000). Likewise, an institution that sells assets to rebuild its balance
sheet puts downward pressure on asset prices, which contributes to
weakening the balance sheets of other institutions and may force them
to engage in further asset sales, the so-called fire-sale externality (see
Krishnamurthy forthcoming). Through these and similar mechanisms,
risks taken by individual institutions may be ultimately borne by the
system as a whole.

One important lesson from the crisis is that regulation should cover
all systemically relevant financial intermediaries and not only deposit-
taking banks. In contrast with most previous episodes of systemic
turbulence,[2] nondeposit institutions such as Lehman Brothers and AIG
arguably played the key role in the 2008–09 meltdown. This accords with
the fact that in the United States (and other advanced economies), deposit

banks have steadily lost ground over time relative to other financial intermediaries (Adrian and Shin 2009). The implication is that the so-called perimeter of regulation needs to be correspondingly enlarged to encompass all relevant nondeposit intermediaries.

There is a raging academic and policy debate on the pros and cons of various specific macroprudential reforms, including some comprehensive proposals advanced in the Geneva Report (Brunnermeier and others 2009), the report of the Group of Thirty (2009), and the NYU-Stern report (Acharya and others 2009). The common objective of all these proposals is the realignment of the incentives and constraints faced by individual institutions in their decisions, so that they adequately reflect their systemwide consequences.

Reform proposals target a wide variety of features of financial institutions including their capital, the liquidity of their assets and liabilities, their leverage, their size, their complexity, and their interconnectedness. To make sense of them, one must distinguish two dimensions of system risk.[3] The first is the cross-sectional dimension: how risk is distributed across the financial system at a given time. The focus here is on the correlated exposures of financial intermediaries, their vulnerability to common shocks, and the mechanisms that generate risk spillovers across institutions. The second is the time dimension: how systemic risk evolves over the cycle. The key issues here are the amplification of system risk over the cycle through feedback across the financial system and between macroeconomic and financial variables, and in particular the booms and busts in credit and asset prices.

In the cross-sectional dimension, reform proposals aim to make each institution internalize its contribution to systemwide risk, by means of capital requirements, taxes, or similar regulatory charges commensurate with its systemic impact. Of course, an essential requirement for this is an appropriate measure of the contribution of intermediaries to systemic risk. Overall balance sheet size can offer a rough indicator, but with the caveat that "big" is not necessarily the same as "systemic." Intuitively, what matters is interconnectedness rather than size per se. Indeed, various observers have pointed out that Lehman Brothers and AIG, both of which played a key role in the propagation and amplification of the global crisis, were not inordinately large, yet they were deeply intertwined with the global financial system.

Alternative indicators of systemic risk have been proposed. For example, the conditional value-at-risk measures an institution's contribution to systemic risk by the value-at-risk of the entire system conditional on the institution in question being in distress.[4] In turn, the Systemic Expected Shortfall focuses on each institution's estimated contribution to systemwide capital shortage in the event of systemic distress.[5] These measures, however, are based on correlations constructed from historical data, and as such, they may not be reliable under rare extreme events and acute turbulence. A third alternative, advanced by the International Monetary Fund (IMF 2010), overcomes this difficulty by examining in detail the cross-exposures in the balance sheets of individual institutions.

While conceptually appealing, these various proposals also highlight the considerable informational requirements that an accurate assessment of the contribution of intermediaries to systemic risk may pose to the regulator. Hence, the appeal of simpler measures related to the size of balance sheets (or specifically, the uninsured portion of the liability[6]), leverage, and, especially, maturity mismatches. Indeed, the global crisis has shown that short-term financing in wholesale markets can be a major source of systemic vulnerability, because it leaves intermediaries engaged in maturity transformation open to creditor runs. These are similar to classic bank runs, but—as in the events of 2008–09—can affect a much broader range of institutions. The failures of Bear Sterns, Lehman Brothers, and Northern Rock, for example, can all be traced to their massive reliance on short-term funding. Discouraging such an unstable form of financing may be an effective way of limiting systemwide risk. One way to achieve this objective is by penalizing maturity mismatches in intermediaries' balance sheets (Brunnermeier and others 2009).

What tools should be used for this purpose? In principle, externalities can be contained through appropriate capital surcharges (Brunnermeier and others 2009), taxes (Acharya and others 2010b), or tight quota restrictions on leverage, liquidity, and so on. However, quotas are typically distortionary and easy to evade by intermediaries not subject to strict monitoring. Capital surcharges are themselves taxes (to the extent that capital is costly), but systemic taxes on unstable funding might be the option easiest to administer (Perotti 2010), and would yield revenue to the authorities that could help cover the costs of emergency intervention at times of distress.

Of course, there is little if any experience with any of these schemes, and it is unclear if in practice they would achieve their desired objectives. Hence, some qualified observers have called for simply placing limits on the size of financial institutions and breaking up those that exceed such limits. This seemingly offers an expedient way of dealing with the "too big to fail" problem, although (as already noted) interconnectedness, and not only size, is what matters for systemic risk.[7]

We now consider the time dimension of macroprudential regulation. Financial crises do not occur at random times; they almost invariably follow booms, as documented, for example, by Schularick and Taylor (2009). Measured risks decline in the boom; asset prices rise; and lending, leverage, and short-term funding become mutually reinforcing. The opposite happens (often more abruptly) in the collapse, in which a vicious circle arises between deleveraging, asset sales, and deteriorating real conditions.[8] In particular, the evidence shows that these credit cycles are larger, more persistent, and more asymmetric in emerging economies than in advanced economies (Mendoza and Terrones 2008).

The objective of macroprudential regulation is to mitigate these boom-bust cycles. However, it is important to keep in mind that the procyclical behavior of the financial system has multiple causes. On the one hand, fundamentals are procyclical: investment opportunities and credit demand rise in the upswing, while the riskiness of prospective borrowers declines. On the other hand, inadequate regulatory policies tend to accentuate the procyclical behavior of the financial system. For example, the risk-weighted capital requirements adopted by the Basel Committee on Banking Supervision under Basel II tend to decline in the boom (owing to the decline in measured risks and the improvement in conventional risk ratings) and rise in the slump, and the empirical magnitude of the effect is substantial (Repullo and Suárez 2010). Fair value accounting has similar consequences, since asset prices rise in the upswing, prompting further balance sheet expansion, and decline in the downswing, forcing deleveraging. Finally, externalities across financial intermediaries and between the financial and real sides of the economy provide another source of procyclicality.

Regulatory reform should focus on the latter two sources of procyclicality.[9] The thrust of reform in this area is the buildup of capital or liquidity buffers, or both, in good times, to cushion the adjustment in bad times. Two concrete proposals that have gained broad support are the use of procyclical capital requirements (Brunnermeier and others 2009), and procyclical bank provisioning.[10] Under these proposals, capital requirements or provisions, or both, for loan losses would be scaled up or down according to cyclical conditions, such as measures of aggregate credit expansion, growth of gross domestic product, and so forth.

At present, there is limited analytical research, and no actual experience, on the workings of procyclical capital requirements. In turn, procyclical provisioning has seen some actual use, notably in Spain and more recently in Peru and Colombia.[11] There is consensus, especially in the case of Spain, that the provisioning scheme allowed banks to enter the downswing in more robust shape than they would have otherwise. However, there is much less evidence that countercyclical provisioning had any material effect on the credit cycle or that it helped in any significant way to contain Spain's real estate bubble over the 2000s (Caprio 2010). Little is known about how the cycle should be measured for these purposes or what degree of cyclical sensitivity regulations should have.

The same applies to other measures that have seen some limited application, such as countercyclical loan-to-value ratios and direct controls on specific credit flows—for example, mortgages or consumer credit—that have been employed by emerging markets in Asia (Caruana 2010). The extent to which they have been effective in mitigating credit and asset price booms remains an open question.

These reforms will tend to complicate the task of regulators and supervisors, and place additional burdens on their capacity. Moreover, experience shows that procyclical tightening of prudential regulation will encourage disintermediation[12] to less-regulated institutions (or countries), limiting its effectiveness. Finally, the political economy challenges should not be ignored. Attempts by the authorities to rein in credit expansion in good times, in the absence of obvious symptoms of inflationary or financial distress, will meet strong resistance from both lenders and borrowers riding the boom and from policy makers crediting the boom to their good policies. The reliance of regulators on well-defined rules (rather than discretionary regulatory changes) and independence from government may be helpful in this regard, as would strong incentives for regulators, which are lacking in most countries. It is important to recall that countercyclical regulatory changes would have been possible in many countries in the run-up to the global financial crisis, yet very few made use of them.

How Can Macroeconomic Policy Help?

It is still unclear what precise form macroprudential regulation of the financial system may take and how much it will contribute to financial stability. This means that other policy tools may need to be deployed in pursuance of macroprudential objectives. The leading candidate is monetary policy, which at least in theory could contribute to financial stability by becoming more "symmetric" over the financial cycle, that is, more restrictive during a credit and asset price boom, just like it almost invariably becomes accommodative in a crash (Papademos 2009).

The conventional view is that monetary policy should focus exclusively on inflation of goods prices, and not react to asset prices or other financial variables; in particular, it should not attempt to lean against the buildup of financial risks and asset bubbles, except to the extent that conventional Taylor rules dictate such a course of action in light of inflation and output gap trends (Bernanke and Gertler 2000). The reason is that it is very difficult to establish whether asset prices are out of line with fundamentals in a timely manner, when intervention might help. Moreover, little is known about the timing and magnitude of the monetary policy impacts on asset prices. Hence, in this view the authorities should adhere to the "Tinbergen principle," gearing monetary policy to goods price stability and macroprudential regulation to financial stability.

However, absent better macroprudential tools, an emerging view holds instead that monetary policy should also react to the buildup of risk in the financial system. This can be reconciled with inflation targeting over a longer horizon—that is, taking into account the inflation that would otherwise result from unavoidable monetary easing in the crash. There is some evidence that monetary policy has a significant effect on the acquisition of assets by leveraged intermediaries (Adrian and Shin 2009) and the quality of those assets (Maddaloni, Peydró, and Scopei forthcoming). Hence, timely monetary tightening might be effective at containing the cyclical expansion of leverage, credit, asset prices, and risk taking. This means that there might be a role for balance sheet aggregates in the determination of monetary policy, echoing the once-popular targeting of monetary aggregates, although for reasons of financial stability rather than price stability. But from a practical point of view, little is known about the complexities that implementing such policy could involve; its likely effects; or the short-run tradeoffs it might impose among financial stability, price stability, and output stability, to the extent that these various objectives could demand policy changes in different directions.

While the question of the appropriate role of monetary policy is being debated primarily in advanced countries, it is no less relevant for emerging markets, particularly those that adopted inflation-targeting regimes in recent years. One additional concern for them is that gearing the policy stance to correct hard-to-identify asset price misalignments may detract from its transparency and predictability, which may be especially worrisome for countries still at the early stage of establishing monetary policy credibility or, more generally, their commitment to price stability. It might also hamper the beneficial effects of financial development, which might be reflected in seemingly "excessive" credit growth.

Aside from monetary policy, fiscal policy can also contribute to financial stability. The global crisis has brought under the spotlight the potential of countercyclical fiscal policy, and in particular the need to create room to maneuver through fiscal tightening in the boom, which helps mitigate its amplitude and generates buffers for a fiscal loosening in the downswing. Some emerging markets (for example, Chile) have benefited from strict adherence to this course of action, which allowed them to support aggregate demand in the crash and, in some cases, to finance the measures needed to shore up the financial system as well. Yet the crisis has also shown that the deployment of discretionary fiscal policy often faces considerable delays, which makes it unsuitable for counteracting the financial cycle in a timely manner more generally. This underscores the need to build up self-deploying automatic stabilizers, which are still weak in most developing countries (Debrun and Kapoor 2010).

Apart from the countercyclical deployment of fiscal policy, other fiscal measures can still contribute to financial stability. Most important, the removal of widespread tax incentives to borrowing by the corporate sector, through the favorable tax treatment of debt relative to equity financing, and to households in the form of tax exemptions of interest payments on mortgages could discourage credit growth and have effects qualitatively analogous to those of the Pigouvian tax schemes[13] that have been proposed by some experts to contain the externalities behind the credit cycle.

Finally, the role of external financing policies from the point of view of financial stability has also attracted renewed attention. Emerging markets, notably in Asia, hoarding large amounts of foreign reserves, were better able than the rest to weather the global deleveraging. In part this was a reaction to the East Asia crisis of the 1990s, in which countries whose financial systems had borrowed massively abroad were hit hard by foreign creditor runs, leading to exchange rate crashes and financial distress. Indeed, evidence from a large number of credit booms episodes shows that in emerging markets, booms are often preceded by surges in capital inflows—more so than by financial reforms or productivity gains (Mendoza and Terrones 2008).[14]

Self-insurance against foreign creditor runs through reserve hoarding involves significant opportunity costs, which are likely to mount in view of the growing size of precautionary reserve pools across the developing world, partly driven by the "fear of losing reserves" underscored by some observers. Of course, international insurance arrangements would provide a much more efficient solution. But in spite of some promising developments (such as the International Monetary Fund's new contingent credit facility), they are still far from offering a real alternative to self-insurance, which is likely to be further encouraged after the crisis.

Measures to discourage external borrowing, in particular at short maturities, might offer another way to limit the self-insurance cost incurred by countries and the international propagation of turbulence. For example, Pigouvian taxation of external borrowing to make borrowers internalize the social cost of eventual deleveraging would likely reduce the extent of borrowing and implicitly help finance the precautionary liquidity hoarding (Aizenmann forthcoming). However, as with other macroprudential proposals, the effectiveness of such measures remains to be established.

Concluding Remarks

The 2008–09 global financial crisis has underscored the devastating macroeconomic effects of inadequate prudential regulation. In its wake, the design of a macroprudential framework capable of moderating boom-bust financial cycles has become a top priority in the international policy agenda. There is a raging debate around a variety of reform options, but the design of such a framework is still in its early stages. There are strong hints that international regulatory bodies will opt for some form of cyclically sensitive capital charges or provisioning schemes, and perhaps a tax on financial intermediation. However, the eventual effectiveness of such measures at containing systemic risk is largely unknown.

Although the spotlight is on macroprudential regulation, behind the scenes other tools may have to do much of the work to dampen the financial cycle in the coming years. They include countercyclical deployment of fiscal policy; reduction of tax incentives to borrowing; attention to financial stability in the formulation of monetary policy; and external financial policies that contain external borrowing, particularly short term.

Among developing countries, macroprudential reform ranks high on the policy agenda for emerging markets, particularly those with large and sophisticated financial systems. It is a less urgent priority for countries that were less exposed to the global turmoil and for countries with less developed financial sectors and more limited capacity for regulatory policy design and implementation. For the latter, fiscal, monetary, and external financial policies are likely to keep the greater role.

Heterogeneous regulation naturally encourages migration of intermediation activities across types of financial institutions and regulatory jurisdictions, toward less regulated ones. In this regard, it is not clear how nondeposit institutions will be affected by reform trends. Even more important, there is a distinct danger that, in the absence of a quick international agreement on reform standards, country-specific regulatory initiatives will rush ahead and lead to regulatory protectionism, inconsistent rules, and regulatory arbitrage across jurisdictions, shifting bubbles and risk-taking to countries with less strict regulation and less capable enforcement.

Looking ahead, it is likely that tighter macroprudential requirements on financial intermediaries—in the form of capital charges, liquidity requirements, and taxes—will raise their funding costs and limit their lending capacity. This may have an adverse effect on the global supply of financing and, other things being equal, restrain global growth. This could be particularly costly to developing countries with large financing needs. It is obviously very difficult to assess how large such effect might be and how it would compare with the benefit of reduced likelihood of financial meltdowns that the reforms seek to achieve.

Notes

1. Brunnermeier (2009) highlights the role of spillovers and externalities in the propagation of the global crisis.
2. Perhaps the closest case was the Long-Term Capital Management episode of 1998.
3. This distinction is taken from Borio (2003).
4. More precisely, the relevant magnitude is the difference between the conditional systemwide value-at-risk and the value-at-risk of the institution under consideration (see Adrian and Brunnermeier 2009).
5. See Acharya and others (2010a). For estimates of the systemic risk of U.S. institutions based on the Systemic Expected Shortfall, visit http://vlab.stern.nyu.edu/analysis/RISK.USFIN-MR.MES.
6. The underlying logic is that the insured portion, that is, commercial bank deposits, already incurs regulatory charges.
7. In fact, some of the largest banks may have instead become "too big to save," in the sense that their size exceeds the resources that their home-country governments could deploy to stabilize the financial system (Demirgüç-Kunt and Huizinga 2010). This would offer an independent reason for size limits and/or penalties.
8. The analytical underpinnings of these "financial accelerator" effects are examined by Kiyotaki and Moore (1997).
9. But reform should not focus on the first one. Some procyclicality may be desirable, and not all credit booms end in crashes; in fact, many of them arise from the process of financial development. For example, Barajas, Dell'Ariccia, and Levchenko (2009) examine multiple episodes of booming credit across the world and find that only one in five end up in financial crises.
10. Taxation schemes to discourage borrowing in the boom have also been proposed (see, for example, Jeanne and Korinek 2010).
11. See Fernández de Lis and García-Herrero (2010) for a comparative perspective on these three experiences.
12. Disintermediation is the shift of financial activity out of (regulated) financial institutions.
13. A Pigovian tax (named after economist Arthur Pigou) is a tax levied on a market activity that generates negative externalities. The objective of the tax is to correct the socially inefficient market outcome.
14. However, the evidence also shows that credit booms preceded by large capital inflows are not significantly more likely to end in financial crashes than other

booms. The key propitiating factors are instead the duration and scale of the boom and the quality of financial supervision (Barajas, Dell'Ariccia, and Levchenko 2008).

References

Acharya, V., L. Pedersen, T. Philippon, and M. Richardson. 2009. "Regulating Systemic Risk." In *Restoring Financial Stability: How to Repair a Failed System*, ed. V. Acharya and M. Richardson, 283–304. Wiley Finance Series. Hoboken, NJ: John Wiley and Sons.

———. 2010a. "Measuring Systemic Risk." Unpublished manuscript, Stern School of Business, New York University, New York.

———. 2010b. "A Tax on Systemic Risk." Unpublished manuscript, Stern School of Business, New York University, New York.

Adrian, T., and M. Brunnermeier. 2009. "CoVaR." Staff Report 348, Federal Reserve Bank of New York.

Adrian, T., and H. Shin. 2009. "Financial Intermediaries, Financial Stability, and Monetary Policy." Staff Report 346, Federal Reserve Bank of New York.

Aizenmann, J. Forthcoming. "Macro Prudential Supervision in the Open Economy and the Role of Central Banks in Emerging Markets." *Open Economies Review.*

Allen, F., and D. Gale. 2000. "Financial Contagion." *Journal of Political Economy* 108: 1–33.

Barajas, A., G. Dell'Ariccia, and A. Levchenko. 2009. "Credit Booms: The Good, the Bad, and the Ugly." Unpublished manuscript, International Monetary Fund, Washington, DC.

Bernanke, B., and M. Gertler. 2000. "Monetary Policy and Asset Price Volatility." NBER Working Paper 7559, National Bureau of Economic Research, Cambridge, MA.

Borio, C. 2003. "Towards a Macro-prudential Framework for Financial Regulation and Supervision." Working Paper 128, Bank for International Settlements, Basel, Switzerland.

Brunnermeier, M. 2009. "Deciphering the Liquidity and Credit Crunch 2007–08." *Journal of Economic Perspectives* 23 (1): 77–100.

Brunnermeier, M., A. Crockett, C. Goodhart, A. Persaud, and H. Shin. 2009. "The Fundamental Principles of Financial Regulation." *Geneva Reports on the World Economy* 11.

Caprio, G. 2010. "Safe and Sound Banking: A Role for Counter-cyclical Regulatory Requirements?" Policy Research Working Paper 5198, World Bank, Washington, DC.

Caruana, J. 2010. "Macroprudential Policy: Working toward a New Consensus." Bank for International Settlements, Basel, Switzerland.

Debrun, X., and R. Kapoor. 2010. "Fiscal Policy and Macroeconomic Stability: Automatic Stabilizers Work, Always and Everywhere." IMF Working Paper 10/111, International Monetary Fund, Washington, DC.

Demirgüç-Kunt, A., and H. Huizinga. 2010. "Are Banks too Big to Fail or too Big to Save?" International Evidence from Equity Prices and CDS Spreads." Discussion Paper No. 7903, Center for Economice Policy Research, Washington, DC.

Fernández de Lis, S., and A. García-Herrero. 2010. "Dynamic Provisioning: Some Lessons from Existing Experiences." Working Paper Series No. 218, Asian Development Bank Institute, Tokyo.

Group of Thirty. 2009. *Financial Reform: A Framework for Financial Stability.* Washington, DC: Group of Thirty.

IMF (International Monetary Fund). 2010. *Global Financial Stability Report, April 2010.* Washington, DC: International Monetary Fund.

Jeanne, O., and A. Korinek. 2010. "Managing Credit Booms and Busts: A Pigouvian Taxation Approach." Unpublished manuscript, University of Maryland, College Park, MD.

Kiyotaki, N., and J. Moore. 1997. "Credit Cycles." *Journal of Political Economy* 105: 211–48.

Krishnamurthy, A. Forthcoming. "Amplification Mechanisms in Liquidity Crises." *American Economic Association Journals—Macroeconomics.*

Maddaloni, A., J. Peydró, and S. Scopei. Forthcoming. "Does Monetary Policy Affect Bank Credit Standards?" Unpublished manuscript.

Mendoza, E., and M. Terrones. 2008. "An Anatomy of Credit Booms: Evidence from Macro Aggregates and Micro Data." NBER Working Paper 14049, National Bureau of Economic Research, Cambridge, MA.

Papademos, L. 2009. "Monetary Policy and the 'Great Crisis': Lessons and Challenges." Speech at the 37th Economics Conference, "Beyond the Crisis: Economic Policy in a New Macroeconomic Environment." Österreichische Nationalbank, Vienna, May 14. http://www.ecb.int/press/key/date/2009/html/sp090514.en.html.

Perotti, E. 2010. "Serious Reform Starts with a Systemic Tax." VoxEU. http://www.voxeu.org/index.php?q=node/5021.

Repullo, R., and J. Suárez. 2010. "The Procyclical Effects of Bank Capital Regulation." Paper presented at the "Conference on Procyclicality and Financial Regulation," University of Tilburg, March 11–12.

Schularick, M., and A. Taylor. 2009. "Credit Booms Gone Bust: Monetary Policy, Leverage Cycles and Financial Crises, 1870–2008." Working Paper 15512, National Bureau of Economic Research, Cambridge, MA.

8

Finance in Crisis: Causes, Lessons, Consequences, and an Application to Latin America

Augusto de la Torre and Alain Ize

Why and how have the Latin American financial systems managed to survive more or less unscathed the biggest financial crisis the world has known since the Great Depression? Will the 2008–09 crisis affect the future of financial development in the region? Is financial development in Latin America after the crisis destined to continue to lag that in many other parts of the world, or is a rapid catch-up now more likely than before?[1] Answering these interrelated questions requires looking back at the recent economic history of the region and examining the possible lessons one can draw from the crisis as regards the inner dynamics of financial development and financial stability.

There is little disagreement that financial development has lagged in the region due to a history of acute macroeconomic volatility combined with misconceived microeconomic policies. These resulted in repressed financial systems during the 1970s and 1980s, a situation that eventually led to a shift in favor of a two-tiered policy for financial development that emerged clearly during the 1990s and that has prevailed until now. The conventional wisdom became *Get the macro right, and let those markets go free!*

Yet, the crisis has led to a questioning of this policy. It was precisely the combination of stable, successful macroeconomic policies during a long period of "great moderation" and largely free but inadequately regulated financial markets that were at the core of the dynamics of the crisis. What does this mean, then, for the future of financial development in Latin America? Should the conventional wisdom that prevailed prior to the crisis be revisited and reshaped? Or is the region still at a level of financial development where crisis lessons from the center are only marginally, if at all, relevant to the periphery?

This chapter argues that the above-mentioned precrisis tenets of financial development policy will continue to hold at the core, but that that will not be enough. They will need to be complemented and revisited at the edges.

On the macro side, the stable policies of the recent past will need to be supported by the introduction, or in some cases strengthening, of macroprudential instruments. As for industrial countries, these instruments will need to boost the resilience of financial systems of Latin America and the Caribbean (LAC) to endogenous risk dynamics. But they will also need to strengthen their independence from imported perturbations. Given the sharper constraints faced by the monetary policies of the region, arising in particular from concerns about the adverse effects on growth of excessive exchange rate volatility, the use of these instruments may be even more crucial in Latin America than in industrialized countries. At the same time, a minimum degree of currency independence will continue to be needed to limit the cross-border regulatory arbitrage resulting from more active and independent macroprudential policies.

On the microprudential side, contestable, deeper, more innovative financial markets should remain the order of the day. However, a more attentive, forward-looking, and smarter presence of the state will be crucial to maintaining financial markets pointed in the right direction. This will require a closer monitoring and control of systemic risk, both over time and across institutions. While many of the policy implications will be similar to those being debated in industrial countries, several issues, such as devising appropriate countercyclical prudential norms, introducing Pigovian taxes[2] to induce intermediaries to internalize the adverse systemic effects of their actions, revisiting the perimeter of regulation to limit dynamic regulatory arbitrage, and remolding prudential supervision to enhance systemic monitoring, should have a distinct regional flavor in view of the more limited financial development or generally weaker institutions.

Other issues are more clearly Latin America–specific. For instance, should the region revisit certain dimensions of its insertion into global financial markets? In particular, should it continue with the trend of increasing its net creditor position in debt contracts vis-à-vis the rest of the world while at the same time continuing to raise its net debtor position in equity contracts? And should it rethink the role of foreign banks in local markets and perhaps ring-fence them from the pressures faced by their parent banks abroad? More broadly, should Latin America's regulatory framework deviate from the one currently taking shape in the industrial world?

As regards the role of the state in financial development, should Latin America revisit the mission of public banks to emphasize their catalytic and countercyclical leveraging capacity? (This latter capacity was de facto amply used during the recent crisis.) And should the region use regulatory or tax policy, or both, more actively to internalize externalities? (Unlike the debate in industrial countries, which is mainly centered on stability issues, the discussion in Latin America should also address developmental aims.) Many of these issues are quite contentious and likely to remain at the center of the regional agenda for years to come.

The Precrisis Conventional Wisdom in Latin America

The recurrent currency and banking crises that hit the Latin American region during the 1980s and 1990s confirmed that poor macroeconomic fundamentals are particularly dangerous in open financial systems. Ex ante, the uncertainty resulting from macroeconomic volatility—particularly high and unpredictable inflation—was deleterious to financial development, most of all at the longer maturities. It corroded the role of money as a store of value, leading to a gradual buildup of currency and duration mismatches, often associated with a displacement of domestic intermediation by cross-border intermediation. It also induced a drastic shortening of funding that exposed financial systems across the region to recurrent roll-over and liquidity risks.

Ex post, inflexible exchange rate regimes—adopted in part to bring down inflation expectations in the midst of rising international financial integration—became extremely vulnerable to self-fulfilling attacks. This compounded the proneness to currency crashes associated with unsustainable fiscal positions. In turn, widespread currency, duration, and maturity mismatches boosted the fragility of financial systems and their susceptibility to currency upheavals, interest rate volatility, and runs on banks. In addition to thwarting and setting back financial development by years at a time, the repeated financial crises led to multiple ownership changes. By facilitating the entry of often unfit, improper, or poorly capitalized bankers, some re-privatizations of banking systems in turn compounded the brittleness of financial development.

The policy response to such problems—which became increasingly better defined as the 1990s unfolded—rested on two pillars: *Get the macro right, and let those markets go free!*[3] The first pillar reflected the dominant perception that unlocking the process of financial development had necessarily to start with macro stability at home. The latter was recognized as an essential precondition for financial stability, which in turn was the key to financial development. Therefore, over the past 20 years or so, ensuring stable and low inflation—increasingly through the introduction of inflation targets and a flexible exchange rate regime—became the first order of business toward unleashing the forces of financial development. Fiscal reform and the development of local currency public bond markets were viewed as the natural complements to a successful monetary reform.

A cautious, hands-on prudential oversight, buttressed by sufficient capital and liquidity buffers, was also viewed as an indispensible complement to ensure that financial institutions withstood systemic turbulence. The program to make this a reality included efforts to adopt the international prudential standards emanating mainly from the Basel Committee on Banking Supervision. These efforts began in the early 1990s, but were visibly deepened after the Asian and Russian crisis in the latter part of that decade. They went in tandem with a global push for convergence toward a large battery of international standards and codes and with a shift of emphasis toward risk-sensitive capital requirements and risk-based supervision. They increasingly aimed at monitoring the activities of financial conglomerates on a consolidated basis.

Paradoxically, this Basel-inspired program, although aimed at systemic stability, was focused on the measurement and management of the idiosyncratic risks faced by the individual institution (or conglomerate), thereby largely ignoring the oversight of systemic risk. However, this was partially compensated in the region by efforts to address liquidity risks, mainly via substantial liquidity and reserve requirements, particularly on dollar liabilities. At the same time, the entry of reputable foreign bankers with deep pockets was viewed as an obvious response to the twin problems of inexperienced bankers and recurrent deposit outflows.

The emphasis on macroeconomic and financial stability and the consequent priority given to the modernization of the prudential oversight framework were accompanied by a similarly drastic shift of the microeconomic paradigm (that is, resource allocation). The shift favored a frankly market-based approach to financial development—the second pillar of the precrisis consensus. The conventional wisdom thus drifted away from the predominance that had been previously given to state-owned financial institutions and state *dirigisme* in the mobilization and allocation of finance and toward the promotion of market forces and private intermediation.

This market orientation helps explain why Latin America's quest for systemic financial stability through macroeconomic stability was nonetheless accompanied by a Basel-inspired prudential agenda that ignored systemic risk. The implicit premise was that, given Basel norms and sufficient information disclosure, disciplined markets would spawn and self-regulate, with the consequence that risks would be appropriately priced and managed. Sound financial institutions would add up to a sound system that would, in turn, buttress the financial stability achieved through macro policy rectitude.

The "let competitive markets breathe" motto of the microeconomic paradigm implied a reform agenda geared at fostering and strengthening the multiple facets (institutional, informational, contractual) of the enabling environment. As noted, this was naturally accompanied by efforts to sharply reduce or eliminate the direct intervention of the state in financial activities, including the state's tendency to quickly bail out troubled institutions.[4] Rapid financial market liberalization and a more cautious yet widespread adherence to the dynamics of financial globalization were viewed as necessary complements toward an efficient and sound path of financial development.[5] And to maintain the course, prudential regulation was supposed to be increasingly focused on fostering of market discipline by ensuring adequate buffers of risk-sensitive capital ("skin in the game") and the continuous upgrading of information and transparency standards.

This precrisis consensus on the stability-oriented and market-friendly tenets of financial development policy was legitimized by the visible successes achieved in stabilizing and reducing the vulnerability of financial systems across the region. The newly gained resiliency paid off handsomely during the 2008–09 global crisis, as Latin America avoided financial crises at home while the rich economies saw the crippling of their financial systems. However, the depth and reach of financial intermediation in the region in the years prior to the crisis remained limited, partly explaining its greater resilience during the crisis. Moreover, much of the growth was concentrated in consumer lending. Hence, especially as the new millennium dawned, the need to expand financial inclusion and broaden the access to financial services became a central source of concern. The latter was increasingly added to the financial development agenda *as an objective*, albeit with limited clarity and consensus on the policy reform agenda.[6]

Causes and Lessons from the Global Financial Crisis

The 2008–09 global financial crisis seems to have turned the links among macroeconomic stability, financial stability, and financial development on their heads. Rather than macro stability feeding both financial stability and financial development, macro stability actually fed an unsustainable process of financial development in rich-country financial systems, particularly the United States, which culminated in catastrophic financial instability. At the same time, macro stability interacted with a regulatory architecture predicated on a strong belief in the self-disciplining role of markets, to unleash a series of new market failures that fueled ultimately perverse dynamics.

Such new market failures included novel varieties within the traditional paradigm of *asymmetric information*, around which most of the precrisis prudential policy was established. For example, as the "skin in the game" thinned for the various agents acting at the nodes of the originate-and-distribute model (mortgage originations, lenders, packagers, rating agencies, investment banks, providers of credit default protection, and so forth), incentives to take advantage of the less informed swelled, fueling excessive risk taking with someone else's money. At the same time, the multiplication of agents and complex instruments aggravated the problems of asymmetric information by producing an increase in systemic opacity (Ashcraft and Schuermann 2008; Gorton 2008).

The emergence of these "second-generation" asymmetric information problems runs contrary to the naive view that the reduction in transaction (including informational) costs should gradually dilute the agency problems associated with asymmetric information. While it seemed natural to expect that better and cheaper information would give the agent a better handle on the principal, better information and lower transaction costs also attracted new agents and promoted new instruments. Thus, the new nodes of agency frictions (along the originate-and-distribute chain, for example) arose at a faster pace than the ability of principals to catch up.

However, new market failures also proliferated, and perhaps more treacherously, well beyond the confines of the information asymmetry paradigm, deeply involving the newer and less familiar territory of the *collective cognition* and *collective action* paradigms, as discussed below.[7]

The apparent success of monetary policy in stabilizing inflation and smoothing out the business cycle fueled a mood of excessive optimism and exuberance, reflecting *collective cognition failures* associated with uncertainty and bounded rationality. As the observed macrofinancial volatility declined, making pricing more predictable and deepening market liquidity, financial innovation was quickened, risk appetite boosted, and highly procyclical leveraging stimulated. The low-volatility environment had the immediate mechanical effect of reducing values at risk, and the more it persisted, the more it fed collective cognition failures and mood swings. The prevailing feeling was that "this time around, things are different and the good times are here to stay." Of course, when unexpected icebergs popped up on the horizon (say, an initial but nationwide downturn in housing prices in the United States), moods swung sharply to panic.

These cognition failures fed on the process of financial innovation. It privately paid to develop new instruments; it did not pay to fully understand their potentially adverse systemic implications. More broadly, it generally paid to understand how risks and returns compared across a range of possible investments at any point in time, but it did not pay to investigate and understand how the system as a whole was wired and what the systemic tail risks laying ahead (perhaps years away) might be. Private costs clearly exceeded private returns. Furthermore, such collective cognition failures were concealed under an impressive apparatus of complex risk measurement systems and value-at-risk analysis, which created the impression that risk pricing and management was under scientific control.

The adverse side effects of macro stability on financial development (the unsustainable systemic risk buildup) were also driven by *collective action failures* linked to a fundamental asymmetry in the underlying process of market completion. While market forces incessantly pushed for completing markets through new instruments and forms of intermediation, they did not provide the tools or markets that would be needed to fully insure against systemic risks. What individuals did in the pursuit of their private risk and return calculus directly conflicted with the welfare of the group, raising a growing asymmetry between private market completion and social market completion. This situation was likely exacerbated by what Caballero and Krishnamurthy (2009) call the "other imbalance," namely, an "insatiable demand for safe debt instruments," which advanced financial systems tried to satisfy but at the expense of generating systemic risk in the process.

Specifically, financial frictions and the lack of systemic insurance led to amplification effects that were not properly internalized by individual agents. This led them to undervalue the social benefits of liquidity in crisis states and to take on socially excessive levels of systemic risk, chiefly by leveraging up steeply and with undue reliance on wholesale short-term funding (Brunnermeier 2008; Brunnermeier and Pedersen 2008; Korinek 2010). The shift from relationship lending (based on private information) to arms-length lending (based on public information) accentuated these effects by limiting the net private benefits of monitoring (market discipline). Instead, it encouraged wholesale investors to keep a tight leash on their borrowers by free riding on publicly available information and maximizing the option to lend-short-and-run (the dark side of wholesale finance) (Huang and Ratnovski 2008). In the process, they failed to internalize the systemic cost of eventual and sudden deleveraging. These problems were compounded by the inability of financial intermediaries to coordinate in the face of neck-to-neck competition driven by short-term returns (the famous quote by Charles Prince from Citigroup that you need to keep dancing until the music stops). More generally, the gap between private and social market completion manifested itself through the asymmetry between the positive private externalities of market depth and institutional interconnectedness in the good times (the bright side) and the negative social externalities when everybody was running for his or her life (the dark side).

An equally important consequence of uninternalized externalities was their implication for regulatory arbitrage. The intent of the Glass-Steagall Act—to shift risk away from regulated intermediaries to capital markets and unregulated intermediaries—was in this sense fundamentally misguided. While it could presumably have solved the agency problem (by shifting risks to the land of the well informed), it exacerbated the externalities problem. Well-informed investors had no incentives to internalize systemic liquidity risk and other externalities. The side-by-side existence of a regulated sector—where systemic concerns were partially factored in—and an unregulated sector—where externalities were not at all internalized—created a wedge in returns between the two worlds, giving rise to a *fundamentally unstable construct* where shadow banking grew rapidly out of proportion (Adrian and Shin 2007).

On the micro, resource allocation side, the lessons of the crisis were equally stark and similarly conflicted with the precrisis conventional wisdom. First and most remarkably, of course, market efficiency was severely put to the test. During the upswing, markets were prone to deviate from fundamentals and feed the bubbles; during the downswing, markets became panic stricken and failed to properly allocate resources. At the same time, the crisis tore to shreds the perception that a comprehensive statistical price history (presumed to be normally distributed) is all you needed for good risk management. Instead, it brought to the surface the specter of a world populated by high-likelihood (fat tails) and truly unexpected (black swans) catastrophic events (Taleb 2007). The crisis also brought to an end the widely shared perception that the resiliency of a financial system depended on the resiliency of each of its components. Instead, the crisis clearly demonstrated that the sum of individual protection of financial institutions was not equivalent to the protection of the system as a whole. The preconception that not everything could go wrong at once and that diversification (splicing, dicing, and spreading risk across market participants) always helped, failed. Indeed, the crisis showed that everything could go bad at the same time and interconnectedness could be lethal.

Finally, the crisis turned the spotlight on the inherent difficulties of regulatory reform in a multiparadigm world where the policy prescriptions to fix the main failures of regulation often conflict across paradigms. For example, a prudential norm seeking to limit rollover risk, while desirable from a collective action perspective, is undesirable from an information asymmetry perspective where short-term funding plays an important market-disciplining function. In the past, such tensions originated wide swings in regulation that, by seeking to address the central problem under one paradigm, made the problems under the others worse. The path ahead will ultimately require difficult judgment calls as to whether the benefits of a regulation on account of one paradigm will exceed the potential costs on account of another.

Implications for Latin America

Why have the region's financial systems weathered the crisis so successfully? Much has been said, and rightly so, about the dividends of a decade of sensible, cautious macro policies, anchored on flexible exchange rates, high international liquidity, low public debts, and more assertive and countercyclical monetary policies. The wisdom of stable macroeconomic policies was confirmed since they clearly helped cushion the blow (Porzecanski 2009; IMF 2010; World Bank 2010).

While macroeconomic turbulence might be lower in absolute terms for LAC going forward, the 2008–09 global crisis suggests that the future sources of turbulence are more likely to be imported than domestic, partly reflecting the continuously rising exposure to financial globalization. It is the growing interconnectedness of financial institutions—either within or across borders—that exacerbates systemic risk, given the mentioned market failures. But for the region, the cross-border interconnectedness and substitutability of domestic and cross-border intermediation will likely be of greater relative relevance, at least transitorily as its domestic systems deepen and broaden. These cross-border exposures are also ripe with the type of externalities (both positive and negative) and other collective action and collective cognition failures (including shifting capital flows driven by external mood swings) that characterized the subprime malaise.

A second key realization is that the small size and simplicity (including the dearth of complex derivatives and structured products) of Latin American financial systems will not in the future remain a continuous source of sturdiness, as was arguably the case during the 2008–09 crisis. Hence, the risks associated with financial innovations turned sour (reflecting collective cognition failures) are likely to become increasingly relevant for the region going forward. Indeed, the difficulties experienced at the outset of the global crisis by some of Mexico's and Brazil's largest nonfinancial corporations in the foreign exchange derivatives markets or by Mexican non-deposit-taking finance companies (Sofoles) in the commercial paper and bond markets can be viewed as good first examples of endogenous financial shocks (Jara, Moreno, and Tovar 2009). Such shocks are likely to become increasingly relevant as financial markets, encouraged by the more stable macro environment, deepen and become more complete. As was the case for the United States, the rising gap between private market completion and social market completion is likely to open up cracks through which the crises of tomorrow may materialize.

To meet these new challenges—in Latin America as in industrialized countries—a monetary policy aimed at stable and low inflation will need to be complemented by macroprudential instruments directly targeting financial stability. But in the region, the case for macroprudential tools is even stronger than in rich countries. This is because Latin America's monetary policy is relatively more constrained and burdened as a result of the region's exposure to capital flows and the potentially adverse implications for growth of excess exchange rate volatility. Macroprudential instruments can in these circumstances even contribute to mitigating inflationary pressures and dampening the business cycle without appreciating the exchange rate, thereby partly unburdening monetary policy. Indeed, this sort of situation explains the active use in recent years of reserve requirements as a countercyclical (macroprudential) tool in several countries of the region, including Brazil, Colombia, and Peru.

At the same time, however, a more aggressive use of macroprudential tools, while allowing in principle for a more independent monetary policy stance, will unavoidably raise incentives for cross-border regulatory arbitrage, potentially exacerbating systemic risk. By boosting currency risk and limiting the substitutability of domestic and cross-border intermediation, floating currencies should help attenuate such problems. Thus, while the building up of a macroprudential capability in LAC should help contain excess exchange rate volatility, it is important for its success that exchange rates retain a significant degree of flexibility.

On the microprudential side, the challenges brought about by external shocks or local financial innovations will also require an ambitious policy response. The region's conservative prudential response to its long history of truly systemic perturbations (that is, periods of acute stress affecting the whole financial system) puts it naturally ahead of the curve and should provide a good base on which to build. Indeed, the resilience of local financial systems to the crisis can also be partly attributed to the fatter systemic cushions (particularly as regards liquidity), a more hands-on supervisory style, and tighter leashes on financial innovations imposed by many Latin American supervisory authorities. Moreover, and somewhat ironically, the region's more limited reliance on market valuations and statistics, reflecting the thinness of many of its markets, may in hindsight be seen as a relative strength. Latin American supervisors often had to rely more on their judgment than on allegedly unquestionable "market truths." Nonetheless, much remains to be done.

For starters, in LAC as in the rest of the world, the powers and systemic responsibilities of the supervisor will need to be expanded and strengthened. In view of the region's traditionally weak and often conflicted institutions, finding the institutional setup most conducive to a proper mix of rules versus discretion will likely be one of the trickiest challenges.

As regards regulation, it should be clear that an uneven regulatory treatment of functionally equivalent financial services provided by different entities will unleash the forces of dynamic regulatory arbitrage. This may breed systemic risk, like the migration of activities to the less-regulated field of shadow banking did in the United States. While specificities and speeds of adjustment may differ, reflecting different stages of financial development, this issue is as present in Latin America as it is in the industrialized countries.

For curbing of dynamic regulatory arbitrage while strengthening systemic oversight, a repositioning of the perimeter of prudential regulation will thus be required. On the one hand, the silo-based regulation (that is, regulation by institution and according to the type of license) that currently prevails in most of the region will need to gradually give way to a unified regulation that focuses on functions (rather than on license) with full consolidation of financial groups. On the other hand, the border between financial and nonfinancial corporations (such as department stores) will need to be better defined and made more watertight. In addition, a line will need to be traced to separate from the rest the very small financial institutions (microlending institutions, credit coops, and the like) that can thrive in the region's more limited financial environment.

In turn, the issue of regulatory arbitrage connects with a deeper theme of crucial relevance across the region: to what extent should Latin America's regulation deviate from that taking shape in the center? Should not regional peculiarities (different risks that reflect different stages of financial development and different macrofinancial environments) lead to a tailor-made set of regulations? A different regulation would not arguably be needed if risks were measured uniformly across the world and the way they interact is sufficiently linear, so that the same Basel II–type approach can be uniformly applied across the board. If so, the end result (say, the capital adequacy ratios) could differ across regions, yet the regulation would remain one and the same. It would bite equally at the margin. However, neither of these assumptions may hold, raising the issue of whether and to what extent a different regulation could be adopted regionally without unleashing the demons of cross-border regulatory arbitrage. As in the case of macroprudential instruments, the argument can be made that more independent and credible currencies should help provide a degree of regulatory independence.

Financial globalization raises a number of additional issues. First, should Latin America continue with the trend of increasing its net creditor position in debt contracts vis-à-vis the rest of the world while at the same time continuing to raise its net debtor position in equity contracts? (This would require the further, energetic development of long-term local-currency debt markets and accumulation of international reserves, coupled with aggressive strategies to attract foreign direct investment.) Second, should LAC more explicitly add Chilean-style capital controls to its standard policy toolkit? (The systemic stability benefits would need to outweigh the efficiency costs and questionable effectiveness of such controls.) Third, should the role of foreign banking in the region be rethought and purposeful measures taken to ring-fence these banks from the pressures coming from their headquarters at times of trouble?[8] (While this may be good from a short-term stability perspective, it could affect the willingness of foreign banks to invest in the region.) The tradeoffs involved in the mentioned amendments to the texture of international financial integration imply a difficult balancing act that calls for careful assessment and even more careful implementation.

Finally, reopening the debate on the role of the state in financial development is likely to be unavoidable. The key issue here will be the determination of the conditions under which the state may adopt more active catalytic and risk-absorption roles that clearly go beyond its unquestionable responsibility in improving the enabling environment. In this connection, the mission and importance of development banks in the postcrisis world of market failures are also likely to become two of the most lively and potentially contentious issues in the region. The advocates of development banking clearly see, now more than before, the need to preserve a sizable countercyclical capacity as a primary reason for maintaining a large public presence even in normal times. As the rationale goes, how else can one mount large and effective lending programs in troubled times? In particular, how can one limit the basic problems of asymmetric information that are likely to plague public lending in times of stress if public banks do not already know markets and customers by lending to them in normal times?

Yet, in view of the declining importance of relationship lending and the rising importance of broader risk management issues, the question arises as to whether it is not more important for development banks to know how private banks manage their risk (that is, to know their risk management systems) than to build proprietary information on particular customers in direct competition with private banks. Arguably, development banks that do not directly compete with private institutions in normal times may in the end be better able to have access to private banks' information. This could help development banks overcome problems of asymmetric information in troubled times and without which they could not sensibly control their risk exposure when lending countercyclically.

In effect, private institutions would feel less threatened by—hence, more willing to cooperate with—development banks whose exclusive vocation is to expand the frontier of finance by creating public goods, mobilizing synergies, and spilling over positive externalities.

A final related issue is the use of tax and subsidy policy. Taxes and subsidies should in principle have an increasing role to play in fostering stability and development in financial systems where the importance of externalities rises. Indeed, this will be the case to the extent that financial development breeds network and scale effects and greater needs for coordination. Thus, for example, should capital gains taxes be used as an instrument to help develop capital markets? And shouldn't Pigovian taxes be put in place to induce financial intermediaries to better internalize the adverse systemic implications of their individual actions?

Yet LAC's history and record of state interventions aimed at fostering development through taxes and subsidies is worrisome. The downside risks of using taxes and subsidies are all too clear for Latin Americans, making this topic highly contentious. As in the case of development banks, it also raises particularly thorny issues of measurement. How can tax incentives be designed that do not cause more harm than good, and how can their social impact be measured over time in a way that allows for a proper calibration? While these are hardly new issues, the 2008–09 global financial crisis has thrown a new light on them, stressing the need for a second and deeper look.

Notes

1. Credit to the private sector in Latin American countries has hovered around 30 percent of gross domestic product (GDP) during the past 25 years, in sharp contrast with rising trends in East Asian and G-7 countries (Canada, France, Germany, Italy, Japan, the United Kingdom, and the United States), where bank credit to the private sector has reached 76 percent and 126 percent of GDP, respectively.
2. A Pigovian tax (named after economist Arthur Pigou) is a tax levied on a market activity that generates negative externalities. The objective of the tax is to correct the socially inefficient market outcome.
3. A detailed discussion of the evolution of financial development policy in LAC, along with relevant references to the copious literature on the subject, can be found in de la Torre, Gozzi, and Schmukler (2006).
4. The thrust of this microeconomic paradigm is at the core of World Bank (2001).

5. See de la Torre and Schmukler (2007, chapter 4) for a characterization of the financial liberalization sequencing debate, along with the relevant references.

6. The microfinance revolution provided considerable momentum to the access ("inclusive finance") agenda. A comprehensive review of the state of the art in measuring analytical and policy issues in access to financial services can be found in World Bank (2007).

7. In the asymmetric information paradigm, the better informed intentionally take advantage of the less informed or farther removed. In particular, they expect to capture the upside while leaving the downside to others (moral hazard). In the collective action paradigm, individuals are free agents who have no ill intent but focus only on their private costs and benefits. Failure to internalize externalities or to coordinate individual behaviors leads to outcomes that are suboptimal for society as a whole. In the collective cognition paradigm, a constantly evolving, uncertain world of rapid financial innovation leads to inefficient equilibria and mood swings driven by rational but poorly informed decision making, bounded rationality, or emotional decision making. This paradigm is naturally associated with bouts of risk euphoria followed by episodes of sudden alarm and deep risk retrenchment. For interpretations of the 2008–09 crisis according to each of these paradigms, and a detailed discussion of their prudential implications, see de la Torre and Ize (2010).

8. The fact that foreign banks in Latin America financed their domestic operations mainly with domestic local currency deposits, rather than imported dollar funds (as in most Eastern European countries), provided a good measure of stability (Raddatz 2009; Kanales-Kriljenco, Coulibaly, and Kamil 2010). Nonetheless, some large foreign-owned banks were pressured by their parent companies to limit their risk and transfer some of their liquidity abroad (Ortiz 2009).

Bibliography

Adrian, T., and H. S. Shin. 2007. "Liquidity and Leverage." Federal Reserve Bank of New York and Princeton University, Princeton, NJ.

Ashcraft, A., and T. Schuermann. 2008. "The Seven Deadly Frictions of Subprime Mortgage Credit Securitization." Federal Reserve Bank of New York.

Brunnermeier, M. 2008. "Deciphering the Liquidity and Credit Crunch 2007–08." Working Paper 14612, National Bureau of Economic Research, Cambridge, MA.

Brunnermeier, M., and L. Pedersen. 2008. "Market Liquidity and Funding Liquidity." Working Paper 12939, National Bureau of Economic Research, Cambridge, MA.

Caballero, R., and A. Krishnamurthy. 2009. "Global Imbalances and Financial Fragility." *American Economic Review* 99 (2): 584–88.

de la Torre, A., J. C. Gozzi, and S. Schmukler. 2006. "Financial Development in Latin America: Big Emerging Issues, Limited Policy Answers." Policy Research Working Paper WPS3963, World Bank, Washington, DC.

de la Torre, A., and A. Ize. 2010. "Regulatory Reform: Integrating Paradigms." *International Finance* 13 (1): 109–39.

de la Torre, A., and S. Schmukler. 2007. *Emerging Capital Markets and Globalization: The Latin American Experience.* Washington, DC: World Bank; and Stanford, CA: Stanford University Press.

Gorton, G. 2008. "The Subprime Panic." Working Paper 14398, National Bureau of Economic Research, Cambridge, MA.

Huang, R., and L. Ratnovski. 2008. "The Dark Side of Bank Wholesale Funding." Risk Analysis and Management Conference, World Bank and International Monetary Fund, Washington, DC, October 2–3.

IMF (International Monetary Fund). 2010. *Regional Economic Outlook: Western Hemisphere.* Washington, DC: International Monetary Fund.

Jara, A., R. Moreno, and C. Tovar. 2009. "The Global Crisis and Latin America: Financial Impact and Policy Responses." *BIS Quarterly Review* (June): 53–68.

Kanales-Kriljenco, B. Coulibaly, and H. Kamil. 2010. "A Tale of Two Regions." *Finance and Development* 47 (1): 35–36.

Korinek, A. 2010. "Systemic Risk-Taking: Amplification Effects, Externalities, and Regulatory Responses." University of Maryland, College Park.

Ortiz, G. 2009. "The Global Financial Crisis—A Latin American Perspective." Speech given at the conference on "Financial Globalization: Culprit, Survivor, or Casualty of the Great Crisis?" Yale University, New Haven, CT, November 12–13.

Porzecanski, A. 2009. "Latin America: The Missing Financial Crisis." Studies and Perspective Series No. 6, Economic Commission for Latin America and the Caribbean (ECLAC), Washington, DC.

Raddatz, C. 2009. "When the Rivers Run Dry: Liquidity and the Use of Wholesale Funds in the Transmission of the U.S. Subprime Crisis." World Bank, Washington, DC.

Taleb, N. N. 2007. *The Black Swan: The Impact of the Highly Improbable.* New York: Random House.

World Bank. 2001. *Finance for Growth: Policy Choices in a Volatile World.* Policy Research Report Series. Washington, DC: World Bank.

———. 2007. *Finance for All? Policies and Pitfalls in Expanding Access.* Policy Research Report Series. Washington, DC: World Bank.

———. 2010. *From Global Collapse to Recovery: Economic Adjustment and Growth Prospects in Latin America and the Caribbean.* Semiannual Report, Office of the Chief Economist for Latin America and the Caribbean Region. Washington, DC: World Bank.

Part 2
Governments

9

Tales of the Unexpected: Rebuilding Trust in Government

Nick Manning and Deborah L. Wetzel

"Much of the strength and efficiency of any Government in procuring and securing happiness to the people, depends on opinion, on the general opinion of the goodness of the Government."
—Speech delivered for Pennsylvania delegate Benjamin Franklin by James Wilson on September 17, 1787, the last day of the Constitutional Convention

The headlines surrounding the 2008–09 financial sector crisis seemed clear—the crisis had allegedly further damaged an already unraveling sense of public trust in the competence of developed country governments, and the consequences in the developing world had undermined the already low standing of governments with their publics.

It seems that little of this is true. In the Organisation for Economic Co-operation and Development (OECD) countries, for example, whether the public gave as much credit to governments and regulators for preventing disaster as it blamed them for allowing disaster to come perilously close, it seems that the public did not lose confidence in their governments. However, this does not mean that governments are out of the woods yet in relation to their public's trust. In the OECD countries, there is some evidence of a long-term decline in "Trust in Government."

In the middle-income countries, there is little evidence of any major loss of trust or, in fact, of any major change in any direction—a significant problem when trust is very low. In low-income countries, the data are insufficient to pronounce any overall trends, but the phenomenon of poorly performing governments retaining trust remains.

This chapter looks at Trust in Government in the OECD countries;[1] in middle-income countries, using the example of Latin America; and in low-income countries. It notes some ironies and some pointers for public management in "the day after tomorrow" if Trust in Government is to be maintained at a healthy level or, in some cases, restored or redirected toward a more balanced trust in institutions rather than people.

Trust in Government—What Is It and Why Worry about It?

Trust in Government means that citizens expect the system and political incumbents to be responsive, honest, and competent, even in the absence of constant scrutiny (Miller and Listhaug 1990). However, while the concept is clearly important, there are some major definitional problems, as well as some associated questions about the strength of any metrics that can be used to capture it. The various measures of Trust in Government that result from surveys are often unclear about the unit of analysis (what is being trusted?), and whether respondents understood trust or confidence in the same way as the interviewers.

For the purposes of this chapter, Trust in Government is taken to be a general public assessment of government's current entitlement to be in a position to enforce its policy decisions on individuals and firms and, more fundamentally, that it is generally felt to be reasonable that government retains a monopoly on the legitimate use of violence in the enforcement of social order.[2]

There is evidence that citizens' low Trust in Government can weaken the social contract and lead to citizen and firm disengagement from the state in several key dimensions:

- As *economic actors*: Firms and individuals resort to informal employment practices, and investors are more hesitant for fear of bad faith on the part of government.

- As *service recipients*: Unless forced to do so through lack of an alternative, in low-trust environments, citizens frequently avoid state services, leading primarily to the exit of the middle class from state services with a consequent reduction in influential pressure for service improvements.
- As *taxpayers*: Low trust in government is strongly associated with resistance to paying taxes.[3]
- As *civic actors*: Low trust can coincide with less compliance with legal obligations such as military conscription, less likelihood of engaging in political movements, and so forth.[4]

Recent anecdotal evidence suggests that a significant absence of public trust may lower the morale of civil servants, with the perverse possibility that demoralized civil servants will communicate their dissatisfaction to the public, thereby further lowering public confidence in the institution.

While the measures might be imperfect, there is strong evidence that survey respondents clearly distinguish between different public institutions: Eurobarometer data indicate that twice as many Portuguese trust the army as trust the judicial system, 50 percent more Danes trust the police than the civil service, and four times more Finns trust their police and army more than their political parties. There is remarkable uniformity across OECD countries in the pattern of relative trust of institutions, and political parties are by far the least trusted institution in every European country except Belgium. The army and the police are the most trusted in almost every case. The judicial system, civil service, parliament, and the executive occupy the middle ground of trust. The civil service tends to be trusted, on average, a little more than parliament and government and somewhat less than the judicial system, but there is some variation across countries. The French, Irish, and Austrians have a particularly high regard for their civil service and Italy and Finland a particularly low regard.

Citizens of the middle-income countries in Latin America distinguish among public institutions just as much as their OECD counterparts. Moreover, this differentiation within countries follows the same pattern across institutions as in the OECD, if slightly less pronounced.

Elected politicians are one particular institution that the public seem to be able to differentiate very clearly from other parts of government, and the data from the OECD countries and Latin America suggest a deep and broad lack of trust in the political class.[5] The data confirm that Trust in Government reflects more than incumbent-specific satisfactions or dissatisfactions (Levi and Stoker 2000).

While some Trust in Government is good, a lot is not necessarily better. Some skepticism about government is in order if its legitimacy is to rest on its programs and policies and not solely on ethnic or patrimonial connections (Cook, Levi, and Hardin (2005). There are good reasons to assume that the balance between trust and skepticism is in permanent flux (Clark and Lee 2001).

There is a frequent assertion that confidence in government has been in decline and it is the task of reformers or incoming governments to correct this trend through some radical reform program (see Nye, Zelikow, and King 1997; Perry and Webster 1999; Kettle 2000:57; Bouckaert, Laegreid, and Van de Walle 2005), even though others point out that this persistent drumbeat of concern has been heard for over 30 years (Crozier, Huntington, and Watanuki 1975). More skeptical observers suggest that decline in trust has been used cynically to legitimize public sector reform by politicians who are keen to deflect criticism from their own inability to avoid inflation, deficits, and economic instability (Suleiman 2005; Garrett and others 2006).

Some Curious Cases of Trust

In relation to their public's trust, governments in the OECD seem to have escaped punishment for recent bad work rather nimbly, but ironically, they have been unrewarded for previous good performance. Thus, despite the dire predictions, the financial sector crisis had until very recently remarkably little impact on public confidence in OECD and other European governments. In fact, following mixed trends in Trust in Government during 2008–09, some countries showed a modest increase in Trust in Government from 2009 to 2010, the Russian Federation and Ireland being major exceptions (Edelman Public Relations 2009, 2010; Eurobarometer 2009).[6] However, even though high- and many upper-middle-income country governments may have gotten off lightly in terms of the crisis, the bulk of studies subscribe to a view that while levels of Trust in Government vary among countries, in most OECD countries there has been a persistent decline in the last three to four decades of the 20th century.[7]

This is a somewhat bitter pill for those OECD countries that have been working on improving public sector performance for at least 30 years. There have been both productivity and quality improvements over the past three decades, and while some of this is due to investment in human capacity and information technology, at least some of the progress is due to managerial reforms. So while the evidence of a long-term decline in trust might be overplayed, there is certainly no hint of a "trust return" on the performance improvement investment.

Middle-income countries in Latin America seem to be locked into what might be termed "structured distrust." As in OECD countries, there is little evidence of a major drop in Trust in Government in Latin American countries as a result of the financial sector crisis. In fact, newspaper commentaries suggest the reverse, with implicit praise for governments that seem to have avoided the financial sector deregulatory sins of their richer neighbors. The situation in Latin America seems to be one of persistently low levels of trust in public institutions compared to other regions of the world, including Africa and East Asia (figure 9.1).[8]

The question is why Latin America seems to have been unable to shift the long-term low levels of Trust in Government. Historically, the

Figure 9.1 Trust in National Institutions: Regional Averages

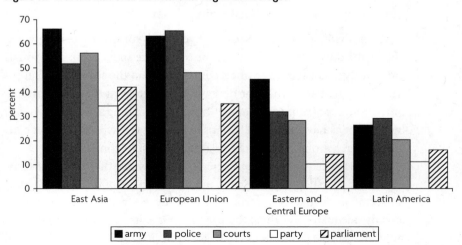

Source: Blind 2006:10, based on data from the Inter-Parliamentary Union.

return to democracy and economic stability in the late 1980s might be expected to have been reflected in increased levels of measured trust. But in Argentina, trust fell considerably from 1984 to 1999. In Mexico, it remained steady from 1990 to 2000. In Chile, in the same period, trust declined somewhat. There is certainly no evidence of any increase (Arancibia 2008:75). There are some recent, very partial signs that significant and rapid increases in service delivery performance in some Brazilian states might be associated with an increased level of trust in the state institutions. However, this is an early finding and time will tell whether this is sustainable.

In some low-income countries, high levels of trust can be distinctly unhelpful. While the data on Trust in Government in low-income countries are too limited to map trends over time or intercountry differences, the striking phenomenon in many developing countries is the degree to which the public trusts an apparently nonperforming government. There is strong evidence that patterns of clientelism in weak institutional environments lead to considerable trust in individual political incumbents—who foster that trust through targeted goods such as jobs and public works projects (Keefer 2007). The question here is whether that personalized form of trust can evolve over time into trust in institutions.

Explaining Trust

At the individual level, one possible hypothesis for this surprisingly forgiving attitude of the OECD public is that in the short term, individuals are quickly reassured when uncertainty ends, and the scale of the happiness "bounces back" when the downward trajectory of the crisis bottoms out. Another possibility is that the "headline-grabbing actions" proposed by politicians have managed to "mislead taxpayers" who have been convinced that action has been taken (Boone and Johnson 2010).

In a review of the longer-term trends, it is possible that OECD governments had a particularly tough job in impressing the public through public sector performance improvements because services, generally, were already adequate, and thus, the proportionate improvement was rather modest. Also, the public might have grown accustomed to a certain annual performance improvement and, thus, discounted the improvement.

The possibility of a long-term decline in Trust in Government in the OECD also raises questions concerning demographic and cultural changes and concerning some particular aspects of recent public management reforms. The demographic and cultural changes that might be contributing to this decline can be summarized as follows:

- *A postwar entitlement generation that will never be happy:* A generational shift occurred toward "postmaterialist" values related to self-expression and self-fulfillment, accompanied by less concern with economic security (less materialism) than the previous generation. A related but alternative explanation is that young OECD citizens now take their material possessions for granted, feeling so entitled that they no longer need to worry about such things, and so can move on to less tangible goals (Inglehart 1997, 2008).
- *The seemingly decreased relevance of national governments in the face of global security concerns:* As the world grows in complexity, it may be that systemic risk is perceived to outweigh other concerns—hence, anxieties about terrorism, genetically modified crops, or climate change seize the public imagination more than improvements in social services.
- *Overextended governments:* A concern is that the current levels of spending (and most recently, deficits) have stretched the social contract to the breaking point, and that while government legitimacy may have been adequate for a lower level of taxation, it is not sufficient to justify current levels of taxation (and, through debt, taxation on subsequent generations).

Most ironically, it is possible that the institutional and public management reforms that have delivered the performance improvements carried the seeds of distrust within them. There is a sense that the ends may be seen to have outweighed any concern for the means, while citizens in OECD countries appear to be increasingly insistent on ethical standards (and monitoring these), rather than on capabilities, in government (Warren 2006).[9] In addition, several analysts have voiced concern about the tendency of governments to undermine their own institutions while promoting reforms, making citizens doubt the competency and honesty of government overall (Goodsell 1994).

In parallel, there have been somewhat ambiguous signals about the state of public service values, with an attempt to replace or reinforce the unwritten rules with explicit codes of ethics (OECD 2005), conflict of interest policies (OECD 2003), and defined principles of public life (OECD 1996). These developments form part of an array of measures that convey an ambiguous message. On the one hand, it signals that some constraints on behavior are being tightened, but on the other hand, it serves as a standing reminder that these are now needed in a way that was perhaps not thought necessary 20 years ago. Related to this, some new public sector performance approaches have unsettled citizens who had an emotional link to the traditional service, with reforms suggesting that traditional institutions were old fashioned at best and dysfunctional at worst (Hood 1995; Kaboolian 1998). The image of the empowered and entrepreneurial public manager is somewhat at odds with clear accountability (Terry 1998). In addition, to the extent that performance improvements have been achieved through a commodification of public services, this might undermine a sense that the client matters individually and that the service provider has an interest in the client's personal well-being.[10]

Finally, recent assessments of major government reforms reviews conclude that there is what amounts to a deluge of reform that may have created confusion within government and the public about the strategy and the immediate purpose of all reforms (Light 2006; Pollitt 2007).

The problem for the OECD governments is that, put broadly, the public is unimpressed by several decades of efforts to improve services. However, in contrast to the OECD—where the possibility of a *decline* in Trust in Government is provoking a debate about the role and authority of government—in the middle-income countries of Latin America, it is the *consistency* in the low Trust in Government figures that is often associated with the alleged inability, or unwillingness, of governments to address poverty, income maldistribution, and poor public services. History has provided Latin America with a long tradition of concerns about elite capture, and the persistent and significant inequality in the region seems to signal a state that is unable or unwilling to address this through fair or efficient redistribution. The better off, who could contribute most to redistribution through more taxes, feel this lack of trust more strongly than the poor who would benefit. This might be a justified perception held by a group whose members have more insider knowledge of the state than the poor, or it might be an excuse proposed by a group that recognizes that it would, in simple financial terms, be on the losing side of redistribution (Graham and Felton 2006).

That lack of redistribution in the face of significant levels of inequality in the region might partially account for the low levels of trust in public institutions. Some evidence suggests that inequality is a causal factor in low trust in Europe.[11] However, this is a rather nuanced point since perceptions of inequality can be fitted within many preexisting narratives. If there is a popular perception that inequality is coexisting with a tradition of social mobility, then inequality can be taken as evidence of that mobility. In that storyline, inequality is the price to be paid for an economically and socially vibrant society with opportunities for all.[12] If, however, the preexisting narrative is one of elite capture, then persistent inequality signals that this is indeed the case (Graham and Felton 2006).

The consistently poor Trust in Government figures in Latin America are also seen as part of a vicious circle in which low trust is reflected in the very low fiscal capacity of the state, and the limited capacity to raise tax revenues limits public spending and, hence, improvement of services. Certainly tax revenues in Latin America are distinctively low; at an average of 18 percent, they are around half that of the OECD, at 36 percent.

This limited willingness to pay taxes is one particular case of a more general phenomenon of low citizen engagement with government in Latin America. This limited engagement can be seen in several dimensions reflecting unwillingness to enter into dealings with the state—as economic actors, as service recipients, and as taxpayers. Labor and firm informality is prevalent. Workers are often in informal jobs, with no state-mandated benefits; small firms avoid labor and other regulation; and larger firms "hide" the extent of their employment and their profits when possible. In addition, unless forced to do so through lack of an alternative, citizens frequently avoid state services.

Disengagement is linked to the low levels of trust, driven in turn by the perceptions of corruption, and to the concern that the state is to some degree "captured" by organized interests and run for the benefit of the few. In this context, noncompliance with economic and labor regulations and unwillingness to pay taxes are rational responses. "Non-compliance is then further compounded by the suspicion that others are not complying either . . . ." (Perry and others 2007:13). The signs of disengagement from the state show up economically in the scale of the shadow economy.

In weak institutional environments in low-income countries, excessive trust in individuals within government shows up most among the rich, who have important elite connections, and the poor, who feel that a stable patrimonial connection with a local politician is their best hope of obtaining some basic services that often include public employment (Espinal, Hartlyn, and Kelly 2006; Cleary and Stokes 2009).

So Where Should Public Management Go?

Through better understanding of the diverse patterns of Trust in Government, public management reforms can then be structured to achieve something nearer to an appropriate balance between trust and skepticism.

Public management and public policy are clearly implicated in changes in Trust in Government, although their impact is rather long term since trajectories of trust show few sudden movements. Broadly, governments have two types of levers by which they can influence trust over time: *performance* and *accountability*—what government does and how it does it. Both are implicated, but both provide an imperfect link to trust—there are many other factors at work, and the direction of causality is far from straightforward (Pollitt 2009:2–3). Summarizing the data concerning Trust in Government, a broad story emerges:

- *Accountability matters distinctively for trust in OECD countries.* Survey evidence from those settings strongly suggests that perceived deterioration in values in public life undermines any gains in trust resulting from performance.[13]
- *The contribution of performance to trust erodes over time, even if the performance itself remains constant.* The perception of performance is readily affected by the views of others about the same service. The more varied that service recipients' experiences are, the more diverse are opinions that any individual will hear within their social network. Since hearing negative experiences has more weight than hearing positive experiences, the effect of hearing a larger range of comments on the service is always negative on balance (Kampen, Van de Walle, and Bouckaert 2006).
- *Improving performance in some services matters more than in others.* Citizens are less able to discern the performance in some opaque policy areas compared to others (market regulation compared to health

provision, for example), thus misestimating variations in service delivery. In addition, citizens have at best a moderate understanding of who provides which services. Dinsdale and Marson (2000) and Swindell and Kelly (2000) note that citizens have increasing problems attributing service provision correctly to the public and private sectors. Services that are more directly related to the provision of better opportunities for the next generation are generally more appreciated by citizens.[14]

- *Performance expectations matter.* The paradox of the improving performance–nonincreasing trust in the OECD can be partially explained by an inflationary tendency in performance expectations—what was achieved through much effort "last year" is simply this year's baseline. In other words, there are diminishing returns as citizens perceive less change than in earlier stages of policy development (Graham and Pettinato 2001).

- *The trust benefits of both performance and accountability improvements can be readily squandered.* Overstated political rhetoric about improvements to be attained from reforms can devalue the credibility of the result and create a cynical and mistrusting public. Most low- and middle-income countries have not experimented as significantly with the more strongly managerialist approaches as the OECD and, thus, may have avoided this problem. In any reforms, suspicions of gaming quickly undermine the credibility of performance information and, hence, undermine any potential impact on trust.[15]

- *Performance and accountability improvements have to overcome their own history.* Some individuals will become impervious to any positive developments because they have generalized distrust in government to the extent that any action by government will be regarded negatively (Levi and Stoker 2000).

One implication of this summary is that Trust in Government is likely facilitated by public management and other institutional reforms in quite different ways:

- *In OECD and similar countries,* (re)building Trust in Government will require a strong focus on accountability; there may be many grounds for continuing to improve service delivery performance, but the trust reward is likely to be slim.

- *In some middle-income countries with distinctively low levels of trust* and stable equilibria of low revenue collection and modestly funded services, performance may well be a far more significant driver of trust, not least because the marginal impact of a performance improvement will be significantly greater than in the OECD.

- *In many low-income countries with weak institutional environments,* improvements in both performance and accountability are key if citizens are to be convinced that it is safe to abandon stable clientelist relationships with politicians.

Notes

1. Analysis of the trust in government data for the OECD countries and the European Union draws on an earlier draft paper by Geoffrey Shepherd, a consultant to the World Bank.
2. Trust is the key foundation of legitimacy as defined by Rheinstein (1968:212–16) and Levi and Sacks (2005).
3. From at least Weber on, some form of willing or quasi-voluntary compliance has been considered an important outcome of Trust in Government and legitimacy (Levi 1988; see also Glaser and Hildreth 1999). A 2009 International Monetary Fund publication highlights the particular challenges of tax collection during an economic crisis because, among other reasons, changing social norms lead to the conclusion for individual taxpayers that others are also evading taxes (Brondolo 2009).
4. See Levi and Sacks (2009) and Cleary and Stokes (2009) concerning trust in government and taxation in Africa and Latin America, respectively. See Van de Walle, Van Roosebroek, and Bouckaert (2005:16) concerning civic engagement. See Maxfield and Schneider (1997) and Cai and others (2009) concerning trust in government and firm and investor behavior.
5. See Pollitt and Bouckaert (2004:152) and the Pew Research Center for the People and the Press (1998:98).
6. These surveys covered "informed publics" who, among other factors, are college educated and have a household income in the top quartile of their country (per age group).
7. See, for example, Nye, Zelikow, and King (1997) and Dalton (2005). However, Van de Walle, Van Roosbroek, and Bouckaert (2008) see a much more mixed picture, perhaps because they are writing a few years later.
8. The data in figure 9.1 are from the Inter-Parliamentary Union. Mishler and Rose (1997:421, figure 3) similarly report lower trust in the public institutions of the transition countries of Eastern Europe than in those of Western Europe. Arancibia (2008:450), using the mean of confidence in parliament and the civil service in 50 democracies (from World Values Survey data), finds Trust in Government lowest in Latin America, middling in the Eastern European countries, and highest in the advanced countries.

9. This point is highlighted by recent work that sought to disentangle the specific driver of mistrust in the United States following the 2008–09 financial sector crisis. Sapienza and Zingales (2009) noted that the perception that government was captured by business was a significant driver.

10. Taylor-Gooby (2006) and Taylor-Gooby and Wallace (2009) report this in relation to the U.K. National Health Service, where performance improvements and spending increases have been associated with a significant drop in public confidence in the service.

11. Using surveys conducted during 2002–03 in 20 European democracies, Anderson and Singer (2007) examine the effect of income inequality on people's attitudes about the functioning of the political system and trust in public institutions. They find that citizens in countries with higher levels of income inequality express more negative attitudes toward public institutions.

12. Anderson and Singer (2007:1) note that "the negative effect of inequality on attitudes toward the political system is particularly powerful among individuals on the political left."

13. However, there may also be a J-curve effect in terms of political returns to such efforts. If expectations and knowledge about public services are low, first-order efforts to make improvements—which also likely impart knowledge, such as test scores in education—may initially increase frustration along with expectations. While not an excuse for not pursuing essential rewards, it is fair warning that the trust returns to some efforts may be very long term—Trust in Government may actually decrease before it increases (Graham and Lora 2009).

14. It is this relationship that might link the problem of trust to that of inequality. When citizens feel that the prevailing economic and social structures give them little opportunity for social mobility, then the impact of public services on improving the mobility prospects of their children assumes a particular significance. Preliminary evidence for Latin America using trust measures (from Latinobarometro surveys) and the World Bank's Equality of Opportunity Index (Paes de Barros and others 2009) reinforces this hypothesis at the empirical level.

15. "[A] Eurobarometer survey showed that in 2007 the U.K. was ranked the lowest of all European countries on the trust that its citizens have in government statistics. If the public don't believe the public service performance numbers, gaining a positive political payoff from publishing them seems unlikely" (Hood, Dixon, and Wilson 2009:3).

Bibliography

Anderson, C. J., and M. M. Singer. 2008. "The Sensitive Left and the Impervious Right: Multilevel Models and the Politics of Inequality, Ideology, and Legitimacy in Europe." *Comparative Political Studies* 41(4–5): 564–99.

Arancibia, C. S. 2008. "Political Trust in Latin America." PhD dissertation, 197, University of Michigan.

Blind, P. K. 2006. "Building Trust in Government in the Twenty-First Century: Review of Literature and Emerging Issues." Report prepared for the "7th Global Forum on Reinventing Government: Building Trust in Government," Vienna, Austria, June 26–29, 2007. http://unpan1.un.org/intradoc/groups/public/documents/UN/UNPAN025062.pdf.

Boone, P., and S. Johnson. 2010. "The Doomsday Cycle." VOX. http://voxeu.org/index.php?q=node/4659.

Bouckaert, G., P. Laegreid, and S. Van de Walle. 2005. "Trust, Quality Measurement Models, and Value Chain Monitoring: Symposium Introduction." Public Performance and Management Review 28 (4): 460–64.

Brondolo, J. 2009. Collecting Taxes during an Economic Crisis: Challenges and Policy Options. Washington, DC: International Monetary Fund.

Cai, H., Y. Chen, H. Fang, and L.-A. Zhou. 2009. "Microinsurance, Trust, and Economic Development: Evidence from a Randomized Natural Field Experiment." NBER Working Paper 15396, National Bureau of Economic Research, Cambridge, MA. http://www.nber.org/papers/w15396.pdf?new_window=1.

Clark, J. R., and D. R. Lee. 2001. "The Optimal Trust in Government." Eastern Economic Journal 27 (1, Winter): 19–34. http://college.holycross.edu/RePEc/eej/Archive/Volume27/V27N1P19_34.pdf.

Cleary, M. R., and S. C. Stokes. 2009. Democracy and the Culture of Skepticism: Political Trust in Argentina and Mexico. New York: Russell Sage Foundation.

Cook, K. S., M. Levi, and R. Hardin. 2005. Cooperation without Trust? New York: Russell Sage Foundation.

Crozier, M., S. P. Huntington, and J. Watanuki. 1975. The Crisis of Democracy. New York: New York University Press.

Dalton, R. J. 2005. "The Social Transformation of Trust in Government." International Review of Sociology 15 (1): 133–54. http://www.socsci.uci.edu/~rdalton/archive/int_soc05a.pdf.

Dinsdale, G., and B. D. Marson. 2000. "Citizen/Client Surveys: Dispelling Myths and Redrawing Maps." Canadian Centre for Management Development, Ottawa.

Edelman Public Relations. 2009. 2009 Edelman Trust Barometer. Washington, DC: Edelman Public Relations. http://www.edelman.com/trust/2009/docs/Trust_Book_Final_2.pdf.

———. 2010. 2010 Edelman Trust Barometer. Washington, DC: Edelman Public Relations. http://www.edelman.com/trust/2010/.

Espinal, R., J. Hartlyn, and J. M. Kelly. 2006. "Performance Still Matters: Explaining Trust in Government in the Dominican Republic." Comparative Political Studies 39 (2): 200–23. http://www.unc.edu/depts/polisci/hartlyn/Perf%20Matters%20CPS%20March%202006.pdf.

Eurobarometer. 2009. "Public Opinion in the European Union Autumn 2009." Public Opinion Analysis Sector, European Commission—Directorate General Communication, Brussels.

Garrett, R. S., J. A. Thurber, A. L. Fritschler, and D. H. Rosenbloom. 2006. "Assessing the Impact of Bureaucracy Bashing by Electoral Campaigns." *Public Administration Review* 66 (2): 228–40.

Glaser, M. A., and B. W. Hildreth. 1999. "Service Delivery Satisfaction and Willingness to Pay Taxes." *Public Productivity and Management Review* 23 (1): 48–67.

Goodsell, C. T. 1994. *The Case for Bureaucracy.* London: Chatham House.

Graham, C., S. Chattopadhyay, and M. Picon. 2010. "Does the Dow Get You Down? Happiness and the U.S. Economic Crisis." Brookings Institution, Washington, DC.

Graham, C., and A. Felton. 2006. "Inequality and Happiness: Insights from Latin America." *Journal of Economic Inequality* 4 (1): 107–22.

Graham, C., and E. Lora. 2009. *Paradox and Perception: Measuring Quality of Life in Latin America.* Washington, DC: Brookings Institution Press.

Graham, C., and S. Pettinato. 2001. *Happiness and Hardship: Opportunity and Insecurity in New Market Economies.* Washington, DC: Brookings Institution Press.

Hood, C. 1995. "The 'New Public Management' in the 1980s: Variations on a Theme." *Accounting, Organizations, and Society* 20 (2/3): 93–109.

Hood, C., R. Dixon, and D. Wilson. 2009. "'Managing by Numbers': The Way to Make Public Services Better?" http://www.publicservices.ac.uk/wp-content/uploads/policy-briefing-nov2009.pdf.

Inglehart, R. F. 1997. "Postmaterialist Values and the Erosion of Institutional Authority." In *Why People Don't Trust Government,* ed. S. Nye, P. D. Zelikow, and D. C. King, 217–36. Cambridge, MA: Harvard University Press.

———. 2008. "Changing Values among Western Publics from 1970 to 2006." *West European Politics* 31 (1–2): 130–46.

Kaboolian, L. 1998. "The New Public Management: Challenging the Boundaries of the Management vs. Administration Debate." *Public Administration Review* 58: 189–93.

Kampen, J. K., S. Van de Walle, and G. Bouckaert. 2006. "Assessing the Relation between Satisfaction with Public Service Delivery and Trust in Government: The Impact of the Predisposition of Citizens toward Government on Evaluations of its Performance." *Public Performance and Management Review* 29 (4): 387–404.

Keefer, P. 2007. "Clientelism, Credibility, and the Policy Choices of Young Democracies." *American Journal of Political Science* 51 (4): 804–21.

Keefer, P., and S. Khemani. 2005. "Democracy, Public Expenditures, and the Poor: Understanding Political Incentives for Providing Public Services." *World Bank Research Observer* 20 (1): 1–27. http://wbro.oxfordjournals.org/cgi/content/short/20/1/1.

Kettle, D. F. 2000. *The Global Public Management Revolution: A Report on the Transformation of Governance.* Washington, DC: Brookings Institution Press.

Levi, M. 1988. *Of Rule and Revenue.* Berkeley, CA: University of California, Berkeley.

Levi, M., and A. Sacks. 2005. "Achieving Good Government and Maybe Legitimacy." In *New Frontiers in Social Policy*, A. Dani and A. Varshney. Washington, DC: World Bank.

———. 2009. "Legitimating Beliefs: Sources and Indicators." *Regulation and Governance* 3: 311–33.

Levi, M., and L. Stoker. 2000. "Political Trust and Trustworthiness." *Annual Review of Political Science* 3: 475–507.

Light, P. C. 2006. "The Tides of Reform Revisited: Patterns in Making Government Work, 1945–2002." *Public Administration Review* 66 (1): 6–19.

Maxfield, S., and B. R. Schneider, eds. 1997. *Business and the State in Developing Countries*. Ithaca, NY: Cornell University Press.

Miller, A. H., and O. Listhaug. 1990. "Political Parties and Confidence in Government: A Comparison of Norway, Sweden and the United States." *British Journal of Political Science* (20): 357–86.

Mishler, W., and R. Rose. 1997. "Trust, Distrust, and Skepticism: Popular Evaluations of Civil and Political Institutions in Post-Communist Societies." *Journal of Politics* 59 (2): 418–51.

Nye, S., P. D. Zelikow, and D. C. King. 1997. *Why People Don't Trust Government*. Cambridge, MA: Harvard University Press.

OECD (Organisation for Economic Co-operation and Development). 1996. "Ethics in the Public Service: Current Issues and Practice." Public Management Occasional Paper 14, OECD, Paris. http://www.oecd.org/dataoecd/59/24/1898992.pdf.

———. 2003. *Managing Conflict of Interest in the Public Service. OECD Guidelines and Country Experiences*. Paris: OECD.

———. 2005. *The OECD Human Resources Working Party: A Summary Retrospective and an Agenda for Action*. Paris: OECD.

Paes de Barros, R., F. H. G. Ferreira, J. R. Molinas Vega, and J. Saavedra-Chanduvi. 2009. *Measuring Inequality of Opportunities in Latin America and the Caribbean*. Washington, DC: World Bank.

Perry, G. E., W. F. Maloney, O. S. Arias, P. Fajnzylber, A. D. Mason, and J. Saavedra-Chanduvi. 2007. *Informality: Exit and Exclusion*. Washington, DC: World Bank.

Perry, P., and A. Webster. 1999. *New Zealand Politics at the Turn of the Millennium: Attitudes and Values about Politics and Government*. Auckland: Alpha Publications.

Pew Research Center for the People and the Press. 1998. *Deconstructing Distrust: How Americans View Government*. Washington, DC: Pew Research Center for the People and the Press. http://people-press.org/report/95/.

Pollitt, C. 2007. "New Labour's Re-Disorganization: Hyper Modernism and the Costs of Reform—A Cautionary Tale." *Public Management Review* 9 (4): 529–44.

———. 2009. "Evidence-Based Trust—A Contradiction in Terms?" Herbert Simon Institute Workshop, "Trust and Confidence: A New Agenda for the Public Services," Manchester Business School, Manchester, England, October 19.

Pollitt, C., and G. Bouckaert. 2004. *Public Management Reform: A Comparative Analysis.* Oxford, U.K.: Oxford University Press.

Rheinstein, M., ed. 1968. *Max Weber on Law in Economy and Society.* New York: Simon and Schuster.

Sapienza, P., and L. Zingales. 2009. "A Trust Crisis." Booth School of Business, Chicago, January 27. http://faculty.chicagobooth.edu/brian.barry/igm/atrustcrisis .pdf.

Suleiman, E. 2005. *Dismantling Democratic States.* Princeton, NJ: Princeton University Press.

Swindell, D., and J. M. Kelly. 2000. "Linking Citizen Satisfaction to Performance Measures: A Preliminary Evaluation." *Public Performance and Management Review* 24 (1): 30–52.

Taylor-Gooby, P. 2006. "The Rational Actor Reform Paradigm: Delivering the Goods but Destroying Public Trust?" *European Journal of Social Quality* 6 (2): 121–41.

Taylor-Gooby, P., and A. Wallace. 2009. "Public Values and Public Trust: Responses to Welfare State Reform in the UK." *Journal of Social Policy* 38 (3): 1–19.

Terry, L. D. 1998. "Administrative Leadership, Neo-Managerialism, and the Public Management Movement." *Public Administration Review* 58: 194–200.

Van de Walle, S., S. Van Roosebroek, and G. Bouckaert. 2005. "Annex: Data on Trust in the Public Sector." Paper prepared for the OECD Ministerial Meeting, "Strengthening Trust in Government," Organisation for Economic Co-operation and Development, Paris, November 28. http://www.modernisinggovernment.nl/html/ oeso/document_download.cfm?doc=A5091E33-F206-B8C5-1E0E14BF 3BE25BD6.PDF&doc_name=5%20Analytical%20Annex%20E.

———. 2008. "Trust in the Public Sector: Is There Any Evidence for a Long-Term Decline?" *International Review of Administrative Sciences* 74 (1): 45–62.

Warren, M. E. 2006. "Democracy and Deceit: Regulating Appearances of Corruption." *American Journal of Political Science* 50 (1): 160–74.

10

Fiscal Quality: A Developing Country's Priority

Marcelo Giugale

> "Fiscal policy may be taken to embrace all government transactions
> which have as their objective the support of general economic policy . . .
> [which] is geared to promote growth with stability and to increase welfare
> through a more equal distribution of available (spendable) incomes."
> —*Development Finance*, by Ursula Hicks (p. 61)

Developed and developing countries came out of the 2008–09 global crisis with diverging macroeconomic policy needs. The former find themselves with enormous fiscal deficits and exploding debt burdens (figure 10.1). For them, fiscal consolidation (read, painful adjustment) is inescapable; the alternative involves sovereign crises of unimaginable consequences. Their priority is quantity—more tax collection, less expenditures. On the other hand, developing countries, on average, came in and out of the crisis with relatively strong fiscal positions,[1] and they are now poised for a period of commodity-fueled growth that will both appreciate their currencies and significantly bulk up their treasuries.[2] For them, the issue will be how best to manage solvency. Their priority is quality more than quantity. But, will the developing world actually

The author is indebted to Eduardo Ley for insightful inputs and comments and to Riccardo Trezzi for superb research assistance.

Figure 10.1 Comparison of Advanced and Emerging Economies after the 2008–09 Financial Crises: Fiscal Imbalances and Public Debt

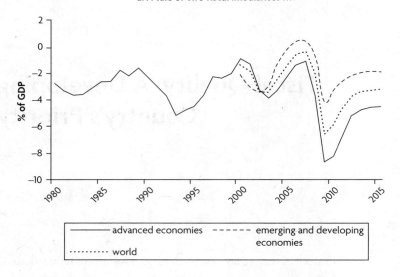

a. A tale of two fiscal imbalances ...

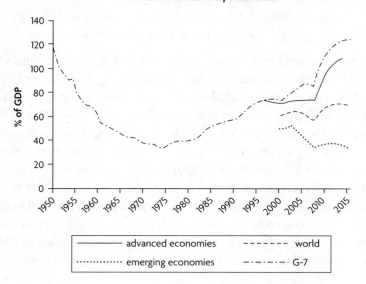

b. ... and a tale of two public debts

Source: International Monetary Fund, World Economic Outlook database, April 2010.
Note: G-7 = Canada, France, Germany, Italy, Japan, the United Kingdom, and the United States; GDP = gross domestic product.

enter a period of better fiscal management, a period of more stability, more efficiency, and more transparency in public finance? Probably, yes. This chapter discusses the reasons for cautious optimism.

Leaning against the Wind

The crisis showed the value of saving in good times to spend more during downturns—the value of anticyclical fiscal policy. Most countries, rich and poor, tried to stimulate their domestic demand through fiscal means, whether temporary reductions in taxes (typically, in the value-added tax) or increases in expenditures (primarily, public investment). For most, the impact in terms of employment creation was bound to be limited, because open borders meant that much of the stimulus went to absorb more imports. Still, the political pressure to be seen "doing something" about the imminent recession was strong. But not every country was able to finance an enlarged deficit at the high interest rates that prevailed during the peak of the crisis (nor did they want to set such an expensive precedent for their future borrowing). Fiscal stimulation was much easier for those governments that could tap previously accumulated funds (Chile, China, and Mexico); they were the "visionaries" that reaped the largest political rewards for their response.

All this suggests future imitation, especially by the average developing country at the receiving end of the commodity bonanza. In fact, some of the mechanisms to ensure that the fiscal accounts move anticyclically ("lean against the wind") are already in place. The use of medium-term fiscal frameworks was widespread well before the crisis; most governments already publish estimates of their multiyear spending plans and borrowing needs. Societies and markets value, and demand, that clarity and penalize deviations. To underpin those frameworks, a universe of fiscal rules has proliferated—placing ceilings on expenditures, deficits, debt, and other aggregates—many of which are enshrined in so-called "fiscal responsibility laws" (figure 10.2). These laws usually prescribe enforcement mechanisms, like surveillance mandates and penalties for nonobservance, which, while not always respected, put the political spotlight on irresponsible behavior.

A more advanced group of countries (Chile, Finland, Norway, and Switzerland[3]) have even experimented with structural fiscal balances,

Figure 10.2 Number of Countries with Fiscal Rules

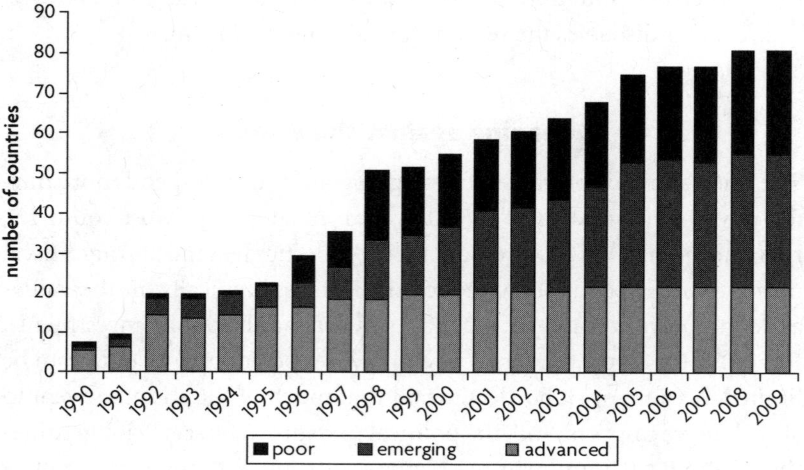

Source: Author.

that is, with keeping the accounts in order whatever the fluctuations of the economy. This has helped anchor macroeconomic expectations regarding fiscal policy—much like inflation-targeting frameworks did for monetary policy. It has also forced more transparent and predictable budget processes. The search for fiscal stability has even triggered an interesting debate about fiscal flexibility: should rules be respected even when unusual, unexpected, and massive shocks ("black-swan events") occur, or should some form of "escape hatch" be available (as it is in Peru and Turkey)?

All this newly acquired fiscal technology, by itself, will generate neither discipline nor anticyclicality—it amounts to no more than "trainer wheels." However, it is difficult to imagine that political leaders operating in democracies could backtrack. More probably, the wish to be ready to respond to the next crisis may move forward a series of associated institutional reforms: better and faster public investment systems; swifter and more powerful automatic stabilizers (notably, unemployment insurance); more buoyant and broader tax bases; fewer earmarks, entitlements, and preassignments; and better federal coordination with subnational entities (smarter decentralization).

Independent Fiscal Agencies

Governments in developing countries will lose their monopoly on fiscal reporting (or what is left of it). The myriad laws, rules, and frameworks that have been, and will continue to be, imposed over fiscal accounts will call for neutral oversight and verification by independent fiscal agencies. These technical institutions (both public and private) will increasingly monitor fiscal developments, assess compliance with precautionary norms, evaluate actual and proposed expenditures, cost out legislative initiatives, and validate the assumptions on which the budget is built. They are unlikely to have policy power, and in that sense, they will not be "authorities" but "councils." Their power will come precisely from their capacity and credibility to issue independent opinions. Many examples already exist, including the peer-review Fiscal Council of the European Union, the decision-making Fiscal Council of Nigeria, the Congressional Budget Office of the United States, the Office of Budget Responsibility of the United Kingdom, the expert forecast panels of Chile, and the self-surveillance mechanism of New Zealand.

This trend is bound to accelerate, especially in developing countries with large commodity revenues. Part of the acceleration will be due to imitation under political pressure ("Why is the government of our neighbors so much more transparent than ours?"). But part will be due to dissatisfaction with the recent performance of private, for-profit, early-warning mechanisms—namely, with credit rating agencies.

Will fiscal agencies over time become to fiscal policy what the new generation of central banks became to monetary policy? Will they mutate into decision-making bodies? Maybe. Contrary to central banks, whose mandate can be defined around a numerical inflation target that enjoys political consensus (who can be against price stability?), fiscal decisions involve objectives that are more difficult to agree on, especially in terms of income distribution, regional disparities, and national priorities. Democratic debate through congresses seems necessary. However, it is not unthinkable that portions of fiscal policy be delegated in the future to independent institutions mandated to achieve specific targets. For example, if additional public investment outlays are meant to close output gaps (as they were during the 2008–09 crisis), they could well be decided upon and executed by a technical agency free of political interference. This will not only increase badly needed implementation speed, but also contribute to the stability and predictability of growth.

Sovereign Wealth Funds

The combination of, on the one hand, fiscal rules and independent over-seers and, on the other, high commodity prices will give momentum to another quality-enhancing tool for fiscal policy in resource-rich countries: the accumulation of revenues into sovereign wealth funds. Put simply, some of the money will have to be saved. In the past, developing countries were not very successful at putting resources aside. When the accumulation got too tempting, political leaders found ways to "raid the kitty." Still, the rapid surge in the number of sovereign funds world-wide is telling (figure 10.3).

The policies and oversight systems that govern these funds are not trivial and require fluid coordination with concomitant liability man-agement strategies (should you accumulate cash or pay off debt?). Norms governing investment decisions can be contentious, especially when, for macroeconomic reasons, it is advisable to park capital abroad (for

Figure 10.3 Sovereign Wealth Funds

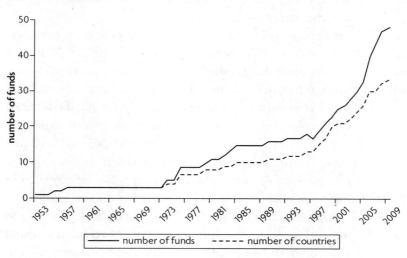

Source: Author.

instance, to avoid appreciation of the local currency). And it is not certain that most developing countries have sufficient institutional capacity to maximize the value of having a sovereign fund.

However, as an additional tool for moderation and control, the contribution of sovereign wealth funds will be significant. The media tend to keep an eye on how much has been accumulated and to let voters know fairly quickly if there is a decline. Intergenerational considerations enter the debate, not least when tax hikes on current workers are at play. The idea that a "rainy day fund" exists reduces borrowing costs for long-term projects. And the pressure (and the training) to be transparent in the operation of the fund gradually permeates to other fiscal areas (from strategic planning to auditing of budget execution).

The Balance Sheet of the State

Better debt management among developing countries (perhaps with the exception of Eastern Europe) has been the unheralded public policy success revealed by the 2008–09 crisis. Not only did most of those countries reduce their public debt burdens compared to the size of their economy (and in some cases, reduced the size of the debt itself), but they also improved the terms of the remaining liabilities, through longer maturities, lower rates, and more reliance on local currencies. Attention was given to the whole liability side of the ledger, even to the more hidden or contingent debts—like pension promises and guarantees to investors in infrastructure projects. Debt offices were professionalized, clearly mandated, and given room to do their job. The natural next step is to begin to pay the same attention to the assets of the state, to take a broader "balance sheet" approach.

Few governments in the developing world can account fully for their state assets—what they are, how much they are worth, what returns they give. This is particularly true for nonfinancial assets, like real estate and machinery. Look to countries that have undergone banking crises, and you are likely to find large inventories of repossessed collaterals that ended up in public hands following bailouts. They sit idle for years on the treasury's books, when they are on the books at all.

What will make policy makers manage state assets more proactively than in the past? The mix of tighter fiscal rules, better own capacity, and nosier independent fiscal agencies will. It will, for example, be odd for a country with a well-scrutinized sovereign wealth fund to be ignorant of or even opaque about its minority stakes in privately controlled enterprises or to closely track the accumulation in that fund and, at the same time, tolerate secrecy in the state-owned company that generates most of the accumulation (say, in the oil sector). Have many developing economies shown progress in this more holistic approach to fiscal policy in "patrimonial accounting" of the state? No, but some have (for instance in Colombia), and more will follow.

Show Me Results

Few signs of fiscal quality are clearer than the results governments achieve with the money they spend. Voters in the developing world are beginning to notice those signs. Politicians that have committed to specific results (that have "a contract with the people") and deliver them, are doing remarkably well. They tend to belong to subnational levels of government, where their closer proximity to the constituents helps accountability (Brazilian states and Colombian cities are good examples). The technological breakthrough that has made all this possible is the advancement in the definition, measurement, and dissemination of standards—in education, health, logistics, security, and virtually any other public service. Now people know what to expect. More powerful information technology tools, coupled with smarter financial management, have added to the process.

The instrument through which results are entering public finance is performance-based budgeting. Is a change in budgeting technique really that important? Even if it is, will the developing world embrace it? Focusing on results implies a new conception of the state: it becomes a transformer of inputs into outcomes, not just outputs. Money flows toward desired impacts, not just toward projects or sectors. Monitoring and evaluation becomes central, to see what is working and what needs correcting. Control and compliance give room to performance and accountability.

In various forms, management by results is already being embraced by emerging economies. For starters, those that have practiced inflation targeting have de facto signed a performance contract with their central banks—with much success. Vast improvements in household surveys over the past decade allowed for results-based programs in human development, where demographic and social data are key (Brazil, China, and Uganda did it for health). Even in infrastructure, where public-private partnerships carry specific performance targets, the results approach has made inroads. As tighter, overall fiscal discipline takes deeper roots, more areas of public action will be subjected to some form of performance contract. It is difficult to imagine that many countries will want (or be able) to keep the old, no-questions-asked, tax-and-spend approach to public administration.

Decentralize, Devolve

Over the past 30 years, the spread of democracy among developing countries opened the door to fiscal decentralization. Competences and resources that were once kept by the central (federal) government were passed down to newly elected local authorities. Provinces and municipalities became responsible for public services like education, water, and disaster prevention. The idea was that local accountability would enhance service quality. The outcome has been mixed. But decentralization itself proved popular and is bound to continue apace. It will gradually take the form of "devolution."

Some 30 countries (there were only three in 1997) have in the past decade set up logistical mechanisms to transfer resources directly to the poor. Through a debit card or through a cell phone, it is now possible to give to each beneficiary the funds necessary to buy or the right to access almost any public service, from vaccinations to secondary education. This new relationship between the state and the individual, without intermediaries, is generating a wealth of information—about costs, needs, impacts, preferences—and can be extended easily to all social strata. More important, it is rendering irrelevant what level of government is responsible for the service.

As devolution proceeds (and not just in developing countries), the quality of fiscal outlays will improve. With the individual as client, duplications and overlaps in social expenditures will be easier to eliminate. Those expenditures will also become more progressive, since there will be no justification for blanket subsidies that are given to all citizens irrespective of their wealth (think of free public universities). Informality and tax evasion will be easier to spot, since baseline data on the recipients of public transfers will be available. And geographic disparities will be easier to even out: It will be known who lives where in what conditions.

Concluding Remarks

This chapter has made a rather optimistic case for the advent of fiscal quality in the developing world. If one looks both at the initial conditions (less debt, better policies) and at the drivers of change (from the spread of fiscal rules to the reality of devolution), some optimism is indeed in order. Naturally, not all countries will move along this path at the same speed; many will probably move in the opposite direction for a while. But the crisis, with all its lessons, seems to have confirmed that the path forward leads through better management of the public treasury.

Notes

1. Eastern Europe is the exception.
2. "Commodities" are understood here to include also nonprimary commodities, that is, manufactured goods with little or no qualitative differentiation across a market, such as computer RAM chips.
3. *Chile* has adopted a structural balance with an independent body (agency) providing key input. Under the structural balance rule, government expenditures are budgeted ex ante in line with structural revenues, that is, revenues that would be achieved if (a) the economy were operating at full potential, (b) the prices of copper and molybdenum were at their long-term levels, and, more recently, (c) the return on accrued financial assets were in line with the long-term interest rates. Between 2002 and 2007, a surplus of 1 percent of gross domestic product (GDP) was targeted; in 2008, 0.5 percent of GDP; and in 2009, 0 percent of GDP. *Finland* targets a structural fiscal surplus of 1 percent of potential GDP. Cyclical or other short-term deviations are allowed if they do not "jeopardize" the reduction of the central government debt ratio. In *Norway*, the non-oil structural deficit of the central government should equal the long-run return of the government pension fund. In *Switzerland*, the structural balance rule is as follows: one-year-ahead ex-ante ceiling on central government expenditures equals predicted revenues, adjusted by a factor reflecting the cyclical position of the economy. Any deviations of actual spending from the ex-ante spending ceiling are accumulated in a notional compensation account.

Bibliography

Aguiar, M., and G. Gopinath, 2007. "Emerging Market Business Cycles: The Cycle Is the Trend." *Journal of Political Economy* 115: 69–102.

Alberola, E., J. M. Gonalez Minguez, P. Hernandez de Cos, and J. M. Marques. 2003. "How Cyclical Do Cyclically Adjusted Balances Remain? An EU Study." *Hacienda Pública Española* 166: 151–81.

Besley, T., and A. Scott. 2010. "A New Watchdog Would Guard Us from Debt." *VOX.* http://www.voxeu.org/index.php?q=node/4680.

Bird, R. 2010. "Smart Tax Administration." Unpublished document, World Bank, Washington, DC.

Blanchard, O. 1990. "Suggestions for a New Set of Fiscal Indicators." Working Paper 79, Organisation for Economic Co-operation and Development, Paris.

Calmfors, L., G. Kopits, and C. Teulings. 2010. "A New Breed of Fiscal Watchdogs." *EuroIntelligence*, May 13. http://www.eurointelligence.com/.

Chaudhury, N., J. Hammer, M. Kremer, K. Muralidharan, and F. H. Rogers. 2006. "Missing in Action: Teacher and Health Worker Absence in Developing Countries." *Journal of Economic Perspectives* 20 (1): 91–116.

Hicks, U. 1965. *Development Finance: Planning and Control.* Oxford, U.K.: Clarendon Press.

IMF (International Monetary Fund). 2010. *World Economic Outlook.* Washington, DC: IMF. http://www.imf.org/external/pubs/ft/weo/2010/01/index.htm.

King, M. 2010. "Uncertainty in Macroeconomic Policy Making: Art or Science?" Lecture delivered at the Royal Society Conference on "Handling Uncertainty in Science," London, March 22. http://www.bankofengland.co.uk/publications/speeches/2010/speech432.pdf.

Kopits, G. F. 2001. "Fiscal Rules: Useful Policy Framework or Unnecessary Ornament?" In *Fiscal Rules,* Banca d'Italia. Rome: Banca d'Italia.

———, ed. 2004. *Rules-Based Fiscal Policy in Emerging Markets: Background, Analysis, and Prospects.* London: Palgrave Macmillan.

Kopits, G. F., and S. A. Symansky. 1998. "Fiscal Policy Rules." Occasional Paper 162, International Monetary Fund, Washington, DC.

Orphanides, A., and S. van Norden. 2002. "The Unreliability of Output-Gap Estimates in Real Time." *Review of Economics and Statistics* 84: 569–83.

Simpson, H. 2009. "Productivity in Public Services." *Journal of Economic Surveys* 23 (2): 250–76.

11

Public Expenditure after the Global Financial Crisis

Jim Brumby and Marijn Verhoeven

The public finance responses to the 2008–09 global financial crisis are still evolving as many countries move from a concern to stimulate economic activity to one of reestablishing fiscal solvency. This transition in focus has implications for public finance in terms of aggregate fiscal management (Level 1), the prioritization of expenditures (Level 2), and the technical efficiency of government delivery (Level 3). During the period ahead, the management of public finances will need to take account of the links among these three levels for a successful transition.

The first-stage response to the crisis in developing countries was focused on letting automatic stabilizers work to the extent the available fiscal space allowed. This was supplemented in some cases (mainly in emerging markets and energy exporters) with directed stimulus measures. While there were high-profile cases of concern for the quality of spending, in many cases it appeared that countries were mainly concerned with getting money out the door as fast as possible and communicating a commitment to "protect" the population against some aspect of the distress that would otherwise have occurred. Initial hopes that stimulus measures could be designed to meet longer-term growth objectives, through the rapid implementation of "shovel-ready" investment projects, as well as demand management objectives, turned out to be too ambitious in both developing and advanced countries.

But as the fiscal effects of the crisis continue to crystallize, especially through reduced revenues, larger calls for spending on benefits and other crisis-related items, and servicing of higher debt levels, the unease with unsustainable fiscal aggregates is becoming palpable. As countries begin to make the transition back to sustainability, they will need to reexamine the soundness of their expenditure allocations and decide if the operations of government can be harnessed in efficient ways, with a resulting dividend in terms of fiscal discipline and enhanced efficiency.

As the effects of the crisis mature, it is more likely that higher-income countries will curtail spending as well, perhaps to very significant degrees. The required adjustment in structural primary balance in G-20 emerging economies during 2010–20 to protect fiscal sustainability is 2.6 percent of gross domestic product (GDP) compared to a much more substantive 9.3 percent in high-income G-20 countries[1] (IMF 2010). To achieve this adjustment, these emerging economies appear likely to rely mostly on revenue, while high-income countries plan a larger contribution from expenditure. Whether countries will be able to implement these plans remains to be seen; experience suggests that expenditure reform is an essential ingredient of successful large fiscal adjustment.

Done well, expenditure curtailments provide opportunities for countries to spring-clean their policies, improve targeting of core spending, introduce more effective budgetary institutions, and sponsor the sorts of public sector reforms that should see a lowering in the unit costs of service delivery. Done poorly, opportunities to improve aggregate fiscal management through improvements in Levels 2 and 3 are lost, with resulting costs for the population, especially the most vulnerable. Part of this process requires putting everything on the table—including transfers and subsidies—with revenue and expenditure restraint contributing to some form of social contract in which all sides have an incentive to negotiate a comprehensive package of reforms (OECD 2010:9)

The Prioritization of Expenditures

The global crisis has challenged countries to sustain spending that promotes future economic growth and poverty reduction. In particular, countries have made efforts to safeguard expenditure for health, education, and investment. As the crisis was unfolding, the need to support aggregate demand mitigated pressures on public expenditures. But in the aftermath of the crisis, the need for fiscal consolidation will put renewed pressure on public expenditure in many countries.

Across-the-board cuts and freezes that indiscriminately affect programs and services can have perverse effects and may not actually help fiscal sustainability through time. Poor-quality cuts tend not to stand the test of time, often being reversed once rational analysis prevails. While top-down approaches are generally considered an appropriate tool in times of fiscal austerity, it is important that decision makers are aware of the links between the sinking lids provided to line ministries and the activities that are being identified for cuts. While efficiency measures and internal reallocations away from lower-priority policies may not generally make a large contribution to deficit reductions, they are nevertheless unambiguously beneficial for value for money and for the credibility of the fiscal path.

The good news is that countries have become more sophisticated at crisis management over time. This time around, countries are (temporarily) expanding safety nets, protecting social sector spending through loans, redirecting funding to retain social spending, and harnessing the crisis to achieve major reforms that improve efficiency and quality. A harbinger of this evolution is the case of Argentina in 2001. The government increased transfers to the provinces by 70 percent in real terms for nutrition, maternal and child health services, and the acquisition of essential drugs, in sharp contrast to earlier across-the-board cuts with little concern for the incidence of government actions. Countries appear to be relying more heavily on data and policy research in making spending allocations as budgets contract, replacing the ax with a scalpel to drive policy and future directions for their country.

Core Spending

The growth path of public expenditure on health and education (social spending) was interrupted by the global economic crisis. In the earlier part of the 2000s, social spending in developing countries (in 2005 constant prices at purchasing power parity [PPP] exchange rates) grew by an average of 4 to 10 percent. These rates are estimated to have fallen in

2009 to below 2 percent (see figures 11.1 and 11.2).[2] As economic growth recovers from the crisis, social spending growth is also likely to recover, but it will take some years before spending growth returns to precrisis levels. The growth interruption due to the crisis was not severe enough to force declines in spending levels—education and health spending continued to rise as a share of GDP and in per capita terms (in PPP dollars; see figure 11.1).

The decline in spending growth rates due to the crisis risks setting back achievement of human development goals, because these depend on the rapid spending increases achieved in the 1990s and the earlier part of the 2000s. In fact, the present estimates of the impact of the crisis on spending are consistent with an earlier World Bank analysis that found that financing shortfalls to cover at-risk core spending on health, education, safety nets, and infrastructure amount to about US$11.6 billion for the poorest countries during 2009–10 (World Bank 2009).

Recovery of public health and education spending after the crisis is likely to be unevenly distributed between regions and developing countries at different levels of income. Countries in the Europe and Central

Figure 11.1 Public Social Spending (Averages for Developing Countries)

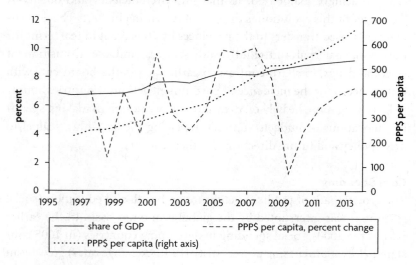

Source: Lewis and Verhoeven 2010.

Figure 11.2 Public Spending

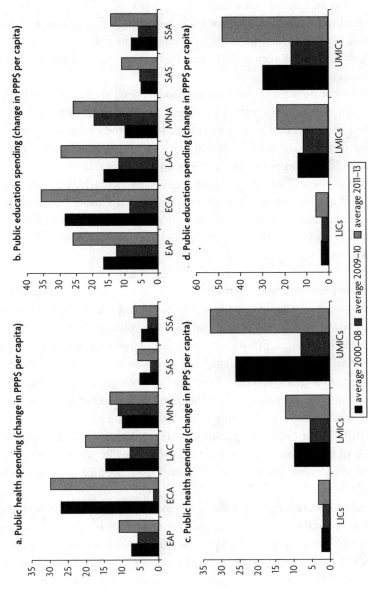

Source: Lewis and Verhoeven 2010.

Note: EAP = East Asia and Pacific, ECA = Europe and Central Asia, LAC = Latin America and the Caribbean, LICs = low- income countries, LMICs = low- and middle-income countries, MNA = Middle East and North Africa, SAS = South Asia, SSA = Sub-Saharan Africa, UMICs = upper-middle-income countries.

Asia region faced the biggest fiscal challenges during the crisis, which has been reflected in comparatively large drops in the growth rates of education and health spending during 2009–10. These countries will also find it hardest to regain precrisis spending growth rates. This protracted bending of the growth path of spending could have a substantial impact on the accumulation of human capital and future growth prospects.

Expenditure reforms, such as initiated by several countries in Europe and Central Asia, are critical to mitigate the impact on human and economic development. Latvia, for example, is using the stringencies imposed by the crisis to rightsize its teaching force, and Romania substantially reduced education personnel in 2009, largely by curtailing supplements to base salaries. Countries in other regions, particularly the Middle East and North Africa, were not as affected by the crisis and have not seen an interruption in the growth of their social spending. In other regions, growth in social spending during 2011–13 is projected to rapidly return to close to precrisis rates.

Public Investment Management

Government investment, as measured by the net acquisition of physical assets,[3] was less affected than social spending during the financial crisis. Stimulus spending kept up investments in a large number of developing countries, to an average growth rate of government net investment in per capita PPP terms of about 13 percent in 2009 and 2010 (see figure 11.3). In low-income countries (LICs), the increase in government investment substantially accelerated during 2009–10, and reached an average of over US$10 PPP per capita. Upper-middle-income countries (UMICs) and low- and middle-income countries (LMICs) saw larger increases in per capita investment, but this was still down from average increases earlier in the 2000s.

The prospects for government investment during the postcrisis period are less favorable. Fiscal consolidation is projected to further reduce investment spending growth rates during 2009–13. The drop is likely to be particularly severe in LICs. Under these circumstances, reforms in investment budgeting and implementation will be critical for increasing the efficiency of government investment and its impact on growth and development.

Figure 11.3 Government Investment as Net Acquisition of Physical Assets

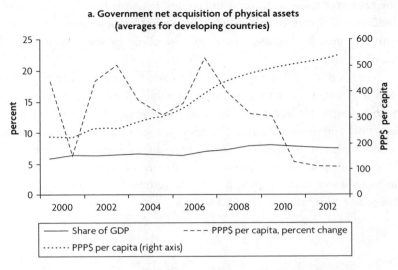

a. Government net acquisition of physical assets
(averages for developing countries)

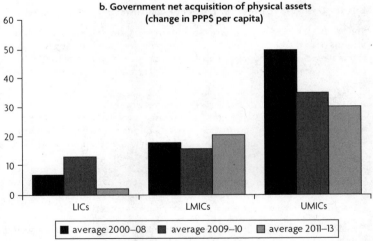

b. Government net acquisition of physical assets
(change in PPP$ per capita)

Source: International Monetary Fund, World Economic Outlook database 2010.
Note: LICs = low-income countries, LMICs = low- and middle-income countries, UMICs = upper-middle-income
countries.

While improving the performance of investment is always important,
it is particularly so in the current period of severe economic and fiscal
challenge. Given the reduction in resources and the increase in urgency,
it is imperative that public investment projects are delivered at the least

possible cost and on time and that maximum output is received from the resources invested. Careful and comprehensive project selection procedures will therefore be needed to help identify those projects that not only will give the highest return but also could be implemented more quickly.

Based on its global experience, the World Bank has identified key desirable features of a well-functioning public investment system, along with a diagnostic framework for assessing the quality of public investment management efficiency. The resultant "gap" analysis can be used to identify structural aspects of public investment decisions and management processes that may be weak and in need of attention and reforms to focus scarce managerial and technical resources where they will yield the greatest impact (see box 11.1).

Box 11.1 Desirable Features for Efficient Public Investment Management

The World Bank has developed guidance to help formulate a pragmatic and objective assessment of the quality of public investment efficiency in a context where governments are seeking to mobilize additional fiscal resources for investment. An indicator-based approach has been developed around a set of core "must-have" dimensions. These are as follows:

- Investment guidance and preliminary project screening
- A formal project appraisal process (with cost-benefit analysis being best practice)
- Independent review of appraisals (for example, including consideration of alternatives)
- Project selection and budgeting that establish envelopes for public investment so that a sustainable investment program can be undertaken
- Realistic implementation plans
- Adjustment for changes in project circumstances
- Facility operation (asset registers need to be maintained and asset values recorded)
- Evaluation (to ensure that there is some learning and feedback).

This approach is designed to provide a basis both for an objective assessment and for highlighting of weaknesses that should be addressed if the use of fiscal resources is to enhance public sector assets and economic growth. An assessment might therefore help to identify "quick win" reforms to accelerate investment spending during a crisis. While the approach does not seek to identify best practice, Organisation for Economic Co-operation and Development countries commonly provide guidelines and seek to strengthen their management capacity around similar dimensions.

Source: Rajaram and others 2009.

Emerging Lessons So Far[4]

The worldwide crisis has required a country-led response. The role that core social spending and investment can play in the crisis response has also varied considerably. Future crises need to be approached on the same basis.

Governments are making a variety of interventions to try to achieve the best possible outcomes for their countries. An effective international response does not mean that all countries should have to take identical actions—for example, middle- and low-income countries may be more constrained, in terms of both fiscal space and capacity to design and deliver effective policies, and need to carefully sequence their response. Countries that entered the crisis in vulnerable states had less freedom and will need to focus more rapidly on the path back to sustainability. Fiscal actions should also take account of country needs, including the disparate impact of the crisis among countries.

1. *Investment and core social spending may be at risk if the global recession double dips and public finances weaken further.* Many governments are likely to come under increasing pressure to lower financing requirements. In such a situation, there is a real temptation to cut spending on investment as a first resort, since this is seen as being easier than raising taxes or cutting social expenditure or public service wages and salaries. If pressure on public finances were to become particularly acute, there is a risk that governments might be induced not only to postpone investment in new infrastructure, but also to reduce spending on maintaining existing infrastructure and facilities (Ferris 2009) and to cut down on core social spending.

2. *In spite of the urgency of responding to macrofiscal challenges as they arise, governments should focus on delivering good projects and improving the delivery of public services.* The scarcity of fiscal resources suggests that it is critical to focus on delivering public investment projects and social services at the least possible cost and that maximum output is received from the resources invested. Public investment must be focused on building capacity in key areas, such as infrastructure, education, and energy efficiency, and spent strategically in order to generate jobs for those hardest hit by the

recession. If investment in such areas can be delivered in a timely way and bottlenecks can be avoided, it can be an effective tool for stimulating economic activity and raising employment in the short run (OECD 2009).

3. ***Medium-term budgetary frameworks should be strengthened and should be consistent with a credible path for deficit reductions.*** A crisis can make it easier to adopt a deficit reduction plan, but also requires policy and administrative acuity. Having a central government ministry act as an active gatekeeper of the medium-term fiscal position provides useful discipline and reinforces the selection of efficient policy and delivery mechanisms. Usually this requires the finance ministry or its offshoots to be at the center of the process, acting within the context of a national plan for economywide development priorities and the protection of the fiscal position. Medium-term budget frameworks should provide forward visibility regarding resource availability and predictability of investments. Put another way, public investment projects and emerging social spending needs should fit with credible medium-term forecasts and comprehensive economic policy—that shows how the budget can be financed in a sustainable way—in order to ensure that there is capacity to accommodate such items (Flyvbjerg 2007; OECD 2010).

4. ***Spending decisions will be better if investment choices are assessed in terms of costs and benefits, and if the ministry of finance has the expertise to challenge the policies of line ministers and ministries.*** Ministries of finance can use the relative shortage of fiscal resources as a means to get tougher on poor-quality policies or expensive delivery mechanisms. As the Organisation for Economic Co-operation and Development has commented, development of savings proposals cannot be left solely to officials in line ministries; savings proposals may need to come from the center, but be supported with information flows from the line ministries. In this realm, countries are experimenting with service delivery units and reestablishing fundamental review mechanisms. Everything should be on the table. Governments need to identify not only which projects will give the highest return, but also which projects can be implemented more rapidly. To do this, they need to establish good guidance systems to deal with the technical aspects of project appraisal that are appropriate to the technical

capacity of their ministries. It is also important that there is rigorous, independent review of all public investment projects before they get the "go-ahead," in order to ensure that they have the potential to yield the maximum economic and social benefits. Under the current circumstances, where speed is important, it may be necessary to develop standardized, if simpler, methods for project appraisal (that is, cost-effectiveness, multicriteria, and so forth) and standardized reference projects.

5. *There may be increased scope for public-private partnerships, but beware the folly of rushing into long-term contracts without proper considerations of fiscal risk.* Many governments now recognize that the involvement of the private sector is critically important in bringing their infrastructure up to world-class standards and in assisting in the delivery of public services. However, the crisis in financial markets meant that bank lending to the private sector declined. In a recent report (PPIAF 2009), the Public-Private Infrastructure Advisory Facility pointed out that, although it is still too soon to assess the full impact of the current crisis on new public-private infrastructure projects, there is strong evidence of lower rates of financial closure and of projects being postponed and cancelled, mainly in energy and transport. In an environment where private investment continues to be depressed, government expenditure will remain the only contributor to GDP growth in many countries.

6. *A good response would focus on improving organizational capacity and bolstering institutions.* Improvements in technical, financial, and managerial capacity can certainly help to increase a country's capability and flexibility to deliver public investments and core social spending. The ongoing risks to the economic and fiscal outlook suggest (a) a strong benefit from well-functioning forecasting and oversight institutions and (b) an arrangement of institutions to support the professionalization rather than the politicization of that task. A number of countries have moved in this direction, such as Hungary, which has created a new independent institution to monitor fiscal developments. Significant capacity building in terms of deepening project management and implementation skills is not an easy task. But it is necessary, particularly in line ministries and public agencies that undertake public investment.

7. *Initiatives associated with transparency and accountability can provide benefits to private actors; fiscal rules have been tested and found wanting in many countries.* More and more, electorates look to be informed of what policies governments are implementing. Also, confidence in the way the economy is being managed can help encourage consumers, businesses, and financial markets to spend, subsequently supporting the recovery. And governments are responding. An example is the American Recovery and Reinvestment Plan. Another is Brazil's Growth Acceleration Program, which shows progress in implementing the accelerated program of public works. At the start of June 2010, the U.K. Treasury announced the opening of the Combined Online Information System database. By comparison, fiscal rules have proved quite ineffective in guiding policy in the presence of major external shocks, because policy makers and circumstances have conspired to allow for a substantial deviation in the track of fiscal progress and the path allowed via rules. While a sluggish economy may make it difficult to implement a deficit reduction plan, it does not preclude the announcement of such a plan. Indeed, transparency concerning such plans can assist in moving market expectations in line with the regaining of sustainability. Rules may assist in the restoration process.

8. *Countries have made core social spending a priority, but uncertainties remain concerning donors.* Donor funding, which is an important component of social spending in many developing countries, tends to decline significantly when Organisation for Economic Co-operation and Development countries face a downturn. In the aggregate, rich countries do not respond to the needs of countries affected by global or regional crisis. However, there are specific instances where they have provided relief and support to individual countries, and in this crisis, consistency in HIV/AIDS funding is a departure from past practices of reneging on promises when banking crises hit donor economies (Lewis and Verhoeven 2010). While enhancing development effectiveness should include providing a source of support in times of crisis, domestic politics can make this problematic. Protection of progress toward the Millennium Development Goals could usefully be considered an overriding objective for the efforts in high- and low-income countries.

While the current crisis is not over, encouraging evidence suggests that social spending is increasingly a priority for countries (Green, King, and Miller-Dawkins 2010; IMF 2010). The big challenge is how well countries spend available funds and implement public programs. The rate of spending is only part of it.

Notes

1. Members of the G-20 are Argentina, Australia, Brazil, Canada, China, France, Germany, India, Indonesia, Italy, Japan, the Republic of Korea, Mexico, the Russian Federation, Saudi Arabia, South Africa, Turkey, the United Kingdom, the United States, and the European Union.
2. Estimates are based on panel analysis for 108 developing countries for 1980–2007. Estimates of health and education expenditure for the forecast period (2008–13) are based on income per capita in PPP terms and aggregate government spending from the International Monetary Fund's World Economic Outlook database.
3. Data are based on the International Monetary Fund's World Economic Outlook database estimates and forecasts.
4. This section draws from Thomas and Ferris (2009).

Bibliography

Ferris, Tom. 2009. "Implications of Recession for Public Investment." *Public Affairs Ireland Journal* (55).

Flyvbjerg, B. 2007. "Policy and Planning for Large-infrastructure Projects: Problems, Causes, Cures." *Environment and Planning B: Planning and Design 2007* 34 (4): 578–97.

Green, D., R. King, and M. Miller-Dawkins. 2010. "The Global Economic Crisis and Developing Countries: Impact and Response." International Research Report, Oxfam International, New York. http://www.oxfam.org.uk/resources/policy/ economic_crisis/downloads/rr_gec_and_developing_countries_full_ en_260510.pdf.

IMF (International Monetary Fund). 2009. *Creating Policy Space—Responsive Design and Streamlined Conditionality in Recent Low-Income Country Programs.* Washington, DC: IMF.

———. 2010. *Fiscal Monitor: Navigating the Fiscal Challenges Ahead.* Washington, DC: IMF.

Lewis, M., and M. Verhoeven. 2010. "Financial Crises and Social Spending: The Impact of the 2008–2009 Crisis." Unpublished paper, World Bank, Washington, DC.

OECD (Organisation for Economic Co-operation and Development). 2009. *Going for Growth 2009.* Paris: OECD.

————. 2010. "Restoring Fiscal Sustainability: Lessons for the Public Sector." Public Governance Committee, Working Party of Budget Officials, OECD, Paris.

PPIAF (Public-Private Infrastructure Advisory Facility). 2009. *Financial Crisis Affecting New Private Infrastructure Projects*. Washington, DC: PPIAF.

Rajaram, A., T.-M. Le, N. Biletska, and J. Brumby. 2009. "A Diagnostic Framework for Assessing Public Investment Management." Public Sector and Governance Unit, Poverty Reduction and Economic Management Network, World Bank, Washington, DC.

Thomas, T., and T. Ferris. 2009. "Review of Public Investment Management Performance (PIMP) in an Economic Crisis." Global Expert Team Brief, World Bank, Washington, DC.

World Bank. 2009. "Protecting Progress: The Challenge Facing Low-Income Countries in the Global Recession." Background paper prepared by World Bank Group staff for the G-20 Leaders' Meeting, Pittsburgh, PA, September 24–25.

12

Debt Management and the Financial Crisis

Sudarshan Gooptu and
Carlos A. Primo Braga

Until the eve of the financial crisis, sovereign debt management in developing countries was being carried out under favorable circumstances. The period 2000–07, for example, was characterized by lower local interest rates and a reduced reliance on short-term external borrowing. The increased availability of local currency financing, reflecting the development of domestic capital markets, and the globalization of the corporate sector in emerging market economies underscored the changing landscape of development financing.

The global financial crisis is changing this landscape once again. Since 2007, the world economy slowed significantly—global output declined 0.6 percent (a 3.2 percent contraction in the case of advanced economies) in 2009. Although the global economy is expected to return to a positive growth path in 2010 (4.2 percent), future prospects remain uncertain (World Bank 2010). Moreover, advanced economies are expected to face large public debts, rising real interest rates, and slower growth. The International Monetary Fund (IMF), for example, projects that annual gross

This paper relies extensively on Primo Braga (2010) and Gooptu, Suri, and van Doorn (2010).

domestic product (GDP) growth rates in advanced countries will be about a half percentage point less, on average, than precrisis levels.

There is also broad consensus that many dangers remain ahead in terms of the sustainability of the recovery, including the challenges in implementing exit strategies from the massive government interventions that took place since 2008 (Primo Braga 2010). In spite of the first signs of attenuation of the crisis in the third quarter of 2009, economic indicators still point to significant levels of unemployment and social distress around the world. So far, this crisis has not yet evolved into a systemic sovereign debt crisis.[1] The rapid accumulation of public debt and growing fiscal imbalances in many countries, however, and historical precedent suggest that one cannot simply dismiss such a possibility. Interestingly enough, for the first time over the past four decades, concerns about debt sustainability seem to be concentrated in high-income economies. It is true that developing economies entered this crisis in a much stronger financial position, reflecting better macroeconomic policies, improved debt management practices, and, in the case of heavily indebted poor countries, debt relief. Still, the severity of the crisis and the growing tensions in public debt markets in Organisation for Economic Co-operation and Development (OECD) countries underscore the fact that there is no room for complacency. In what follows, we document evolving debt and fiscal trends and identify some of the emerging challenges faced by debt managers in developing markets.

Emerging Issues

The first years of the 21st century were characterized by more prudent macroeconomic policies in the developing world, the positive impact of debt relief on low-income countries, and positive growth trends for the world economy, in spite of the puncturing of the high-tech "bubble" in OECD countries. Many emerging economies were able to reduce the vulnerabilities of their debt portfolios over the past decade. Average maturities increased, reflecting increases in the maturities of new debt issuances, and as a consequence, many countries entered the crisis facing lower rollover risks.

Figure 12.1 captures some of the key debt and fiscal variables for a relevant set of advanced and emerging countries in 2007, immediately

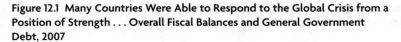

Figure 12.1 Many Countries Were Able to Respond to the Global Crisis from a Position of Strength . . . Overall Fiscal Balances and General Government Debt, 2007

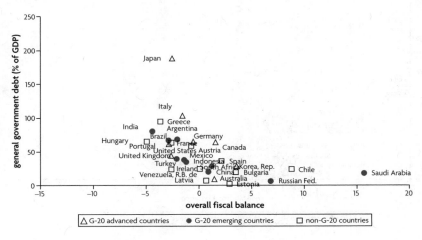

Source: Authors' calculations.

Note: Debt measures for Bulgaria, República Bolivariana de Venezuela, and Chile are gross public debt, external debt, and public sector gross debt, respectively.

before the onset of the crisis. As illustrated by the location of a large number of economies in the right quadrant of the graph—with fiscal surpluses and debt-to-GDP ratios below 60 percent—many countries were able to respond to the crisis from a position of strength. Figure 12.2 shows that by the end of 2009 the picture had changed significantly with many countries now displaying fiscal deficits of more than 5 percent and debt-to-GDP ratios well above 60 percent. In other words, *the scope for further expansionary interventions, be it on the monetary or on the fiscal fronts, is much more limited now*. The situation is particularly complex in some countries in the eurozone where existing social entitlements and low productivity growth prospects make debt-to-GDP reduction exercises quite difficult.

Confidence in the strength of the recovery of advanced economies remains a question, and the process of deleveraging of the private sector in many OECD countries is ongoing. Accordingly, although the debate about the proper timing to unwind public interventions remains fierce (see, for example, Hannoun 2009), it was clear by May 2010 that

Figure 12.2 But this Fortunate Position Is Rapidly Changing . . . Overall Fiscal Balances and General Government Debt, 2009

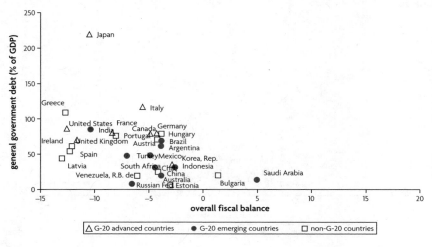

Source: Authors' calculations.

Note: Debt measures for Bulgaria, República Bolivariana de Venezuela, and Chile are gross public debt, external debt, and public sector gross debt, respectively. Greek deficit figure for 2009 revealed by government sources in November 2009, reported by the *Financial Times*, February 3, 2010.

developments in European markets had increased the need for credible plans for fiscal consolidation.

Given the growing levels of debt, several questions emerge in a medium-term context. These include: What if the fiscal stimulus programs were to continue for an additional two to four years more than currently projected? What will happen to public debt if there is no adjustment to the primary fiscal balances in the medium term? What is the degree of fiscal adjustment that countries need to make to either reduce their public debt stock to historical average levels or stabilize it around a certain fiscally sustainable target? If the adjustment is deemed too large to be deemed credible from a political economy standpoint, what will be the effect of a more gradual adjustment on debt sustainability? While this chapter does not aim to answer these important questions, some preliminary findings on some of them have already started to appear in the literature. A recent study undertaken for a sample of 20 middle-income countries (MICs), for example, shows that the fiscal policy responses in 2008 and 2009 and the related external financing packages have contributed to higher public and external debts in several countries (figure 12.3) (Gooptu, Suri, and van Doorn 2010).

Hypothetical scenarios that were examined in this study—to assess the staying power of these fiscal stimulus programs in this sample of countries—suggest that if a growth recovery is not sustained in advanced countries and the global outlook remains fragile, the primary balances that most of these countries will need to run in the medium term will be significantly higher than what they have done in the recent past. Moreover, if the prolonged downturn leads to even more debt accumulation, this will make it more difficult for several of these countries to reach their respective debt targets if rising international interest rates, foreign exchange risk, and a continuous repricing of risk of sovereign credits characterizes the new postcrisis reality (figure 12.4).

In the case of low-income countries, the global financial crisis has also affected their debt positions and associated vulnerabilities. This group of countries is likely to face tighter external financing—dwindling foreign direct investment, commercial lending, and (potentially) smaller aid flows—and contractions in export income. Several of them have increased

Figure 12.3 The Crisis Has Brought with It Increased External and Public (Including Domestic) Debt Levels in MICs

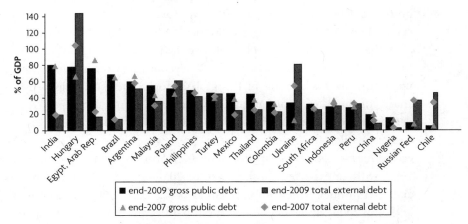

Sources: Gooptu, Suri, and van Doorn 2010; International Monetary Fund, World Economic Outlook database.

Figure 12.4 Significant Divergence of Required Postcrisis Primary Balances from Countries' Past Levels

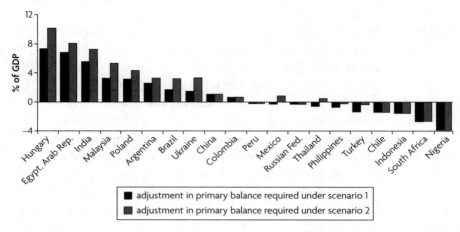

Sources: Gooptu, Suri, and van Doorn 2010; International Monetary Fund, World Economic Outlook database.

Note: Assumptions: Debt target is 40 percent of GDP by 2020 if the country's gross public debt was above 40 percent of GDP at end-2009, or to stabilize debt at its end-2009, level if debt was below 40 percent of GDP at end-2009. Adjustment is the difference between the required primary balance to reach the debt target under the two hypothetical scenarios and the country-specific historical primary balance (that is, average of 1996–2001 for countries marked with an asterisk; average of 2002–07 for all other countries). Light shaded bars indicate that the historical primary balance is larger than the required primary balance, so, in principle, no unprecedented fiscal adjustment will be needed in these countries.

their reliance on domestic debt to close their widening fiscal financing needs. A recent joint World Bank–IMF study reviewed debt sustainability analyses (DSAs) for 32 low-income countries (LICs) for which pre-and postcrisis debt sustainability analyses were available. Like the MICs, the external and fiscal financing requirements of LICs have also increased after the global crisis (World Bank and IMF 2010). In addition, their future levels of GDP, exports, and fiscal revenues are expected to be permanently lower as a result of this global shock. The World Bank–IMF study concludes that, on average, LIC debt ratios are also expected to deteriorate in the near term, particularly for public debt.

Meanwhile, the surge in gross borrowing needs of advanced economies—from US$9 trillion in 2007 to roughly US$16 trillion in 2009, with an expected similar level for 2010—is adding to the financial stress under which public debt is being managed (Blommestein and Gok 2009). If general government debt ratios in advanced economies are to be brought back to the precrisis average of 60 percent of

GDP by 2030, it will require an 8 percent swing in the fiscal balance from an average deficit of 4 percent in 2010 to a fiscal surplus of 4 percent by 2020 and then maintaining of this surplus for the ensuing decade (Lipskey 2010). The growing level of public debt suggests that the spread between long-term and short-term interest rates is likely to increase over time, even though quantitative easing may delay such a trend. This is likely to imply higher borrowing costs and shortening maturities for developing-country new borrowings. Developing countries will be affected not only by the implications of these developments for the cost of capital and by less dynamism in the world economy, but also by the massive public interventions of the past two years—in the absence of an orderly unwinding—that will foster asset bubbles and speculative waves. Exchange rate misalignments can also contribute to the tensions in the system. Speculative attacks against currencies in highly leveraged economies can add to risks by further contributing to the deterioration of private sector balance sheets and may evolve into sovereign debt crises. All these risks need to be managed on a continuous basis going forward. This should be accompanied by credible medium-term debt management practices and financing strategies to support the fiscal spending and postcrisis recovery efforts.

Adopting a Sovereign Balance Sheet Approach to Minimize Fiscal and Debt Risks

The debt and fiscal paths reviewed in the previous section underscore the importance of renewed attention to sovereign debt management. The traditional external debt sustainability assessments will continue to be an important ingredient of the analytical toolkit, but they need to be complemented by closer examination of public debt (that is, encompassing both domestic and external debts) and medium-term fiscal sustainability analyses by the respective authorities on a regular basis. Special attention will now need to be given to managing not only the composition of sovereign debt portfolios, but also the expanding array of contingent liabilities incurred by governments in the context of their responses to the crisis.

Conventional debt sustainability assessments for low- and middle-income countries highlight the country-specific characteristics, focusing on the nature and size of shocks that affect a country's debt and debt service profile and on the potential for fiscal response to these shocks, given its fiscal space at any point in time. However, the lessons from the East Asian financial crisis of the late 1990s and the recent global financial crisis underscore the need for debt sustainability analyses to consider the wider liabilities of the public sector. Countries with high sovereign debt ratios, large fiscal deficits, and growing contingent liabilities are especially at risk of contagion since heightened market uncertainties in international capital markets lead to a flight to quality. Investors are wary of rising interest rates across countries and stringent fiscal consolidation ahead unless growth resumes in their respective economies.[2]

The ability of governments to make payments on their debt obligations (domestic and external), and to minimize future risks to their public finances, can be enhanced by implementing a credible medium-term debt management strategy and creating an institutional capability to monitor and manage its contingent liabilities. To this end, a sovereign balance sheet approach to debt management will be useful in managing the financial and credit risks associated with carrying out their regulatory and macroeconomic functions. This approach helps one to look into the nature of the risk characteristics of assets and obligations that the government manages, and the types of financial flows associated with them. In practice, this entails an examination of the cash flows generated by the key assets (or asset classes) of the government and monetary authorities, noting how sensitive they are to changes in real interest rates, currency movements, and shifts in terms of trade (Wheeler 2004, 77–90).

Concluding Remarks

The coordination of exit policies from the massive fiscal interventions of the past few years will pose major challenges for governments around the world. While simultaneous fiscal expansion helped thwart the global economic slowdown in 2008–09, the story is more complicated when it comes to unwinding these fiscal programs and entering a path of fiscal consolidation. Simultaneous fiscal consolidation is likely to constrain the dimensions of economic recovery at least in the initial stages of fiscal retrenchment. A case can be made that if the fiscal consolidation is focused on stabilizing entitlement-spending-to-GDP ratios (a must for countries facing demographic pressures) and letting discretionary interventions expire, the required adjustment can be achieved. The difficulties of dealing with entitlement reforms (for example, pension and health reforms) and the temptation to postpone adjustment in view of continued weaknesses in the private sector (reflecting the ongoing deleveraging process), however, underscore how challenging the political economy of fiscal consolidation will be.

Markets will be closely monitoring the evolution of fiscal positions around the world, and those economies that are not able to implement their consolidation plans will face increasing difficulties in financing their debts. In this context, international coordination (and monitoring) can play a positive role in helping enhance the credibility of national strategies and by giving "ammunition" to financial authorities to resist short-term pressures associated with political cycles.

Finally, with the increasing importance of infrastructure spending by the public sector to renew the growth process in several countries through the issuance of sovereign guarantees or by the reliance on public-private partnerships, the role of contingent liabilities requires renewed attention. They may pose substantial balance sheet risks for a government. As the experience of the East Asian Financial Crisis in 1997 bears witness, when contingent liabilities are realized, they become a potential source of future call on tax revenues and can be a major factor in the buildup of public sector debt. Experience shows that particularly important in this regard have been contingent liabilities associated with capital injections into the banking system or in the recapitalization of public sector enterprises (Wheeler 2004, 103–10). The rapid buildup of public debt that has been observed in advanced countries and is now being witnessed in middle-income countries is highly correlated with these "hidden deficits."

Experiences of many countries, such as Colombia, Hungary, New Zealand, South Africa, and Sweden, suggest that the government's exposure to contingent liabilities can be substantially reduced through better, more complete monitoring and reporting; better risk-sharing arrangements; improved governance and regulatory regimes for entities that benefit from such contingent liabilities of the government; and sound economic policies that minimize the possibility of these contingent liabilities from being realized in the first place. Debt managers around the world will have to pay close attention to the evolution of contingent liabilities and their impact on public debt in order to avoid surprises.

Notes

1. There is extensive literature on the correlation between banking crises and sovereign debt crises. See, for example, Reinhart and Rogoff (2009).
2. Blanchard, Dell'Ariccia, and Mauro (2010) have noted that the degree of post-crisis fiscal adjustment that will be necessary is "formidable" if one were to consider the aging-related challenges in pensions and health care that the advanced economies face. They highlight the importance of creating ample fiscal space by harnessing future economic booms and by adopting credible commitments to reduce their debt-to-GDP ratios, including through frameworks (and fiscal rules) that help limit spending increases in economic boom periods. Better automatic stabilizers will help as well.

Bibliography

Blanchard, O., G. Dell'Ariccia, and P. Mauro. 2010. "Rethinking Macroeconomic Policy." IMF Staff Position Note SPN/10/03, International Monetary Fund, Washington, DC.

Blommestein, H. J., and A. Gok. 2009. "The Surge in Borrowing Needs of OECD Governments: Revised Estimates for 2009 and 2010 Outlook." *OECD Journal: Financial Market Trends* 2009 (2).

Gooptu, S., V. Suri, and R. van Doorn. 2010. "Implications of the Fiscal Responses to the Global Financial Crisis: The Case of Middle-Income Countries." Paper presented at the World Bank–Asian Development Bank Conference on "Sovereign Debt Crisis: Is This Time Different?" Tunis, Tunisia, March 29–30.

Hannoun, H. 2009. "Unwinding Public Interventions after the Crisis." Speech delivered at the International Monetary Fund High Level Conference, "Unwinding Public Interventions—Preconditions and Practical Considerations," Washington, DC, December 3.

Horton, M., M. Kumar, and P. Mauro. 2009. "The State of Public Finances: A Cross-Country Fiscal Monitor." IMF Staff Position Note SPN/09/21, International Monetary Fund, Washington, DC.

IMF (International Monetary Fund). 2010. *World Economic Outlook.* Washington, DC: IMF. http://www.imf.org/external/pubs/ft/weo/2010/01/index.htm.

Lipskey, J. P. 2010. "Fiscal Policy Challenges in the Post-Crisis World." Speech delivered at the Council on Foreign Relations, China Development Forum, Beijing, March 21. http://www.cfr.org/publication/21712/imf.html.

Primo Braga, C. A. 2010. "The Great Recession and International Policy Coordination." Paper prepared for the First International Research Conference of the Reserve Bank of India: "Challenges to Central Banking in the Context of Financial Crisis," Mumbai, India, February 12–13.

Reinhart, C. M., and K. S. Rogoff. 2009. *This Time Is Different: Eight Centuries of Financial Folly*. Princeton, NJ: Princeton University Press.

Wheeler, G. 2004. *Sound Practice in Government Debt Management*. Washington, DC: World Bank.

World Bank. 2010. *Global Monitoring Report: The MDGs after the Crisis*. Washington, DC: World Bank.

World Bank and IMF (International Monetary Fund). 2010. "Preserving Debt Sustainability in Low-Income Countries in the Wake of the Global Crisis." World Bank and IMF, Washington, DC.

13

Subnational Debt Finance:
Make It Sustainable

Otaviano Canuto and Lili Liu

This chapter explores the impact of the 2008–09 global financial crisis on subnational debt financing[1] through the following questions: Why is subnational debt financing important? What are the impacts of the crisis on the fiscal balance and financing cost of subnational governments (SNGs)? What explains the variations across countries in the ability of SNGs to proactively address the threat of fiscal deterioration? And what are the long-term structural challenges facing SNGs in sustainable financing of infrastructure and social services?

The Rising Importance of Subnational Debt Finance

State and local debt and debt of quasi-public agencies have been growing in importance. In Brazil, subnational debt accounts for about 30 percent of total public sector net debt. The debt of Indian states is about 27 percent of gross domestic product (GDP) (the number would be higher if debt on the balance sheets of companies such as power and water, which are wholly or largely owned by the states, were included). The rising share of subnational

The authors would like to thank Xiaowei Tian of the Economic Policy and Debt Department of the World Bank for excellent research support in the production of this paper.

finance in consolidated public finance is not limited to federal countries. In France, SNGs account for more than 70 percent of public investment. Even in countries where varying degrees of fiscal decentralization have been recent, SNGs account for an increasing share of public investments—for example, approximately 50 percent in Indonesia and Turkey.[2]

Three structural trends have contributed to the rising share of subnational finance, including SNG debt as a share of general public debt. First, decentralization in many countries has given SNGs certain spending responsibilities, revenue-raising authority, and the capacity to incur debt. With sovereign access to financial markets, SNGs are pushing for access to these markets as well, particularly given the rising regional and subnational political power that is a driving force in decentralization.

Second, the unprecedented scale of urbanization in developing countries requires large-scale urban infrastructure financing to help absorb massive influxes of rural populations. Borrowing enables SNGs to capture the benefits of major capital investments immediately, rather than waiting until sufficient savings from current income can be accumulated to finance them. Infrastructure investments benefit future generations that therefore should also bear the cost. Subnational borrowing finances infrastructure more equitably across multigenerational users of infrastructure services because the debt service can match the economic life of the assets that the debt is financing. Infrastructure services thus can be paid for by the beneficiaries of the services.

Third, the subnational debt market in developing countries has been going through a notable transformation. Private capital has emerged to play an important role in subnational finance in countries such as Poland, Romania, and the Russian Federation. Subnational bonds increasingly compete with traditional bank loans. Notwithstanding the temporary disruption of the subnational credit markets during the crisis, the trend toward more diversified subnational credit markets is expected to continue. SNGs or their entities in various countries have already issued bond instruments (for example, in China, Colombia, India, Mexico, Poland, Russia, and South Africa). More countries are considering policy frameworks for facilitating subnational debt market development (for example, Indonesia), whereas others are allowing selected subnational entities to pilot test transaction and capacity-building activities (for example, Peru).

The Financial Crisis: Impact and Response

The global financial crisis has had a profound impact on subnational finance across countries. Slower or negative national and regional economic growth has generally reduced the SNGs' own revenues; the exact impact is influenced by the revenue structure of the SNG. SNGs with strong dependence on revenues from highly cyclical economic activities such as housing and commodity exports will have experienced more negative impact than will the SNGs that have more stable revenue sources such as property taxes based on delayed assessment. SNGs relying heavily on sales tax, the value-added tax, and income taxes also have experienced reduced revenues. Fiscal transfers that are based on formulas with a time lag will suffer less immediate impact, although the pressures are only being delayed.

The deterioration in primary balance is driven by declining revenues combined with expenditure rigidity or continuing expenditures. In general, the fiscal needs of countries are rising but fiscal space is narrowing, resulting in deteriorating fiscal positions across regions and tiers of government. In the BRIC countries (Brazil, China, India, and Russia) and four advanced economies (Australia, Canada, France, and Spain), the rising fiscal deficit happened across all these countries except Brazil from 2008 to 2009.[3]

All major rating agencies have viewed the impact of the economic downturn on the credit qualities of SNGs as significant (Fitch Ratings 2009; Moody's Investor Service 2010; S&P 2010). From October 2008 to January 2010, Moody's rating actions affected 72 SNGs, or 24 percent of the rated universe outside the United States. Ninety-six percent of the actions were in a downward direction.[4] There was a general shift toward negative outlooks for 2009 in the Fitch ratings of European SNGs, and the downward pressure continued into 2010. Similarly, S&P's negative rating actions for European SNGs largely exceeded positive ones in 2009, and the trend was present in the first half of 2010.

A liquidity squeeze and lower risk appetite generally led to higher financing costs at the height of the crisis, as measured by the cost of subsovereign bond issuances.[5] Although the cost of financing has declined since mid-2009, the rapid increase in public debt levels across many countries is likely to raise longer-term interest rates (Blommestein forthcoming).

Yield spread for subnational bond issuance (outside the United States) steadily increased from the first quarter of 2008 to the second quarter of 2009, whereas maturity exhibited a generally declining trend from the third quarter of 2007 to the first quarter of 2009. If one further decomposes yield spread, the rising spread was driven mainly by the rising spread of bonds with a maturity of less than seven years, while the impact on those with maturity of seven years or longer has not been as significant. However, the share of subnational bonds with a maturity of seven years or more declined from 60 percent in 2007 to 41 percent in 2009. In the United States, the spread for AAA-rated 10-year U.S. municipal general obligation bonds increased by 200 basis points from the fourth quarter of 2007 to the fourth quarter of 2008.[6] There are, however, significant variations in the access to and cost of SNG debt financing across and within countries.

To counter the global financial crisis, countries have launched countercyclical macroeconomic policies. The ability of SNGs to cushion the impact of the crisis is framed by national-level responses. Central governments have launched a range of measures to help SNGs weather the crisis. These include relaxing fiscal and indebtedness targets and broadening the fiscal space for new borrowing (for example, Brazil and India), creating a credit line for SNGs that have suffered a loss of fiscal transfers (for example, Brazil), providing low-cost loans for SNGs and increasing fiscal transfers (for example, Russia), providing financing for SNG infrastructure spending and other core services, and expanding SNG access to capital markets through subsovereign bond issuance (for example, China). In the United States, the American Recovery and Reinvestment Act of 2009 provided nearly US$135 billion in emergency funding, helping states avoid draconian cuts in services.[7]

Long-term Structural Issues

If one looks beyond the crisis and stabilization, a series of long-term structural issues with respect to SNG debt finance will occupy developing countries. Rapid urbanization, with unprecedented rural-to-urban migration, will continue to demand massive urban infrastructure investments—investments that largely have been decentralized to SNGs in many countries. Developing countries invest an annual average of 3 to 4 percent of GDP on infrastructure, well short of what is considered to be required. The scale and sustainability of SNG infrastructure financing will critically depend on the macroeconomic fundamentals of the sovereign, the regulatory frameworks for subnational borrowing, the management of implicit and contingent liabilities, and the development of competitive and diversified subnational credit markets.

Macroeconomic Fundamentals

The sovereign's macroeconomic fundamentals will continue to be vital to the fiscal sustainability of SNGs. With the gradual withdrawal of fiscal stimulus packages and the ending of monetary easing, pressures on SNGs' fiscal space could increase through various channels, such as reduced fiscal transfers and higher borrowing costs.

Major international rating agencies (Fitch, Moody's, and S&P) cap subsovereign credit ratings by the sovereign credit ratings, and rarely do subsovereign ratings exceed that of the sovereign (figure 13.1). A country's

Figure 13.1 Correlation between Sovereign and Subsovereign Ratings of European Countries

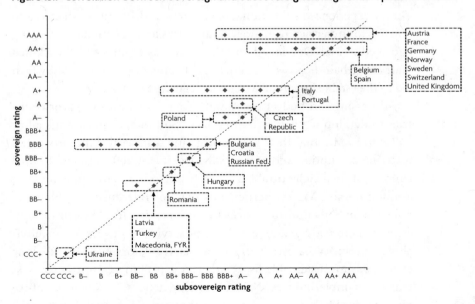

Source: Standard & Poor's, http://www.standardandpoors.com.

Note: The sample size is 141 subsovereign governments from 22 European countries. One dot can represent multiple subsovereigns because many of them share the same sovereign and subsovereign ratings. The only subsovereigns whose ratings exceed their sovereign rating are the Autonomous Community of Basque Country and Navarre of Spain (the dot below the 45° line). Ratings used are as of February 23, 2010.

macroeconomic management and countrywide risks not only affect the broader economic, fiscal, and financial conditions under which an SNG operates, but also place restrictions on an SNG's ability to raise funds. The national government typically has a wide range of constitutional powers giving it first claim over the country's foreign reserves and other resources. Thus, in a financial crisis, the national government would likely be able to fulfill its external or domestic debt obligations ahead of the SNG. The rating "ceiling" relationship applies less strongly to domestic currency debt instruments. Even in cases where the SNG possesses foreign currency reserves that are out of reach of the national government, the national government nevertheless could impose nationwide capital or exchange controls to restrict capital outflows and thereby disallow the SNG from repaying its foreign debts. In short, the sovereign is unlikely to default before any SNG does.

Regulatory Frameworks for Subnational Debt Financing

With subnational debt financing comes the risks of insolvency. During the 1990s, countries such as Brazil, Hungary, India, Mexico, Russia, and Turkey experienced subnational fiscal stress or debt crises, which led to reforms to strengthen regulatory frameworks for subnational borrowing and credit risks. Developed countries such as France and the United States have had their own experiences of subnational insolvency, which led to the establishment of systems to regulate the risks.[8]

Addressing soft budget constraints is a strong motivation for countries to develop regulatory frameworks.[9] Soft budget constraints allow SNGs to live beyond their means, negating competitive incentives and fostering corruption and rent-seeking (Weingast 2007). Unconditional bailouts of financially troubled SNGs by the central government create a moral hazard. Market participants may tolerate unsustainable fiscal policy of an SNG if history backs their perception that the central government implicitly guarantees the debt service of the SNG (Ianchovichina, Liu, and Nagarajan 2007). However, regulatory frameworks alone cannot ensure sustainable fiscal policy. A gap-filling grant transfer system, for example, induces SNGs to run fiscal deficits. Lack of own-source revenues for SNGs in many countries undermines their ability to make fiscal corrections. Furthermore, a competitive capital market prices risks and returns of subnational lending, helping discipline subnational borrowing from the capital market side. But this market discipline could be undermined by monopoly supply of credits to SNGs (Liu and Waibel 2008).

Regulatory frameworks consist of two components: (a) ex-ante fiscal rules for SNGs, stipulating purposes and types of and limits for debt instruments, and issuance procedures; and (b) ex-post debt restructuring in the event that SNGs become insolvent. Insolvency mechanisms increase the pain of circumventing ex-ante rules for both lenders and borrowers, thereby strengthening preventive rules. Regulatory frameworks in many countries are still evolving, and the pace of putting together a full range of regulatory elements varies.

Liu and Waibel (2008) point out some key common elements in ex ante borrowing regulation across countries. First, long-term borrowing should be only for public capital investments, that is, a balanced budget net of public investment.[10] Second, limits should be imposed on key fiscal variables such as debt service ratios and ceilings on guarantees.[11] Third, increasingly, legal frameworks include procedural requirements that SNGs establish a medium-term fiscal framework and a transparent budgetary process.[12] This requirement is intended to ensure that fiscal accounts move within a sustainable debt path and that fiscal adjustment takes a medium-term approach to better respond to shocks and differing trajectories for key macroeconomic variables. It also fosters a more transparent budgetary process through longer-view debates by executive and legislative branches on spending priorities, funding sources, and required fiscal adjustments.

Ex-ante fiscal rules for SNG debt financing can also be supported by regulations on lenders. To improve fiscal transparency, Mexico introduced a credit-rating system for SNGs. Although subnational participation in the credit rating is voluntary, the requirements of the capital-risk weighting of bank loans introduced in 2000 and of loss provisions introduced in 2004 aim at imposing subnational fiscal discipline through the market pricing of subnational credits. In Colombia, the Fiscal Transparency and Responsibility Law (2003) tightened the regulations on the supply side. Lending to SNGs must meet the conditions and limits of various regulations, such as Law 617 and Law 817. Otherwise, the credit contract is invalid and borrowed funds must be restituted without interest or any other charges.

Ex-post regulation—that is, an insolvency mechanism—deals with insolvent SNGs.[13] It serves multiple objectives: to enforce hard budget constraints on SNGs, to maintain essential services while SNGs undergo debt restructuring, and to restore the financial health of the SNGs so that they reenter the financial market. The need for a collective framework for resolving debt claims is driven by conflicts between creditors and debtor, and among creditors. Creditors' remedies in contract laws, instead of bankruptcy mechanisms, are effective for enforcing discrete unpaid obligations. However, individual lawsuits or negotiations become ineffective if there is a general inability to pay. Individual creditors may have different interests and security provisions for the debt owed to them and may often demand preferential treatment and threaten to derail debt restructurings voluntarily negotiated between a majority of creditors and the subnational debtor—the so-called holdout problem (McConnell and Picker 1993). This problem causes uncertainty and prolongs the debt restructuring process. The holdout problem is not as serious if debts are concentrated in a few banks. However, a collective framework for insolvency restructuring takes on more importance as the subnational bond markets develop—with thousands of creditors.

Key design considerations arise concerning insolvency procedures—namely, the fundamental difference between public and private insolvency, the choice between judicial or administrative approaches (including the extent to which the legal authority of SNGs to govern may be effected judicially or administratively), and the operation of the insolvency procedure itself. On the first, the public nature of the services provided by governments explains the fundamental difference between public and private insolvency. When a private corporation goes bankrupt, all assets of the corporation are potentially subject to attachment. By contrast, the ability of creditors to attach assets of SNGs is greatly restrained in many countries. Thus, the insolvency mechanism for subnationals generally involves reorganization, not asset liquidation.

The choice of approaches varies across countries, depending on history, political and economic structure, and motivation for establishing an insolvency mechanism.[14] Judicial procedures place courts in the driver's seat. Courts make key decisions to guide the restructuring process, including when and how SNG insolvency is triggered (a priority structure for allocating credits among competing claims), and which services will be maintained. Because the debt discharge is highly complex, the judicial approach has the advantage of neutralizing political pressures during the restructuring. However, because mandates for budgetary matters lie with the executive and legislature in many countries, the courts' ability to influence subnational fiscal adjustment is limited. Administrative interventions, by contrast, usually allow a higher level of government to intervene in the entity concerned, temporarily taking direct political responsibility for many aspects of financial management.[15]

Managing Implicit and Contingent Liabilities

The global financial crisis reaffirmed the importance of managing implicit and contingent liabilities that are off budgets and balance sheets of official financial accounts. Beyond the well-known liabilities that are not captured by official accounting (such as deficit financing through arrears due to a cash accounting framework), two types of subsovereign fiscal risks and two types of contingent liabilities are likely to grow in importance in developing countries.

First, SNGs have undertaken a large share of infrastructure investments in many countries.[16] SNGs often create special-purpose vehicles (SPVs) to undertake infrastructure and other public investments. Such vehicles can play an important role in developing infrastructure networks that cut across the boundaries of subnational administrations, since the latter may not be compatible with the technological nature of infrastructure networks. In the United States, revenue bonds of SPVs accounted for about two-thirds of about a US$400 billion annual issuance of subnational bonds during 2005–09.[17] In France, *sociétés d'économie mixte locales* (SEMs)—private-public companies with SNGs owing a majority share—are a main instrument for delivering infrastructure such as waste management and water supply across a large number of small municipalities.[18] In Fitch's ratings of 13 French SNGs in 2008, net debt outstanding by SEMs, including guarantees provided by SNGs to SEMs, was close in amount to net debt outstanding directly by SNGs.[19] In China, debt financing through subnational SPVs has been instrumental in unprecedented large-scale urban infrastructure transformation over the past two decades, and the subsovereign debt (SPVs) is reportedly larger than the sovereign debt.[20] Since the late 1990s, SPVs have become important infrastructure-financing vehicles of Indian states and municipalities. SPVs often form partnerships with private financiers and operators. Public-private partnerships experienced a sevenfold increase in developing countries during 2006–08 compared to 1990–92 (Engel 2008).

Notwithstanding the tremendous benefits of SPVs, significant fiscal risks exist. Often SNGs provide explicit or implicit guarantees for market borrowings of SPVs. Countries such as India and Poland have regulations on explicit guarantees.[21] Challenges arise from implicit guarantees, which influence creditors' risk assessment. Moreover, there is a lack of standardized accounting, recording, collecting, and disclosing of such debt incurred by off-budget financing vehicles in many developing countries.[22] These tasks are challenging because of arrays of complex arrangements of SPVs. SPVs may have different quasi-fiscal relations with the budgets of their owners—SNGs. Adding to the complexity is wide varieties of legal contractual relationships in public-private partnerships. There is no standard uniformity in these contractual relationships; they vary across sectors and within sectors.

Second, land financing of infrastructure can also carry fiscal risks (Peterson and Kaganova 2010).[23] SNGs in developed and developing countries have used various instruments (such as land sales, lease auctions, and sale of rights to more intensive land development) to generate revenue from publicly owned land assets. Today, land is often the most important public contribution to public-private joint ventures that build metro (subway) lines, airports, or other large infrastructure projects. Properly managed, the use of land-based revenues for capital finance should reduce overall capital financing risk. Land transactions of this kind complement borrowing by reducing the uncertainty surrounding future debt repayment capacity. Land transactions in the past few years in cities such as Cairo, Cape Town, Istanbul, and Mumbai have generated revenues much greater than the prior annual capital spending of the city. Chinese SNGs have also used land-related instruments in financing large-scale urban infrastructure investments.[24]

There are, however, significant fiscal risks related to the land financing instruments. Unlike the regulations on direct borrowing, there is a general lack of regulatory frameworks for managing fiscal risks from land financing in many developing countries. Revenues from the sale of land assets exert a much more volatile trend and could create an incentive to appropriate auction proceeds for financing operating budgets, particularly at a time of budget shortfalls during economic downturns. Land sales often involve less transparency than borrowing. When sales are conducted off-budget, it is easier to divert proceeds into operating (non-capital) budgets. Transactions by different development agencies and public entities may be ad hoc without a coherent city- and regionwide medium-term capital investment framework. Furthermore, bank loans for financing infrastructure are often backed by land collateral and expected future land-value appreciation. This can lead to excessive borrowing, and the volatility of land and real estate markets can create risk of nonperforming loans, which, in turn, can create contingent liabilities and macroeconomic risks for national governments.

It is critical to develop ex ante prudential rules, comparable to those governing borrowing, to reduce fiscal risks and contingent liabilities associated with land financing of infrastructure. Key guiding principles would include asset sale proceeds that must be used to finance investment, with exceptions given only for key, one-time institutional reforms; collateral-to-loan ratios linked to prudential banking regulations; linking of land financing with medium-term fiscal framework and capital budgeting; all information on public land inventories, public land valuations, land sales, and land contributions to public-private joint ventures or subsidiaries to be conducted through standardized instruments, be reflected in the budget or its annexes and financial statements; and transparent governance structure for land financing transactions.

In addition to the above risks, pension liabilities for subnational civil servants are a challenge for some developing countries. Pension and health care obligations are a serious long-term fiscal challenge for advanced economies, according to Cecchetti, Mohanty, and Zampolli (2010), whose study focused on central government liabilities. Which level of government is responsible for pension liabilities of subnational civil servants depends on the framework for administrative and fiscal decentralization in each country. In a federal system such as Brazil, India, and the United States, states are responsible for the pensions of their civil servants. Health care costs and unfunded pension liabilities are long-term fiscal problems confronting the states and local governments in the

United States. It is also a generic issue for some European Union countries (for example, Germany, Italy, and Spain). Comprehensive data on
subnational pension liabilities are not available for developing countries.
However, available work shows that subnational pension liabilities are a
challenge for many SNGs in, among others, Argentina, Brazil, India, and
Mexico.[25]

Finally, structured financial products contributed significantly to the
global financial crisis and led to large liabilities of national governments. SNGs are not immune to these products. Developing countries
can learn from the lessons of risky structured products used by some
SNGs in developed countries such as France, Italy and the United
States.[26] As SNGs search for innovative financing tools, instruments
such as swaps and other derivative instruments can be tempting. However, they carry significant risks by, for example, swapping long-term
higher fixed interest rates into lower variable rates with counterparty
risk and threshold indexing to variables such as exchange rates that can
be volatile. Public accounting standards have not kept pace in reflecting
developments in these new products, and their costs and risks have not
been fully evaluated.

Developing Competitive Subnational Credit Markets

The global financial crisis has brought home the importance of developing domestic financial markets, including subnational credit markets. A
competitive and diversified subnational credit market can help ensure
the lowest cost and the sustainable availability of credit. Diversified subnational credit markets can also provide more choices of investment
instruments for institutions (such as insurance companies and mutual
funds) and individual investors.

There are two major models of subnational credit markets (Peterson
2002). The first model is bank lending, which financed municipal investment in Western Europe throughout most of the 20th century and is still
the primary source of local credit financing there (Peterson 2002). Over
the past 10 years, SNGs in Europe have been diversifying debt instruments, with bond issuance increasing from less than US$20 billion in
2000 to US$61.8 billion in 2003 to more than US$100 billion in 2009. The
second model is the United States, which has relied on its deep and competitive capital market to finance SNG borrowing. Annual issuances of

SNG bonds have been about US$400 billion in the past 5 years.[27] Individual investors are the largest holders of U.S. subnational bonds, followed by mutual funds, bank trust accounts, banks, insurance companies, and corporations (Maco 2001).

According to Peterson (2002), there is a policy argument for having municipalities borrow at the true market cost of capital. There are also counterarguments in favor of subsidizing loans under some conditions. This issue has been the subject of continuing policy debate. However, it is generally agreed that significant movement toward market pricing of subnational debt would be economically efficient, at least for those SNGs that are creditworthy. This means opening access on equal terms to bank lending and bond issuance, prohibiting monopolies of "municipal banks." As articulated by South African policy makers, "Active capital markets, with a variety of buyers and sellers, and a variety of financial products, can offer more efficiency than direct lending. First, competition for municipal debt instruments tends to keep borrowing costs down and create structural options for every need. Second, an active market implies liquidity for an investor who may wish to sell. Liquidity reduces risk, increases the pool of potential investors, and thus improves efficiency" (South Africa National Treasury 2001:192).[28]

Though bank loans still dominate SNG borrowing in many developing countries, various countries have been moving toward more diversified instruments including bonds, with China leading in this direction. Total SNG bond issuance in developing countries reached US$45.1 billion from 2000 to 2007, and US$102.8 billion from 2008 to 2010, first quarter, with China being the largest and dominant issuer followed by Russia.[29]

Developing competitive subnational capital markets would require securities regulations that in many ways are similar to those for sovereign and corporate bonds. The market infrastructure such as regulations on credit rating agencies, broker-dealers, underwriters, and auditors, is similar across sovereign, subsovereign, and corporate bonds. However, securities laws cannot replace rules for prudent fiscal management of SNGs and for corporate governance of SPVs. What security laws contribute is enforcing disclosure requirements and antifraud practices. Over the long term, the development of subnational credit markets would also benefit from self-regulation and a "buyer beware" approach. Many U.S. regulations were developed by market players themselves; for example, the Government Finance Officers Association in the United States developed many municipal bond disclosure rules and practices that were adopted in the industry.

Finally, competition in and access to financial markets can be a challenge for smaller SNGs or those in less developed regions. For the former, developing models of pooled finance can reduce financing cost, as shown by experiences in Italy and the United States. For the latter, fiscal transfers will continue to play an important role in the basic provision of services.

Conclusions

The financial crisis has had a significant impact on many SNGs, as a result of slowing economic growth, rising cost of borrowing, and deteriorating primary balances. Beyond the crisis, structural trends of decentralization and urbanization are likely to continue with force, requiring massive infrastructure investments. Pressures on subnational finance are likely to continue—from potentially higher cost of capital, the fragility of global recovery, refinancing risks, and sovereign risks.

A range of middle-income countries, and low-income countries in transition to market access, are contemplating expanding subnational borrowing and debt financing. Before doing so, the first priority should be to establish clear fiscal rules for SNGs and to account for and manage fiscal risks coming from off-budget financing vehicles and other hidden liabilities. It would take time to develop effective ex-post insolvency mechanisms, which help anchor the expectation of borrowers and creditors and enforce hard budget constraints.

Subnational credit risks are intertwined with broader macroeconomic and institutional reforms. Macroeconomic stability and sovereign strength cap the credit ratings of SNGs and influence the availability and cost of funds for them. Moreover, the intergovernmental fiscal system underpins the fundamentals of the subnational fiscal structure. Without increased fiscal autonomy and greater own-source revenues, SNGs will rarely be in a position to borrow sustainably on their own. Effective management of subnational default risks goes in tandem with broader development of subnational credit markets for efficient intermediation of savings and investments.

Notes

1. The term *subnational* refers to all tiers of government and public entities below the federal or central government. Subnational entities include states or provinces, counties, cities, towns, public utility companies, school districts, and other special-purpose government entities that have the capacity to incur debt.
2. Data are from government Web sites and World Bank country teams.
3. See Canuto and Liu (2010) for details. For Brazil, the improvement in 2009 was largely the result of a fall in interest payments as a share of GDP (from 1.85 percent in 2008 to 0.47 percent in 2009). This decline is linked to deflation in the General Price Index, which indexes state debts with the federal government.
4. For example, 31 percent of the rated SNGs in Central and Eastern Europe and the Commonwealth of Independent States experienced downward rating actions. By comparison, 6 percent of rated SNGs in the Latin American region had downward rating actions.
5. It is difficult to obtain comprehensive data on the cost and structure of bank loans to SNGs.
6. The source for SNG bonds issued outside the United States is DCM Analytics. Data coverage for bond issuances with a maturity of less than three years is incomplete. Data may not include entities largely or wholly owned by SNGs (such as public utilities) except for China and India. Data for the United States are from Bloomberg. Municipal bonds in the United States include those issued by states, municipalities, districts, and special-purpose vehicles of SNGs. The 200-basis-point increase was from -28 to 170. The yield for 10-year treasury bonds declined by 45 percent while the yield for AAA-rated 10-year municipal general obligation bonds increased by 5 percent from the fourth quarter of 2007 to the fourth quarter of 2008.
7. Data are from government Web sites, Fitch Ratings (2009), NGA/NASBO (2009), and World Bank country teams.
8. With over 200 years of subnational capital market development, the United States implemented a series of legal and institutional reforms. Among them were many states' imposition of constitutional limits on their debt in the 1840s after the states' debt crisis (Wallis 2004), the enactment of Chapter 9 of the Bankruptcy Code during the Great Depression (McConnell and Picker 1993), and an Internet-based disclosure system (Haines 2009). Decentralization in France started in 1982. After episodes of SNG insolvency in the early 1990s, a regulatory system was developed.
9. In the United States, the no-bailout principle was established during the states' defaults in the 1840s (Wallis 2004). In Hungary, a motivation for establishing a bankruptcy framework for subnationals was to impose a hard budget constraint for SNGs and change the perception among lenders that there was an implied sovereign guarantee. In Brazil, after prior bailouts of SNGs, the federal government in 1997 required subnational fiscal adjustment in return for debt relief.

10. Developing countries that have adopted this "golden rule" include Brazil, Colombia, India, Peru, Russia, and South Africa. Short-term borrowing for working capital should be allowed, but with provisions to prevent governments from rollover borrowing as a way of financing operating deficits.

11. In India, fiscal responsibility legislation of many states specifies eliminating revenue deficits and reducing fiscal deficits. In Colombia, SNGs are prohibited from borrowing if the interest-to-operational-savings ratio is greater than 40 percent and the debt-stock-to-current-revenue ratio is greater than 80 percent. In Brazil, the debt restructuring agreements between the federal government and the states in 1997 established a comprehensive list of targets, including debt-to-net-revenue ratio and personnel spending. In the United States, most states each set fiscal limits for themselves and for their local governments. For more see Liu and Waibel (2008).

12. See, for example, Brazil, Colombia, India, and Peru (Liu and Waibel 2008).

13. For a detailed cross-country comparison of subnational insolvency systems, including design and motivation, see Liu and Waibel (2009).

14. In Hungary, the goal of neutralizing political pressure for bailing out insolvent SNGs favored the judicial approach. South Africa's approach is a hybrid, blending administrative intervention with the role of courts in debt restructuring and discharge. In Brazil, the federal government chose an administrative approach in 1997 and imposed a fiscal and debt adjustment package. Resolving the holdout problem during the Great Depression, when municipal defaults were widespread, was the primary motivation for the United States to enact Chapter 9 (McConnell and Picker 1993). No uniform approach exists across states. State consent is a precondition for municipalities of the state to file Chapter 9 in federal court. Many states have their own system for dealing with municipal insolvency.

15. In some instances, the higher level of government has restructured the subnational's debt obligations into longer-term debt instruments. In the case of New York City's insolvency in 1975, the Municipal Assistance Corporation was set up to issue longer-term bonds of the state to repay maturing short-term obligations of the city, conditioned on the city's fiscal and financial management reforms (Bailey 1984). The 1997 debt agreements between the Brazilian federal government and the 25 states focused on debt restructuring and fiscal reforms.

16. Together with the private sector, SNGs are the main investors in infrastructure in an increasing number of middle-income countries such as China, India, and Indonesia (Asian Development Bank 2007). This pattern is similar to that in the countries of the European Union, where SNGs contribute two-thirds of gross national capital formation (Dexia 2006).

17. Data for 2005–08 are from the Federal Reserve Board. The 2009 data are from Thomson Reuters. The share has been more or less the same since the 1970s.

18. More than 20,000 municipalities have fewer than 500 inhabitants, and 32,000 municipalities have less than 2,000 inhabitants (Direction Générale des Collectivités Locales 2010).

19. See Fitch Ratings (February 28, 2008) and fitchratings.com for a compilation of various reports. Reports for 3 cities out of 13 were in 2007.
20. Sovereign debt was about 20 percent of GDP in 2009.
21. The Fiscal Responsibility and Budget Management Acts of many Indian states set limits and rules on issuing guarantees. The Public Finance Law of Poland (2005) stipulates that guarantees by SNGs be counted within the legal limits for debt services whether or not guarantees are called.
22. China has launched reform efforts to collect data on the debt of SPVs (through Urban Development and Investment Corporations).
23. The discussion on land financing is drawn from Peterson and Kaganova (2010).
24. The city cases are from Peterson (2009). As an example, an auction of 13.0 hectares (32.1 acres) of land in Mumbai's new financial center in 2006 and 2007 by the Mumbai Metropolitan Regional Development Authority (MMRDA) generated US$1.2 billion to primarily finance transport projects. The proceeds are 10 times MMRDA's total capital spending in fiscal 2005.
25. Information on the United States is from the U.S. Government Accountability Office (2010) and the Pew Center on the States (2010). Information on selected developing countries is from the World Bank country teams.
26. The Orange County bankruptcy in California in 1994 is the largest filing of Chapter 9 to date, since the Great Depression in the United States. The bankruptcy was caused by derivative instruments in the municipal investment portfolio. Jefferson County in Alabama could become the largest subnational default in U.S. history. To reduce interest rates, the county refinanced its debt using adjustable-rate demand notes. Rising interest rates related to the adjustable-rate demand notes has led to debt distress.
27. The SNG bond issuance data for Europe are from DCM Analytics. The U.S. data before 2009 are from the Federal Reserve Board, and the 2009 data are from Thomson Reuters.
28. In South Africa, private lending to municipalities from 1997 to 2000 was stagnant, and the expansion in municipal debt was driven by growth in public sector lending, particularly by the Development Bank of South Africa. The government was concerned about the lack of private financing and stressed the importance of private investments and a competitive capital market (South Africa National Treasury 2001:192–93).
29. Data are from DCM Analytics.

Bibliography

Asian Development Bank. 2007. *Market Survey of Subnational Finance in Asia and the Pacific*. Manila: Asian Development Bank.

Bailey, R. W. 1984. *The Crisis Regime: The MAC, the EFCB, and the Political Impact of the New York City Financial Crisis*. Albany: State University of New York Press.

Blommestein, H. J. Forthcoming. "Public Debt Management and Sovereign Risk: Crisis Experiences and Lessons from the OECD Area." In *Sovereign Debt and the Financial Crisis*, ed. C. A. Primo Braga and G. A. Vincelette. Washington, DC: World Bank.

Canuto, O., and L. Liu. 2010. "Subnational Debt Finance and the Global Financial Crisis." *Economic Premise* Note 13, May, World Bank, Washington, DC.

Cecchetti, S. G., M. S. Mohanty, and F. Zampolli. 2010. "The Future of Public Debt: Prospects and Implications." Paper for the Reserve Bank of India conference, "Challenges to Central Banking in the Context of Financial Crisis," Mumbai, India, February 12–13.

Dexia. 2006. *Subnational Public Finance in the European Union: Subnational Governments. European Leaders in Public Investment.* Paris: Dexia.

Direction Générale des Collectivités Locales. 2010. *Les Collectivités Locales En Chiffres.* Paris: Direction Générale des Collectivités Locales.

Engel, E. 2008. "Public-Private Partnerships: When and How." Paper with assistance of R. Fischer and A. Galetovic, Yale University, New Haven, CT.

Fitch Ratings. 2009. "European Local and Regional Government Outlook 2010." Fitch Ratings, New York.

———. 2010. "Spanish Autonomous Communities' 2010 Budget: Deficit to Grow Further." Fitch Ratings, New York.

Haines, M. 2009. "Regulation of the Sub-national Securities Market in the USA." Presentation to the International Forum on Subnational Debt Management, Zhuhai, China, September 25.

Ianchovichina, E., L. Liu, and M. Nagarajan. 2007. "Subnational Fiscal Sustainability Analysis: What Can We Learn from Tamil Nadu?" *Economic and Political Weekly* 42 (52): 111–19.

Liu, L. 2008. "Creating a Regulatory Framework for Managing Subnational Borrowing." In *Public Finance in China: Reform and Growth for a Harmonious Society*, ed. J. Lou and S. Wang, 171–90. Washington, DC: World Bank.

Liu, L., and K. S. Tan. 2009. "Subnational Credit Ratings: A Comparative Review." Policy Research Working Paper 5013, World Bank, Washington, DC.

Liu, L., and M. Waibel. 2008. "Subnational Borrowing, Insolvency, and Regulation." In *Macro Federalism and Local Finance*, ed. A. Shah, 215–42. Washington, DC: World Bank.

———. 2009. "Subnational Insolvency and Governance: Cross-Country Experiences and Lessons." In *Does Decentralization Enhance Service Delivery and Poverty Reduction?* ed. E. Ahmad and G. Brosio, 333–76. Cheltenham, U.K.: Edward Elgar.

Maco, P. S. 2001. "Building a Strong Subnational Debt Market: A Regulator's Perspective." *Richmond Journal of Global Law and Business* 2 (1): 1–31.

McConnell, M., and R. Picker. 1993. "When Cities Go Broke: A Conceptual Introduction to Municipal Bankruptcy." *University of Chicago Law Review* 60 (2): 425–35.

Moody's Investor Service. 2010. "Sub-Sovereign Outlook 2010: Challenges Persist and Downward Ratings Actions Expected." Moody's Investor Service, New York.

NGA/NASBO (National Governors Association and National Association of State Budget Officers). 2009. *The Fiscal Survey of States, Fall 2009*. Washington, DC: NGA/NASBO. http://www.nasbo.org/Publications/FiscalSurvey/tabid/65/Default.aspx.

Peterson, G. E. 2003. "Banks or Bonds? Building a Municipal Credit Market." In *Local Government Finance and Bond Markets*, 1–18, ed. Y.-H. Kim. Manila: Asian Development Bank.

———. 2009. *Unlocking Land Values to Finance Urban Infrastructure*. Washington, DC: World Bank and Public-Private Infrastructure Advisory Facility.

Peterson, G. E., and O. Kaganova. 2010. "Integrating Land Financing into Subnational Fiscal Management." Draft paper, Economic Policy and Debt Department, World Bank, Washington, DC.

Pew Center on the States. 2010. *The Trillion Dollar Gap: Unfunded State Retirement Systems and the Roads to Reform*. Washington, DC: Pew Center on the States.

S&P (Standard & Poor's). 2010. "The Outlook for Europe's Local and Regional Governments Is Broadly Stable in 2010, But LRGs in Spain and Russia Face Pressures." S&P, New York.

South Africa National Treasury. 2001. *Intergovernmental Fiscal Review 2001*. Pretoria: Formset Printers Cape.

U.S. Government Accountability Office. 2010. "State and Local Governments Fiscal Outlooks." U.S. Government Accountability Office, Washington, DC.

Wallis, J. J. 2004. "Constitutions, Corporations, and Corruption: American States and Constitutional Changes, 1842–1852." NBER Working Paper 10451, National Bureau of Economic Research, Cambridge, MA.

Weingast, B. 2007. "Second Generation Fiscal Federalism: Implications for Development." Stanford University, Palo Alto, CA.

14

Sovereign Wealth Funds in the Next Decade

Stefano Curto

Data across the globe for the first half of 2010 indicate that the global economic recovery from the 2008–09 financial crisis is under way. However, many analysts anticipate that the recovery will be particularly uneven: strong growth will resume in developing countries, with emerging Asian economies leading the way out of global recession, and developed countries will continue to struggle with a fragile situation and no appetite by the central banks to raise rates in the near future.

Interest rate differentials can be expected only to widen—creating opportunities for arbitrage that produce a resurgence of unsustainable capital flows to developing countries, exacerbate exchange rate pressure and sterilization policies, and intensify global imbalances and reserve accumulations. This macroeconomic and financial landscape is set to create mounting incentives for the central banks of emerging markets to allocate even more foreign reserves into sovereign wealth funds (SWFs) to release the pressure on money supply; reduce the cost of sterilization; and use reserves in excess of prudential levels more productively, away from low-yield, dollar-denominated securities.

Sovereign Wealth Fund Assets and Portfolios

Precrisis estimates of SWF assets ranged from US$13.4 trillion to US$17.5 trillion by 2017.[1] If the foreign assets under SWF management were to be invested under the reasonable assumption of a mix between the portfolio allocations of Singapore and Norway before the crisis,[2] we could expect SWFs to invest about 20 to 30 percent of their assets in developing countries, of which 45 percent would be allocated into equities, 45 percent into bonds, and 10 percent into private equity, real estate, and commodities. At least US$2.7 trillion to US$5.0 trillion of total assets theoretically could be invested in developing countries by 2017 (equally split between equities and bonds). If one excludes the regions where these funds originate (that is, Asia and the Middle East), these assets could represent 8 to 16 percent of the combined gross domestic product (GDP) in developing countries in Latin America, Africa, and Eastern Europe; 1 to 2 percent of their market capitalization of traded companies; and 10 to 19 percent of the total debt securities in these regions.

However, no one knows with certainty the pace of reserves accumulation and the size of SWF increases at the margin. On the one hand, external imbalances are expected (hoped) to somehow diminish in the medium term, because surplus countries may be under pressure to increase internal demand. On the other hand, the crisis and its associated policy response actions to support the global economy might create mounting incentives for central banks to allocate even more foreign reserves into SWFs, and for the SWFs to seek higher yields and diversification.

Quite naturally, where SWFs invest is also going to be governed by a number of considerations. Although developed countries, and the United States in particular, have been the main recipients of SWF investments to date, a shift in attention toward developing-country securities is likely to increase because of the economic prospects of developed countries in the medium and long terms. Despite differences in investment strategies and appetite for risk and liquidity—reflecting different objectives, liabilities structure, and so forth—the desire to diversify their portfolios in the hope of maximizing returns for acceptable levels of risk is a common feature of all SWFs and will support such a shift (albeit gradually). In September 2009, the move by China Investment Corporation (CIC) to take a US$1 billion minority stake in the Hong Kong,

China–based Noble Group, a commodities trading and supply chain manager, was a step in this direction. J.P. Morgan calculates that other deals worth US$50 billion of investments are likely to materialize between the CIC and companies in developing countries.

In addition to maximizing portfolio performance, portfolio allocations may also have strategic considerations, like future access to commodities. Despite its early, visible stakes in Blackstone, Morgan Stanley, and other financial institutions in the United States, the CIC has also focused on other areas—namely, natural resources (Wei 2007). Before the crisis, for instance, East Asia accounted for more than a quarter of global demand for commodities and a significant portion of demand for agricultural commodities (Lyons 2007). Gaining access to strategic commodities and resources will require not only contracts, but also mergers and acquisitions. In this regard, it has been reported that a number of Chinese companies already have been securing strategic assets in energy and raw material supplies in Africa and Latin America, with the backing of China's government; the Industrial and Commercial Bank of China's investment in Standard Chartered was seen by many market analysts as China's strategic entry point into the African continent, using the bank as the principal investment agent.

In addition to US$1.6 billion of acquired assets at the end of 2005, an additional US$2.3 billion has been invested by China National Offshore Oil Corporation in Nigerian oil and gas exploration (Trinh 2006; Broadman 2007). China Development Bank also has launched a US$5.0 billion China-Africa Development Fund to finance the investment of Chinese companies in Africa, following up what was agreed to at the Beijing Summit of the Forum on China-Africa Cooperation. According to China's Xinhua News Agency, Chinese and African companies and governments at that summit signed 14 agreements worth US$1.9 billion for projects in infrastructure, telecommunications, and other fields. A deal to build a US$8.3 billion railway in oil-rich Nigeria was announced, as were joint China-Africa plans to explore energy development (China's Xinhua News Agency). In February 2010, the oil industry in India called for the government to use parts of the US$278 billion in foreign exchange reserves to create an SWF to compete with China in the race to secure global energy assets.

SWFs could, of course, play a role in purchasing government bonds issued by the G-7 countries[3] (projected by the International Monetary Fund to rise from precrisis levels by an average of 40 percent of GDP by 2014). But a gradual shift toward the investments of developing countries may be the most likely outcome. As reserves accumulate, SWF strategy will focus initially on a rebalancing from low-yield assets into high-yield equities. Diversification away from the G-7 is definitely going to be more gradual and incremental. SWFs will avoid a further depreciation of U.S. dollars, and that, in turn, could generate large revaluation losses for the central banks' dollar-denominated assets and a slowdown in the accumulation of future reserves. As long as countries in which SWFs are fed by the accumulation of reserves resist the appreciation of their currencies, a full diversification away from the dollar will be difficult. At the consolidated level (including central bank purchases), there is already some evidence of portfolio rebalancing. The sale of Chinese holdings of U.S. Treasury debt in December 2009—ceding its place as the world's biggest foreign holder of U.S. debt to Japan—provides clues about China's appetite for loaning money to the United States. China pared its Treasury holdings by US$34.0 billion, to US$755.4 billion. Japan's holdings total US$768.8 billion, according to U.S. Treasury estimates.

Opportunities and Challenges for Host Countries

Over the 2010–20 decade, SWFs have the potential to boost global wealth by helping recycle large savings in surplus countries toward more productive investments, particularly in the developing world. Over the medium term, many developing countries will continue to depend on external savings to finance critical investment, since excluding China and major oil exporters, developing countries are (on average) net importers of capital. On the supply side, major fiscal stimulus packages in advanced economies are likely to result in a general re-pricing of sovereign debt risk and the associated cost of borrowing and in more limited access to and a crowding-out of credit for developing-country borrowers, forcing some of them into fiscal austerity if they do not find alternative resources.

In this context, SWFs could bridge the gap between the growing investment needs and the reduced supply of external resources, thereby sustaining growth, accelerating progress toward the Millennium Development Goals, increasing economic integration, and helping build the foundations for a multipolar world. Africa, in particular, may benefit most from SWF resources, given its relatively weak starting point in trade, regional integration, infrastructure, and private sector development. The World Bank's (2010) *Global Economic Prospects 2010* estimates that most of the 53 developing countries that faced an external financing gap in 2009 had current account deficits of 5 percent or more, with private-sourced net-debt inflows financing equivalent to about 2.2 percent of GDP (0.8 percent if Central Asia and Europe are excluded).

Although SWFs could help recycle large savings generated in surplus countries toward the developing world where capital might be socially and economically more productive, several concerns remain, and the memory of the 1980s debt crisis fueled by the recycling of the savings of oil countries is still vivid.

Debt Run-up

The current global savings glut may have similarities with the recycling of the savings of oil countries that fueled the debt crisis in the 1980s. In the 1970s and early 1980s, these windfalls were deposited in banks in the West and were eventually on-lent to developing countries in Latin America and elsewhere. Today, these windfalls may take the form of SWFs directed, for example, to African countries that are becoming increasingly attractive investment destinations, are growing at the fastest rates in the past four decades, are reforming institutions and improving governance, and, most important, have had their government balance sheets virtually wiped free of external debt as a result of the Heavily Indebted Poor Countries and Multilateral Debt Relief initiatives.

Three important factors should be considered.

- First, even though their external debt may have been slashed, many countries are burdened by domestic debt and contingent liabilities related to loss-making state-owned companies or possible banking system problems.
- Second, the institutional capacity of countries to select high-rate-of-return projects is often limited. Besides, the projects have to be

implemented, monitored, and maintained. In other words, the paucity of investment funds may not be the binding constraint to growth and development.

- Third, portfolio shifts by SWFs may put some upward pressure on the prices of riskier asset classes, such as equities, and downward pressure on bonds, thus increasing yield.

Again, the impact on developing countries will not be negligible in terms of the cost of borrowing, for instance, and of inflated equity prices. Warnock and Warnock (2005) underscore that total foreign buying (private and official) of U.S. bonds in the years leading up to 2005 kept the 10-year Treasury yield 150 basis points lower than it would have been without foreign inflows. The same study estimates that without foreign official buying, long-term rates would have been 60 basis points higher. Miles and Jen (2007) estimate that, all other things being equal, the emergence of SWFs could push up "safe" bond yields over the next 10 years by 30 to 40 basis points and could reduce the equity risk premium by 80 to 110 basis points.

Financial Stability

There are also concerns about the impact of SWF investments on the financial stability recipients, particularly those that have more shallow financial markets. Limited information about SWF objectives, strategies, institutional structure, and investment management may reinforce the unfavorable opinions about how SWFs behave.

Procyclicality and Herding. SWFs are believed to be countercyclical in supporting prices and markets, since they have traditionally had buy-and-hold strategies. However, procyclical behavior cannot be excluded. Individual transactions undertaken by an SWF may disrupt more shallow financial markets either because the funds might mirror hedge fund strategies of portfolio rebalancing against possible losses or because perceived shifts or rumors and second-guessing about SWF investment decisions may cause volatility and herding. For example, the sale by Singaporean SWF Temasek Holdings of its shares in two big Chinese banks (Bank of China and China Construction Bank) and in Asia's largest container-shipping group, Cosco, created rumors about the health of the banking sector and the belief that several areas of the Chinese economy had reached their cyclical peak. That occurred despite Temasek's statements that the sale was just "part of our ongoing rebalancing of the portfolio against new opportunities" (Burton 2007).

Short Positions. We also cannot assume that taking short positions in quick win-win situations will not occur in the future, rather than waiting to step in when asset prices fall. For instance, *The Economist* (2008) mentioned that, four years ago, Norway's SWFs began to sell short the bonds of Iceland's banks when a slowdown of the economy was foreseen. Anecdotal evidence suggests that SWFs farm out part of their assets to highly leveraged funds. For instance, a quarter of Singapore's SWF is believed to be channeled and invested through hedge funds that use this strategy. Jen (2008) estimates that SWFs may outplace 20 percent or more of assets with external investors.

Opportunities and Challenges for Home Countries

The idea behind SWFs is quite simple: divert reserves in excess of those needed for short-term current and capital account requirements (Guidotti-Greenspan rule) or for stabilizing exchange rate movements toward long-term diversified portfolios of equities and bonds. In line with long-standing tradition, reserves are invested in safe but low-yield U.S. Treasury bills; when converted into local currency terms, the return could be close to zero or negative because of the depreciation of the dollar. This might be aggravated by sterilization policies intended to maintain price and exchange rate stability.

The Bank for International Settlements has estimated costs of sterilization to be roughly 0.5 to 2.0 percent of GDP for 14 emerging markets. Similarly, Summers (2006) suggests that central bank portfolios have earned around 1 percent real returns annually over the past 60 years compared with about 6 percent for a portfolio diversified in stocks and bonds. With foreign exchange reserves at 50 percent of GDP, in a country like China, a difference of 500 basis points on the returns to reserves amounts to 2.5 percent of GDP a year. This is more risky than investing in U.S. Treasury bills in the short term, but is also likely to yield higher returns over the long haul. However, although the idea is appealing and some benefits are undeniable, the following challenges are worth mentioning.

Net Wealth, Repatriation of Assets, and Dutch Disease

When a substantial amount of the reserve buildup has been the counterpart of the sterilization of central banks, SWF assets can be considered as a purchase with government debt. An analysis conducted by the Bank for International Settlements suggests that, during January 2000 to May 2006, sterilization might have offset as much as 85 to 95 percent of changes in net foreign assets in India; the Republic of Korea; Malaysia; Singapore; and Taiwan, China; and over 70 percent and 60 percent, respectively, in the case of China and the Russian Federation. Therefore, a careful analysis of government whole-balance-sheet effects is necessary to assess real net wealth, which may not be as large as it first appears. The joint balance sheet of government and the central bank actually would worsen with domestic currency appreciation and high domestic interest rates.

A potential currency mismatch is of particular concern for developing countries in light of repatriation of returns on investments, because a country's future needs (SWF liabilities) are denominated in domestic currency while SWF assets are denominated in foreign currencies. Real convergence and catching up in emerging markets inevitably would force domestic currencies to appreciate in real terms relative to those of developed currencies (the Balassa-Samuelson effect), reducing the real (or nominal, or both) value of repatriated funds. In addition, as SWF returns are repatriated, the influx of dollars cannot avoid the need for an adjustment when dollars are spent, putting additional upward pressure on their currencies and undermining the competitiveness of the traded goods sectors. Bourdet and Falck (2006) studied the effect of Cape Verde remittances on the traded goods sector. As local incomes rose with a doubling of remittances from abroad, the Cape Verde real exchange rate appreciated 14 percent during the 1990s. The export sector of the Cape Verde economy suffered a similar fall in productivity during the same period—a fall caused entirely by capital flows. In the long run, it seems that some form of Dutch Disease is unavoidable for oil-exporting countries whose intention in setting up SWFs is to avoid real exchange rate appreciation.

Opportunity Costs

The issue of investable surplus and real net wealth hints to the opportunity costs attached to the alternative uses of SWF assets. Those opportunity costs arise from the fact that in countries with underdeveloped social and economic infrastructure, social and economic return on investment at home may exceed the return on investing foreign reserves abroad, regardless of the nature of that investment and of the intergenerational preference of the government. In 2006, several authors attempted to measure the opportunity cost of reserves accumulations. For instance, Rodrik (2006) shows that there is a "social cost" to reserves accumulation to the extent that the private sector borrows at a higher rate than what the central bank earns on its foreign currency assets. Similarly, Summers (2006) suggests higher costs based on the foregone return on infrastructure projects.

Since 2003, China has used foreign exchange reserves to support domestic policies, including through the recapitalization of the Agricultural Bank of China and the China Development Bank with capital from the CIC. Russia has taken advantage of run-ups in oil prices to pay down its external debt, and some other governments (such as Brazil) have considered the possibility of using a share of their international reserves in a fund geared toward the promotion of industrial policy. The use of foreign exchange reserves for domestic purposes has its merits but can also be problematic for monetary policy. For commodity SWFs, investing foreign reserves domestically is also a fiscal policy issue because foreign currency accrues directly to the government and is not converted into domestic currency unless it is spent by the treasury.

Concluding Remarks

A prolonged and multispeed recovery period, its associated policy response, and the new global financial landscape might have important bearing on the size and allocation of SWF assets. SWFs could become a driving force in South-South flows, boosting global wealth by helping recycle large savings in surplus countries toward more productive investments. While they indeed represent a new opportunity for developing countries, they also carry challenges for both home and host countries.

Notes

1. Projections are by Morgan Stanley, Standard Chartered, and Merrill Lynch. The International Monetary Fund estimated that foreign assets under the management of SWFs could reach US$12 trillion by 2012.

2. Before the crisis, Singapore's Government Investment Corporation operated along lines similar to most private investment management companies, allocating resources across a range of asset classes and regions. The corporation was reported to have around 50 percent in equities; 20 to 30 percent in bonds; and 20 percent in private equity, real estate, and commodities. By region, 45 to 50 percent of assets are reported to be in the United States; 30 percent in Europe; 10 percent in Japan; and 10 percent in Asia, excluding Japan. Similarly, Norway's Government Pension Fund was operating similarly to a pension fund with assets reported to be 50 to 70 percent in fixed-income securities and 30 to 50 percent in equities. Forty to 60 percent of the equity portfolio is invested in currencies and markets in Europe, 25 to 45 percent in the Americas or Africa, and 5 to 25 percent in Asia and Oceania. Where fixed-income securities are concerned, 50 to 70 percent has been invested in currencies and markets in Europe, 25 to 45 percent in the Americas or Africa, and up to 15 percent in Asia and Oceania.

3. Members of the G-7 are the Canada, France, Germany, Italy, Japan, the United Kingdom, and the United States.

References

Bourdet, Y., and H. Falck. 2006. "Emigrants' Remittances and Dutch Disease in Cape Verde." *International Economic Journal* 20 (3): 267–84.

Broadman, H. G. 2007. *Africa's Silk Road: China and India's New Economic Frontier.* Washington, DC: World Bank.

Burton, H. 2007. "Temasek Sale a Fresh Sign of China Doubts." *Financial Times,* November 30.

Economist. 2008. "Asset-Backed Insecurity." January 17.

Jen, S. 2008. "How Much Assets Could SWFs Farm Out?" Briefing Note, Morgan Stanley, New York.

Lyons, G. 2007. "State Capitalism: The Rise of Sovereign Wealth Funds." Standard Chartered Bank, London.

Miles, D. K., and S. Jen. 2007. "Sovereign Wealth Funds and Bond and Equity Prices." Morgan Stanley, *Global Economic Forum,* June 1. http://www.morganstanley.com/views/gef/archive/2007/20070601-Fri.html#anchorf40f6046-419e-11de-a1b3-c771ef8db296.

Rodrik, D. 2006. "The Social Cost of Foreign Exchange Reserves." *International Economic Journal* 20 (3): 253–66.

Summers, L. 2006. "Reflections on Global Account Imbalances and Emerging Market Reserve Accumulation." Speech delivered at the L.K. Jha Memorial Lecture, Reserve Bank of India, Mumbai, March 24.

Trinh, T. 2006. "China's Commodity Hunger: Implications for Africa and Latin America." Deutsche Bank Research, Frankfurt am Main, Germany.

Warnock, F. E., and V. C. Warnock. 2005. "International Capital Flows and U.S. Interest Rates." International Finance Discussion Paper 840, Board of Governors of the Federal Reserve System, Washington, DC.

Wei, T. 2007. "China's CIC Likely to Diversify Away from Further U.S. Banking Sector Investments." *Financial Times*, December 30.

World Bank. 2010. *Global Economic Prospects 2010: Crisis, Finance, and Growth.* Washington, DC: World Bank.

15

Poverty, Equity, and Jobs

Ana Revenga and Jaime Saavedra-Chanduvi

Until the 2008–09 global financial crisis, developing countries were making good progress on reducing poverty. Between 1981 and 2005, the share of the population in the developing countries living below US$1.25 a day was more than halved from 52 percent to 25 percent. This amounted to a decline of about 1 percentage point per year in the aggregate poverty rate, reducing the number of the world's poor from 1.9 billion to around 1.4 billion. At the standard of US$2 per day, which is more appropriate for regions such as Latin America and Eastern Europe, the share of the population classified as poor fell from 70 percent in 1981 to 47 percent in 2005, while the number of people below this line remained unchanged at around 2.5 billion (Chen and Ravallion 2008).

The decline in poverty between 1981 and 2005 varied considerably across regions (figure 15.1). Driven by China, the East Asia and Pacific Region made dramatic progress, with the incidence of US$1.25 a day poverty dropping from 78 percent to 17 percent. In China alone, 400 million people were lifted out of poverty. Trends in East Asia, and in China in particular, explain a large proportion of the reduction in the number of global poor (figure 15.2). At the other extreme, in Sub-Saharan Africa, poverty remained basically stagnant, affecting half of the population. The poverty rate fell in South Asia, Latin America and the Caribbean, and

Figure 15.1 Poverty Rates in the Developing World: People Living on Less than US$1.25 a day

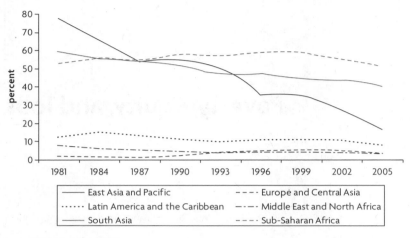

Source: World Bank PovcalNET.

Figure 15.2 Regional Poverty (US$1.25 a day)

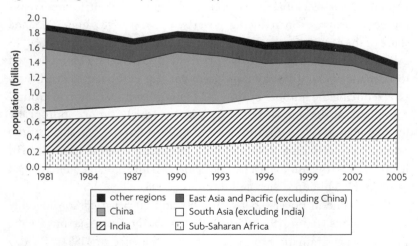

Source: Chen and Ravallion 2008.

the Middle East and North Africa during the same period, although due to population growth, the total number of poor did not decline.

Additional data using national poverty figures up to 2008 or 2009 confirm a pattern of accelerated poverty reduction until the crisis (figure 15.3). In many middle-income countries, particularly in Latin America, East

Figure 15.3 Annualized Poverty Headcount Change (US$2.50 a day) Early 2000s to late 2000s

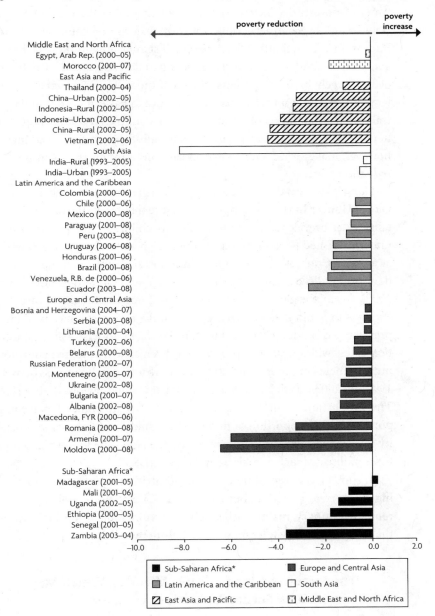

Source: Own calculations based on PovcalNET.

* Poverty line for Sub-Saharan African countries is set at US$2 per day .

Asia, and Eastern-Central Europe, poverty has continued to fall. In Latin America, poverty declined sharply in Brazil, Colombia, Peru, and República Bolivariana de Venezuela, while the vast majority of countries showed improvements. In South Asia, poverty fell significantly in India, Pakistan, and Sri Lanka. Although poverty reduction in East Asia and the Pacific was driven largely by developments in China, Indonesia and Vietnam registered impressive improvements. Performance in Eastern Europe and Central Asia was heterogeneous, but in all cases, countries saw some reduction in poverty. A weak statistical base in many Sub-Saharan African countries, however, makes it difficult to extrapolate more recent trends in poverty reduction there.

Hunger has also diminished, but numbers remain extremely high. The Global Hunger Index—a composite measure that tracks the under-5 mortality rate, prevalence of underweight in children, and proportion of undernourished—has declined by almost 25 percent since 1990. However, at a current rate of 15.2, the index indicates that much still needs to be done to eradicate hunger (Von Braun, Vargas Hill, and Pandya-Lorch 2009). Again, the global picture masks a high degree of regional variation. Progress in South Asia has been good, but the region still has the highest prevalence of underweight children in the world. In East Asia, malnutrition is less widespread, but progress has been slow despite the enormous improvements in poverty. In Sub-Saharan Africa, overall progress between 1992 and 2003 was small compared with that in other regions (figure 15.4). The proportion of undernourished people fell by about 4 percentage points, but the proportion of underweight children and the child mortality rate showed almost no improvement, the latter due to the high prevalence of diseases such as malaria and HIV/AIDS.

In sum, global trends in poverty, malnutrition, and hunger are heading in the right direction, but too large a share of the global population remained hungry, malnourished, poor, or vulnerable to poverty—more than what is socially tolerable—even before the crisis hit.

The Picture on Inequality Is Mixed ... Which May Slow Future Reductions in Poverty

What lies behind the reduction in global poverty? Some factors are common to all countries: macroeconomic stability, better policy and

Figure 15.4 Indicators of Global Hunger

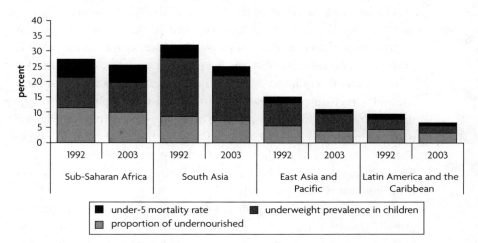

Source: Ahmed, Hill, and Wiesmann 2007.

institutional frameworks in the developing countries, faster global integration, and sustained economic growth. But countries differed broadly
in how growth was distributed and experienced quite different trends in
inequality. The only region in which inequality fell in most countries was
Latin America, albeit from extremely high levels (Gasparini and others
2009; Lopez-Calva and Lustig 2010). In other regions, there was a much
greater mix of rising inequality in some countries (China, India, Vietnam,
several countries of Eastern Europe and Central Asia) and declining
inequality in a few others (Thailand and Sri Lanka).

One interesting, albeit often-used, comparison is that of Brazil and
China, both strong emerging economies with successful poverty reduction records. China, a country that started with low levels of inequality
and relatively similar access to economic opportunities, has achieved
incredible outcomes in terms of poverty reduction—reducing its poverty to about a quarter of its 1990 level in two decades. Part of its success
was due to its relative equality at the start—for example, relatively equal
access to productive inputs (such as land, education, and health), coupled with an initial emphasis on agricultural and rural development,
meant that the poor were able to share more fully the gains of growth
(Ravallion 2009a). But the pattern of growth in China also triggered an

increase of income inequality, with the Gini coefficient rising from 0.29 to 0.42 between the onset of the reforms and 2005. Growth in the primary sector (largely in rural areas) slowed in the late 1980s and was dwarfed by growth in manufacturing and services sectors located mainly in urban and coastal areas. While the growth process was partly market driven, it was also induced by deliberate policies, such as subsidies, credits, and a regulatory framework that favored the development of the urban, large-scale, nonfarm sector. This rising inequality might have a negative impact on growth and poverty reduction in the future—especially if (as seems to be the risk in China) it translates over time into highly unequal access to health and education and, hence, into "structural" inequality of opportunity.

By contrast, falling inequality will tend to enhance the impact of growth. Growth must be pro-poor and, if accompanied by redistributive policies, may be even more successful. In many instances, growth is inevitably uneven, but redistribution might bring balance and allow providing opportunities to all to be part of the growth process. Brazil's experience demonstrates how even in a highly unequal economy the combination of growth plus redistributive policies can help to ensure that growth does lead to a reduction of both poverty and inequality. In an environment of healthy growth, Brazil universalized a minimum pension; expanded its conditional cash transfer (CCT) scheme, *Bolsa Familia*; and increased productive investments at the local level. At the same time, the country began to harvest long-term investments in education. Poverty fell at a rate of 3.2 percent per year between 1981 and 2005 (Ravallion 2009a), and while incomes of the top decile grew at the same rate as average German per capita income, incomes of the bottom decile grew at a pace akin to China's.

Of course, all gains are relative: Brazil's educational levels are still 25 years behind Chile; and despite dramatic improvements, inequality in access to basic services remains among the highest in Latin America. Moreover, Brazil's current level of inequality is still far higher than China's (figure 15.5), and its levels of poverty (relative to its gross domestic product [GDP] per capita) are arguably worse than those in China. Nonetheless, the experience of Brazil illustrates how, with the right policies, high (and entrenched) initial inequality may not pose an insurmountable barrier to poverty reduction. In Brazil, the government successfully seized

Figure 15.5 Inequality in Brazil and China

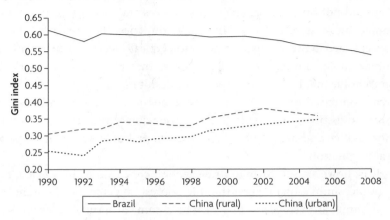

Sources: Instituto de Pesquisa Económica Aplicada (IPEA) and PovcalNET.

opportunities to ensure that growth was pro-poor, and this led to falling inequality in incomes and to reductions in the gaps in access to basic services between the rich and the poor.

Then the Crisis Came, Hitting Not Only the Poor and the Hungry

The 2008–09 global financial crisis has slowed the pace of poverty reduction, but the degree to which the crisis hit the poor remains unclear. Simulations on precrisis data for Bangladesh, Mexico, and the Philippines demonstrate multiple potential channels of impact. In Bangladesh, 50 percent of the average loss in per capita household income associated with the crisis may have happened through a slowdown in the growth of remittances; in Mexico and the Philippines, 90 percent was attributable to a fall in labor income. In many developing countries, this decline in earnings from labor reflects less a rise in unemployment and more a shift from higher-paying to lower-paying jobs and a reduction in the number of hours worked (Khanna, Newhouse, and Paci 2010).

Relative to other crises, there is some evidence to suggest that the chronic poor will be less affected by the current crisis than the working poor and middle classes, for several reasons. Unlike previous crises, this crisis did not originate in macro imbalances and has not been accompanied by massive inflation. In many countries, its impact has been concentrated in the manufacturing sector, typically located in urban areas. For example, simulation models suggest that 60 percent of Turkish households that have become poor as a result of the crisis live in urban areas compared to 30 percent of the general population. On average, households that are likely to become poor due to the crisis tend to be more skilled and urban than the chronic poor, but less so than the general population.

It is, however, too early to draw general conclusions. In Mexico, for example, simulations suggest that the poorest 20 percent of households could suffer an average loss in per capita income of about 8 percent compared to 5 percent for the entire population, even after existing safety net transfers are taken into account. And preliminary evidence suggests a significant impact of the crisis on the rate of poverty reduction and the number of the poor in many countries. A lower rate of poverty reduction as a result of the crisis has been estimated to translate into an estimated 1.4 million and 2.0 million additional poor people in the Philippines and Bangladesh, respectively, in 2010, relative to a precrisis growth scenario (Habib and others 2010a). In Mexico and in Turkey (Hentschel and Aran 2009), where the crisis has had a stronger impact, the poverty rate is projected to rise by nearly 4 percentage points and 4.5 percentage points, respectively, between 2008 and 2010. In Latvia, simulations suggest that the crisis may have induced a sharp rise (6 percentage points) in poverty rates to 20 percent, along with an increase in the depth of poverty and income inequality (Ajwad, Haimovich, and Azam, forthcoming). And in addition to its impact on income poverty, the crisis may also slow progress in human development, due to the combination of falling incomes, lower capacity for human capital accumulation, and limited coping mechanisms.

Beyond poverty reduction, the relatively good performance on hunger reduction in previous decades might have been thwarted by the double jeopardy of the food and financial crises. The Food and Agriculture Organization (FAO) estimates that in 2007 there were 923 million undernourished people; Tiwari and Hassan (2010) estimate that the incidence of undernourishment could have increased by 63 million in 2008 due to the global food price spike. And some 40 million more people went hungry in 2009 than would have been the case had the economic crisis not taken place. The bottom line is that despite improvements, food security and nutrition are still key issues on the development agenda. The reality of almost a billion people experiencing hunger globally while others enjoy unprecedented wealth is a vivid illustration of high global- and country-level inequality and of deeply entrenched differences in people's opportunities to participate in global growth.

By the end of 2010, an estimated additional 64 million more people are expected to be living in extreme poverty than would have been the case before the crisis. Nonetheless, the developing world as a whole appears to be on track to attain the income poverty target of Millennium Development Goal 1. According to a 2010 baseline forecast by the World Bank, global extreme poverty is likely to drop to about 920 million (15 percent) by 2015. In a low-growth scenario, it is estimated to drop to about 1.13 billion (18.5 percent). These projections are lower than the precrisis, high-growth trend forecast of 865 million (14 percent), but nevertheless come in below the Millennium Development Goal target rate of 21 percent. This positive forecast has been initially reinforced by early postcrisis data for the largest developing economies—China, Brazil, and India—and other middle-income countries in Latin America and Asia, which show very quick economic recoveries by 2010. However, nothing is certain; continuing a path of poverty reduction requires sustained growth, and current developments do not yet assure sustained global growth in the coming years.

Increasing Welfare for All Will Not Be Possible if Inequality of Opportunities Persists

Postcrisis macro stability and a continuation of reforms are needed to sustain growth. Growth patterns will differ across and within countries and will likely be sectorally uneven. Export development zones, shifts from agriculture to other sectors, and high-tech services growth make some sectors grow faster than others, and that is, in most cases, economically efficient. As such, the spatial map of economic opportunities can be very bumpy (World Bank 2009) across and within countries. But the map of human opportunities should not be uneven.

All individuals should have equal opportunity to expand their individual capabilities, shape their futures, and pursue a life path of their choosing. Universal access to key goods and services such as clean water, minimum nutrition, basic education, basic health services—at acceptable quality standards—and citizenship are critical steps toward a world of justice, fairness, and equal opportunity—goals that few societies would disagree with. But all over the world, and particularly in the developing world, access to key goods and services is far from universal. Moreover, the ability to access key goods and services is correlated with circumstances that are beyond the control of individuals, such as gender, parental background, race, or ethnicity. For example, in Chile, a poor child is half as likely to finish sixth grade on time as a well-off child, and in Brazil, a poor child is only one-tenth as likely to do so (figure 15.6).

An equitable development process should seek to ensure that opportunities are allocated equally and are not detrimental to any particular social group. The ultimate goal should be universality. If universal access to basic goods and services is to be considered a major development goal, then it is critical to measure progress toward its accomplishment. The Human Opportunity Index (HOI), presented by Barros and others (2009) and Molinas and others (2010), considers two aspects of opportunity: first, how far a country is from the goal of providing universal access to a set of key goods and services to all (specifically, access to basic education, clean water, sanitation, and electricity); and second, the degree to which each child has an opportunity to access those goods and services, irrespective of circumstances: gender, parental education and income, area of residence, and family structure. It shows that in Latin America, beyond the huge inequalities in income and living standards, there are also huge inequalities in opportunities. Access to services is limited to a fraction of the population, and variables such as gender, family background, and area of residence matter in explaining that access. The HOI, which ranges from 0 to 1, varies from 0.95 in relatively opportunity-egalitarian Chile to around 0.55 in Guatemala, Honduras, and Nicaragua. But it also shows progress, with very fast increases in Brazil, Ecuador, Peru, and Mexico.

Still, at the current pace of growth, on average it will take about a generation to universalize access to those key goods and services. The analysis

Figure 15.6 Differential Probability of Completing Sixth Grade on Time, Circa 2005

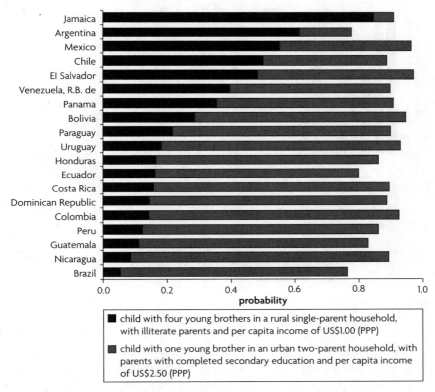

child with four young brothers in a rural single-parent household, with illiterate parents and per capita income of US$1.00 (PPP)

child with one young brother in an urban two-parent household, with parents with completed secondary education and per capita income of US$2.50 (PPP)

Source: Barros and others 2009.

of specific services, such as access to sanitation, reveals even starker inequality and large differences across countries and regions (figure 15.7). In one region alone—Latin America and the Caribbean—the HOI for access to sanitation varies from 0.93 in Costa Rica to 0.11 in Nicaragua, and differences across countries in the world are extremely high.

How Can Societies Improve Both Opportunities and Outcomes?

Development requires growth to be an instrument to reduce poverty and improve welfare for all. It follows that in addition to sustaining of the recovery of growth, a key element of the postcrisis agenda is to provide

Figure 15.7 Human Opportunity Index for Access to Sanitation

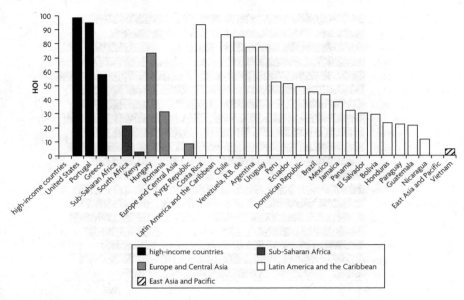

Source: Molinas and others 2010.

opportunities widely to ensure growth is inclusive. Opportunities must be provided to both young and adult workers (both male and female, skilled and unskilled workers) through the labor market since labor is the main source of income for most people; to those who need access to efficient factor markets to undertake productive investments; and to children so that the playing field is leveled from birth. Multiple factors underpin a process of inclusive growth, but history and empirical evidence suggest three aspects are critical[1]:

- Ensuring of equality of opportunity in access to key basic goods and services (most notably education, health, basic water and sanitation, basic infrastructure)
- Pattern of growth that translates into "good" income-earning opportunities, which means primarily good employment opportunities
- Effective protection against shocks.

The state has a role to play in ensuring that these three factors materialize.

Resources and Policies to Enable Opportunities. The creation of opportunities for all is no mean feat. Implicit in the task is providing everyone with the potential to accumulate assets, which in turn requires sufficient human capital (through the provision of health, education, and basic services), to enable engagement in high-productivity activities. It often requires an investment in infrastructure to connect people to markets and an expansion of social safety nets to protect the vulnerable and promote risk-taking (see below). All this, in turn, demands fiscal space and a structure of taxes and transfers that can allow for the required investments, while remaining consistent with long-term growth objectives. And in the final analysis, the creation of equality of opportunity also requires political and social commitments to redistribution.

In both Latin America and South Asia, tax-to-GDP ratios are low compared to other developing countries with similar income levels. Excluding Brazil, which has a tax pressure above 35 percent, the average rate in Latin America is around 15 percent. The tax pressure in South Asia varies from 8 to 12 percent of GDP in countries other than India, where it reaches 19 percent.

So in many countries, increasing the fiscal space to facilitate redistribution is a critical challenge. And in many of these countries, the prominence of the informal economy represents a major obstacle to domestic resource mobilization. But the challenge is not just one of expanding fiscal space. Above all, each society must arrive at its own dynamic social contract, determining which goods and services should be provided to all and how public resources will be used in order to redistribute them to improve the allocation of opportunities. The redistributive patterns observed in developing economies do not point toward a state that is doing enough. Figure 15.8 shows the structure of social spending and taxes by quintile in Mexico and the United Kingdom, suggesting a pattern of redistribution toward the poor, in the form of access to education, health, assistance, and social protection much better targeted in the United Kingdom.

But it is not only a matter of resources or a matter of willingness to redistribute resources to provide opportunities for all. In many cases, better knowledge about which policies work is limited. Evidence suggests that technology enables individuals to connect to markets, that some nutritional interventions can prevent undernourishment, and that

Figure 15.8 Social Spending and Taxes by Quintile as a Percentage of GDP Per Capita

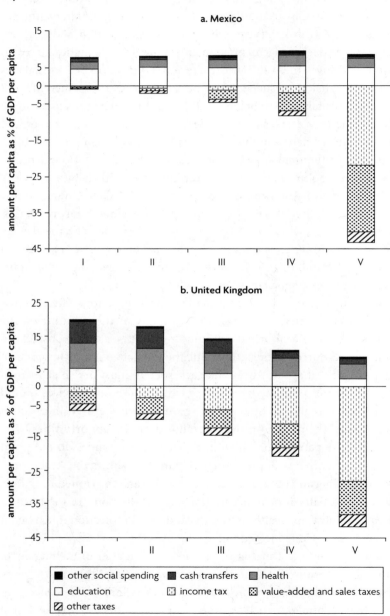

Sources: Breceda, Rigolini, and Saavedra 2009.

CCTs can have a net positive effect on human capital accumulation. But our knowledge of the effectiveness of a number of interventions remains much more limited. Therefore, a crucial step in advancing equality of opportunities is advancing a research agenda to understand which policies work and to expand the implementation of policies whose design is firmly based on evidence.

Promoting the Growth of "Good" Jobs. Labor income is the dominant source of income for households everywhere, but labor markets are even more essential in developing countries with widespread poverty. Because poor households have few other assets to rely on but their labor, employment opportunities will be their only route out of poverty. When one looks at employment in developing countries, it is critical to look not only at employment, but also at the characteristics of that employment—specifically, labor productivity and earnings. In the poorest developing countries, poverty rates tend to be higher for the employed because labor markets are dominated by low-earning, low-productivity jobs. Unemployment tends to be a luxury that only the well-off can afford.

Growth can increase either the number of jobs (higher employment elasticity) or labor productivity (higher output per hour worked or per worker). In recent years, countries with higher growth rates have not always seen higher job creation than others. Nor has the capacity of economic growth to generate employment increased over time (Johansson and Paci 2010). For example, Albania, Bangladesh, and Rwanda (in the 2000s) and Vietnam (in the 1990s) all witnessed comparatively jobless growth, as employment rates fell or stagnated. However, per capita GDP grew significantly and the poverty headcount index fell in each of these countries due in part to an increase in labor productivity. In contrast, employment rates increased in Madagascar and Nicaragua while the poverty headcount index stagnated in the former and increased in the latter (table 15.1). So what matters for poverty reduction is not the number of jobs generated by growth but the productivity of that employment.

Employment in low-income economies is dominated by low-productivity primary sector activities, mainly in agriculture. Outside of agriculture, employment tends to be informal and characterized by unregulated working arrangements and limited access to formal credit or programs, which may limit the scope for productivity growth. Partly

Table 15.1 GDP Growth, Employment Growth, and Poverty Reduction

Country	% change per year		Employment elasticity	% change in poverty headcount index per year			Poverty elasticity	Period
				International				
	GDP	Employment		$1.15/day	$2.00/ day	National		
Albania	3.1	1.8	0.6	n.a.	n.a.	−10.1	−3.3	2002–05
Vietnam	8.3	2.6	0.3	n.a.	n.a.	−8.4	−1.0	1993–98
Pakistan	4.7	3.6	0.8	−9.0	−4.0	n.a.	−0.9	1999–2005
Bangladesh	5.1	2.1	0.4	n.a.	n.a.	−3.5	−0.7	2000–05
Sri Lanka	4.0	2.3	0.6	−2.6	−2.6	n.a.	−0.7	1996–2002
Nepal	4.0	2.6	0.7	−2.7	−1.6	n.a.	−0.4	1996–2004
Rwanda	6.3	2.5	0.4	n.a.	n.a.	−1.0	−0.2	2000–06
India	6.5	1.8	0.3	−1.5	−0.7	n.a.	−0.1	1994–2005
Madagascar	1.3	2.8	2.2	n.a.	n.a.	−0.5	−0.4	2001–05
Nicaragua	3.4	3.9	1.1	n.a.	n.a.	0.0	0.1	2001–05

Source: Johansson and Paci 2010.
Notes: n.a. = not applicable.

as a result, workers in the informal sector are typically more vulnerable than those in formal employment, are more exposed to variability in their earnings, and are more constrained by their initial endowments. The job creation challenge for most countries is addressing the constraints to productivity growth in both formal and informal employment.

Evidence from the more successful emerging economies suggests that the key to creating better-quality jobs is embarking on a pattern of growth that is consistent with comparative advantage and that facilitates the shift of workers from lower-productivity to higher-productivity activities. Some of this may take the form of intersectoral shifts, for example, from agriculture to manufacturing or services. But it will in part also come from within-sector flows of resources from lower-productivity firms and enterprises to higher-productivity ones. In low-income countries and regions, most notably in Africa, there are three challenges: to raise productivity in activities that will continue to engage large fractions of the workforce for a long time, namely agriculture; to foster the creation of nonagricultural wage jobs on a massive scale, possibly by relying on labor-intensive exports; and to avoid falling into (fiscal) quick wins from mineral and extractive natural resources without paving the way for longer-term job creation.

Meeting this job creation challenge will require action on both the labor demand and the labor supply sides. On the demand side, macro stability and a stable investment climate are key, along with reforms to enhance the competitiveness of product and factor markets and to support infrastructure. On the supply side, ensuring that the workforce has appropriate skills is often the principal challenge, but efforts to address social norms that act as labor market barriers (such as discrimination by gender or ethnicity) can also prove crucial.

Expanding Protection. The food and financial crises highlight the fragility of progress in the fight against global poverty. Moreover, the experience of previous crises shows that even temporary deterioration in incomes and the quantity and the quality of employment can leave lasting scars on human capital accumulation and future labor productivity. These scars are often particularly damaging to the poor. Within this context, safety nets can play three broad roles. First, they can redistribute income to the poorest and most vulnerable. Second, they can enable households to make better investments in education and health. Third, they can help manage risk so that the poor have an element of insurance against sudden shocks.

The most effective safety nets should be flexible enough to be scaled up quickly in times of need and phased out when the crisis passes. They cannot be built overnight: setting up a sound safety net program from scratch usually requires at least four to six months, with a longer period for refinement. Although they do not necessarily require large amounts of resources, effective safety nets require administrative systems for enrolling beneficiaries, making payments, and monitoring. Because of this, the immediate response to a crisis will often be constrained by what is already in place, while any additional safety nets will have to be implemented in phases.

A key question for safety nets in the midst of a crisis is whom to target. In a crisis, poor households usually become poorer while previously nonpoor households can slip into poverty, for example, through loss of employment, sharp drops in real wages, or declines in remittances. Catering to the newly poor in the midst of a crisis is not always easy; for instance, access to formal unemployment benefits involves administrative costs to confirm eligibility before transfers can start. On the other hand, self-selection into public works programs can ensure that newly poor households receive rapid assistance (provided institutional capacity to launch large-scale programs exists), as in the Republic of Korea following the 1998 economic crisis. The technical difficulties with targeting are typically compounded by political economy issues in the midst of a crisis that often result in pressures to protect broader, and politically vocal, sections of the population.

Within the range of possible safety net responses, some programs offer distinct advantages over others. Targeted cash transfers of adequate coverage, generosity, and quality are in general the best option. Targeted cash transfers are preferable to in-kind programs because they allow consumer sovereignty, usually have lower administrative costs, and are more amenable to payment systems that may guard against diversion of benefits. Some countries, however, may prefer near-cash instruments for political reasons; food stamps, for example, have been used successfully in a number of countries. In cases of high inflation, or where markets are functioning poorly, or where strategic grain reserves need to be rotated, in-kind food distribution may be appropriate. For instance, with inflation eroding the value of the cash component of the largest safety net program in Ethiopia in 2008–09, participants have requested in-kind transfers. In-kind transfers may also fulfill nutritional objectives more effectively if the food grains provided are fortified with essential micronutrients.

An obvious but important insight into safety nets is that they must be designed to best meet the chosen objective. For instance, CCTs have a proven track record of reducing poverty and contributing to human development outcomes (Fiszbein and Schady 2009) and can be scaled up in response to crises (as has happened in many Latin American countries following both the food and the financial crises). But since a key to successful CCTs is careful targeting, rapid expansion to newly poor households in the wake of a crisis is infeasible. By contrast, public works programs can effectively absorb those affected by a crisis that generates unemployment, but are not ideal responses to crises that trigger a decline in real wages without much change in levels of employment.

A general rule is that luck favors the prepared: it is much easier to adapt and expand an existing sound policy framework than to establish it from scratch in times of emergency. Having safety net systems in place, and working on their design and implementation in good times, is key to maintaining the asset accumulation process, particularly of the poor.

Concluding Remarks

Poverty reduction, elimination of hunger, and equality of opportunity are essential elements of development. Growth is essential for these development objectives to be attained. The postcrisis agenda requires setting the conditions for sustained growth through deeper integration into global markets and reducing factor market inefficiencies. But it also requires setting the conditions for this growth to be translated into jobs that are accessible to the poor and jobs that have increasing levels of productivity to help people move sustainably out of poverty. Growth at the same time will provide the fiscal space needed to improve equality of opportunities and give all people a chance. For growth to translate into opportunities for all, a redistributive process is critical. It entails building a social contract that is perceived by most as sufficiently fair and worth committing to both financially and politically. Equity is an essential ingredient of development, together with growth. And to make progress in the equity agenda, it is likely that the reliance on the state to foster and guide that process will have to be higher.

Note

1. These three critical pillars were already at the core of the strategy for sustained poverty reduction and inclusive growth identified in the *World Development Report 1990* on poverty (World Bank 1990) and were reinforced by the *World Development Report 2000/2001* (World Bank 2001) on poverty 10 years later.

Bibliography

Acevedo, J. P., E. Molina, J. Newman, E. Rubiano, and J. Saavedra. 2009. "How Has Poverty Evolved in Latin America and How Is It Likely to Be Affected by the Economic Crisis?" Poverty Reduction and Gender Group Latin America, World Bank, Washington, DC.

Ahmed, A., R. V. Hill, and D. Wiesmann. 2007. "The Poorest and the Hungry, Looking beyond the Poverty Line." International Food Policy Research Institute, Washington, DC.

Ajwad, M. I., F. Haimovich, and M. Azam. Forthcoming. "The Employment and Welfare Impact of the Financial Crisis in Latvia." Washington, DC: World Bank.

Barros, R. P., F. Ferreira, J. R. Molinas, and J. Saavedra. 2009. *Measuring Inequality of Opportunities in Latin America and the Caribbean*. Washington, DC: World Bank.

Breceda, K., J. Rigolini, and J. Saavedra. 2009. "Latin America and the Social Contract: Patterns of Social Spending and Taxation." *Population and Development Review* 35 (4): 721–48.

Chen, S., and M. Ravallion. 2008. "The Developing World Is Poorer than We Thought, but No Less Successful in the Fight against Poverty." Policy Research Working Paper 4703, World Bank, Washington, DC.

Fiszbein, A., and N. Schady. 2009. *Conditional Cash Transfers: Reducing Present and Future Poverty*. Washington, DC: World Bank.

Gasparini, L., G. Cruces, L. Tornarolli, and M. Marchionni. 2009. "A Turning Point? Recent Developments on Inequality in Latin America and the Caribbean." Working Paper 81, Centro de Estudios Distributivos, Laborales y Sociales (CEDLAS), Universidad Nacional de la Plata, Argentina.

Habib, B., A. Narayan, S. Olivieri, and C. Sanchez-Paramo. 2010a. "Assessing ex ante the Poverty and Distributional Impact of the Global Crisis in a Developing Country: A Micro-Simulation Approach with Application to Bangladesh." Policy Research Working Paper 5238, World Bank, Washington, DC.

———. 2010b. "Assessing ex ante the Poverty and Distributional Impact of the Global Crisis in the Philippines: A Micro-Simulation Approach." Policy Research Working Paper 5286, World Bank, Washington, DC.

Hentschel, J., and M. Aran. 2009. "A Methodology Note on Assessing Employment and Poverty Implications of a Possible Growth Slowdown in Turkey." World Bank, Washington, DC.

Johansson, S., and P. Paci. 2010. "Beyond Job Creation: Revisiting the Employment Agenda in Developing Countries." Unpublished document.

Khanna G., D. Newhouse, and P. Paci. 2010. Forthcoming. "Fewer Jobs or Smaller Paychecks? Labor Market Impacts of the Financial Crisis in Middle-Income Countries." In *The 2007–09 Financial Crisis: Labor Market Impacts and Policy Responses*, ed. D. Newhouse, P. Paci, and D. Robalino. Washington, DC: World Bank.

Lopez-Calva, L., and N. Lustig. 2010. *Declining Inequality in Latin America: A Decade of Progress?* Washington, DC: Brookings Institution Press.

Molinas, J. R., R. P. Barros, J. Saavedra, and M. Giugale. 2010. *Do Our Children Have a Chance? The 2010 Human Opportunity Report for Latin America and the Caribbean*. Washington, DC: World Bank.

Ravallion, M. 2009a. "A Comparative Perspective on Poverty Reduction in Brazil, China, and India." Policy Research Working Paper 5080, World Bank, Washington, DC.

————. 2009b. "Why Don't We See Poverty Convergence?" Policy Research Working Paper 4974, World Bank, Washington, DC.

Tiwari, S., and Z. Hassan. 2010. "The Impact of Economic Shocks on Global Undernourishment." Policy Research Working Paper 5215, World Bank, Washington, DC.

Von Braun, J., R. Vargas Hill, and R. Pandya-Lorch, eds. 2009. *The Poorest and Hungry: Assessment, Analyses, and Actions.* Washington, DC: International Food Policy Research Institute.

World Bank. 1990. *World Development Report 1990.* Washington, DC: World Bank.

————. 2001. *World Development Report 2000/2001.* Washington, DC: World Bank.

————. 2009. *World Development Report: Reshaping Economic Geography.* Washington, DC: World Bank.

16

Investing in Gender Equality: Looking Ahead

Mayra Buvinic, Trine Lunde, and
Nistha Sinha

The realities of the world after the 2008–09 global financial crisis call for greater attention to gender, both to address the vulnerability of countries to global shocks and to reach growth and poverty reduction goals. Investments in girls and women need to be scaled up substantially in response to the recent crisis and, looking ahead, to alleviate demographic stresses and harness demographic opportunities for growth. This is because the fate of women and girls, especially in low-income countries and low-income households, is closely linked to the economic prospects of these countries and these households.

The Business Case for Gender Equality

Gender equality, embedded in the behavior of the family, the market, and society, affects prospects for poverty reduction and growth by stimulating productivity and earnings and improving child development outcomes (figure 16.1). In particular, the added advantage of increased

The authors are grateful to Ursula Casabonne for undertaking the analysis of demographic trends presented in this chapter.

Figure 16.1 Women's Earnings, Children's Well-being, and Aggregate Poverty Reduction and Economic Growth—the Gender Pathways

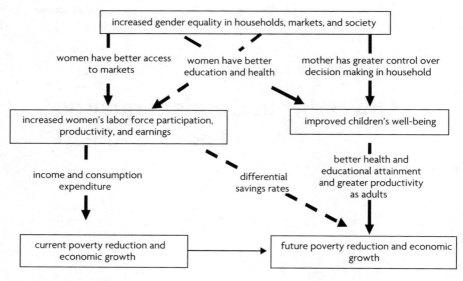

Source: World Bank 2007a.

gender equality in the intergenerational transmission of wealth, through its effect on child well-being (the pathway depicted on the right in figure 16.1), is a potentially significant policy lever to minimize the long-term negative consequences of the crisis on human development.

Impact of Food, Fuel, and Financial Crises

The impacts of the food, fuel, and financial crises at the end of the 1990s have highlighted the vulnerability of developing countries to global shocks and their gender dimensions—the latter especially in relationship to the labor market, agricultural production, and human development outcomes.

In the *labor market*, where women's participation is below that of men in virtually all developing countries and is concentrated in specific sectors, economywide shocks affect their labor force participation in specific ways. Evidence shows that during crises, particularly in vulnerable households where the main wage earner has lost a job or faces reduced earnings, women will look for work to maintain household consumption (Sabarwal, Sinha, and Buvinic 2009). At the same time, lower aggregate demand also affects jobs and earnings of self-employed women in the informal sector. And employment losses in export sectors directly affected by lagging global demand can especially hurt women, who often make up a large proportion of the workforce in export manufacturing (as in Bangladesh, Cambodia, Nicaragua, and the Philippines) and high-value agricultural exports (as in Ecuador, Thailand, and Uganda).

The food and fuel crises and the opportunities brought about by the growing markets for tropical high-value produce have encouraged renewed attention to *agriculture, food security, and rural development* and to the role of female farmers. In many low-income countries, particularly in Sub-Saharan Africa, agriculture is the most important sector as a share of gross domestic product (GDP) and employment, elevating the importance of broad-based growth in agricultural incomes for stimulating economic growth. In many of these countries, women make up 60 to 80 percent of the workforce in agriculture and have a large role in food production. Yet, they continue to have less access to land, fertilizers, seeds, credit, and extension services than do men. Furthermore, women's access to output markets and profitable cash crops and their control over household resources tend to be constrained, affecting productivity and efficiency in the agricultural sector (World Bank 2007b). More equitable access for women to economic opportunities and resources would make agriculture a more efficient vehicle for promoting shared economic growth, reducing poverty, and improving food security.

Crises also affect *human development* outcomes, especially the survival of infant girls. Friedman and Schady (2009) estimate that the growth slowdown in 2009 will result in 28,000 to 49,000 excess deaths in Sub-Saharan Africa, most of them infant girls. An analysis of 59 low-income countries estimates that a 1 percent drop in per capita GDP raises infant mortality by 0.27 deaths per 1,000 births for boys, but double that (0.53) for girls (Baird, Friedman, and Schady 2007). An analysis by Buvinic (2009) of the progress of countries toward the Millennium Development Goals suggests that girls in poor households in countries with high child mortality rates or low female schooling rates are especially vulnerable to the effects of the global economic and food crises.

Figure 16.2 Impact of the Crises: Countries' Progress toward the Millennium Development Goals

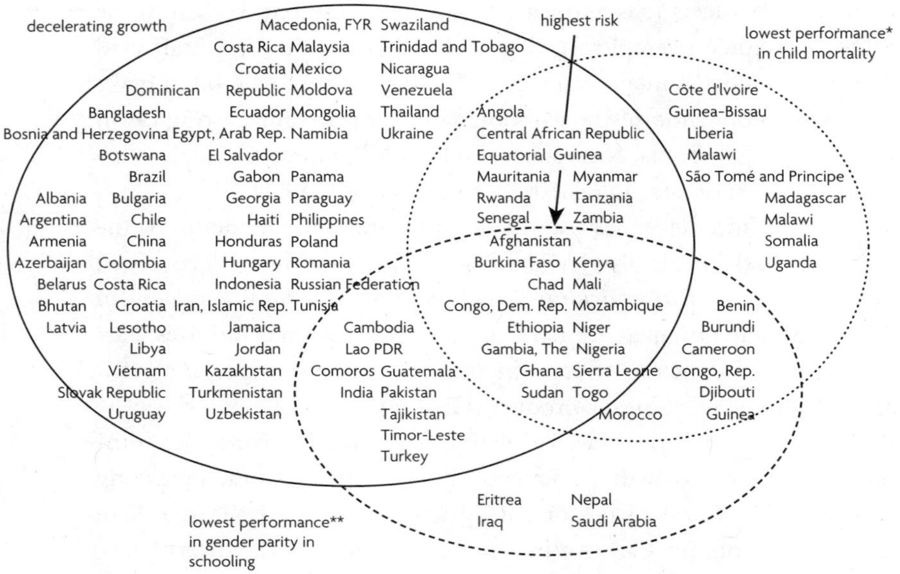

decelerating growth

Macedonia, FYR Swaziland
Costa Rica Malaysia Trinidad and Tobago
Croatia Mexico Nicaragua

highest risk

lowest performance*
in child mortality

Dominican Republic Moldova Venezuela
Bangladesh Ecuador Mongolia Thailand Angola
Bosnia and Herzegovina Egypt, Arab Rep. Namibia Ukraine Central African Republic

Côte d'Ivoire
Guinea-Bissau
Liberia

Botswana El Salvador Equatorial Guinea Malawi
Brazil Gabon Panama Mauritania Myanmar São Tomé and Principe
Albania Bulgaria Georgia Paraguay Rwanda Tanzania Madagascar
Argentina Chile Haiti Philippines Senegal Zambia Malawi
Armenia China Honduras Poland Afghanistan Somalia
Azerbaijan Colombia Hungary Romania Burkina Faso Kenya Uganda
Belarus Costa Rica Indonesia Russian Federation Chad Mali
Bhutan Croatia Iran, Islamic Rep. Tunisia Congo, Dem. Rep. Mozambique Benin
Latvia Lesotho Jamaica Cambodia Ethiopia Niger Burundi
Libya Jordan Lao PDR Gambia, The Nigeria Cameroon
Vietnam Kazakhstan Comoros Guatemala Ghana Sierra Leone Congo, Rep.
Slovak Republic Turkmenistan India Pakistan Sudan Togo Djibouti
Uruguay Uzbekistan Tajikistan Morocco Guinea
Timor-Leste
Turkey

Eritrea Nepal
Iraq Saudi Arabia

lowest performance**
in gender parity in
schooling

Sources: For decelerating growth: growth estimates based on the International Monetary Fund World Economic Outlook database 2009 projections and on World Bank staff estimates and data from the World Development Indicators database 2009; for child mortality rates and schooling, WDI 2009.

Note: Countries with high infant mortality rates are those in the highest quartile of the distribution of under-5 mortality rates (per 1,000 live births) for 151 developing countries in 2007. Countries with low female schooling rates are those in the lowest quartile of the distribution of the ratio of girls to boys in primary and secondary enrollment for 131 developing countries for the latest available data between 2004 and 2007.

* Lowest performance in child mortality measured by dividing 151 developing countries in quartiles based on under-5 mortality rate (per 1,000) in 2007.

** Lowest performance in gender parity in schooling measured by dividing 131 developing countries in quartiles based on ratio of girls to boys in primary and secondary enrollment (percent) for the latest year between 2004 and 2007.

Their situation is most precarious in the 15 countries, mainly in Africa, that are affected by high child mortality rates, low female schooling rates, and decelerating growth (figure 16.2).[1]

Crisis Priorities

If left unaddressed, these gender-specific consequences of crises will contribute to current poverty and imperil future development. Fortunately, policy responses (summarized in table 16.1), which build on the role of women as economic agents and their preference for investing

Table 16.1 Priorities for Crisis-Response Activities

Impact area of crisis	Key issues	Priority investments
Labor markets	• Women in the informal sector, particularly the self-employed, lose jobs or face a decline in earnings. • Men lose jobs or their earnings fall; women not previously in the labor force search for jobs to maintain household consumption. • Sectors that are large employers of women, such as export manufacturing, lay off workers or reduce salaries.	• Public works programs are designed to reach women seeking jobs (offering appropriate work and facilities such as child care). • Cash transfer programs and other safety nets maximize impact of cash transfer programs by channeling resources through mothers. • Access to credit and savings for women.
Human development outcomes	• Families cut back on food consumed by mothers and children; likely increase in infant mortality. • Child labor increases. • Investments in children's (male and female) education fall.	• Nutritional supplementation and feeding programs are for mothers and children. • Cash transfer programs and other safety nets maximize impact of cash transfer programs by channeling resources through mothers.
Agricultural production	• Farmers, especially women farmers, face reduced access to inputs.	• Fertilizer and seed distribution programs are designed to ensure women farmers' access. • Better access for women farmers to rural services and finance, training, and markets is crucial for gender equality.

Source: Authors' compilation.

resources in child well-being, are promising and can go a long way toward mitigating these negative effects.

Harnessing of Demographic Trends for Development in a Postcrisis World

Over the longer term, demographic trends help countries prioritize gender mainstreaming in sectors likely to have the greatest impact on development effectiveness and poverty reduction. Demographic processes affect the share of the working-age population and the fiscal space (both in total fiscal resources and priorities) and, therefore, influence the prospects of countries for poverty reduction and economic growth. Demographic stresses caused by high fertility rates or high young adult mortality rates can be eased by investments in gender equality. And investments to expand women's ability to earn and control income can strengthen prospects for gains when demographic conditions improve (Buvinic, Das Gupta, and Casabonne 2009).

Trends in fertility and mortality rates are reflected in four demographic scenarios: *demographic explosion* (countries with a high fertility rate and more than 40 percent of the population below age 20 and, thus, with high youth dependency ratios); *demographic transition* (countries where a declining fertility rate has led to a high proportion of working-age adults relative to children and the elderly); *demographic implosion* (countries where the population is aging rapidly as a result of continuing low fertility and declining adult mortality rates); and *demographic hourglass* (countries where the prime working-age population has been affected by premature adult mortality, from armed conflict or disease, such as HIV/AIDS). Table 16.2 lists countries by their demographic status.

Demographic Explosion

Of the 134 countries for which we have complete data, 43 countries, mostly in Sub-Saharan Africa, are in the demographic explosion stage. The number of children and young people in these countries is at an all-time high: 450 million, of a total population of 830 million, are under age 20. The high adolescent fertility rate is a concern in these countries (figure 16.3, panel a). The rate declined only marginally during 1990–2006 (World Bank 2009a). Births to mothers ages 15–24 account for 30 to 50 percent of all births in more than half of the countries at the explosion stage.

Teenage mothers are more likely than older mothers to die of pregnancy-related causes, a major cause of death in high-fertility settings (Conde-Agudelo, Belizan, and Lammers 2005; WHO 2004). At the same time, pregnant women in demographic explosion countries face much higher maternal mortality risks than do their counterparts in other countries (see figure 16.3, panel b). An important reason is low access to prenatal care and to skilled health care providers during childbirth (figure 16.3, panel d). New estimates show that many countries have made

Table 16.2 Developing Countries by Demographic Setting, 2010 and 2015

	Explosion 2010, explosion 2011	Explosion 2010, early transition 2015	Early transition 2010, early transition 2015	Early transition 2010, transition 2015	Transition 2010, transition 2015	Transition 2010, implosion 2015	Implosion 2010, implosion 2015
AFR	Angola*	Congo	Botswana*	South Africa*	Mauritius		
	Benin	Eritrea	Burundi*				
	Burkina Faso	São Tomé and Príncipe	Cape Verde				
	Cameroon**	Sudan	Comoros				
	Central African Republic**	Swaziland*	Djibouti				
	Chad	Togo	Gabon*				
	Côte d'Ivoire	Zimbabwe**	Namibia*				
	Congo, Dem. Rep.*		Ghana				
	Ethiopia		Mauritania				
	Equatorial Guinea						
	Gambia, The						
	Guinea						
	Guinea-Bissau						
	Kenya						
	Lesotho**						
	Liberia*						
	Madagascar						
	Malawi**						
	Mali						
	Mozambique***						
	Niger						
	Nigeria						
	Rwanda*						
	Senegal						
	Sierra Leone*						
	Somalia						
	Tanzania**						
	Uganda**						
	Zambia**						
EAP	Timor-Leste	Samoa	Cambodia	Fiji	China		
	Tonga		Lao PDR		Indonesia		
			Micronesia		Korea, Rep.		
			Papua New Guinea		Malaysia		
			Philippines		Mongolia		
			Solomon Islands		Myanmar		
			Vanuatu		Thailand		
					Vietnam		

(continued)

	Explosion 2010, explosion 2011	Explosion 2010, early transition 2015	Early transition 2010, early transition 2015	Early transition 2010, transition 2015	Transition 2010, transition 2015	Transition 2010, implosion 2015	Implosion 2010, implosion 2015
ECA		Tajikistan		Uzbekistan	Albania, Armenia, Azerbaijan, Belarus, Kazakhstan, Kyrgyzstan, Macedonia, FYR, Moldova, Montenegro, Turkey, Turkmenistan	Bosnia and Herzegovina, Georgia, Poland, Russian Federation, Serbia	Bulgaria, Croatia, Romania, Ukraine
LAC	Guatemala**		Belize, Bolivia, Haiti, Honduras, Nicaragua, Paraguay	Dominican Republic, Ecuador, El Salvador	Argentina, Brazil, Chile, Colombia, Costa Rica, Grenada, Guyana, Jamaica, Mexico, Panama, Peru, Saint Lucia, Saint Vincent and the Grenadines, Suriname, Trinidad and Tobago, Uruguay, Venezuela, R.B. de		
MENA	Yemen, Rep.	Iraq**	Egypt, Arab Rep., Jordan, Syrian Arab Republic		Algeria, Iran, Islamic Rep., Lebanon, Libya, Morocco, Tunisia		
SAR	Afghanistan*	Nepal*, Pakistan	Bangladesh, Bhutan, India		Maldives, Sri Lanka		

Source: Authors' analysis based on data from the United Nations Population Division 2009.

Notes: Explosion: over 40 percent of population below age 20; Early transition: over 40 percent of population ages 20–59; Transition: over 50 percent of population below age 20, but with 45 percent or more ages 20–59; Transition: over 50 percent of population ages 20–59; Implosion: over 20 percent of population above age 60. AFR = Africa, EAP = East Asia and Pacific, ECA = Europe and Central Asia, LAC = Latin America and the Caribbean, MENA = Middle East and North Africa, SAR = South Asia. **Countries affected by violent conflict. ***Countries affected by both high HIV-AIDS and violent conflict.

*Countries affected by high HIV-AIDS.

significant headway in reducing maternal mortality in recent decades, indicating that the problem is not intractable. Nevertheless, the gap between rich and poor countries remains alarmingly high; for instance, for every 100,000 live births in West Africa, 629 mothers die, compared to 7 mothers in Western Europe (Hogan and others 2010).

Low access to skilled health care providers, whether in the form of skilled attendance at birth or access to prenatal care services, is an important reason underlying the poor maternal mortality outcomes and the

Figure 16.3 Gender Gaps in Development Outcomes Vary by Countries' Demographic Stage

a. Adolescent fertility rate, 2003–08

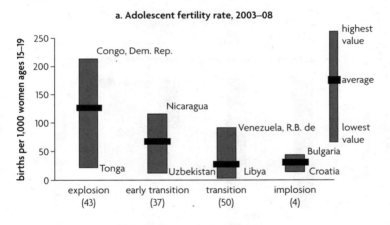

b. Maternal mortality rate, 2003–08

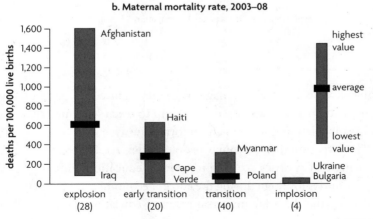

(*continued*)

Figure 16.3 Gender Gaps in Development Outcomes Vary by Countries'
Demographic Stage (*continued*)

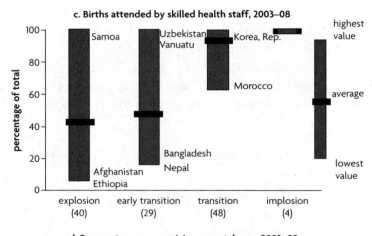

c. Births attended by skilled health staff, 2003–08

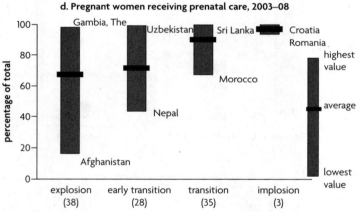

d. Pregnant women receiving prenatal care, 2003–08

Source: World Bank 2009b.
Note: Data are population-weighted averages.

high risks associated with teenage pregnancy (figure 16.3, panel c). Young
women are therefore an important group to reach with maternal health
and family planning services and information.

The large number of young people under age 20 presents a major
challenge as countries struggle to provide education and employment
opportunities for them during the current economic and financial crisis.
Reflecting the push for universal primary education, girls' enrollment

rates in demographic explosion countries rose substantially, reducing the gap between girls' and boys' primary and secondary school enrollment by 10 percentage points during 1991–2006. Yet a large gap remains, particularly in Afghanistan and the Republic of Yemen, and primary school completion rates are lower for girls (50 percent) than for boys (63 percent; figure 16.4). Secondary school enrollment also remains very low in Sub-Saharan Africa (24 percent for girls and 33 percent for boys).

By 2015, nine explosion countries will face improved demographic conditions and enter the demographic transition stage characterized by a youth bulge and greater opportunities for growth and poverty reduction. At the same time, spikes in premature adult mortality caused by violent conflict or HIV/AIDS exacerbate demographic stresses in nearly a third of countries in demographic explosion.

Hourglass Scenario

Among countries in demographic explosion and early transition are 24 countries faced with high levels of adult mortality, often predominantly of one gender, due to armed conflict or disease such as HIV/AIDS. With economies depleted of working-age adults, these countries are the most demographically stressed countries.

Nine low-income countries have an HIV/AIDS prevalence rate among adults of greater than 5 percent. By 2020, some of the worst-affected countries (Botswana, Lesotho, Swaziland, and Zimbabwe) will have lost an estimated 35 percent or more of their working-age populations (ILO 2006). Moreover, many more women than men are affected and at a younger age. The Joint United Nations Program on HIV/AIDS estimates that women make up three-quarters of Africans aged 15–24 who are HIV positive (UNAIDS 2008). Yet wars tend to affect men, especially young men, much more than women. Either way, families and economies end up losing members who play an essential role in the household or economic structure. Conflict and high HIV/AIDS prevalence have a large negative impact on GDP growth through loss of labor productivity because of illness and death and increased health care expenditures that lead to dissaving and lower capital accumulation and expenditures on schooling (Corrigan, Glomm, and Mendez 2005).

Figure 16.4 Primary, Secondary, and Tertiary School Enrollment and Completion Rates for Girls and Boys, 2003–08

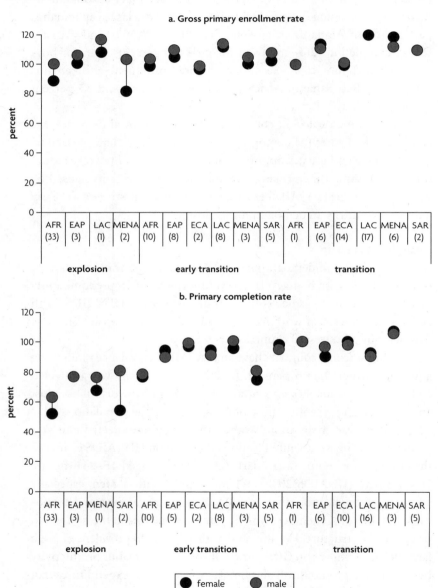

a. Gross primary enrollment rate

b. Primary completion rate

● female   ● male

(continued)

Figure 16.4 Primary, Secondary, and Tertiary School Enrollment and Completion Rates for Girls and Boys, 2003–08 (*continued*)

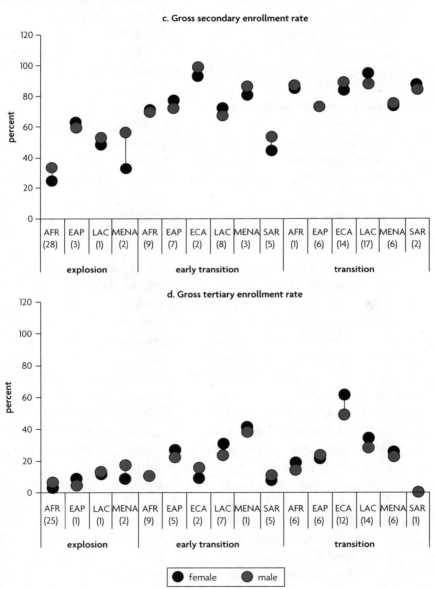

Note: Data are population-weighted averages. Numbers in parentheses are number of countries in each region. AFR = Africa, EAP = East Asia and Pacific, ECA = Europe and Central Asia, LAC = Latin America and the Caribbean, MENA = Middle East and North Africa, SAR = South Asia.

In postconflict countries, additional challenges include the level of violence against women and the rehabilitation and demobilization of ex-combatants. An estimated 300,000 children under age 18 are fighting in wars or have recently been demobilized (World Bank 2006). Initiatives to reintegrate ex-combatants into society include a range of second-chance programs, including medical and psychosocial support.

Demographic Transition

Eighty-seven countries—65 percent of the countries for which we have complete data—are currently in the early or middle phases of a demographic transition, with large working-age populations relative to children and elderly persons. By 2015, five will have moved into the implosion stage.

Although fertility rates are lower in countries experiencing a demographic transition, poor maternal health remains a concern. Among countries that have just entered this phase (early transition), use of maternal health services (skilled attendance at birth and prenatal care) remains low (see figure 16.3, panels c and d). Moreover, in some demographic transition countries such as Bangladesh, India, and Nicaragua, births to young women still make up a large share of all births. Thus, a focus on reproductive health of young women and adolescents remains a priority for this group of countries as well.

The window of opportunity for high growth and poverty reduction—the demographic dividend—provided by a large and young workforce has opened for 37 low-income countries. But if this opportunity is to result in accelerated growth, governments need to invest in these potential entrants to the workforce and to facilitate their participation in the labor force by expanding employment opportunities.

Gender inequality in schooling and employment can limit the potential for economic growth by reducing labor productivity. At this point, the biggest challenge for countries in demographic transition is to raise secondary enrollment and completion rates for both boys and girls, especially in Sub-Saharan Africa, East Asia and Pacific, and South Asia, where secondary enrollment rates are at 30–40 percent in countries at the early stage of transition. Tertiary enrollment is also extremely low in low-income countries, at less than 20 percent for countries in early transition.

The ratio of employment to population in demographic transition countries in South Asia is 24.4 percent for young women ages 15–24 and more than twice that (58.4 percent) for young men (figure 16.5). Facilitating the entry of young women into the labor force and expanding their employment opportunities are crucial for early transition countries to reap the full benefit of their investments in girls' education and to take advantage of the acceleration in growth offered by the demographic dividend. Investing in adolescent reproductive health to address early childbearing is another way to ease women's transition from school to work.

With fewer children than before, women are better placed to enter the labor market. However, with the exception of Sub-Saharan African and East Asian countries, women's labor force participation in demographic transition countries is far below that of men (figure 16.6). This implies considerable scope for designing labor market policies and policies to encourage entrepreneurship (including expanding access to technology

Figure 16.5 Ratios of Employment to Population Are Much Lower for Young Women than for Young Men Ages 15–24

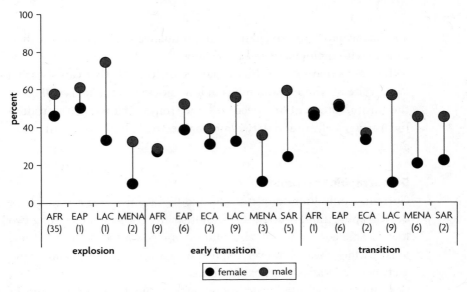

Source: World Bank World Development Indicators database 2008.
Note: Data are population-weighted averages. Numbers in parentheses are number of countries in each region.

Figure 16.6 Labor Force Participation Rate by Region and Demographic Stage, 2003–08

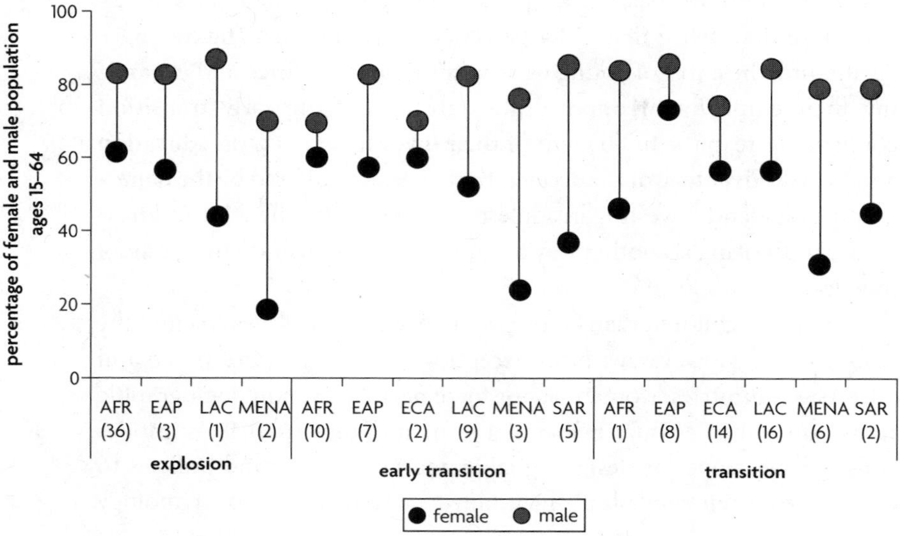

Source: World Bank 2009b.

Note: Data are population-weighted averages. Numbers in parentheses are number of countries in each region.

and finance) to help women invest in productive skills and allocate their time to self-employment and wage labor.

Because expansion of the formal sector to levels that can absorb a large share of women (and men) in low-income countries is still far in the future, interventions need to target improving women's productivity in agriculture and in the informal sector, in both rural and urban areas.

Demographic Implosion

Currently, only four countries (all middle income) face a scenario of demographic implosion. By 2015, another five countries, including two low-income countries, will also find themselves in this scenario. If one looks further ahead, however, population aging is a major phenomenon and will accelerate in the next 25 years.

Women constitute by far the greater number and proportion of older populations in these countries, especially in Eastern Europe and the Former Soviet Union. The average life expectancy for women in Bulgaria, Croatia, Poland, Romania, the Russian Federation, Serbia, and Ukraine combined is 75 years compared to 65 for men. The central issue of the aging population is increased poverty and vulnerability. These problems are more acute for women, not only because they tend to live longer than men, but also because women tend to be disadvantaged in the patriarchal societies in which they live. The consequences of gender roles (men as "breadwinners," women as "housekeepers") become explicitly apparent. In situations where pension schemes accrue mainly to employees, women who have not worked for most of their adult lives become even more heavily reliant on their husbands' status and pensions. Older women who are single, widowed, or divorced are especially vulnerable, receiving few or none of the entitlements received by men. But there is also a future cohort of older men that may be particularly vulnerable in the few societies where the "culling" of infant girls will result in sharp sex-ratio imbalances, and older, single men will be left to fend for themselves without the old-age protection traditionally afforded by the family (Ebenstein and Sharygin 2009).

Countries with rapidly aging populations face the challenge of designing affordable old-age support policies with expanded coverage to include these growing elderly cohorts. Gender-informed design and targeting should increase the reach and affordability of these policies.

Postcrisis Priorities

While in the short run, investments in gender equality should focus on minimizing the negative impacts of the recent crises on development, in the long run, countries will need to step up investments in gender equality that respond to specific country circumstances and are framed to address the demographic stresses and opportunities associated with specific demographic scenarios. Table 16.3 defines priority investments in gender equality for the four different demographic scenarios identified in this chapter. These priority investments are either proven to be effective (such as conditional cash transfers) or show promising results. In most cases, countries will need to improve women's earning opportunities and the quality of their jobs, but they will also need to intensify gender integration in social sectors, particularly in reproductive health,

Table 16.3 Priorities for Investments in Gender Equality over the Longer Term

Scenario	Key issues	Priority investments
Demographic explosion	• Lower per capita resources for investment in human capital and growth • Poorer health and lifetime earnings for women and children, greater household vulnerability to poverty	• Family planning programs to increase birth intervals, reduce teen pregnancies, and prevent mother-to-child HIV transmission • Basic reproductive health services, particularly those addressing the reproductive health needs of adolescent and young women and men • Investments in schooling that increase education quality for all and reduce gender gaps in school enrollment and completion (both supply and demand considerations such as conditional cash transfers) • Productivity-enhancing and income-earning policies, including those targeting women farmers
Demographic transition	• Potential for rapid economic growth • Additional efforts needed to realize women's contribution to growth	• Policies that expand labor demand and create economic opportunities for women (active labor market programs such as skills training, labor-intermediation programs, trade policies, and access to entrepreneurship and self-employment) • Basic reproductive health services, particularly those addressing the reproductive health needs of adolescent and young women and men • Child care
Countries moving toward implosion	• Strained public and private resources for support • Added resource strains since women live longer and have fewer economic resources	• Safety net and pension options for vulnerable elders, typically older women (but also older men, especially in countries with skewed gender ratios)
Hourglass (due to HIV/AIDS and conflict)	• Lower potential for economic growth, households more vulnerable to poverty • If men missing (due to war), more vulnerability to poverty for female-headed households; if women missing (due to HIV/AIDS or sex selection), deprivation of familial support for unmarried men	• Family planning programs to reduce teen pregnancies and prevent mother-to-child HIV transmission • Investment in schooling, including accelerated learning programs and targeted programs to improve the school-to-work transition and skill deficits of poor young women • Better access to entrepreneurship and self-employment opportunities for women • Antiretroviral therapy • Interventions to address gender issues in conflict prevention (including gender-sensitive Disarmament, Demobilization and Rehabilitation programs)

Source: Authors' compilation.

where development assistance has contracted in recent years. And they will need to address both "first generation" gender equality issues, especially in the demographic explosion and hourglass scenarios, and "second generation" issues, in the advanced transition and implosion cases, including a focus on transferable skills for the modern labor market; access to commercial credit; the formalization of female entrepreneurship; and old-age security for vulnerable widowed women and, in societies with gender-ratio imbalances, also aging protection for vulnerable single, older men with no families.

Concluding Thoughts

While there are gender inequalities in all countries, these inequalities take different forms depending on the country's stage of demographic transition and help to define priority policy responses. Low-income, high-fertility, and hourglass-scenario countries, in particular, need to intensify gender integration in the social sectors. A priority area of intervention (that has suffered contraction in development assistance in recent years) is expanding access to quality reproductive health services and coverage, including services for adolescents. Yet, late-transition and implosion countries need to focus on old-age security and design affordable old-age support policies with expanded coverage, especially for vulnerable widowed women and, in the few societies with sharp sex-ratio imbalances, also aging protection for vulnerable single, older men who have no family support.

The exception to this is empowering women economically, which emerges as a priority regardless of the country's demographic scenario. It is a proven way to manage crises and respond to demographic stresses. The specific nature of the interventions will vary, of course, in response to the different development needs of countries. For example, in low-income countries, providing women with access to basic agricultural inputs and microfinance will continue to be fundamental to their economic empowerment, while in transition and late-transition countries, women's economic opportunities are linked to an increased focus on transferable skills for the modern labor market, access to commercial credit, the formalization of female entrepreneurship, and viable child care options.

In all sectors, but especially for policies aiming to expand women's economic opportunities, there is a continued need to know what works best and under which circumstances. At the same time, evidence-based experience and good practices are emerging in a range of countries. South-South dialogue should be intensified so that new and innovative responses to a changing world can be shared and issues related to gender equality and development more broadly understood.

Note

1. Countries with high infant mortality rates are those in the highest quartile of the distribution of under-5 mortality rates (per 1,000 live births) for 151 developing countries in 2007. Countries with low female schooling rates are those in the lowest quartile of the distribution of the ratio of girls to boys in primary and secondary enrollment for 131 developing countries for the latest available data between 2004 and 2007.

Bibliography

Baird, S., J. Friedman, and N. Schady. 2007. "Aggregate Economic Shocks and Infant Mortality in the Developing World." Policy Research Working Paper 4346, World Bank, Washington, DC.

Buvinic, M. 2009. "The Global Financial Crisis: Assessing Vulnerability for Women and Children—Identifying Policy Responses." Paper prepared for the 53rd Session of the United Nations Commission on the Status of Women, New York, March 2–13.

Buvinic, M., M. Das Gupta, and U. Casabonne. 2009. "Gender, Poverty, and Demography: An Overview." *World Bank Economic Review* 23 (3): 347–69.

Conde-Agudelo, A., J. M. Belizan, and C. Lammers. 2005. "Maternal-Perinatal Morbidity and Mortality Associated with Adolescent Pregnancy in Latin America: Cross-sectional Study." *American Journal of Obstetrics and Gynecology* 192 (2): 342–49.

Corrigan, P., G. Glomm, and F. Mendez. 2005. "AIDS, Human Capital, and Growth." *Journal of Development Economics* 77 (1): 107–24.

Ebenstein, A. Y., and E. J. Sharygin. 2009. "The Consequences of the 'Missing Girls' of China." *World Bank Economic Review* 23 (3): 399–425.

Fraser, A., J. Brockert, and R. H. Ward. 1995. "Association of Young Maternal Age with Adverse Reproductive Outcomes." *New England Journal of Medicine* 332 (17): 1113–17.

Friedman, J. A., and N. Schady. 2009. "How Many More Infants Are Likely to Die in Africa as a Result of the Global Financial Crisis?" Policy Research Working Paper 5023, World Bank, Washington, DC.

Hogan, M., K. Foreman, M. Naghavi, S. Ahn, M. Wang, S. Makela, A. Lopez, R. Lozano, and C. Murray. "Maternal Mortality for 181 Countries, 1980–2008: A Systematic Analysis of Progress towards Millennium Development Goal 5." *The Lancet* 375 (9726): 1609–23.

ILO (International Labour Organization). 2006. *HIV/AIDS and Work: Global Estimates, Impacts on Children and Youth, and Response.* Geneva: International Labour Organization.

IMF (International Monetary Fund). 2009. World Economic Outlook Database. http://www.imf.org/external/pubs/ft/weo/2009/01/weodata/index.aspx.

Sabarwal, S., N. Sinha, and M. Buvinic. 2009. "The Global Financial Crisis: Assessing Vulnerability for Women and Children, Identifying Policy Responses." Policy Brief, Poverty Reduction and Economic Management Network, Gender and Development Group, World Bank, Washington, DC.

Thirumurthy, H., J. Graff Zivin, and M. Goldstein. 2005. "The Economic Impact of AIDS Treatment: Labor Supply in Western Kenya." NBER Working Paper 11871, National Bureau of Economic Research, Cambridge, MA.

UNAIDS (Joint United Nations Programme on HIV/AIDS). 2008. "Addressing the Vulnerability of Young Women and Girls to Stop the HIV Epidemic in Southern Africa." Joint United Nations Programme on HIV/AIDS, Geneva.

World Bank. 1993. *World Development Report 1993: Investing in Health.* New York: Oxford University Press.

———. 2006. *World Development Report 2007: Development and the Next Generation.* Washington, DC: World Bank.

———. 2007a. *Global Monitoring Report 2007: Confronting the Challenges of Gender Equality and Fragile States.* Washington, DC: World Bank.

———. 2007b. *World Development Report 2008: Agriculture for Development.* Washington, DC: World Bank.

———. 2009a. *Global Monitoring Report 2009.* Washington, DC: World Bank.

———. 2009b. *World Development Indicators 2009.* Washington, DC: World Bank.

———. 2009c. World Development Indicators Database. http://databank.worldbank .org/ddp/home.do?Step=12&id=4&CNO=2.

WHO (World Health Organization). 2004. *Adolescent Pregnancy: Issues in Adolescent Health and Development.* Geneva: World Health Organization.

Yamano, T., and T. S. Jayne. 2004. "Working-age Adult Mortality and Primary School Attendance in Rural Kenya." International Development Collaborative Policy Briefs KE-TEGEMEO-PB-05, Michigan State University Department of Agricultural Economics, East Lansing, MI.

17

The Impact of the Global Financial Crisis on Migration and Remittances

Sanket Mohapatra and Dilip Ratha

Remittances sent by international migrants worldwide are an important source of external finance for many developing countries. The 2008–09 global financial crisis raised fears of a slowdown or even a reversal of migration flows and a consequent decline in remittance flows, especially to low-income countries. In this chapter, we present recent trends in, and the outlook for, migration and remittance flows for 2010–11.

Historically, remittances have been noted to be stable or even countercyclical and have tended to rise in times of financial crises and natural disasters because migrants living abroad send more money to help their families back home. For example, remittance inflows increased to Mexico following the country's financial crisis in 1995, to the Philippines and Thailand after the Asian crash in 1997, and to Central America after Hurricane Mitch in 1998.

Unlike past emerging market crises, however, the current crisis started in the high-income countries and has spread to the developing countries,

This note draws on Migration and Development briefs 10 through 12 published by the World Bank between July 2009 and April 2010 (co-authored with Ani Silwal) and on Ratha (2009). http://www.worldbank.org/prospects/migrationand remittances.

resulting in a global crisis. Migrant destinations in both the North and the South have been affected to varying degrees, and that, in turn, is affecting employment and income opportunities for migrants. For the first time since the 1980s, remittances to developing countries are estimated to have declined by a modest 6 percent in 2009. Unlike private capital flows, remittance flows have remained resilient through the crisis and have become even more important as a source of external financing in many developing countries.

Recent Trends in Remittances in 2009

Officially recorded remittance flows to developing countries in 2008 reached US$336 billion (see table 17.1). This is three times as large as overall official development assistance to developing countries, and larger than private capital inflows in many countries. The true size of flows, including unrecorded flows through formal and informal channels, is even larger. For many states, remittances are now the largest and least volatile source of foreign exchange, and for some countries—such as Lesotho, Moldova, Tajikistan, and Tonga—they exceed one-third of national income.

On the basis of high-frequency data for the first three quarters of 2009, we estimate that remittance flows to developing countries reached US$316 billion in 2009, marking a 6 percent decline from 2008. This decline, however, masks significant variation across the developing regions. Remittance flows to South Asia grew strongly in 2008, despite the global economic crisis; but now there are risks that they may slow in a lagged response to a weak global economy. East Asia and Sub-Saharan Africa also face similar risks. By contrast, remittance flows to Latin America and the Caribbean and to the Middle East and North Africa were weaker than anticipated in 2009; but they appear to have reached a bottom already, with the expectation of a recovery in 2010 and 2011.

Remittance flows to South Asia and (to a lesser extent, East Asia) continued to grow in 2009, although at a markedly slower pace than in the precrisis years. Flows to Pakistan and Bangladesh increased by 23.9 percent and 19.4 percent, respectively, in 2009, but the growth of these flows has decelerated since the last quarter of 2009 in a lagged response to the debt crisis in Dubai. In the Philippines, a surge in the last quarter of 2009

Table 17.1 Remittance Flows to Developing Countries, 2006–11

Remittance flows (US$ billions)	2006	2007	2008	2009(e)	2010(f)	2011(f)
Developing countries	235.2	289.6	335.8	315.7	335.4	359.1
East Asia and Pacific	57.6	71.3	86.1	85.7	94.1	102.7
Europe and Central Asia	37.3	50.8	57.5	45.6	48.1	51.7
Latin America and the Caribbean	59.1	63.1	64.4	56.5	59.8	64.5
Middle East and North Africa	26.1	31.7	34.8	32.0	33.1	34.4
South Asia	42.5	54.0	71.7	75.2	78.7	82.8
Sub-Saharan Africa	12.6	18.7	21.3	20.7	21.6	22.9
Low-income countries	19.9	24.7	31.9	32.2	34.6	37.2
Middle-income countries	215.3	265.0	303.9	283.4	300.8	321.8
World	317.4	385.4	443.4	413.7	437.3	464.9
Growth rate (percent)						
Developing countries	18.4	23.1	15.9	−6.0	6.2	7.1
East Asia and Pacific	14.2	23.8	20.7	−0.4	9.8	9.2
Europe and Central Asia	24.1	36.0	13.3	−20.7	5.4	7.6
Latin America and the Caribbean	18.1	6.9	2.1	−12.3	5.7	7.9
Middle East and North Africa	4.6	21.4	9.8	−8.1	3.6	4.0
South Asia	25.3	27.1	32.6	4.9	4.7	5.2
Sub-Saharan Africa	34.8	48.5	14.1	−2.7	4.4	5.8
Low-income countries	23.9	24.0	29.4	1.0	7.2	7.7
Middle-income countries	17.9	23.0	14.7	−6.7	6.1	7.0
World	15.6	21.4	15.0	−6.7	5.7	6.3

Source: Ratha, Mohapatra, and Silwal 2010.
Note: e = estimate; f = forecast. Remittances are defined as the sum of workers' remittances, compensation of employees, and migrant transfers. For data definitions and the entire dataset, see http://www.worldbank.org/prospects/migration andremittances.

increased remittances by 5.6 percent as migrants sent money to help their families affected by typhoons Ondoy and Pepeng.[1]

Remittance flows to countries in the Latin America and the Caribbean Region in 2009 show larger declines than expected. In Mexico, they fell by 15.7 percent in 2009, and flows to El Salvador decreased by 8.5 percent. However, the decline in flows appears to have bottomed out in most countries across the region. This reflects the fact that the crisis in the United States and Spain (particularly in the construction sector)—key destination countries for Latin American migrants—started sooner than the crisis in other parts of the world. The Europe and Central Asia Region is estimated to have experienced the largest decline in remittance flows among all developing regions in 2009, in part because of depreciation of the Russian ruble relative to the U.S. dollar.

Remittances to the Middle East and North Africa Region were also weaker compared to the previous year. Flows to the Arab Republic of Egypt (the largest recipient in the region) declined by 18 percent, and flows to Morocco fell by 9 percent in 2009. Data on remittance flows to Sub-Saharan Africa are sparse, but these flows appear to have declined only modestly in 2009. Flows to Ethiopia, Kenya, and Uganda show higher growth or smaller declines than expected. Remittances to Cape Verde declined in U.S. dollar terms in 2009 but were almost flat in local currency terms.

Factors that Affected Migration and Remittance Flows in 2009

The trends in global migration and remittance flows in 2009 appear to have been influenced by the following factors: (a) effects of the economic crisis on migrant stocks, (b) diversification of migration destinations, (c) currency effects, and (d) the link between barriers to labor mobility and the impact of economic cycles on remittances. These factors are discussed below.

Effect of Global Financial Crisis on Migration Stocks and Flows. Contrary to popular perception, remittance flows in a given year are not directly related to migration flows during the same year; instead, remittances are sent by almost the entire existing stock of migrants (that is, cumulated flows of migrants over the years; see box 17.1). For an understanding of factors that influence the impact of the 2008–09 financial crisis on remittance trends, it is helpful to examine the impact of the crisis on the stock of international migrants. The following stock-flow equation for migration is useful in this context:

$$M_t = (1 - \delta)M_{t-1} - R_t + N_t, \qquad \text{(Eq. 1)}$$

Box 17.1 Resilience of Remittance Flows Relative to Other Types of Flows during the Current Crisis

Despite the prospect of a sharper decline in remittance inflows than anticipated, these flows have remained more resilient than many other types of resource flows (such as private debt and equity flows and foreign direct investment, which declined sharply in 2009 as foreign investors pulled out of emerging markets). There are several reasons for the resilience of remittances in the face of economic downturns in host countries:

- Remittances are sent by the cumulated flows of migrants over the years, not only by the new migrants of the past year or two. This makes remittances persistent over time. If new migration stops, then remittances may stop growing over a period of a decade or so. But they will continue to increase as long as migration flows continue.
- Remittances are a small part of migrants' incomes, and migrants continue to send remittances when hit by income shocks.
- Because of a rise in anti-immigration sentiments and tighter border controls, especially in Europe and the United States, the duration of migration appears to have increased. Those people staying in the host country are likely to continue to send remittances.
- If migrants do return to their home countries, they are likely to take accumulated savings with them. This may have been the case in India during the Gulf War of 1990–91, which forced a large number of Indian workers in the Gulf to return home (Ratha 2003). Also, the "safe haven" factor or "home bias" may cause remittances for investment purposes to return home during an economic downturn in the host country. Migrants not only bring back savings; they also bring business skills. Jordan's economy performed better than many observers had expected between 1991 and 1993 because of the return of relatively skilled workers from the Gulf.
- Most high-income remittance source countries in the Organisation for Economic Co-operation and Development have undertaken large fiscal stimulus packages in response to the financial crisis. This increase in public expenditure, if directed to public infrastructure projects, will increase demand for both native and migrant workers. Taylor (2000) has found that public income transfer programs in the United States resulted in increased remittances to Mexico: when all other factors are equal, immigrant households that received social security or unemployment insurance were more likely to remit than were other immigrant households. Also, documented migrants are likely to send more remittances to their families to compensate for a fall in remittances by undocumented migrants.

Source: Ratha, Mohapatra, and Silwal 2010.

where M_t = new migrant stock, M_{t-1} = existing stock of migrants, R_t = return migration, N_t = new migration, and δ is the death rate of migrants in the host countries. Equivalently,

$$\Delta M_t = N_t - R_t - \delta M_{t-1}, \tag{Eq. 2}$$

where ΔM_t is the change in migrant stock. In other words, the change in migrant stock equals new migration net of return migration and deaths (and assimilation) of existing migrants.

There is little evidence of return migration (R_t) as a result of the financial crisis in Europe and the United States. On the contrary, there are widespread reports that migrants are unwilling to return to their countries of origin, fearing that they may not be able to reenter once they leave because of tighter immigration controls (Awad 2009; Fix and others 2009; Green and Winters forthcoming). Data from the Mexican Migration Project show that the duration of migration for Mexican migrants in the United States has increased from 8 months in the early 1990s to 15 months more recently (figure 17.1). In part, the reluctance to return also reflects the significantly higher incomes that migrants are earning in the rich countries despite the crisis.

Financial incentives to encourage return migration have also not worked as expected in the Czech Republic, Japan, and Spain. In part because of the weak response to financial incentives, Spain and other European countries have implemented stronger immigration restrictions, even for highly skilled migrants. Anecdotally, employers in the Gulf Cooperation Council (GCC) countries are also offering unpaid leave to migrant workers to encourage them to return home until the economy recovers, but there appear to be few takers.

On average, new migration flows in a given year tend to be small relative to the existing stock of migrants. During 2000–05, for example, new

Figure 17.1 U.S.-Mexico Border Controls and Duration of Stay of Mexican Migrants in the United States

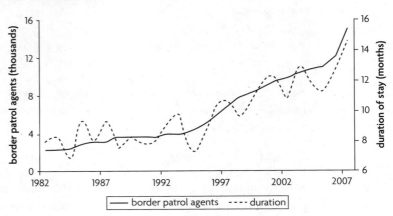

Sources: U.S. Department of Homeland Security; Mexican Migration Project.

migration flows amounted to about 2 percent of migrant stocks in the United States, 4 percent in European Union (EU) countries, and 5 percent in GCC countries. New migration flows (N_t) from many countries appear to have been affected by the financial crisis and weak job markets in the destination countries, although flows are still positive.[2] There has been a large fall in new deployments in many migrant-sending countries; in Bangladesh, for example, migration fell by nearly half in 2009 compared with the number of migrants in 2008. New migration from Poland and other accession countries to the United Kingdom has fallen, and the number of workers from those countries employed in the United Kingdom has plateaued since the start of the crisis.

Developing countries with migrants in the GCC countries, such as Bangladesh, India, Nepal, Pakistan, and the Philippines, have experienced smaller declines in remittance flows. Dubai, which has been severely affected by the crisis, is only one of the seven emirates of the United Arab Emirates and the only one that does not have oil. The substantial financial resources and long-term infrastructure development plans of the GCC countries imply that they will continue to demand migrant workers.

The More Diverse the Migration Destinations, the More Resilient Are Remittances. Remittance flows to Latin America and the Caribbean are highly correlated with the business cycle of the United States. Since economic cycles in the Gulf region are different from those of the United States, remittance flows to countries that send migrants to both the United States and the Gulf (for example, India and the Philippines) tend to be more resilient. The migration destinations of India are diversified, which is one of the reasons why flows to India fell only modestly in 2009. Recent estimates of migrant stocks show that about two-fifth of Indian migrants are in the Gulf and a fifth are in North America, with the remainder in Europe, Australia, Bangladesh, Nepal, and other regions. Filipino migrants are also well-diversified in terms of destinations, with land-based workers in the United States, the Gulf, Europe, and other continents, and a significant number of sea-based workers.

The composition of migration has shifted during the crisis, with migrants switching across sectors and countries. For example, in the

Gulf, after the massive construction projects such as Burj Dubai have been completed and with the debt crisis in Dubai, there is a slowdown in new construction projects and, therefore, in demand for new migrants. Many migrants have moved on to Abu Dhabi and other oil-rich emirates of the United Arab Emirates and to neighboring countries where there are huge infrastructure projects. Since the second half of 2009, the share of remittances from the United Arab Emirates in overall remittance flows from the GCC countries to Bangladesh has fallen, but that of Saudi Arabia has risen. Saudi Arabia has also become an increasingly important destination of migrants from the Philippines; between 2005 and 2008, the percentage of Filipino migrants going to Saudi Arabia increased from 20 percent to 30 percent of all Filipino migrants. Together with the higher level of earnings and sectoral diversification in health, domestic work, and other sectors, this diversification has cushioned overall remittances to the Philippines.

Some developing countries are also important destinations for migrants—for example, India, Malaysia, the Russian Federation, and South Africa. Resource-rich developing countries, such as the Islamic Republic of Iran, Libya, Nigeria, and Sudan, are also becoming attractive destinations for migrants. It is hard to predict how outward remittances from these destination countries in the South will be affected by the crisis, but some interesting cases involving currency effects are discussed below.

Exchange Rate Movements Produce Valuation Effects, but They Also Influence the Consumption-Investment Motive for Remittances. Exchange rate movement can be an important factor affecting the U.S. dollar valuation of remittances. For example, in U.S. dollar terms, remittance flows to the Kyrgyz Republic, Armenia, and Tajikistan declined by 15 percent, 33 percent, and 34 percent, respectively, in the first half of 2009 compared with the same period in 2008. However, the Russian ruble lost 25 percent of its value against the U.S. dollar in the first half of 2009 compared with its average value in the same period the previous year. If measured in ruble terms, remittances to the Kyrgyz Republic actually increased 17 percent in the first half of 2009 on a year-on-year basis. In Armenia, the year-on-year fall in ruble terms was only 8 percent, and in Tajikistan, it was 10 percent. Similarly, a significant part of the decline in remittance flows to Poland can be explained by the weakening of the British pound against the U.S. dollar.

Exchange rate movements also affect remittances through their impacts on consumption and investment motives. The depreciation of the Indian rupee and the Philippine peso produced a "sale effect" on housing, bank deposits, stocks, and other assets back home. Indeed, as the Indian rupee has depreciated more than 25 percent against the U.S. dollar, there has been a surge in remittance flows to India. There are signs that a similar surge in investment-related remittance flows is happening in Bangladesh, Ethiopia, Moldova, Nepal, Pakistan, the Philippines, and Tajikistan.

The Lower the Barriers to Labor Mobility, the Stronger Is the Link between Remittances and Economic Cycles in That Corridor. The impact of the crisis has been more severe in corridors with fewer restrictions on labor mobility. Russia's relatively porous border with neighboring countries allows migrants to move in and out of the country in response to changing economic prospects, with the result that remittances are more correlated with the business cycle in the source country. Remittance outflows from Russia to Commonwealth of Independent States countries fell sharply—by 33 percent—during the first three quarters of 2009. With increasing oil prices, however, outward remittance flows from Russia are starting to recover (figure 17.2). On the other hand, remittances outflows from Saudi Arabia have been less correlated with oil prices. This is in part because of Saudi Arabia's ambitious development plans and countercyclical fiscal policy, but also because of its quotas on immigration that it has strictly enforced.

Because the labor markets are relatively integrated within the EU, migration is more responsive to economic cycles of the destination and source countries. Remittance flows to Poland and Romania fell between 2008 and 2009. This sharp decline is partly due to weak labor markets in Spain and Italy, but also because of the ability of workers within the EU to easily move in and out of countries in response to changes in labor demand.

In countries where it is more difficult to reenter after leaving, migrants have chosen to remain. Many migrants who have lost jobs in Dubai have not left; rather, they are taking lower-paying jobs with other employers and often staying on illegally. Interviews with migrants in

Figure 17.2 Sharp Decline of Remittance Outflows from Russia during the Crisis, but Beginning of Increase with Recovery in Oil Prices and Growth

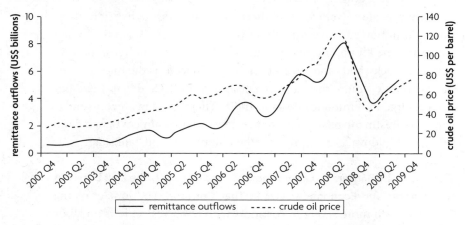

Sources: International Monetary Fund Balance of Payments database; World Bank Development Prospects Group.
Note: Q = quarter.

Dubai suggest that many migrant workers have reduced their daily expenditures in response to wage cuts by employers. Some sent their families back home, so the funds spent in Dubai are now remitted home. Migrants are also sharing accommodations to enable them to send remittances. Migrant workers, from Bangladesh in particular, appear to be stranded in Dubai because they cannot afford to return. Interviews with migrants suggest that it costs about 12,000 dirhams (about US$3,300) to pay recruitment agencies and travel costs. With a monthly income below 900 dirhams (about US$245), and little overtime, a construction worker can easily take three years to save enough to repay the recruitment costs. Even with the crisis, migrants often cannot risk returning home. So many entered into creative arrangements (for example, taking unpaid leave) with employers to simply wait it out in Dubai. Rising living costs in Dubai have also reduced remittances. The price of rice, a staple for many migrants, more than doubled in the past two years. Earlier, a construction worker spent roughly 150 dirhams (about US$40) a month on food; now, he or she is spending between 350 and 400 dirhams (US$95 to US$110). Also, this has increased the time it takes a migrant to pay back the recruitment fees. There are anecdotal reports of family members sending "reverse remittances" to help migrants (see box 17.2).

Box 17.2 Reverse Remittances

There have been several anecdotal media reports about reverse remittances from Mexico and the Dominican Republic to the United States. According to these reports, the economic crisis in the United States is forcing many migrants to dip into their savings and assets back home and to rely on their families for financial help. Also, some migrants have sold their homes in Mexico to make mortgage payments in the United States. There are also anecdotes that some, deciding that returning home was not an option, have brought their family members to join them in the United States. This would imply, again, that they would liquidate assets in the home country and remit the proceeds overseas.

Decline of Nonresident Deposits* in 2008 but Subsequent Rise
US$ billions

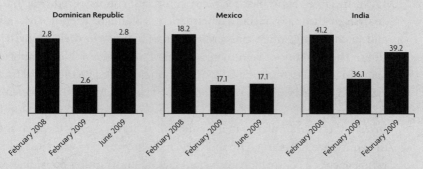

Sources: Central banks of the Dominican Republic, Mexico, and India.
* The Dominican Republic: foreign currency deposits; India: foreign currency and repatriable rupee deposits; and Mexico: foreign currency demand deposits and time deposits from the public. Note that these charts use different scales.

There is no way of judging the extent of such reverse remittances. Data on outward remittance flows are of questionable quality in most of the countries. Also, many large migrant destination countries do not report monthly data on inward remittance flows. A modest, and rather indirect, inference about reverse remittances can be drawn from a decline in foreign currency deposits—which are likely held by migrants or their relatives—in the Dominican Republic and other countries. In 2008, these deposits declined by 7 percent in the Dominican Republic, 12 percent in India, and 6 percent in Mexico (see figure above). However, these deposits have risen since then, indicating perhaps that reverse remittances are slowing because of a bottoming of the U.S. economic downturn. Reverse remittances are most likely miniscule—and they seem to be declining—compared to the size of remittance flows received by developing countries.

Source: Authors.

Leveraging of Remittances for External Financing

The global financial crisis has highlighted the importance of remittances for meeting external financing gaps. Remittances have helped to build up international reserves and have contributed to reducing current account deficits in many developing countries. This has provided a cushion against external shocks during the global economic crisis. In low-income countries, the current account deficit as a percentage of gross domestic product (GDP) would have more than doubled in the absence of remittances in recent years. For some large remittance recipients such as the Philippines, Bangladesh, and Nepal, remittance flows have offset large trade deficits and enabled these countries to maintain a current account surplus (figure 17.3).

Remittances are now factored into sovereign ratings in middle-income countries and debt sustainability analysis in low-income countries (figure 17.4). In large remittance-recipient countries, country creditworthiness analysis by the major rating agencies such as Standard & Poor's, Moody's, and Fitch Ratings often cite remittances as a factor in their rating decisions. The stability of remittances to the Philippines was an important factor in its ability to issue a US$750 million bond despite the global financial crisis. Bangladesh was rated for the first time in April 2010, receiving a BB–rating from Standard & Poor's Investor Service and Ba3 from Moody's Investor Service, similar to many emerging markets. Again, the high share of remittance flows in GDP and their high growth rate was cited by the rating agency as one of the important factors for its rating decision.

As countries have become aware of remittances as a stable source of foreign currency earnings, many countries have started looking at the

Figure 17.3 Offset of Trade Deficits by Remittances in Many Middle- and Low-Income Countries

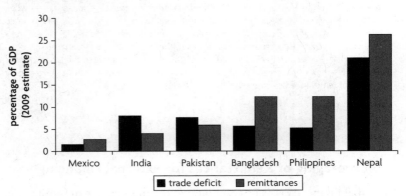

Sources: World Bank, Migration and Remittances Team and Global Economic Prospects 2010 database.

Figure 17.4 Contribution of Remittances to Sovereign Creditworthiness and External Debt

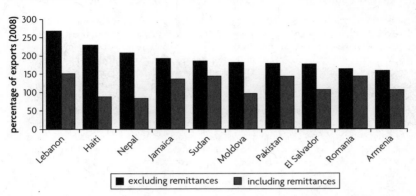

Sources: World Bank Migration and Remittances Team and Global Economic Prospects 2010 database.
Note: External debt is a percentage of exports and remittances. The figure includes countries that received more than US$1 billion in remittances and whose remittances were more than 4 percent of GDP in 2008.

diaspora abroad as potential sources of capital that could be tapped with diaspora bonds. Many countries—for example, El Salvador, Ethiopia, Nepal, the Philippines, Rwanda, and Sri Lanka—have issued or are considering issuing diaspora bonds (see box 17.3).

Structural and Policy Changes in the Remittance Markets

The global financial crisis has intensified efforts to reduce remittance costs and leverage remittances for improving financial access. Many banks and operators are cutting remittance fees. This is partly because of the global financial crisis, which has caused the market to shrink in several corridors (especially from the United States to Latin America), and more intense competition. For example, remittance fees from the United Arab Emirates to South Asia, a high-volume corridor, are often under US$1 per transaction.

Africa is now at the forefront of mobile money transfer technologies. Kenya's M-Pesa now has more than 9 million subscribers. While M-Pesa is mostly focused on domestic money transfers in Kenya with a small pilot scheme for U.K.-Kenya remittances, Kuwaiti mobile operator Zain has expanded to 15 African countries and has 42 million subscribers. It offers

Box 17.3 Diaspora Bonds as a Source of Financing during Difficult Times

In the current environment of a severe crisis of confidence in debt markets, some developing (and even developed) countries are encountering a great deal of difficulty in obtaining private financing using traditional financial instruments. This scarcity of capital threatens to jeopardize long-term growth and employment generation in developing countries, many of which have limited access to capital even in the best of times. Official aid alone will not be adequate to bridge near- or long-term financing gaps. Ultimately, it will be necessary to adopt innovative financing approaches to target previously untapped investors. Diaspora bonds are one such mechanism whereby developing countries turn to borrowing from their expatriate (diaspora) communities. A diaspora bond is a debt instrument issued by a country—or potentially, by a subsovereign public or private entity—to raise financing from its overseas diaspora. In the past, diaspora bonds have been used by Israel and India to raise over US$35 billion of development financing. The proceeds from these bonds were used to support balance-of-payments needs and finance infrastructure, housing, health, and education projects. Several countries—for example, El Salvador, Ethiopia, Nepal, the Philippines, Rwanda, and Sri Lanka—are considering (or have issued) diaspora bonds to bridge financing gaps.

If 200,000 Haitians in the United States, Canada, and France were to invest US$1,000 each in diaspora bonds, it would add up to US$200 million. If these bonds were opened to friends of Haiti, including private charitable organizations, much larger sums could be raised. If the bond ratings were enhanced to investment grade via guarantees from the multilateral and bilateral donors, then such bonds would even attract institutional investors.

For such countries, diaspora bonds represent a stable and cheap source of external finance, especially in times of financial stress. For the diaspora investors, these bonds offer the opportunity to help their country of origin while at the same time offering an investment opportunity. Besides patriotism, diaspora members are usually more interested than foreign investors in investing in the home country. However, in countries that have weak governance and high sovereign risk, diaspora bonds may require support for institutional capacity building, credit enhancement, or both from multilateral or bilateral agencies. Compliance with securities and exchange regulations overseas can also be cumbersome in some migrant-destination countries.

Sources: Ketkar and Ratha 2010; Ratha 2010.

Zain Zap, a mobile remittance service, which, in addition to money transfers, also offers other services such as payment for bills and groceries.

New remittance technologies are also being adopted in South Asia. In Bangladesh, Banglalink, the second-largest mobile operator in Bangladesh after GrameenPhone with 13 million subscribers, is launching mobile remittance services in partnership with several Bangladesh banks. These banks will offer "mobile wallet" accounts through Banglalink, and Banglalink distribution outlets will be used as remittance disbursement cash points. The services will reduce transfer time from four to five days to one day. A remittance card introduced in Bangladesh for existing and prospective migrants allows nominees of the migrant worker to withdraw the remittance through the point-of-sale terminals of bank branches and automatic teller machines. In Pakistan, Telenor, one of the largest mobile operators, has extended its domestic EasyPaisa service from money transfers and bill payments to savings accounts for people who do not have bank accounts.

The Philippines central bank is introducing a lower-cost real time gross settlement system. The Philippine Payments and Settlement (PhilPaSS) system, planned for implementation in the second quarter of 2010, would ensure same-day settlements of transactions and reduce fees to a maximum of 100 Philippines Pesos (about US$2.25) per transaction.

The State Bank of Pakistan, the Ministry of Overseas Pakistanis, and the Ministry of Finance launched a joint initiative called the Pakistan Remittances Initiative to facilitate and support a faster, cheaper, and more convenient and efficient flow of remittances. The initiative reimburses a part of marketing expenses to banks and other entities that work with Pakistani banks in order to reduce costs for the remittance senders and to facilitate flows through formal banking channels. Market competition can often pressure businesses to provide customized remittances and other financial services for the poor at market prices, although businesses usually vie to serve wealthier customers. Competition has pushed many remittance service providers to send remittance agents to the migrant camps to provide remittance services to poor migrant workers from Bangladesh, the Philippines, and other countries. But in addition to providing a standard remittance service, they also provide deposit and loan services customized to the needs of migrants. When small numbers add up to create large profit opportunities, such services are likely to be more sustainable over time than those relying on public or private subsidies. The remittance market in Abu Dhabi and Dubai is large. As information about the size of the market has become more credible, competition among remittance service providers has become intense.

Remittances and Microfinance: A Tenuous Link?

Several pilot programs use remittances to improve the access of households to formal financial services, but the scale of such programs to date remains limited. With the recent increased popularity of microfinance, a number of microfinance institutions are looking into provision of remittance services. Some microfinance institutions are beginning to use the history of remittances as a way to evaluate creditworthiness of their poor customers who often cannot provide proof of income. Also, several microfinance agencies are trying to earn remittance fee income. Early evidence (from 2004 and 2005) from the World Council of Credit Unions showed that when people enter a credit union branch to send or receive remittances, both remittance senders and receivers open an account and leave some money behind for use later.

The Universal Postal Union is also working with a remittance software platform to provide remittance services through member post offices, earn remittance fees, and at the same time cross-sell postal saving products. The World Savings Bank Institute is trying to promote a link with remittances and savings with member savings banks. Cemex, a Mexican cement company, had an early scheme to link remittances to microsaving to try to encourage saving by migrants to build houses. Later a Bancomer affiliate piloted a scheme in New York suburbs to provide housing financing to migrants who send remittances through its branches. There are pilot products linked to (a) remittances to provide car loans to migrants in the United States for purchasing cars in Mexico and in the Gulf for purchasing cars in the Philippines and (b) life insurance to remitters to guarantee the continuation of remittance flows for 12 months or more in the event of remitter's death.

While the goal of expanding remittance services to underserved poor customers is laudable, the idea of using remittance fees to cross-subsidize microfinance products is less appealing because this involves one set of poor people subsidizing another set of poor people. Microfinance customers are also not always remittance recipients, and vice versa, except in communities that have a large concentration of migrants or remittance recipients.

Outlook for Migration and Remittances in 2010–11

Based on our methodology of forecasting remittances using a bilateral migration matrix and the World Bank's forecasts of nominal GDP growth, remittance flows to developing countries are projected to grow by 6.2 percent in 2010 and 7.1 percent in 2011 (table 17.1; see box 17.4

Box 17.4 Revised Forecast Methodology Using New Bilateral Migration and Remittance Matrixes

The forecasts for remittance flows for 2010 and beyond are based on stocks of migrants in different destination countries and estimates of how changes in income of migrants influence remittances sent by these migrants. Remittance flows are broadly affected by three factors: (a) the migrant stocks in different destination countries, (b) incomes of migrants in the different destination countries, and (c) to some extent, incomes in the source country (see Ratha and Shaw [2007] for a discussion of these and other factors). Remittances received by country i from country j can be expressed as

$$R_{ij} = f(M_{ij}, y_i, y_j),$$

where M_{ij} is the stock of migrants from country i in country j, y_j is the nominal per capita income of the migrant-destination country, and y_i is the per capita income of the remittance-receiving country. The bilateral remittance matrix of Ratha and Shaw (2007) is re-estimated using the bilateral migrant stocks data above to arrive at estimates of remittance intensities I_{ij} (the share of remittance outflows in nominal GDP Y_j of each source country j going to receiving country i).

$$I_{ij} = r_{ij} I_j,$$

where r_{ij} is the share of country j's remittances going to country i, and I_j is the share of remittance outflows in nominal GDP of source country j.

During the precrisis period, remittances grew faster than the GDP of remittance-source countries because of a number of factors, including improvements in remittance technologies, falling costs, and the steady increase in migrant stocks. For the postcrisis period (2010 and beyond), the elasticity of remittances (R_j) with respect to migrant incomes (MY_j) is assumed to be half of the precrisis period, with an upper bound of 3 and lower bound of 1, with the view that remittances would grow at a lower, more "sustainable" rate in the postcrisis period. These remittance elasticities are used to forecast remittance outflows from each remittance-source country in 2010 and beyond based on the latest available forecasts of GDP from the World Bank, using the following formula:

$$\hat{R}_j^t = R_j^{t-1} \left(1 + \eta_j \left(I_j \right) log \left(MY_j^t / MY_j^{t-1} \right) \right).$$

The forecasts of outflows and estimated remittance intensities are used to arrive at the estimates of inflows for each remittance-receiving country i.

$$\hat{R}_i^t = \sum_j r_{ij} R_j^t.$$

For this purpose, the bilateral migration matrix developed by Ratha and Shaw (2007) was updated with immigrant stock data from various sources to provide the most comprehensive estimates of bilateral immigrant stocks worldwide in 2010 (*Migration and Remittances Factbook 2010* forthcoming).

Source: Ratha, Mohapatra, and Silwal 2010.

for a description of the forecast methodology). Remittance flows to developing countries are expected to reach US$335 billion in 2010, almost the same level reached in 2008.

The decline in remittance flows to Latin America and the Caribbean appears to have bottomed out. Partly because of the large decline in 2009, flows to Europe and Central Asia by 2011 are unlikely to recover to the precrisis levels of 2008. Flows to other developing regions are expected to remain weak in 2010–11. Although the outcome for remittances in 2009 turned out better than expected, the recovery in the coming years is expected to be more shallow.

One source of risk to this outlook is that the crisis could last longer than expected. The emerging recovery in construction and other sectors in the United States may not be sustained after the effects of the stimulus package wear off. The recovery in construction employment in the United States has been driven in part by a credit to new home buyers that has stabilized migrant employment in that sector. If this subsidy proves unsustainable, it could have a dampening impact on the housing market. The recovery in migrant employment in construction during the summer may also be seasonal. A slowdown in construction activities in the United States tends to affect remittance flows to Mexico with a lag of four to six months (figure 17.5).

Other migrant-sending countries may also experience a lagged slowdown in remittance flows in response to slowing activities in other destination countries. A deceleration in construction activities in the GCC countries may affect migrant-sending countries in East Asia and South Asia. Although a recovery in oil prices and a fiscal stimulus implemented by GCC governments are likely to help maintain employment levels for existing migrants, new migration flows are unlikely to grow over the next two years. Therefore, remittances from the GCC countries may remain stable, but they are unlikely to grow rapidly for a year or two.

A second source of risk to the outlook presented here is that weak job markets and persistently high rates of unemployment in the destination countries may lead to further tightening of immigration controls, especially for low-skilled migrants. Even with projections of economic recovery in the advanced economies, unemployment rates are projected to remain high during 2010 and 2011, with a "jobless" global recovery. The labor market in the United States, the largest migrant-destination country, is expected to remain weak in the medium term, and unemployment rates

Figure 17.5 Correlation between U.S. Construction Sector Activity and Remittances to Mexico

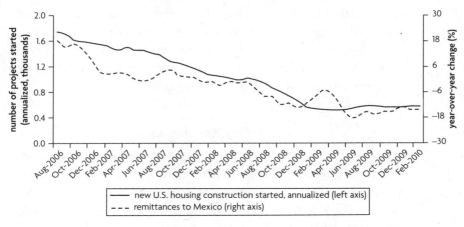

Sources: U.S. Census Bureau 2010; Banco de México 2010.
Note: Three-month moving averages are shown in chart.

Figure 17.6 Reflection of Fall in Demand for (and Supply of) High-Skilled Foreign Workers in Fewer Applications for U.S. Temporary Worker Visas

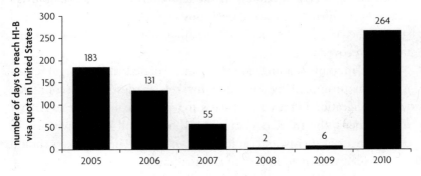

Source: U.S. Citizenship and Immigration Services. http://www.uscis.gov/portal/site/uscis.
Note: The figure shows applications for the upcoming fiscal year, which runs from October to September.

are expected to remain high. The applications from high-skilled foreign workers for temporary worker visas has fallen in the United States, with the number of days to fill the quota rising from two days for the 2008 fiscal year to 264 days for applications for the 2010 fiscal year (figure 17.6). If employment recovers only with a substantial lag to the recovery in economic output, then it is likely to have an impact on the employment levels and incomes of migrants—and, in turn, on their ability to send remittances.

A third source of risk is that currency movements are highly unpredictable. If the currencies of receiving countries start appreciating with respect to the U.S. dollar, then the "sale effect" (remittances for investment in cheaper assets) may reverse. This especially applies to India, which experienced a surge in such flows during 2008. The abnormal surge in remittances to Bangladesh and Tajikistan during 2007–08 may also prove unsustainable for the same reasons.

Policy Responses

With lower levels of foreign aid and investment likely over the short term, remittances will have to shoulder an increasing percentage of local development needs. Unfortunately, the greatest risk to remittance flows does not come from the economic downturn itself; instead, it comes from protectionist measures taken by many destination countries, including those in the developing world. There are risks that more immigration controls to protect native workers might imply a tradeoff between protecting native workers from job competition and protecting businesses facing falling revenues. In the short term, allowing employers flexibility in hiring and firing decisions may help them cut costs and survive the crisis. In the medium term, that might result in a more sustainable recovery.

Many migrant-sending countries are worried about large return migration prompted by weak job markets in destination countries. Return migration in the current crisis appears to be negligible so far, but if it happens, the workers coming back home will return with skills, entrepreneurial energy, and capital (see box 17.3). These workers should be provided with help in setting up small businesses and reintegrating into their communities, not be made the object of envy or fear of job competition.

To compensate for any reduction in new migration flows, some migrant-sending countries are trying to establish guest worker programs with destination countries. India is negotiating mobility partnerships with some European countries. Bangladesh and Nepal are trying to negotiate the continuation of immigration quotas with Malaysia and the Republic of Korea, respectively. The Philippines is actively searching for new migrant destinations.

Several countries are beginning to look at facilitating remittances in the face of external financing constraints, including introducing incentives to send more remittances through formal channels. For example, Pakistan has introduced a program that subsidizes remittance service providers for a certain part of their marketing expenses, depending on the volumes transferred. Countries are also trying to facilitate cheaper and faster remittances. One of the potentially cheapest and quickest options is money transfer using mobile phone networks. However, significant regulatory challenges related to anti-money-laundering initiatives and efforts to counter the financing of terrorism remain for cross-border transfers using mobile phone networks.

A standard remittance is a simple financial transaction that—if lightly regulated and processed using modern technology—can have minimal cost. Many remittance providers currently charge fees of more than 10 percent. Reducing remittance costs would require improving competition and transparency in the remittance market, applying a simpler and identical set of regulations across state and national boundaries, and increasing the use of postal networks and mobile phone companies. Exclusive partnership arrangements between money-transfer companies and the postal and banking networks of most countries are a hindrance to competition among firms offering remittance services. Sharing of payment platforms with multiple partners should be encouraged.

If funds were transferred through banks and other financial intermediaries, migrants and their beneficiaries would be encouraged to save and invest. Intermediary banks could also use remittance inflows as collateral to borrow larger sums in international credit markets for local investments. The development community can leverage remittance flows for development by making them cheaper, safer, and more productive for both the sending and the receiving countries. An "International Remittances Agenda," as summarized in figure 17.7, would involve

- Performing monitoring, analysis, and projections
- Improving retail payment systems through use of better technologies and appropriate regulatory changes
- Linking remittances to financial access at the household level
- Leveraging remittances for capital market access at the institutional or macroeconomic level.

Figure 17.7 International Remittances Agenda

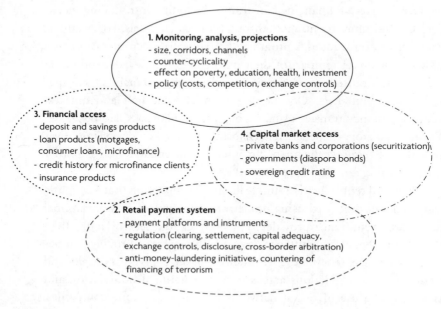

1. Monitoring, analysis, projections
- size, corridors, channels
- counter-cyclicality
- effect on poverty, education, health, investment
- policy (costs, competition, exchange controls)

3. Financial access
- deposit and savings products
- loan products (motgages, consumer loans, microfinance)
- credit history for microfinance clients
- insurance products

4. Capital market access
- private banks and corporations (securitization)
- governments (diaspora bonds)
- sovereign credit rating

2. Retail payment system
- payment platforms and instruments
- regulation (clearing, settlement, capital adequacy, exchange controls, disclosure, cross-border arbitration)
- anti-money-laundering initiatives, countering of financing of terrorism

Source: Authors.

Conclusion

Officially recorded remittance flows to developing countries reached US$316 billion in 2009, down 6 percent from US$336 billion in 2008. With improved prospects for the global economy, remittance flows to developing countries are expected to increase by 6.2 percent in 2010 and 7.1 percent in 2011. The decline in remittance flows to Latin America that began with the onset of the financial crisis in the United States appears to have bottomed out since the last quarter of 2009. Remittance flows to South Asia (and to a smaller extent East Asia) continued to grow in 2009, although at a markedly slower pace than in the precrisis years. Flows to Europe and Central Asia and the Middle East and North Africa fell more than expected in 2009.

These regional trends reveal three features:

- The more diverse the migration destinations, the more resilient are remittances.

- The lower the barriers to labor mobility, the stronger is the link between remittances and economic cycles in that corridor.
- Exchange rate movements produce valuation effects. However, they also influence the consumption-investment motive for remittances.

The resilience of remittances during the financial crisis has highlighted their importance in countries facing external financing gaps. Remittances are now being factored into sovereign ratings in middle-income countries and debt sustainability analysis in low-income countries. Countries are also becoming increasingly aware of the income and wealth of the overseas diaspora as potential sources of capital. Some countries are showing interest in financial instruments such as diaspora bonds and securitization of future remittances to raise international capital.

Notes

1. Remittance flows to Haiti are also likely to surge in 2010, in response to the devastating earthquake in January (see Ratha 2010).
2. Green and Winters (forthcoming) have examined migration trends during several past crises (during 1831–1913 and the Great Depression in the 1930s) and conclude that host-country economic factors usually were a much stronger determinant of migration than were origin-country factors. Passel and Suro (2005) report a similar finding for Mexican migration to the United States during 1992–2004. (See also Hatton and Williamson 2009.)

References

Awad, I. 2009. *The Global Economic Crisis and Migrant Workers: Impact and Response.* Geneva: International Migration Programme, International Labour Organization.

Fix, M., D. G. Papademetriou, J. Batalova, A. Terrazas, S. Yi-Ying Lin, and M. Mittelstadt. 2009. "Migration and the Global Recession: A Report Commissioned by the BBC World Service." Migration Policy Institute, Washington, DC. http://www.migrationpolicy.org/pubs/MPI-BBCreport-Sept09.pdf.

Green, T., and L. A. Winters. Forthcoming. "Economic Crises and Migration: Learning from the Past and the Present." U.K. Department for International Development, London.

Hatton, T., and J. G. Williamson. 2009. "Global Economic Slumps and Migration." Vox EU. http://www.voxeu.org/index.php?q=node/3512.

Ketkar, S. L., and D. Ratha. 2010. "Diaspora Bonds: Tapping the Diaspora during Difficult Times." World Bank, Washington, DC.

Passel, J. S., and R. Suro. 2005. "Rise, Peak, and Decline: Trends in U.S. Immigration 1992–2004." Pew Hispanic Center, Washington, DC. http://pewhispanic.org/files/reports/53.pdf.

Ratha, D. 2003. "Workers' Remittances: An Important and Stable Source of External Development Finance." In *Global Development Finance 2003: Striving for Stability in Development Finance*, 157–76. Washington, DC: World Bank.

———. 2009. "Dollars Without Borders." *Foreign Affairs*, October 16. http://www.foreignaffairs.com/articles/65448/dilip-ratha/dollars-without-borders.

———. 2010. "Mobilize the Diaspora for the Reconstruction of Haiti." *Haiti: Now and Next*, SSRC Features, February 11. http://www.ssrc.org/features/pages/haiti-now-and-next/1338/1438/.

Ratha, D., S. Mohapatra, and A. Silwal. 2010. "Outlook for Remittance Flows 2010–11: Remittance Flows to Developing Countries Remained Resilient in 2009, Expected to Recover during 2010–11." *Migration and Development Brief* 12. World Bank, Washington, DC.

Ratha, D., and W. Shaw. 2007. "South-South Migration and Remittances." Working Paper 102, World Bank, Washington, DC.

Taylor, J. E. 2000. "Do Government Programs 'Crowd In' Remittances?" Inter-American Dialogue and the Tomas Rivera Policy Institute, Washington, DC.

World Bank. Forthcoming. *Migration and Remittances Factbook 2010*. Washington, DC: World Bank.

Part 4
Regions

18

Africa: Leveraging Crisis Response to Tackle Development Challenges

Shantayanan Devarajan and Sudhir Shetty

Until the onset of the food, fuel, and financial crises of 2007–09, the countries of Sub-Saharan Africa were experiencing relatively rapid economic growth for over a decade. Between 1997 and 2007, gross domestic product (GDP) grew at almost 5 percent a year—the same rate as all developing countries except China and India—accelerating to over 6 percent in 2006–07. Poverty was declining: the percentage of Africans living on US$1.25 a day fell from 59 percent to 50 percent. Unlike previous episodes of rapid growth, this one was not driven solely by the boom in oil and commodity prices of the early 2000s. About 22 non-oil-exporting countries, accounting for a third of the African population, averaged better than 4 percent annual growth during 1998–2008. The oil exporters, home to another third of the population, also enjoyed rapid growth—over 6.5 percent annually for the decade—thanks to high oil prices and, as we show below, sound macroeconomic management. To be sure, the remaining third of the population lived in countries that were growing slowly or not at all. Most of these countries were either involved in conflict or emerging from it, although some such as Zimbabwe were simply trapped in a disastrous policy environment.

Africa's precrisis growth and poverty reduction were due to a combination of three, mutually reinforcing factors. First, there was an increase in external resources. Foreign aid, fueled by debt relief, increased by about US$14 billion—although the increase falls about US$11 billion short of the Gleneagles pledge to double aid to Africa by 2010. Private capital flows to Africa also increased, reaching a peak of US$53 billion in 2007. And remittances grew at double-digit rates, peaking at US$20 billion in 2007. Second, African countries benefited from a buoyant global economy and rising commodity prices. But perhaps the most important factor was that the underlying economic policy environment in Africa had, since the mid-1990s, improved significantly. Most countries had undertaken macroeconomic and fiscal policy reforms, and they were beginning to pay off. The median inflation rate in the mid-2000s was half that in the mid-1990s; whereas in 1996 there were 13 African countries with above-20 percent inflation, by 2007 there were only two.

The Crises of 2007–09

The triple crises of 2007–09 threatened to bring Africa's resurgent growth and poverty reduction to an abrupt halt. The doubling of food prices (in dollar terms) in 2007 hurt poor Africans, many of whom spend over half of their budget on food. Analysts estimated that poverty would increase by about 4 percentage points (Ivanic and Martin 2008). Riots broke out in cities such as Ouagadougou, Burkina Faso; Maputo, Mozambique; and Douala, Cameroon. African governments responded by lowering taxes (including import tariffs on food) and, in some cases, increasing existing subsidies. Countries that had reasonably well-functioning safety net programs scaled them up. Ethiopia, for instance, doubled the wage paid to participants in its Productive Safety Nets Program. Unlike in previous crises, very few countries resorted to price controls. Those that introduced export restrictions as a means of keeping domestic prices low soon abandoned them. Nevertheless, the food price crisis highlighted two weaknesses in the African policy environment. One was that poor agricultural infrastructure, not to mention in some cases the abandonment of food production, prevented farmers from benefiting fully from higher food prices. The other was that very little was known about the effectiveness of existing safety nets in Africa, so that it was not clear which ones could be scaled up during a crisis.

The near-doubling of world oil prices in 2007–08 had an asymmetric effect, with oil importers suffering a terms-of-trade shock of 5 to 7 percent of GDP, while oil exporters enjoyed a windfall of double that. The oil importers responded by increasing subsidies or lowering fuel taxes. In contrast to their behavior during previous oil booms, most of the oil exporters saved the additional revenues. When the price of oil was US$140 a barrel, Angola, Gabon, and Nigeria used a reference price of about US$80 a barrel.

The global financial crisis that started in September 2008 initially had only a mild effect on African economies. Most African banks were not sufficiently integrated with the global financial system to suffer from the fallout. The few that were integrated, such as those in Mauritius and South Africa, had strong prudential regulations that protected them.

But when the financial crisis turned into an economic crisis, most African countries were severely affected. Private capital flows, which had been rising faster to Africa than any other region, dried up. The Democratic Republic of Congo saw a decline of foreign direct investment of US$1.8 billion. Kenya and Ghana postponed sovereign bond offerings worth US$800 million. Remittances, which had been rising at about 13 percent a year, slowed to a trickle. Africa was particularly hard hit because 75 percent of its remittances come from the United States and Western Europe, the epicenter of the crisis. The decline in commodity prices reversed the terms-of-trade shock of the previous year, with oil importers gaining and exporters losing. While the savings during the oil boom helped cushion some of these exporters, the fact that their economies were so heavily dependent on oil meant that GDP growth suffered. Angola's GDP, for instance, went from growing at over 15 percent a year during 2004–08 to 1 percent in 2009. Finally, foreign aid was unlikely to increase given the fiscal problems in donor countries.

Policy Responses to the Global Financial Crisis

The net result was that Africa's GDP growth rate fell from 5.8 percent in 2008 to 1.4 percent in 2009. Although growth was still positive (in contrast to most of the developed world), the decline in per capita GDP meant that poverty would rise. An estimated additional 7–10 million Africans would be thrown into poverty. Furthermore, such sharp declines in growth are associated with increases in infant mortality: some 30,000 to 50,000 additional infants were likely to die before their first birthday. Perhaps most troubling was the prospect that the economic reforms, which had been delivering strong growth and poverty reduction until 2008, would be slowed or reversed. The payoffs to these reforms had suddenly disappeared. And the policies being pursued by developed countries—increasing fiscal deficits and nationalizing banks—were precisely in the opposite direction of what African governments were undertaking.

Significantly, these policy reversals did not happen. Those African countries that had some fiscal space (thanks to debt relief and prudent macroeconomic management before the crisis) ran modest countercyclical policies, dampening the impact of the global crisis on the domestic economy. Zambia, for instance, ran a fiscal deficit of 2.6 percent of GDP. Most of the increase in the fiscal deficit (which averaged about 2 percentage points) was due to the decline in government revenues. Government expenditures did not increase because implementation difficulties would have prevented them from stimulating the economy. The increased deficits were financed by a combination of domestic borrowing (which expanded by 2 percentage points of GDP) and front-loaded, concessional resources from the World Bank and the African Development Bank.

Furthermore, those countries that did not have fiscal space chose to run contractionary fiscal policies to maintain long-term sustainability. For example, Ghana, which had a fiscal deficit of 14 percent of GDP in 2008 (which was unrelated to external shocks), has now embarked on a program to reduce that deficit by 2 percentage points a year for the next six years.

Not only did African countries respond quickly and pragmatically to the global crisis, but many of them innovated and, in some cases, accelerated reforms. Tanzania, for instance, introduced an emergency program for the banking sector that provides loan guarantees that are strictly time bound—two years—a feature that is lacking in comparable programs in the United States and Europe. Recognizing that public investment typically suffers in recessionary times, South Africa provided countercyclical funds of about US$100 billion exclusively for public investment (this was also necessary so the country could host the 2010 Soccer World Cup).

Mauritius introduced an innovative burden-sharing program among business, labor, and government to restructure distressed companies. Finally, Nigeria used the weakness in oil prices to begin deregulating its downstream petroleum sector.

Longer-Term Challenges and Opportunities

The growth recovery across a large swath of the continent since the mid-1990s and the pragmatism that has characterized the policy responses of most countries to the crises of 2008–09 are encouraging. Nevertheless, much of the African continent continues to face a number of challenges in the medium term. In what follows, four such challenges are noted, along with the opportunities to address them, with recognition that the specifics will necessarily differ across countries.

Infrastructure Gaps. In almost every African country, the lack of physical infrastructure is a constraint to growth and poverty reduction. Infrastructure is not only lacking, but also much more expensive than elsewhere in the developing world. Average electricity costs of US$0.18 per kilowatt hour are about double that of other developing countries. Infrastructure gaps are largest by far in energy, with citizens in 30 of the 47 countries in Sub-Saharan Africa facing regular power shortages and power interruptions. Furthermore, only one in four Africans has access to electricity. Collectively, the countries of the subcontinent (with more than 800 million people) have about the same power generation capacity as that of Spain (with a population of about one-twentieth).

Filling these gaps and lowering service costs will require both more money and reforms in the provision of infrastructure. The additional money will need to come from domestic and external sources, including donors. And there will need to be a balance between new investment and spending on operations and maintenance so that the latter is not crowded out. To raise the level of infrastructure of all African countries to the level of that of Mauritius, countries will need an additional US$48 billion per year, a third of which will be needed to cover maintenance needs. The complementary policy and institutional reforms in infrastructure sectors will both ensure that new investment is well spent and help bring the private sector into financing and operating these facilities. Nevertheless, even if potential efficiency gains are fully realized, a funding gap of about US$31 billion will remain.

A specific aspect of these infrastructure investments that will be important in almost every African country will be the expansion of irrigation. Despite its importance to economic activity and its potential role in reducing poverty, agriculture in most African countries has been ignored until relatively recently, the adverse implications of which became clearest during the food crisis of 2008. And with less than 5 percent of cultivated land irrigated, African agriculture remains extremely vulnerable to the effects of global climate change—more frequent floods and droughts, as well as what appears to be a long-term drying trend in many parts of the continent.

Demographic Transition and Job Creation. In many countries in Sub-Saharan Africa, the demographic transition has not even begun. There are still many Sahelian countries, such as Mali, Niger, and Burkina Faso, where the population growth rate is over 3 percent per year with total fertility rates of over 7 births per woman. Even where the transition has started, there is a bulge in the under-15 population that will work its way into the labor force in the coming decades. These factors will exacerbate the problem of youth unemployment with 7 million to 10 million young people entering the labor force every year and formal-sector job growth not rising fast enough to absorb them. The creation of productive employment opportunities, especially for the youth, will be an important economic and political challenge for African governments.

Part of the answer will be to reduce the demographic pressures, especially where fertility rates are still high. These efforts will need to go beyond providing access to and information about family planning services to also cover the empowerment of girls and women, including through access to education. There will also need to be efforts to increase the demand for youth labor, including in the informal sector where most jobs in low-income African economies are created. The informal sector is estimated to employ about 80 percent of Africa's labor force. Improving the investment climate is critical in this regard for both formal and informal sector firms. And targeted efforts to expand youth employment, such as wage subsidies or vocational training schemes, will need to take account of and build on global experience with such interventions.

Governance and State Capacity. The challenges of governance and limited state capacity are starkest in the 20 fragile states of Africa—be they due to earlier conflicts, such as those in the Democratic Republic of Congo and the Central African Republic, or ongoing conflict, such as that in Somalia. But as with the issue of job creation, the challenges cut across Africa. Many resource-rich countries show significant weaknesses in governance, which means they gain much less than they should from their natural resource wealth. In general, and although there are exceptions such as Mauritius, the quality of public sector management and institutions is lower in Sub-Saharan Africa than in other regions. The most significant adverse reflection of these governance weaknesses is seen in the poor quality of service delivery in health, education, and water and sanitation. Public school teachers in Uganda are absent about 20 percent of the time. In Chad, the share of nonwage public health resources that reaches the primary clinics is 1 percent. These service delivery failures have hindered faster progress toward the Millennium Development Goals.

Improving governance will necessarily be a long-term and country-specific effort. In general, however, where conflict is still prevalent, as in the Democratic Republic of Congo, or the risks of resumption high, as in Sudan, the root causes will still need to be addressed, including through long-term coordinated support from development partners. In resource-rich economies, priority needs to be placed on ways of increasing transparency, promoting accountability, and improving decision making throughout the chain of resource extraction and use. This will cover such areas as the awards of licenses and contracts, the macroeconomic management of windfall revenues, and public spending decisions. In all countries, there must be a focus on efforts to enhance the capabilities and incentives of the public sector to better plan and implement development policies, tailored to country circumstances.

Aid Volumes and Modalities. Much of Africa will remain aid dependent in the medium term. However, as the full impact of the financial crisis becomes apparent in Organisation for Economic Co-operation and Development countries, aid flows from the Development Assistance Committee donors are not likely to grow as robustly as they have over the past decade. Even before the crisis, projections were that overseas development assistance would be about US$20 billion short of the Gleneagles commitment to double aid to Africa by 2010. With the impact of the crisis, the gap has only widened. Alongside tightening aid budgets, there is also a backlash emerging against budget support as the preferred modality of aid provision in many Western European countries—despite the evidence that this instrument lowers transaction costs, supports capacity building, and helps harmonize donor support. Ironically, these developments are happening when the productivity of aid to Africa—as a result of the policy reforms undertaken over the past 15 years and the continued pursuit of prudent policies during the crisis—has never been higher.

Conclusion

Africa is the world's poorest region and faces development challenges of monumental proportions. But the fact that policy reforms generated relative rapid economic growth and poverty reduction before the global crisis, and that policy makers by and large continued to pursue these policies during the crisis, means that the continent's prospects for resuming growth are good. It also means that there is increasing political support for pro-poor reforms—the very reforms that will help the continent address the challenges of infrastructure, job creation, governance, and shrinking aid. If the international community continues to support Africa, the combination of additional resources and policy reforms could launch the continent on a path of sustained, rapid growth and poverty reduction.

Reference

Ivanic, M., and W. Martin. 2009. "Implications of Higher Global Food Prices for Poverty in Low-Income Countries." *Agricultural Economics* 39 (1): 405–16.

19

East Asia and the Pacific Confronts the "New Normal"

Vikram Nehru

The developing countries of East Asia and the Pacific are leading the world out of the 2008–09 global economic and financial crisis. While the region's gross domestic product (GDP) growth slowed from 8.5 percent in 2008 to 7.0 percent in 2009, the region is expected to bounce back to 8.6 percent in 2010. But in an unusually diverse region, averages mask wide differences across countries. China, boosted by its unprecedented fiscal and monetary stimulus package, registered 8.7 percent GDP growth in 2009, down from 9.5 percent in 2010 but still an exceptional performance in a contracting global economy. Remove China from the East Asia aggregate, however, and the rest of the region grew by only 1.3 percent in 2009, much lower than South Asia and only just higher than Sub-Saharan Africa (table 19.1).

The reality is that East Asia's performance was decidedly mixed in 2009. Indonesia, the Lao People's Democratic Republic, Papua New Guinea,

---

This chapter is a shortened version of the publication of the World Bank's East Asia Region, "East Asia and the Pacific: Emerging Stronger from the Crisis," World Bank, Washington, DC, April 2010, at: http://web.worldbank.org/WBSITE/EXTERNAL/COUNTRIES/EASTASIAPACIFICEXT/EXTEAPHALFYEARLYUPDATE/0,,contentMDK:20275253~pagePK:64168427~piPK:64168435~theSitePK:550226,00.html.

Table 19.1 Thanks to China, Developing East Asia as the Fastest Growing Developing Region
percentage change year-on-year

	2007	2008	2009
Developing East Asia	11.4	8.5	7.0
Developing East Asia excluding China	6.2	4.7	1.3
Europe and Central Asia	7.1	4.3	−6.2
Latin America and the Caribbean	5.5	3.9	−2.6
Middle East and North Africa	5.3	5.8	2.9
South Asia	8.5	5.7	5.7
Sub-Saharan Africa	6.5	4.9	1.1
High-income countries	2.6	0.4	−3.3

Sources: World Bank 2009; World Bank staff estimates and projections.

Timor-Leste, and Vietnam did well to maintain robust growth rates (table 19.2). But the upper-middle-income economies of Malaysia and Thailand, and the low-income economies of Cambodia, Fiji, and Mongolia, contracted in 2009. The Philippines barely registered positive growth.

Even so, by the end of 2009, most countries in the region had resumed robust growth and many had reached their precrisis peaks in industrial production and GDP. Strong growth in private consumption, resumption in export growth, and inventory accumulation drove GDP growth sharply upward in the fourth quarter of 2009. Importantly, the economies of the region are emerging from the crisis with manageable fiscal deficits, relatively low government and external debt burdens, and benign rates of inflation.

Helping this quick recovery were four factors. First, most East Asian economies entered the crisis from positions of strength—rapid growth, low fiscal and external debt, external current account surpluses, large external reserves, low inflation, and well-capitalized banks with little or no exposure to toxic assets. Second, policy makers took quick action to counteract the forces of contraction emanating from the advanced countries, with virtually every East Asian country introducing fiscal and monetary stimulus packages. Third, China's rapid growth sucked in imports from around the world, including East Asia, providing much-needed external demand. By end-2009, China's import growth was an astonishing 56 percent (year-on-year),[1] helping lower the trade balance to 4 percent of

Table 19.2 Bright Prospects for East Asia and Pacific
year-on-year percentage change unless indicated otherwise

	2008	2009	2010f	2011f	Forecasts for 2009	
					December 2008	November 2009
					2009	2009
Developing East Asia	8.5	7.0	8.7	8.0	6.7	6.7
China	9.6	8.7	9.5	8.7	7.5	8.4
Indonesia	6.1	4.5	5.6	6.2	4.4	4.3
Malaysia	4.6	−1.7	5.7	5.3	3.7	−2.3
Philippines	3.8	0.9	3.5	3.8	3.0	1.4
Thailand	2.6	−2.3	6.2	4.0	3.6	−2.7
Vietnam	6.2	5.3	6.5	6.5	6.5	5.5
Cambodia	6.7	−2.0	4.0	6.0	4.9	−2.2
Lao PDR	7.5	6.7	7.7	7.8	6.0	6.4
Timor-Leste	12.8	7.4	7.5	7.4	1.4	7.4
Mongolia	8.9	−1.6	7.3	7.1	7.5	0.5
Fiji	−0.1	−2.5	2.0	2.2	1.1	−0.3
Papua New Guinea	6.6	4.5	6.8	5.1	5.0	3.9
Memoranda						
Developing East Asia Middle-income countries	8.6	7.2	8.7	8.0	6.8	6.9
Low-income countries	6.3	4.3	6.3	6.4	6.1	4.5
Developing East Asia excluding China	4.7	1.3	5.5	5.2	4.1	1.1
Middle-income countries	4.5	0.9	5.4	5.1	3.8	0.7
G-3	0.3	−3.5	1.7	2.0	−0.4	−3.5
Global trade volumes	3.0	−14.4	4.3	5.3	−2.1	−11.4

Sources: Datastream; Development Prospects Group in the Research Department (DECPG) of the World Bank; World Bank staff estimates and projections.
Note: f = forecast; G-3 = Eurozone, Japan, and the United States.

GDP (down from 6.7 percent of GDP in 2008). Fourth, remittances to many countries in the region remained remarkably resilient.

The crisis slowed the pace of poverty reduction in the region, but did not stop it. Our simulations suggest that the number of poor increased by 9 million in the region compared to the counterfactual of continued trend growth, but that still represents a decline in the number of poor from an estimated 508 million in 2008 to 477 million in 2009 (around 200 million in China alone).[2] These aggregate numbers, however, underestimate the welfare consequences of the crisis on the poor and near poor in the region. Micro-evidence from several countries shows that while formal wages and unemployment remained virtually unchanged, furloughs and cuts in overtime reduced take-home pay, especially in export firms and small and medium enterprises, forcing labor to seek work in the informal sector or in unskilled agriculture. Wages in the informal sector inevitably declined; for example, construction wages in Cambodia fell by a third and off-farm rural wages declined by around 13 percent.

A Key Challenge in the Short Term

Now that the region's economies are moving at a rapid clip, the attention of policy makers is naturally turning toward tightening the monetary and fiscal policies that proved so effective in boosting economic activity during the crisis. Indeed, signs of rising inflation in some countries have already prompted central banks to tighten credit growth. Indonesia has raised reserve requirements, and Vietnam and Malaysia have raised policy rates.

But the world's focus is on China's monetary policy. There, a large part of the stimulus was delivered through a 30 percent expansion in credit growth. The inflation rate became positive in November 2009 and has been inching up since (reaching 2.7 percent in early 2010). More important, property sales climbed 75 percent in value and 42 percent in space during 2009. Urban property prices increased 10.7 percent (year-on-year) in end-February 2010, with prices rising in all 70 cities and reaching 50 percent in Hainan Island. In response to these rising prices, construction activity surged after September 2009, and in the first two months of 2010, it had climbed 37 percent.

In October 2009, China's central bank started mopping up excess liquidity (through open-market operations and foreign exchange swaps); raised the required reserve ratio twice; and introduced selective credit controls, especially for the real estate sector. As a result, credit growth is slowing, although it still remains relatively high (figure 19.1). Further tightening is expected.

The authorities in the region have been more reluctant to tighten fiscal policy, and rightly so. Thanks to fiscal stimulus measures that compared

Figure 19.1 Slowdown of China's Credit Growth

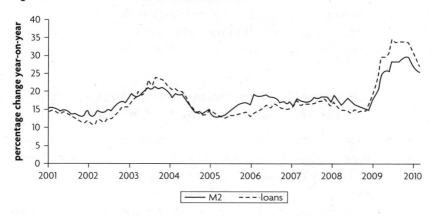

Source: CEIC database.
Note: M2 = a calculation of the money supply that combines money currently in circulation (M1) plus money in accounts that can be quickly converted to spending money.

Figure 19.2 East Asia and Pacific's Fiscal Stimulus Compared with That of Advanced Countries

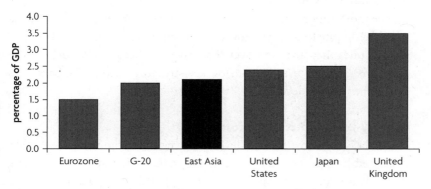

Sources: National authorities; World Bank staff estimates.

favorably with even those of the advanced countries (figure 19.2), economic activity in East Asia moderated by less than many other developing regions. Nevertheless, the pressure on labor markets remains high, and recovery in global markets is not assured. Moreover, most countries have the fiscal space to continue with expansionary fiscal policy, at least through the remainder of 2010 and then assess the need for changes in the fiscal stance in light of domestic and global developments. At the same time, governments need to guard against the view that the world will return to precrisis conditions soon and design their fiscal policies accordingly. The reality is that precrisis growth in the global economy was unsustainable and that the "new normal" will be quite unlike the old.

Confronting the "New Normal": Structural Reforms for Rapid Growth in the Medium Term

Projections describing global economic conditions over the medium term—the new normal—have been revised downward significantly since the crisis. The key reason is expected lower growth in the United States, Japan, and the Eurozone (which together account for three-quarters of global GDP) on account of high public debt burdens, continued rehabilitation of bank balance sheets, increased risk aversion, policy uncertainty about proposed financial reforms, and periodic macroeconomic aftershocks of the crisis. For the developing countries, this will mean slower-growing export markets, costlier international finance, and a difficult trading environment.

The most important question confronting East Asian policy makers is whether, despite these conditions, their economies can resume the rapid growth rates they achieved over the past three decades. We believe the answer is "yes"—but it depends on key structural reforms in countries and at the regional level.

Country-Level Structural Reforms

East Asia is the most diverse developing region in the world—whether measured by size, per capita income, or production structures (figure 19.3). From China (population 1.33 billion) to Palau (population 20,000), the region includes areas with some of the highest population densities in the world (Java in Indonesia) to some of the lowest (Mongolia)—from manufacturing powerhouses to commodity-dependent economies—and the second-highest number of fragile states in the world (after Africa).

No common structural agenda could possibly fit such a diverse group. But it does help to consider the key challenges confronting five subgroups.

China. China deserves to be a subgroup all by itself. In China, the biggest reform challenge is "rebalancing"—and not surprisingly, it is identified

Figure 19.3 More Diversity in East Asia than in Other Developing Regions

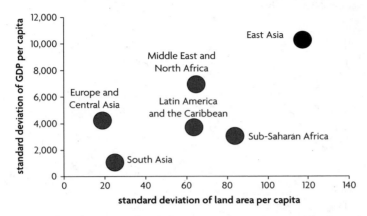

Source: World Bank World Development Indicators database.

as a central objective in the country's 11th Five-Year Plan. It is now broadly accepted in China that while capital-intensive, industry-led, export-oriented growth has been spectacularly successful in increasing incomes, the resulting pattern of production is energy intensive and environmentally unsustainable, does not create enough jobs, has generated increased inequality, and is heavily dependent on external demand (figure 19.4). To correct this, China is seeking to rebalance its growth pattern, with domestic demand (especially consumption) as the main driver and services as the leading sector. This, in turn, is expected (a) to better balance economic growth with resource conservation, energy efficiency, and environmental protection, and (b) to help mitigate the urban-rural divide; promote more balanced regional development; and improve basic public services, especially social protection, health, and education.

The critical nature of this transition toward a more balanced economy cannot be overemphasized. If recent energy consumption patterns continue for another 20 years, China will consume 87 percent of the world's current energy output. The authorities have moved forcefully to boost energy efficiency and improve environmental sustainability. For example, about a third of the stimulus package is for "green investments," a share three times as large as that in the United States. Similarly, in 2009, China doubled yet again its installed wind power capacity, a pace three times as

Figure 19.4 China's Capital-Intensive Industry-Led Pattern of Production in an International Perspective

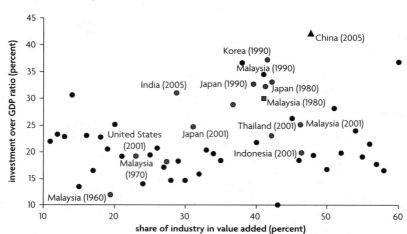

Sources: World Bank World Development Indicators database; NBS (for China); World Bank staff estimates.

fast as that of the world as a whole. China now accounts for a third of global capacity and is just behind the United States.

Although the stimulus package may have helped accelerate public investments in areas important for rebalancing (environment, health, education), other policy reforms in support of rebalancing have been delayed due to the crisis, such as removing distortions in the tax structure and in the price of capital, energy, natural resources, land, and the environment, and scrapping regulatory barriers impeding services development. It is important that these are once again given the priority they deserve.

Middle-Income Countries. The middle-income countries in East Asia—Indonesia, Malaysia, the Philippines, and Thailand—face the medium-term challenge of raising investment in physical and human capital with the intention of moving up the value chain. After their initial export successes (Malaysia and Thailand more than Indonesia and the Philippines), the pattern of labor-intensive production and exports in these countries has remained broadly unchanged for two decades. With the rise of China and India as favored investment locations for labor-intensive manufacturing, the middle-income countries of East Asia have to reinvent themselves if they are to grow rapidly. Put simply, these countries could be caught in a middle-income trap—unable to remain competitive as high-volume, low-cost producers, yet unable to move up the value chain and achieve rapid growth by breaking into fast-growing markets for knowledge- and innovation-based products and services.

Moving up the value chain requires investment—in infrastructure, machinery and equipment, education, skills, information technology, and so on. Yet investment in all these countries *declined* in the decade after the Asian financial crisis, and currently falls well short of levels that existed in the Republic of Korea, Japan, and Singapore when they were at similar per capita income levels. The slowdown in investment does not stem from a lack of savings—indeed, in all these countries, domestic saving exceeds domestic investment, resulting in external current account surpluses. An extreme example is Malaysia, where the current account surplus was 17 percent of GDP in 2008 and 2009.

In fact, there is no single reason for low levels of private and public investment in middle-income countries. In Malaysia, rigidities in the labor market and entry barriers tend to discourage private investors; in Indonesia, public infrastructure appears to be a binding constraint; in Thailand, internal political strife has raised risk and uncertainty; and in the Philippines, it is probably a combination of these reasons.

Resolving these problems is a priority for rapid growth to be sustained over the medium term. The new economic model announced recently by Malaysia is representative of the reforms needed—empowerment of state and local authorities, cluster- and corridor-based economic activities (to capture economies of scale), attraction of local and foreign talent, removal of labor market restrictions, incentives supporting innovation and risk-taking, and a shift in market orientation from the G-3 countries (the United States, Japan, and the Eurozone) to Asia and the Middle East. In Indonesia, urgent attention is being given to the core issue of infrastructure connectivity to lower transport costs and crowd-in private investment. And in all countries, improving access to education, and raising its quality—particularly secondary and tertiary education (since primary education is already universal)—will be central to developing the skilled labor force needed to move up the value chain.

Low-Income Countries. The low-income countries of East Asia—Lao PDR, Cambodia, and Vietnam—are confronted with the task of "breaking in" to the production networks of East Asia. They have already made a remarkably successful start. For their level of per capita income, they are among the countries with the highest share of manufacturing relative to GDP in the world. In Cambodia, value added in industry almost tripled over the past two decades, albeit from a low base, and so did the number of workers. And Vietnam is a favored destination of foreign investors seeking high returns from investments in labor-intensive production (10 percent of GDP in 2008).

These countries will undoubtedly be helped by regional and global forces in the future—a rapidly growing neighborhood; a continued global trend toward specialization in tasks; and rapidly rising labor costs in middle-income countries, including China. Thus far, however, only Vietnam has been able to link to production networks, and that, too, in a limited way. The challenge and opportunity confronting Lao PDR and Cambodia will be to upgrade physical and human capital and embrace regional integration. The development of regional and national infrastructure to improve connectivity and reduce transportation costs across Southeast Asia is a critical step in this direction. This will now need to be complemented by "soft infrastructure"—namely, measures to facilitate trade such as efficient transit arrangements, common border regulations, national single-window facilities for importers and exporters, and customs modernization.

Commodity Exporters. The commodity exporters of the region—Mongolia, Papua New Guinea, and Timor-Leste—need to harness volatile export revenues for sustainable long-term growth. Interestingly, two of the three—Papua New Guinea and Timor-Leste—had already adopted fiscal rules prior to the crisis, as a result of which they sustained rapid growth in 2009 despite the global downturn. Mongolia, on the other hand, implemented expansionary fiscal and monetary policies prior to the crisis on the back of the commodity boom, so that when the crisis hit in late 2008, the economy went into a tailspin and encountered a severe fiscal and financial sector crisis. Mongolia's parliament is now considering a Fiscal Stability Law, but the recent rise in commodity prices (especially copper prices) may make political passage of the bill difficult.

The volatility of commodity prices increased substantially prior to the crisis and is unlikely to abate soon (figure 19.5). This makes the adoption of fiscal rules and a robust fiscal framework all the more important in these countries.[3] Unfortunately, the track record of countries in this regard has been mixed. Even Papua New Guinea, under pressure from the crisis, allowed a budget deficit greater than the limit set by the fiscal rule. In so doing, Papua New Guinea was not unique. Governments invariably find reasons to abandon or circumvent fiscal rules as they become binding.

Although difficult to maintain in good times and equally difficult to defend in bad times, fiscal rules and a sound fiscal framework are essential prerequisites for transforming boom-bust cycles into sustainable revenue streams that can be used productively for long-term development. The emergence of recent best practice in this regard is to combine a medium-term fiscal framework with a fiscal risk statement that reveals the risks attached to particular fiscal trajectories and flags the quantitative impact of known contingent liabilities. Such risk statements can be persuasive in convincing the authorities of the dangers of departing from a fiscal rule.

The Pacific Islands
The Pacific Islands face unusually difficult development and policy challenges, given the small size of their economies and population, the

Figure 19.5 Recent Increase in the Volatility of Commodity Prices

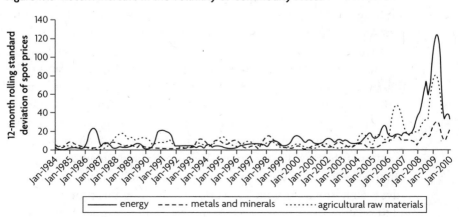

Source: World Bank staff estimates.

significant distance to large markets, and the exceptionally high dependency of their economies on single sectors. The Pacific Islands have a population of about 2 million, a tenth of Jakarta, and yet stretch across an area of ocean that covers one-seventh of the world's surface. Their small economies make them vulnerable to external economic shocks, and diseconomies of size make the unit cost of public service delivery unusually high. As if that were not enough, the fact that many are low-lying islands makes them vulnerable to climate change, and their location makes them prime targets for natural disasters (earthquakes, tsunamis, and hurricanes). And finally, to make matters worse, several Pacific Island states are prone to conflict and political instability. It is hardly surprising, then, that despite being heavily dependent on aid to make ends meet, most Pacific Island countries are off-track in their quest to meet the Millennium Development Goals.

While there are many long-term challenges confronting this subregion, it is worth highlighting three for which potential solutions are feasible. The first is aid coordination and aid predictability. The Cairns Compact on strengthening development coordination in the Pacific is an important step toward implementing the Paris Declaration on Aid Harmonization.[4] The compact calls for frequent collective review of progress in strengthening development coordination, regular peer review of national development plans and budget allocation processes, and annual reports on efforts to reduce aid fragmentation and lower administrative costs. In addition, it is important that aid is predictable if it is to support long-term development efforts and that catastrophic risk insurance instruments are available to provide resources when natural disasters hit.

The second challenge is to overcome the costs of distance and isolation by facilitating the quiet telecommunications revolution taking place in the Pacific, which is reducing costs of transactions, information flows, and service delivery. Long-distance learning through the Internet has taken off, enabling students in the Pacific Islands to obtain degrees at a fraction of the cost of attending in person. Similarly, medical diagnoses can now be made on the basis of images transmitted from the islands to advanced hospitals around the world. Accelerating this process requires additional investments in telecommunications and greater coordination and integration of national efforts within the subregion.

The third challenge is the importance of subregional economic integration. Significant progress has been made in this regard, but much more can be done. Most important among these are efforts to (a) implement subregional agreements on the management, conservation, and development of fisheries; (b) develop regional arrangements for marine mineral resource management; and (c) implement key regional agreements to promote the freer movement of goods and services. There is also considerable potential for deepening integration with the nearest large market, which for the Pacific Islands mostly means integration with Australia and New Zealand. Most recently, temporary migration schemes with New Zealand and Australia have been at the forefront of this agenda. New Zealand now runs a Recognized Seasonal Employer program that allows up to 8,000 temporary migrants from the Pacific Islands to work in the country's horticulture sector. Such efforts can be expanded, particularly given Australia's need for large numbers of temporary agricultural laborers.

A Common Regional Agenda

In addition to structural reforms needed at the country level (in the case of the Pacific Islands, at the subregional level), there are many reforms and actions that cut across countries and need to be taken at the regional level. Fortunately, East Asia is served by two active and effective regional organizations—the Association of Southeast Asian Nations (ASEAN) and Asia-Pacific Economic Cooperation. ASEAN, in its various manifestations (ASEAN+3, ASEAN+6, the East Asia Summit) covers most of East Asia, while Asia-Pacific Economic Cooperation broadens East Asia's partnership with the North American continent and Latin America. We highlight here two high-priority items on the regional agenda that both these organizations are promoting—regional economic integration and climate change.

Regional economic integration has been instrumental in driving much of East Asia's growth over the last three decades. Intraregional trade has grown faster here than in any other region in the world and is gradually approaching levels achieved in the European Union (figure 19.6). ASEAN member countries have made significant progress in cutting tariff and other barriers at the border in line with the Common Effective Preferential Tariff Scheme. Yet, per capita income in East Asia is much

Figure 19.6 The Quick Rise of Intraregional Trade in East Asia and the Pacific, Surpassing That of NAFTA

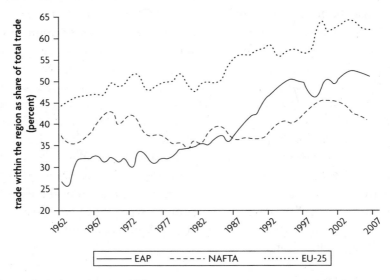

Source: Alavi, Nehru, and van Dorn 2008.
Note: EU-25 = European Union 25. NAFTA = North American Free Trade Agreement.

more dispersed than in Europe, suggesting that there remains considerable scope for more integration (figure 19.7).

The agenda for further economic integration can be advanced along five fronts. First, improvements in logistics and behind-the-border reforms are a priority. Logistics in the region cost twice as much as in the advanced countries. For example, in terms of averages for all products, logistics account for about 8 percent of landed costs from East Asia compared to about 4 percent in the developed world. Similarly, behind-the-border procedures and rules need to be simplified and made more predictable. These include streamlining documentary requirements for import and export transactions, reducing the number of border agencies with which firms must interact, and eliminating hidden trade barriers. Such reforms will increase predictability, reduce the cost of doing business, lower export and import delays, remove uncertainty surrounding unofficial payments, and discourage favoritism in administrative decision making.

Second, barriers to investment need to be lowered. Contrary to expectations, barriers to foreign direct investment in East Asia are the highest

Figure 19.7 Higher Income Disparity in East Asia and the Pacific than in Europe
Coefficient of variation in per capita income

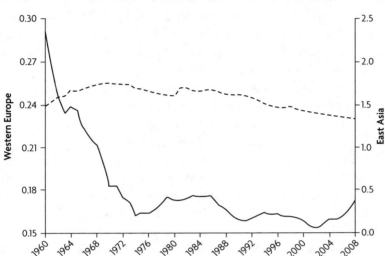

Source: Alavi, Nehru, and van Dorn 2008.

in the world. This outcome is surprising given the role of foreign direct investment in advancing intraregional trade. Removing such barriers will enhance competition and productivity gains from higher foreign direct investment; encourage the use of the region's large savings for investments within the region; and support the spread of new technologies, including "green technologies."

Third, the region needs to promote trade in services. The benefits of doing so could be many times that of reducing barriers to trade in goods. For example, static gains from trade for developing East Asia and Korea arising from services trade liberalization are estimated to be about US$270 billion, or 10 percent of income, by 2015 (World Bank 2002). Interestingly, gains in services trade liberalization tend to accrue largely to the country implementing the reforms. This is because improvements in the efficiency of the services sector not only promote growth in services, but also encourage growth in other sectors that use services as a key input. As regional production networks become the basis for manufacturing strength and competitiveness, weaknesses in the availability of services can become a serious obstacle.

Fourth, the region is moving rapidly toward greater financial integration. The launch of the Chiang Mai Initiative Multilateralization (CMIM) in March 2010 is a significant move toward addressing balance-of-payments and short-term liquidity difficulties in the region, supplementing existing international financing arrangements. The priority now is to establish an independent regional surveillance unit to monitor and analyze member economies and support CMIM decision making. Similarly, the Asian Bond Market Initiative seeks to develop local-currency-denominated bond markets and thereby encourage private savings to be used for regional development. The priority now is to promote the demand for and issuance of local-currency-denominated bonds and to develop the associated infrastructure and regulatory framework. In addition, the ASEAN+3 Finance Ministers' Meeting in Bali in May 2009 endorsed the establishment of the Credit Guarantee and Investment Mechanism as a means to further encourage regional bond markets.

Fifth, addressing key issues associated with intraregional migration could potentially prove to be a win-win proposition. Host countries worry about both the influx of unskilled migrants and their potentially depressing effects on wages and employment opportunities and the burden on public finance and services. Source countries are concerned about brain drain, exploitation of workers, adverse cultural and social effects, and growing dependence on remittance earnings. These issues reached a crescendo during the global crisis and its immediate aftermath. Progress in resolving them should help contribute to regional integration and help reduce labor shortages in some countries and excess labor supply in others. And migrants in manufacturing, especially in companies integrated within production networks, can potentially learn valuable skills that are transferable home where production networks may be making initial inroads.

Climate change and environmental sustainability are global issues that must also be tackled at the regional (and country) level. East Asia's rapid economic development, including accelerating urbanization, has resulted in a tripling of energy consumption over the past three decades, with projections for a further doubling over the next two decades. Unfortunately, the pattern of production and the technologies adopted for energy generation, transport, and infrastructure have resulted in sharp increases in greenhouse gas emissions. And although energy consumption and greenhouse gas emissions per capita are well below levels in advanced economies, developing East Asia has some of the world's most-polluted cities. Under unchanged policies, the World Bank projects that greenhouse gas emissions and local air pollutants will double for all the larger countries in the region by 2030. At the same time, these large increases in greenhouse gas emissions are accelerating global climate change, often with detrimental effects for the region. Whether associated with climate change or not, catastrophic events such as floods, droughts, and storms—especially for countries in the Mekong Delta, Vietnam, Indonesia, the Philippines, and the Pacific islands—appear to be growing in frequency and becoming more deadly.

Mitigation and adaptation measures are, therefore, key priorities for the medium term. Our proposition is that not only can East Asia make these measures work in support of sustainable growth, but they also can actually help accelerate it. In other words, East Asian economies have an opportunity to turn the challenge of climate change into growth. With investment rates in the region higher than in most developed countries and many developing ones, a significant portion of the capital stock can embed "green" technologies within a few years. Already, there is growing evidence that although new green technologies are being created in the advanced countries, they are being applied increasingly in developing countries, especially East Asia. Over a third of China's stimulus package was devoted to green investments compared to just 10 percent in the U.S. stimulus package. China is devoting US$88 billion to high-speed rail compared to US$8 billion in the United States. China, Japan, Korea, and Singapore are already at the forefront of developing energy-efficient and renewable technologies and products, including photovoltaic cells, wind power, biofuels, and hydroelectricity. With the right policies, application of such technologies will gradually spread, leading also to familiarity and eventually mastery. Just as East Asia did in the application of other technologies (such as information and communication technology) in the past, it has the capacity to do so now by leapfrogging over the advanced countries to reach the green technology frontier rapidly. Such a move could possibly give the region a competitive advantage in a sector poised for rapid global growth.

Given the far-ranging adverse impacts of climate change, adaptation must be an integral component of an effective strategy to address climate change, along with mitigation. The Irrawaddy Delta in Burma was devastated by Cyclone Nargis in May 2008, and late in 2009, Cambodia, Lao PDR, the Philippines, Thailand, and Vietnam were hit by Typhoon Ketsana (named "Ondoy" in the Philippines), suffering floods, landslides, and loss of life and property. Densely populated coastal areas are susceptible to the adverse effects of climate-related events. The Irrawaddy, Mekong, and Red River delta regions, for example, and the urban centers of Bangkok, Jakarta, and Manila are extremely vulnerable and are designated as "climate hot spots."

Adaptation is about building resilience and reducing vulnerability. For building of resilience, development is an imperative. In this sense, the rapidly growing economies of East Asia are better positioned than some other developing regions. Not only does development make economies less reliant on climate-sensitive sectors, such as agriculture, but it also increases incomes, health, and education; expands the capacity of households to adapt; improves institutional infrastructure; and enhances the ability of governments to assist. Countries with high levels of investment also hold an advantage, because adaptation also requires new technologies, such as drought- and flood-tolerant crops and climate-proofed infrastructure.

When catastrophic natural disasters have struck the region, countries have pulled together to help the devastated areas and subregions. But in each case, support was coordinated in a relatively ad hoc fashion. Since such disasters could increase in intensity and frequency, regional coordination frameworks are necessary for responding to climate change effects and natural disasters. ASEAN is leading this process in East Asia and recently approved a declaration on climate change that sets out a framework for international cooperation.

Conclusion

Developing East Asia is leading the global economic recovery, although performance varies across the region. In some countries, the monetary stance is already being tightened in light of emerging inflationary pressures, but it is premature to withdraw the fiscal stimulus until the global recovery is on a firmer footing. Fortunately, most countries have adequate fiscal space and relatively low debt burdens. To ensure the momentum of the recovery transitions into sustainable and inclusive growth over the medium term, the governments in the region must once again focus their attention on medium-term structural reforms. This means different policy priorities in different countries—especially given the diversity of the region. In addition, the region faces two common priorities—regional economic integration and climate change. Making progress on both will be critical to the region's medium-term prospects.

Notes

1. Admittedly, imports were at their nadir in December 2008.
2. These data are based on the US$2 a day (in purchasing power parity terms) international poverty line.
3. A robust fiscal framework includes, but is not limited to, a good taxation regime for the natural resource sector; comprehensive government budgets; thorough costing of all government programs; budget and spending transparency; stronger medium-term fiscal and expenditure frameworks; and a robust regime for public investment planning, execution, and monitoring. Fiscal rules are an integral part of the framework.
4. See the final communiqué of the Fortieth Pacific Islands Forum, Cairns, Australia (August 5–6, 2009).

References

Alavi, H., V. Nehru, and R. van Dorn. 2008. "Building the Neighborhood One Policy at a Time: The Case for Deeper Integration in East Asia." World Bank, Washington, DC.

World Bank. 2002. *Global Economic Prospects and the Developing Countries*. Washington, DC: World Bank.

———. 2009. *Global Economic Prospects 2009: Commodities at the Crossroads*. Washington, DC: World Bank.

20

Europe and Central Asia: A Time of Reckoning

Luca Barbone

When the Europe and Central Asia (ECA) region celebrated the 20th anniversary of the fall of the Berlin Wall on November 9, 2009, the celebration occurred, in one of those coincidences of history, when the region was in the midst of its first generalized recession—and the most serious one that most countries had seen since the Soviet Union crumbled.

The convergence toward western European living standards lifted millions out of poverty and created, in recent years, a rapidly growing middle class. This happened in the context of, and facilitated, a remarkable process of (a) political democratization and creation of new institutions that have made governments more accountable to the population; and (b) for several countries, integration into the European Union. But the achievements, of which the region is proud, also masked significant structural weaknesses. Because of its success in integrating into the world economy and in international financial markets, the region had become heavily dependent on external savings and external capital flows. Rapid growth increased public revenues, and this permitted fiscal consolidation, but also postponement of needed program reforms and even unsustainable increases in wages and transfers. When the recession struck, the fiscal position of most countries deteriorated sharply, presenting realities that necessitated sharp adjustments. As a result of the recession and the fiscal retrenchment, some 40 million people now find themselves among the ranks of the poor, and many more are vulnerable.

As the economic performance of the region begins to turn around, these newly manifested weaknesses cast a shadow on the prospects of future growth and social development and point to the need for governments to demonstrate determined leadership and strategic vision. The trajectory over the next decade crucially will depend on how well significant long-term challenges will be tackled. These challenges include the following:

- The aging of the population and the related stress on labor markets, social protection systems, health, and the sustainability of the fiscal accounts
- The challenge of raising productivity in an increasingly interconnected world
- The effects of global warming on the environment and the economic structure of the region.

The Crisis of 2008–10: A Wake-up Call

A Large and Differentiated Region. Spanning from within the European Union to the borders with China, the ECA region is a large (30 countries, 480 million people), economically important (US$3.7 trillion gross domestic product [GDP]), and politically sensitive region that is most noteworthy for its extreme diversity. Hence, it provides both substantial opportunities for and challenges to integration. It includes the world's largest country, the Russian Federation, and some of its smallest, such as Montenegro. Three countries—Russia, Turkey, and Ukraine—account for more than half the region's population, while the smallest 15 account for less than 10 percent. The region ranges from institutionally weak, low-income countries, such as Tajikistan (US$600 per capita), to post-conflict countries, such as Bosnia and Herzegovina (US$4,500 per capita) and Kosovo, to high-income European Union (EU) member states, like Slovenia (US$24,000 per capita). While some ECA countries, particularly Kazakhstan, Russia, and Turkmenistan, hold almost one-third of the world's gas reserves and are key suppliers to Western Europe, energy security is a major concern for others. Reorientation of trade was a key driver of the transition to market economies, but the region now ranges from some of the most open economies in the world, including five EU member states where trade exceeds 100 percent of GDP, to far less integrated economies where trade is less than half of GDP.

After the economic problems experienced during the 1990s, following the break-up of the Soviet Union and the implosion of the economic institutions and arrangements that underlay it, the region's performance starting from 2000 had been impressive. High and sustained growth rates contributed to lifting some 50 million people out of poverty, and they facilitated important social and political transformations, exemplified by the accession to the EU of eight countries in 2004 (the Czech Republic, Estonia, Hungary, Latvia, Lithuania, Poland, Slovak Republic, and Slovenia), followed by two more in 2007 (Bulgaria, Romania), and credible applications for membership from several others. The emergence of a new middle class has generally—but not everywhere—contributed to the creation of new institutions that have increased accountability of governments.

The Crisis of 2008–09. Despite the positive accomplishments just cited, the ECA region experienced the largest reversal in economic growth from 2007 to 2009 of any region in the world. GDP growth declined by 12 percentage points, compared to 5 percentage points in Latin America, 4 percentage points in Africa and the Middle East, and 3 percentage points in developing Asia (figure 20.1). Even though precrisis fiscal deficits were overall smaller than in other regions (with the exception of the Middle East), the sharper economic contraction has led to much larger fiscal deterioration (more than 5 percent of GDP) than in other regions (2 to 4 percent of GDP).

The recession hit the region in different ways, laying bare structural and financial weaknesses that had accumulated during the high-growth years of 2000–07.

In some of the most advanced countries, which had integrated into the global financial markets, the effects of the global deleveraging, together with the reversal of the real estate booms, reduced the willingness of creditors to finance current account deficits. These deficits were, as a percentage of GDP in 2008, at double digits in countries such as Bulgaria, Latvia, Lithuania, Romania, and Serbia and in the high single digits in Estonia, Hungary, and Ukraine.

Figure 20.1 "The Great Recession, 2009"—GDP Growth by Region

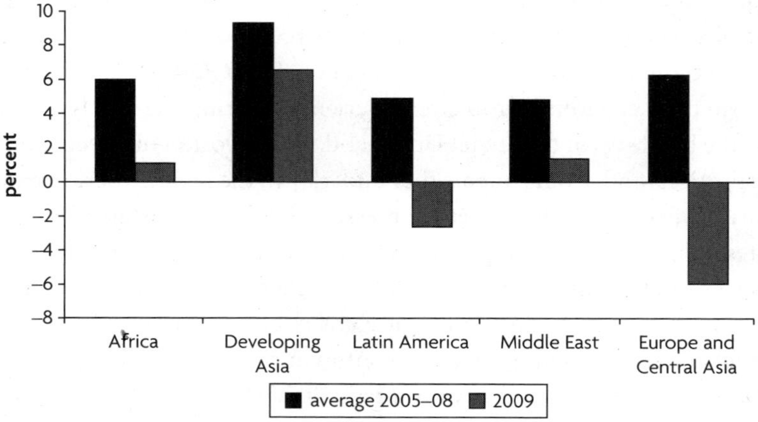

Source: World Bank staff calculations.

A second transmission channel came from the sharp drop in exports to Western Europe and the rest of the world, and had a particularly negative impact on output and employment in small open economies such as the Czech Republic, Estonia, Hungary, and the Slovak Republic, where exports accounted for 70 percent to 80 percent of GDP in 2008. To a somewhat lesser extent, this was also the case in larger economies such as Poland and Romania, where the corresponding share ranged between 30 and 40 percent, and in Turkey.

For the low-income and lower-middle-income countries of the Former Soviet Union, such as Armenia, Georgia, the Kyrgyz Republic, Moldova, and Tajikistan, lower remittance flows (with reductions of some 30 percent or more) severely affected the living standards of the population.

Finally, resource-dependent countries were hit by the sharp declines in commodity prices. In Russia, GDP contracted by more than 7 percent in 2009, a decline compounded by the sharp reduction in credit flows. In Kazakhstan, the crisis started earlier—in 2007—with a sudden stop in capital flows that had financed much of domestic growth, which was then compounded by the commodity crisis of the following year.

The social and economic consequences of the recession have predictably been severe. Households have been hit hard by growing unemployment, poverty, and—as a perverse result of success in building up financial markets—household indebtedness. Unemployment has risen through-out the region, with registered unemployment increasing by about 3 million and millions more in unregistered joblessness. The region's dramatic reduction in poverty has also been partially reversed. The num-ber of poor and vulnerable in 2010 is projected to be higher by almost 30 million compared to precrisis expectations. As a result, 40 million people live below US$2.50 per day in the ECA region, and about 150 million live below US$5.00 per day (figure 20.2).

What Have We Learned from the Crisis?

Many observers in the ECA region have pointed out that the origin of the crisis was largely external. While this is certainly true, it is also true that the crisis unmasked structural weaknesses that could be ignored in the boom times. These factors are not new, but the crisis has refo-cused attention on the unfinished reform agenda and put a premium on faster reform given the tougher growth environment.

The first lesson is that the region's savings deficit was unsustainable. Overreliance on foreign savings—particularly foreign borrowing by the private sector—left both households and firms particularly vulnerable in a world of tighter and more discerning capital markets. The market dominance of foreign banks—itself the result of years of reform and consolidation of domestic banking systems—has been a plus since they were instrumental in the past in introducing better credit instruments and more modern appraisal techniques. Foreign banks have generally maintained their exposure in the region during the crisis, but excessive credit growth destabilized financial sectors in many countries prior to that time. The precautionary fiscal stance needed to offset unsustainable private inflows was largely absent, as governments found it difficult to resist pressures for higher social spending.

The second lesson is thus that the lack of reforms in social sector institutions was masked by high growth rates in the precrisis years. Pub-lic expenditures, mostly on account of social spending, rose in real terms and as a percentage of GDP throughout the region, particularly in the second half of the 2000s. As growth rates declined, the fact that social spending is a bigger share of government expenditure than elsewhere, but lacks better results, has become more apparent. ECA countries spend

Figure 20.2 The Effect of the Crisis on Poverty

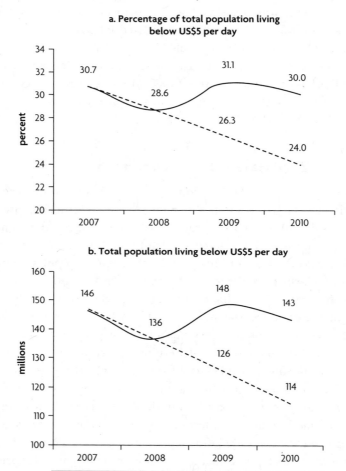

a. Percentage of total population living below US$5 per day

b. Total population living below US$5 per day

Source: World Bank staff calculations.

more on public education than their developing-country counterparts, but outcomes are no better. Hospital-centric systems often result in poor outcomes in basic health indicators despite high levels of public spending. Social protection programs are often poorly targeted and social insurance programs are fiscally unsustainable, but high growth rates and buoyant tax revenues before the crisis decreased the urgency for reform.

High growth rates in the precrisis years—largely the result, on the supply side, of total factor productivity catch-up after the break-up of the early 1990s—masked what have become important barriers to competitiveness in many ECA countries. Infrastructure and a skilled labor force, the positive legacy of socialism, have emerged as the tightest bottlenecks to the growth of firms as indicated by a survey of 10,000 firms in 28 ECA countries. Remarkably, two decades after the fall of the Berlin Wall, infrastructure and labor skills are identified as a bigger constraint in the ECA region than in nontransition economies at similar income levels.

Going Forward—A Renewed Emphasis on Modernization and Integration in an Aging Region

Current growth projections for 2010–14 show that the ECA region is coming out of the recession, but also that its short-term growth prospects are modest, with growth rates averaging 3 to 4 percent during this period, or only half the precrisis level. This year, 2010, is expected to be particularly difficult, with GDP growth forecasts for the ECA of between 1 and 2 percent, less than half of the forecast for the rest of the world.

The reason for such sober forecasts is that many of the factors that contributed to growth during the precrisis years are unlikely to return, at least in a majority of ECA countries. The high growth prior to 2009 was financed by large capital inflows—fueled by world liquidity pressures, euro adoption prospects for some, and commodity price booms for others. World growth (which was exceptionally high during 2000–07), access to capital, and commodity prices are not likely to regain precrisis levels for some time. Foreign direct investment is expected to recover, but most likely not to the levels seen in the precrisis years. In a postcrisis world that is projected to have less global liquidity and more risk aversion, returning to the precrisis model of growth will simply not be an option. This economic environment will challenge governments throughout the region to create the necessary environment to facilitate a more diversified and competitive economy.

Social inclusion and equity issues will likely grow in importance. The increased unemployment, poverty, and household indebtedness arising from the crisis have refocused attention on social issues. In addition, social inclusion and equal access to opportunities will be critical in order to ensure the human capital needed for future growth, particularly in rapidly aging societies. The political economy is also likely to drive the social inclusion and equity agenda, since the political sustainability of economic reforms will require better social outcomes in a world of slower growth and potentially rising inequality. Hot-button issues such as cross-border migration flows and their regulation are bound to come even more to the fore, as the largest countries and economies in the region are projected to lose population (figure 20.3)—and labor force—in important numbers.

The closely linked growth and social agendas will be more difficult to address in a period of inevitable *fiscal consolidation*. The crisis-driven fiscal deterioration will require fiscal consolidation across the region. Four underlying factors will make such consolidation in a period of slower growth particularly challenging: a history of big government (government expenditure averaging 37 percent of GDP over the past decade), social spending that is more than half of government expenditure (higher than other countries at this level of income), a *rapidly aging population* that will further strain fiscal sustainability of social insurance programs,

Figure 20.3 Demographic Projections for Europe and Central Asia Countries

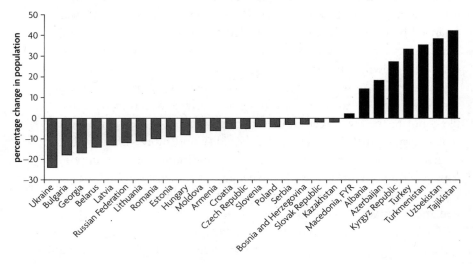

Source: World Bank staff calculations based on United Nations 2005.

and a deterioration in access to financing due to reduced liquidity and more risk-consciousness.

Pressures to face *climate change challenges* will grow rapidly. Inaction will lower future growth and aggravate the global situation. Although the transition to market economies is for the most part accomplished, the central planning legacy of high energy intensity remains. Energy intensity of GDP in the ECA region (0.29 kilograms oil equivalent per dollar of GDP) is similar to that of East Asia or Africa, but double that of Latin America and 50 percent greater than that of South Asia or the Middle East (even taking into account the harsher climatic conditions). Russia alone is the world's third-largest emitter of greenhouse gases. In addition, ambitious EU targets will necessitate enormous smart-energy investments in new member states and candidate countries. Countries will also face near-term challenges brought on by climate change, including winter floods and summer droughts, melting permafrost and glaciers, and hydrological changes.

Postcrisis Strategic Choices for the ECA Region

In the context just discussed of a more difficult external environment and strong domestic pressures, ECA countries will have to struggle to find consensus to tackle a number of reforms for faster and inclusive growth and to tackle climate change issues.

A Long Agenda of Reforms for Faster Growth. Restoring growth and convergence will require tackling bottlenecks to competitiveness, faster productivity growth, and more (not less) integration. The key areas for related sector reform are as follows:

- Innovative policies to promote economic diversification and higher productivity across sectors from information services to agriculture (an agenda that is shared broadly across the region, but is extremely important for resource-dependent countries such as Azerbaijan, Kazakhstan, and Russia)
- The composition and efficiency of public expenditure and revenue mobilization (now that the fall in revenues and the reduced capacity for external borrowing are likely to lead to a long period of fiscal consolidation, largely across the region)

- Stable and efficient financial intermediation (improving regulatory capacity, including macroprudential regulation, and consolidating banking systems), since the crisis has revealed important weaknesses in both regulation and legislation and in the capacity of regulators (witness the severity of the crises in Hungary, Latvia, and Ukraine, to cite a few)
- The investment climate for enterprises (reduction of the regulatory burden, streamlining of tax administration, privatization, and trade and customs reforms)
- Energy and transport infrastructure (ensuring adequate maintenance funding and speeding up implementation of infrastructure projects, improving efficiency in energy production and use, and encouraging private investment through guarantees and improved energy security).
- Regional integration (critical for achieving faster growth, particularly among the Central Asian countries, which have yet to exploit the potential for trade collaboration and proximity to the huge Chinese market).

Inclusive Growth and Better Social Outcomes. Achieving better social outcomes, developing the human capital for growth, and maintaining the political sustainability of reform programs all require better service delivery in education, health, and social protection. Since the low efficiency of public interventions is as big a constraint as the level of resources, the tightening fiscal constraints on ECA countries offers, somewhat paradoxically, an opportunity to address long-standing structural issues in the social sectors. Recent education sector reforms (Bulgaria, Latvia, and Romania), health sector reforms (Latvia and Romania), and pension reforms (Hungary and Romania) exemplify this opportunity to improve the efficiency and quality of public service delivery and continue the convergence to European standards, to face the demographic challenges and ensure sustainability of pensions and social insurance programs, and to strengthen public institutions and governance in the social sectors.

Climate Change for Sustainable Growth. The energy intensity of the ECA region is high, and its carbon footprint is large. Economically sound climate change investments constitute big opportunities. Energy efficiency investments, in particular, offer significant potential for new sources of growth and efficiency in the postcrisis world. The increase in extreme weather events also increases the need for disaster management invest-ments. But even countries and sectors that might benefit from climate change are poorly positioned to do so. The possible gains in agriculture from a warmer climate and more precipitation in the northern part of the region will require massive efforts to reduce the glaring productivity gap in most ECA agriculture.

Conclusion

This chapter ends on a cautionary but optimistic note. The ECA region is clearly facing some of the most difficult challenges of its new history. As we have seen, the "Great Recession" has brought back to the fore old problems and highlighted new ones. The long-term challenges are clearly formidable. However, the region can proudly point to a record of accom-plishment over the past two decades that has allowed its radical transfor-mation and catapulting into a new era. The omens for a successful response to the challenges are good.

Bibliography

Chawla, M., G. Betcherman, and A. Banerji. 2007. *From Red to Grey—The Third Transition of Aging Populations in Eastern Europe and the Former Soviet Union.* Washington, DC: World Bank.

Tiongson, E., A. I. Gueorguieva, V. Levin, K. Subbarao, N. Sugawara, and V. Sulla. 2009. *The Crisis Hits Home—Stress-Testing Households in Europe and Central Asia.* Washington, DC: World Bank.

United Nations. 2005. "World Population Prospects: The 2004 Revision." United Nations Department of Economic and Social Affairs, Population Division. New York: United Nations. http://www.un.org/esa/population/publications/WPP2004/2004 Highlights_finalrevised.pdf.

21

A Brave New World for Latin America

Marcelo M. Giugale

In 2009, Latin America dodged a bullet. Its efforts over the previous decade at better economic management and smarter social policy paid off, and the worst global recession in a generation caused only minor damage. Does this mean that the region will go back to business as usual, back to a commodity-fueled bonanza, back to *la vida loca*? No, it does not. The crisis has opened both challenges that policy makers will be forced to address and opportunities they will be foolish to ignore.

This chapter describes those challenges and opportunities and uses them to visualize how the region's economic policy agenda will change over the coming years. It does not focus on all the issues that will be relevant, but on those that will be relevant and different. Specifically, it will argue that six new issues will appear on the radar of Latin American policy makers: (a) fiscal decision making that smoothes, rather than exacerbates, business cycles; (b) a profound preoccupation with innovation as a means to commercial survival; (c) adaptation to a changing regulatory wisdom in finance; (d) the shifting of social policy from equality to equity; (e) the use of results to rebuild trust in the state; and (f) the realities of having a bigger role in world affairs.

Not all Latin American countries will move along the new agenda at the same speed. A few have already started, and a few may even go for a while in an opposite direction. Overall, however, the picture that emerges is one of second-generation policies, a reflection of well-managed economies making the most of a promising development horizon.

Independent Fiscal Agencies

The global financial crisis has shown the wisdom of governments that save in good times to spend more during downturns—the wisdom of "countercyclical fiscal policy."[1] That simple principle brought huge economic and political rewards to those that practiced it (see Chile). But it did more than that. It opened the door to a new way of thinking about public finance. Much as in the early 1990s, when worries about inflation led many Latin American countries to stop printing money to pay for fiscal deficits and to shift control of the printer to an independent central bank, worries about unemployment may now lead them to link taxation and public investment to growth. In the 1990s, half a dozen Latin American countries adopted "inflation targets" and met them. The time for more independent fiscal decisions that take into account "growth targets" cannot be far away.

Will independent fiscal agencies become common in Latin America? Probably. But they will have advisory, rather than decision-making, roles. That is, they will be fiscal "councils," rather than fiscal "authorities." In fact, two councils already exist (in Brazil and Chile), mostly in the form of technical support for parliaments. As more countries in the region implement fiscal frameworks or fiscal responsibility laws (some 10 already have), independent monitoring will become a necessity, both to judge the realism of budget projections and to hold governments accountable during execution. To some extent, private organizations (for-profit and not-for-profit) have been providing that kind of monitoring service for a while. As pressures mount for fiscal policy to be, and be perceived as, countercyclical, the role of fiscal watchdog will become institutionalized within the apparatus of the state, but outside the control of incumbent governments.

An additional force may be pushing for independent fiscal opinions: the continuing accumulation of commodity-related revenues. In the baseline global scenario, growth in Asia will keep commodity demand strong and commodity prices high. Volumes may also increase, driven by recent discoveries of oil and gas (in Brazil and Colombia). This will translate into fiscal abundance for many Latin American countries. If that happens, some of those monies will have to be saved in sovereign wealth funds, whose rules of operation will be the subject of much debate. Having independent agencies monitor the application of those rules and, at times, provide technical inputs (for example, in forecasting prices) will become a more accepted practice—and a way to avoid political meddling.

Innovate or Perish

Successful Latin American countries will have to learn to live with appreciated currencies. With interest rates in the developed world likely to stay floor-low for a while, money will continue to flow into the region's more promising economies. This will make them less competitive. There is not much they can do about it—accumulate reserves, impose capital controls and taxes, keep banks from credit sprees, and increase productive efficiency. But those are either unsustainable measures or long-term reforms. The reality is that living in, or exporting from, places like Bogotá, Lima, São Paulo, or Santiago will be more expensive in U.S. dollars. It will be more difficult to sell Latin American products in the United States and in any other country that keeps its currency tied to the U.S. dollar, notably China. That is why success in trade will now depend more on new products. While securing additional free trade agreements will still be beneficial, creating new brands will be even better.

The problem for Latin America is that, on the whole, it has not excelled at innovation. It invests too little in research and development, provides few tax incentives, and does not protect intellectual property well, and its universities are disconnected from its businesses. This is reflected in minute levels of patent registration, declining total factor productivity (vis-à-vis the U.S. benchmark), few firms' acquiring of quality certifications (less than a quarter), and a commercial penetration that has been stagnant for decades (only about 5 percent of world trade has a Latin American partner) (figure 21.1). Even the precrisis years of abundant financing saw only a handful of new Latin American business lines come to market—premium foods, medical tourism, aeronautic engineering, software development, and call centers.

It will take years to fix those problems, but the new global reality will make change unavoidable. Will there be a single formula to foster innovation in Latin America? No. Latin American countries differ in terms of technological stock, efficacy of tax systems, quality of human capital, legal predictability, and institutional capacity. But successful innovation strategies show some common features that point the way forward:

- They are priorities of the state (they do not change from government to government).
- They are not based solely on markets.
- They engage all relevant stakeholders (big and small, public and private).

Figure 21.1 Symptoms of Innovation, or Lack of It

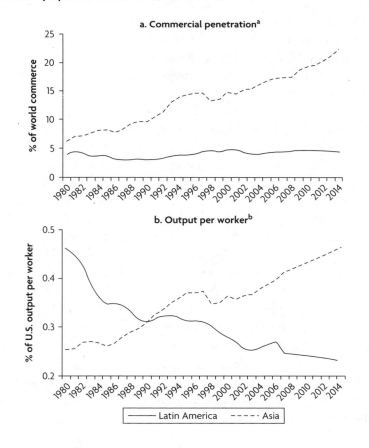

a. Commercial penetration[a]

b. Output per worker[b]

——— Latin America   - - - - - Asia

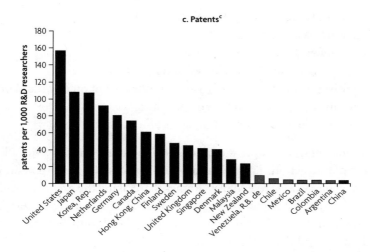

c. Patents^c

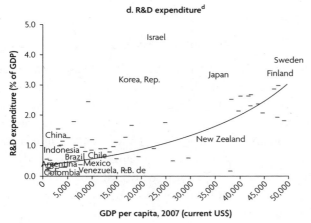

d. R&D expenditure^d

GDP per capita, 2007 (current US$)

Sources: a. World Bank staff calculations and projections on International Monetary Fund (World Economic Outlook) data; b. World Bank staff calculations and projections on Penn World Tables 6.2, University of Pennsylvania; c. World Bank staff calculations on World Intellectual Property Organization (WIPO) and World Bank data; d. World Bank staff calculations on World Bank data.

Note: GDP = gross domestic product; R&D = research and development.

a. Commercial penetration is defined as exports plus imports as a percentage of world commerce.

b. Panel b shows the output per worker as a ratio of the U.S. output per worker over time. The Latin America aggregate is calculated as the unweighted average of Argentina, Brazil, Chile, Colombia, Costa Rica, Ecuador, Mexico, Peru, Uruguay, and República Bolivariana de Venezuela. The Asia aggregate is calculated as the unweighted average of China; Hong Kong, China; India; Indonesia; the Republic of Korea; Malaysia; Singapore; Taiwan, China; and Thailand.

c. Panel c shows the number of patents in the United States per 1,000 R&D researchers using 2007 figures.

d. Panel d shows the relation between R&D expenditure (as a percentage of GDP) and GDP per capita (2007 figures in current U.S. dollars).

- They hold someone accountable for results.
- They are part of a broader effort of integration.
- They are well funded.
- They are continuously evaluated and adjusted.
- They begin with quick wins (usually in the area of quality standards).
- They include reforms in tertiary education.
- They operate within a reliable legal framework.

Interestingly, more private innovation in Latin America will call for better public action. From venture funding to skill improvement, the state will have a new role to play. Rather than taking the exclusive leadership as it tried in the past (with poor results), it will become a catalyzing partner in multi-agent efforts. In some cases, it will contribute resources; in others, it will contribute reforms.

Reinventing Finance

Latin America will be wary of fancy finance. Its banks and bourses sailed through the crisis rather well. There were no subprime surprises in Latin America. In part, that is because its financial sectors are small, unsophisticated, and with limited external connections and, in part, because Latin America still regulates them in a heavy-handed, old-fashioned way. In addition, the remaining publicly owned banks came in handy to keep credit flowing. Meanwhile, the developed world, shocked by the excesses in Wall Street, entered a wide debate about new ways to control financiers without killing their creativity. From how much capital banks should hold to how much bankers should be paid and from who is "too big to fail" to how savers should be protected, it is all up for discussion. Over the next couple of years, governments in the region will have to decide how much of the new thinking to adopt, adapt, or avoid.

In practice, regional policy makers will be dealing with financial issues at both ends of the technical spectrum. On the one hand, postcrisis second-generation questions will have to be addressed, like countercyclical regulation, systemic risk, and nonbank intermediaries. On the other hand, a long list of basic but critical matters that preceded the crisis remains pending, especially in terms of competition and efficiency, access by the poor, and underdeveloped equity markets.

That policy dichotomy will play out at a time when Latin America's financial sector will be under pressure. In the short term, and as described earlier, foreign capital inflows will be abundant. Much of these inflows will be reflected in excess liquidity among domestic banks and in larger domestic lending. Some will flow into the regional equity markets, which, given their relatively small size, may quickly experience a surge in prices. In both cases, the domestic financial sector will be exposed to sudden capital flow reversal. Regulating this risk away will not be easy.

A different challenge emerges in the medium term. The region's largest countries are expected to continue experiencing surpluses in their balance of payments current accounts, led by high commodity prices. The counterpart of those surpluses—large domestic savings—will need to be intermediated. In other words, the balance sheet of Latin America's financial system will expand considerably. Whether this fosters consumption or investment, at home or abroad, by the public sector or by the private sector, will depend on the regulatory parameters under which the system is made to operate. In the recent past, markets could be relied upon to set some of those parameters (for example, through credit ratings); however, the crisis has de facto shifted that responsibility almost entirely back to governments.

Equity: More than Equality

Latin America has learned the value of knowing the poor by name. An estimated 8 million Latin Americans fell into poverty in 2009, and about 5 million missed their chance to leave poverty behind. Those are unfortunate numbers, but, compared to past experience, they are very small. What sheltered the region? It avoided jumps in inflation, so people's purchasing power did not melt. But more remarkably, for the first time, Latin America had effective mechanisms to protect the poor. Thirteen Latin American countries had spent the previous decade identifying the poor one by one and setting up channels to transfer cash to them directly—not an easy task given that the poor rarely have bank accounts or even postal addresses.[2] This has provided a platform for the next big move in Latin American social policy: to focus on equality of opportunity, on giving everybody the same chances rather than the same rewards, on equity rather than equality.

Latin America remains the most unequal region on Earth. Inequality dominates virtually all its development outcomes—income, educational achievement, and landownership. Taxation and public expenditures have made little difference in addressing the problem (figure 21.2).

The result has been acrimonious political disagreement over the proper role of the state: should it redistribute wealth or protect private property? This has weakened confidence in the region's legal security, to the detriment of long-term investment. There is no disagreement, however, over the need to give all Latin Americans the same opportunities, as a matter of social justice or as a call to personal effort. Equity enjoys support across the political spectrum. The problem was that it had never been possible to systematically measure inequality of opportunity, in Latin America or anywhere else. The development profession simply lacked the methodological tools to monitor equity, making it all but impossible to design, implement, and evaluate public policies that target human opportunity.

That changed in 2008. A new technology to measure human opportunity—the Human Opportunity Index (HOI)—became available, the creation of a team of Latin American researchers. In essence, the HOI calculates how personal circumstances (like gender, skin color, or family

Figure 21.2 Gini Coefficients Before and After Public Transfers, Circa 2006

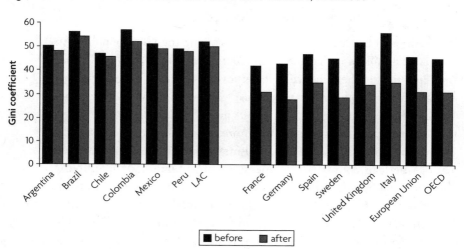

Source: World Bank staff calculations on World Bank and Organisation for Economic Co-operation and Development data.
Note: LAC = Latin America and the Caribbean; OECD = Organisation for Economic Co-operation and Development.

income) impact the probability a child has of accessing the services that are necessary to succeed in life (like timely education, basic health, or connection to electricity). Figure 21.3 shows the 2010 HOI for Latin America.

The HOI, combined with the data and logistics embedded in the direct cash transfer programs that Latin America now has, will make it possible to redirect social policy toward equity (where there is consensus) and away from equality (where there is not). How? Many existing social policies and programs are already equity enhancing. But the focus on equity reveals new points of emphasis along the individual's life cycle. Early interventions, from pregnancy monitoring and institutional births to toddlers' nutrition and neurological development, get a new sense of priority. So do preschool access (such as pre-kindergarten social interaction) and primary school achievement (such as reading standards and critical thinking). The physical security, reproductive education, mentoring, and talent screening in adolescents, all areas that are often overlooked, gain new relevance. A battery of legal and institutional preconditions become sine qua non, from birth certificates, voter registration, and

Figure 21.3 Human Opportunity Index, 2010

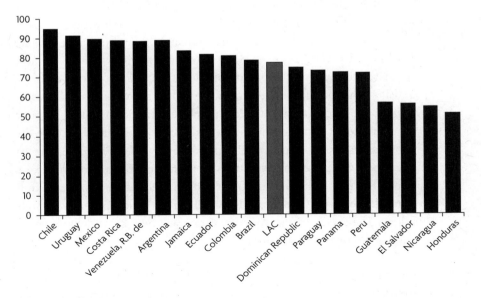

Source: Molinas and others 2010.
Note: LAC = Latin America and the Caribbean.

property titles to the enforcement of antidiscrimination, antitrust, and access-to-information laws. And blanket subsidies that, at the margin, are consumed by those who do not need them (free public college education for the rich, to name one), turn into opportunity-wasting aberrations. If nothing else, the quest for equity will lead to a final push in the decade-long process of subsidy focalization and will spell the end game for a way of giving out public assistance that was blind to the needs of the recipient—a way that was intrinsically unfair.

Trust the State

From now on, people will demand a lot more of the state—to spend more, to regulate more, to protect more. Trust in free markets has been damaged. But Latin Americans never really trusted the state anyway (see figure 9.1 in chapter 9 in this book). That is why they refuse to fund it and remain trapped in a vicious circle of tax evasion and deficient public services. Even progress in fighting corruption (which, unheralded, has occurred) has not done much to rebuild the relationship between the state and the people.

That will need to change soon. Technology and politics will help. New ways to hold public institutions accountable have been penetrating the region for a while, initially among municipalities and provinces, where mayors and governors are in closer proximity to voters. There are now standards to measure the quality of education, infrastructure, security, and any other public service. How many words per minute should a second grader read? At least 60. How much should the cost of logistics be for every dollar exported? No more than 10 cents. What should be the "normal" annual homicide rate? Three for every 100,000 people. The list goes on. Few services in few Latin American countries are, of course, up to par. But political leaders who have committed publicly to these kinds of results do very well in the polls (Brazil, for example). Others will surely follow. The average Latin American state will be increasingly managed and judged by the results it achieves.

There will be another force pushing the state toward results-based management—devolution. Ushered in by the return of democracy in the 1980s, Latin America entered a rapid process of decentralization in the mid-1990s. Tax and expenditure responsibilities were delegated to provinces and municipalities. The quality of public services did not always improve. But decentralization proved popular and is bound to deepen. At the same time, the new ways to do social assistance described earlier showed the possibilities opened by the state's ability to communicate with, and transfer resources to, individual citizens. On a simple magnetic card or even a cell phone, the state can transfer directly to the beneficiary the funds to buy, or the right to access, almost any service, from vaccination to college education. There is no longer a need for intermediaries. Decentralization will be gradually moving down to the citizen level; in a way, it will become devolution. This new, direct relationship between people and the state is generating, and will continue to generate, a wealth of information—about costs, quality, targeting, needs, outcomes, and impacts. Monitoring and evaluation of policies and programs will be much easier. And management by results will become natural.

A Global Player

The 2009 global financial crisis created new forms of external support and integration for Latin America. Its multilateral lenders were promised larger lending capacity and fairer representation. Flexible financing for good performers was quickly offered. The G-20[3] brought Argentina, Brazil, and Mexico to the table where the decisions that will shape the world will be made. In the redesign of financial regulation, the next round of trade negotiation, or the efforts to slow climate change, Latin Americans now have a better opportunity to be heard. They will also count in the rebalancing of the global matrix of saving and consumption; after all, their consumption is larger than China's in absolute dollar terms and as a proportion of gross domestic product. The region is even seeing the emergence of its first, own global leader—Brazil.

But the region's contribution to the global commons will go further. A new generation of former national leaders has left, or will soon leave, office in success and popularity (including Brazil, Chile, Colombia, Costa Rica, Mexico, and Uruguay). Playing by market rules but listening to their people's needs, they delivered prosperity and social progress for their countries. Their governments have not only done well using traditional policy tools, but also pioneered new ones (for example, structural fiscal balances and conditional cash transfers). They are now credible spokespeople for good administration and are much sought after on the international conference circuit. They have become global assets that will give the region a new voice.

This new relevance will bring new disciplines and will reinforce others. It will be more difficult for Latin American countries to backtrack in trade and financial openness, and more painful to lose investment grades. Worldwide rankings will have larger domestic impact (call it "the embarrassment factor"), from those dealing with public transparency to those dealing with the quality of the business environment. And light may begin to shine on long-postponed reforms, without which the benefits of integration are diluted—notably, in education and infrastructure.

Conclusion: If the World Holds, Latin America Will Take Off

The alignment of domestic and external factors augurs well for Latin America's future. Macroeconomic and financial discipline, combined with smarter social policy and a more responsive public sector, may not yet be universal values in the region, but an increasing number of countries are adopting them as part of their development strategies. Latin American voters have begun to reward sensible policy making. At the same time, the rapid growth of the middle classes in Asia should ensure high long-term prices for what Latin America sells. If well managed, this "commodity platform" could be the stepping stone for the region to upgrade its productive capacity, especially its human capital, and expand its brand beyond natural resources.

Are there downside risks? Yes, many. Most come from the global economy. The recovery could be a slow, protracted process, dragged down by balance-sheet adjustments (for example, in mortgage markets) or second-round effects (for example, persistent unemployment). Commodity prices may dive if the liquidity injected by the G-8[4] during the crisis is rolled back too quickly, or if China's domestic consumption does not compensate for the return of its public investment to prestimulus levels. Massive fiscal imbalances in the United States will not be easy to correct, hinting at much higher interest rates (or dollar inflation or both) in the near future. A downgrade of sovereign debt among developed countries could trigger a flight to safety and away from emerging markets. And there are plenty of uncertainties at home: specific countries could still run into overheating and high inflation, breakdowns in internal security, or political turbulence.

Any of those risks could derail Latin America's growth, at least for a while. But for the first time in decades, its fundamentals look solid and the horizon promising. In the base external scenario, and with variations across countries, the region as a whole is converging on a path of sustained development.

Notes

1. The crisis also showed the wisdom of building agile public investment systems. Several countries (Brazil, Chile, Colombia, and Peru) quickly embarked on strengthening those systems.
2. The process of identifying the poor forced a parallel process of integration of individual social records across ministries and agencies. This should further facilitate tailoring social programs to a person's needs.
3. Members of the G-20 are Argentina, Australia, Brazil, Canada, China, France, Germany, India, Indonesia, Italy, Japan, Mexico, the Republic of Korea, the Russian Federation, Saudi Arabia, South Africa, Turkey, the United Kingdom, the United States, and the European Union.
4. Members of the G-8 are Canada, France, Germany, Italy, Japan, the Russian Federation, the United Kingdom, and the United States.

Bibliography

Agosin, M. R., E. Fernández-Arias, and F. Jaramillo. *Growing Pains: Binding Constraints to Productive Investment in Latin America*. Washington, DC: Inter-American Development Bank.

Benavente, J. 2009. "Una Alternativa para la Recuperación y el Crecimiento de Latino-América." Santiago de Chile.

Blind, P. 2006. "Building Trust in Government in the Twenty-First Century: Review of Literature and Emerging Issues." United Nations Department of Economic and Social Affairs, Vienna.

Calvo, G., and C. Reinhart. 2002. "Fear of Floating." *Quarterly Journal of Economics* 117 (2): 379–408.

Commission on Growth and Development. 2008. *The Growth Report: Strategies for Sustained Growth and Inclusive Development*. Washington, DC: World Bank.

———. 2010. *Post-Crisis Growth in Developing Countries: A Special Report of the Commission on Growth and Development on the Implications of the 2008 Financial Crisis*. Washington, DC: World Bank.

Debrun, X., D. Hauner, and M. Kumar. 2009. "Independent Fiscal Agencies." *Journal of Economic Surveys* 23 (1): 44–81.

De la Torre, A., J. Gozzi, and S. Schmukler. 2006. "Financial Development in Latin America: Big Emerging Issues, Limited Policy Analysis." Policy Research Working Paper 3963, World Bank, Washington, DC.

Fukuyama, F., and N. Birdsall. Forthcoming. *New Ideas for Development after the Financial Crisis.* Baltimore: Johns Hopkins University Press.

Gavin, M., and R. Perotti. 1997. "Fiscal Policy in Latin America." *NBER Macroeconomics Annual* 12: 11–61, ed. B. Bernanke and J. Rotemberg. Cambridge, MA: Massachusetts Institute of Technology Press.

Giugale, M. 2009. "Latin America Beyond the Crisis—Impacts, Policies and Opportunities—A Synthesis." In *Latin-America Beyond the Crisis: Impacts, Policies and Opportunities,* 1–6. LCR Crisis Briefs. Washington, DC: World Bank.

Inter-American Development Bank. 2009. *Growing Pains: Binding Constraints to Productive Investment in Latin America.* Washington, DC: Inter-American Development Bank.

Izquierdo, A., and E. Talvi. 2010. *The Aftermath of the Crisis: Policy Lessons and Challenges Ahead for Latin America and the Caribbean.* Washington, DC: Inter-American Development Bank.

Lederman, D., and W. Maloney. 2007. *Natural Resources: Neither Curse nor Destiny.* Stanford, CA: Stanford University Press.

Molinas, J., R. Paes de Barro, J. Saavedra, and M. Giugale. 2010. *Do Our Children Have a Chance? The 2010 Human Opportunity Report for Latin America and the Caribbean.* Washington, DC: World Bank.

Paes de Barros, R., F. Ferreira, J. Molinas Vega, and J. Saavedra. 2009. *Measuring Inequality of Opportunities in Latin America and the Caribbean.* Washington, DC: World Bank.

Pages-Serra, C. 2010. "The Importance of Ideas: Innovation and Productivity in Latin America." In *The Age of Productivity: Transforming Economies from the Bottom Up,* ed. C. Pages-Serra, 223–56. Washington, DC: Inter-American Development Bank.

Rogoff, K. S., and J. I. Bertelsmann. 2010. "The Rationale for Fiscal Policy Councils: Theory and Evidence." Paper presented at the Conference of Independent Fiscal Institutions, Budapest, March 18–19.

Vega, E., and J. Petrow. 2007. *Raising Student Learning in Latin America: The Challenge of the XXIst Century.* Washington. DC: World Bank.

Velasco, A., A. Arenas de Mesa, L. P. Céspedes, and J. R. Cabello. 2007. "Compromisos Fiscales y la Meta de Superávit Estructural." *Estudios de Finanzas Públicas,* May. Ministerio de Hacienda, Chile.

World Bank. 2005. *Inequality in Latin America: Breaking with History?* Washington, DC: World Bank.

Wren-Lewis, S. 2010. "Comparing the Delegation of Monetary and Fiscal Policy." Paper presented at the Conference on Independent Fiscal Institutions, Budapest, March 18–19.

22

The Financial Crisis, Recovery, and Long-Term Growth in the Middle East and North Africa

Ritva Reinikka

The impact of the 2008–09 global financial and economic crisis varied substantially among three country groupings in the Middle East and North Africa (MENA): the Gulf Cooperation Council (GCC), developing oil exporters, and oil importers.[1] Among these three groups, the GCC oil exporters were hardest hit because the crisis affected them directly through two different channels: (a) a negative terms-of-trade shock associated with the drop in oil prices; and (b) a financial shock, which destabilized overextended domestic banks and led to the bursting of a real estate bubble. Growth plummeted for this group of countries from 6 percent in 2008 to less than 1 percent in 2009 (figure 22.1). Ample reserves and repatriated funds enabled the GCC governments to respond quickly with monetary and fiscal stimuli and prevent a deeper deceleration in growth.

Due to the limited integration of their banking sectors into global financial markets, developing oil exporters felt the impact of the crisis mostly through the negative oil price shock. Growth declined only slightly from 2.9 percent in 2008 to 2.2 percent in 2009. Although typically these

The author would like to thank Najy Benhassine, Elena Ianchovichina, Roberto Rocha, Andrew Stone, and Tara Vishwanath whose work was drawn on for this chapter.

Figure 22.1 Real GDP Growth Rates, Middle East and North Africa

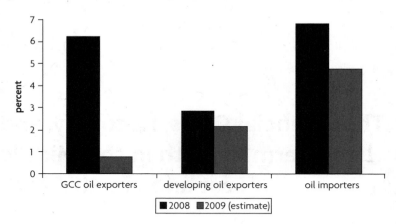

Sources: National agencies and World Bank staff estimates for 2009.
Note: GDP = gross domestic product.

countries pursue procyclical fiscal policies, during this crisis some governments responded with countercyclical measures, but the extent to
which they were able to do so depended on their fiscal space, reserves,
and access to external financing. Strong non-oil gross domestic product
(GDP) growth—at nearly 5 percent in 2009—helped soften the decline
in overall growth (World Bank 2010).

Oil-importing MENA countries were hurt mostly by the secondary
effects of the crisis on trade, remittances, and foreign direct investment
(FDI). Growth, which was high before the crisis, decelerated from close
to 7 percent in 2008, to a moderate pace of 4.8 percent in 2009. Key non-
oil sectors such as services and tourism remained relatively resilient,
while the decline in oil and other commodity prices limited the deterioration of their external balances. Stimulus packages in the Arab Republic
of Egypt, Jordan, Morocco, and Tunisia also helped soften the deceleration in growth.

High unemployment has been a problem in MENA for years, and the
crisis has dimmed prospects for improvement in the near term. While
the impact of the crisis on official unemployment rates has been negligible in most MENA countries, participation rates, which were already
low compared to other countries prior to the crisis, have declined as dis-
couraged workers dropped out of the labor force and decided not to seek
work in the official labor market. In addition, aggregate labor statistics

hide the negative impact on some sectors. Workers in the manufacturing sectors have been especially vulnerable during this crisis, although job losses in these sectors were offset to some extent by the job creation in the nontradable goods and services industries.

Slower growth is expected to result in a decline in the rate of poverty reduction in the region. Because of the economic crisis, approximately 2.6 million more people are likely to fall into poverty in the region by 2011, with nearly half of those in Egypt (Yemtsov and Iqbal 2009). Any weakening of the rate of poverty reduction is a concern because, while absolute poverty in MENA is relatively low (about 5 percent), vulnerability is high. In 2005, 17 percent of MENA's population lived on US$2.00-a-day purchasing power parity (PPP), and a sizable share of the population lived on more than US$2.00-a-day PPP but less than US$2.50-a-day PPP. Limited survey data on household incomes and expenditures, a perennial problem in the region, makes it difficult to assess the impact of the crisis on the poor. These estimates are based on a number of assumptions and past patterns of poverty and growth.

Recovering from the Crisis

The Gulf countries are leading the regional recovery as oil prices have rebounded, and the GCC financial sector is stabilizing. Growth in the GCC countries is projected at 4.4 percent in 2010—a remarkable comeback. The recovery in the GCC countries is expected to have a positive impact on other MENA countries, mainly through increased flows of remittances and FDI. Although Dubai was among those countries in financial crisis, the Dubai World debt restructuring offer has contributed to greater clarity about the prospects of the United Arab Emirates (UAE). The restructuring package is partially funded through loans from Abu Dhabi to Dubai, and its adverse impact on UAE banks is cushioned by the likelihood of increased support to these banks from Abu Dhabi and federal entities. These short-term measures are helping to contain the negative impact of these events on UAE growth. Ongoing large fiscal spending by Abu Dhabi is also expected to help the recovery and support the "service center approach" to integration and economic development. The question remains whether growth of the private sector will pick up when the public sector starts spending less and the effects of the stimulus packages in UAE and Saudi Arabia wear off.

Growth of developing oil exporters is expected to accelerate to 4.2 percent in 2010. The sustainability of their recovery hinges on the evolution in the global demand for oil and oil prices. The Islamic Republic of Iran and Iraq are especially vulnerable to oil price volatility. At present, further upward pressure on oil prices is not expected due to ample spare capacity and little or no growth in oil demand in North America, Europe, and Japan. Temporary spikes, however, cannot be ruled out in response to unanticipated shocks (Samba Financial Group 2010).

The recovery of oil importers in MENA will depend crucially on their key markets, especially the European Union (EU) and the GCC countries. The feeble recovery expected in the Eurozone will drag down growth in the near term, particularly the growth of those with strong links to EU markets. Growth of oil importers is expected to decelerate slightly to 4.5 percent in 2010. Trade is recovering, with export revenue of oil importers expected to grow by 7.7 percent in 2010, after contracting by 13 percent in 2009. Remittance flows are expected to grow by 1.3 percent in 2010, albeit this pace is much slower than the one observed during the precrisis years. The crisis has not led to any major reform reversals, except perhaps a slowing of food and energy subsidy reforms, which have generally been very slow to progress. Some countries have steamed ahead with the reforms started prior to the crisis. These include the financial sector reform in Egypt and trade integration in Tunisia.

Fiscal policy is expected to continue to be expansionary as countries use various measures to stimulate demand and, in some cases, to stimulate the private sector. Expansionary fiscal policy is having an adverse effect on fiscal balances, however. For some countries, including Egypt, Jordan, Lebanon, and the Republic of Yemen, the fiscal space is limited and the fiscal situation risks creating an obstacle to long-term growth. Hence, a painful fiscal adjustment is in store in the coming years.

But fiscal prudence alone will not be enough to return MENA to the rapid growth path that the region experienced briefly in the mid-2000s. So, what should the MENA region do to restore higher growth in the longer term? In a nutshell, the private sector will have to expand and gain new dynamism to be able to create most of the 40 million new jobs that the region needs to create in the next decade.

A More Dynamic Private Sector

Increased openness and liberalization over the past two decades have transformed the economies of MENA from public sector–driven to ones where more than 80 percent of nonhydrocarbon value added is produced by private enterprises. This private sector growth has been fostered by investment climate reforms. For example, Egypt has ranked among the top 10 reformers four times in the past five years on the Ease of Doing Business index published by the World Bank Group, complemented with dramatic changes in taxes, tariffs, selected regulations, and several other key areas of government interaction with private investors. Jordan carried out reforms in 6 of 10 areas measured by the index, and Saudi Arabia has ascended to 13th place in the world among 183 economies evaluated. Among reforms documented by the index, Morocco established a private credit bureau to facilitate access to finance; Tunisia strengthened investor protection and reduced customs processing delays by two days on average; and the UAE sped up its building permit process by putting it online.

Despite reforms and a growing role, the private sector has fallen short of transforming MENA countries into diversified, high-performing economies. Private investment rates have stagnated at around 15 percent of GDP, while dynamic regions like East Asia managed to raise private investment rates close to 30 percent—or double the prevailing MENA rates. MENA's average number of registered businesses per 1,000 people is about a sixth of that in the Organisation for Economic Co-operation and Development (OECD) countries, and less than a third of that in Eastern Europe and Central Asia (World Bank 2009a). Productivity in MENA's average manufacturing firm is about half that of Turkey's manufacturers. Limited productivity is reflected in a weak export base. The most diversified countries in MENA export around 1,500 goods—most of them in low-value-added sectors, compared to close to 4,000 goods in countries like Malaysia, Poland, or Turkey. Diversification is even weaker in oil-rich countries, many of which export less than 500 goods (World Bank 2009b).

World Bank enterprise surveys of about 10,000 firms conducted throughout the region show that MENA has a higher average age of both manufacturing firms and their managers. Firms are almost 10 years older than the average in Eastern Europe and East Asia, and managers on average are seven years older than in these two regions. This disparity occurs despite MENA having one of the youngest populations in the world. In some cases, this reflects dominant and connected firms using a privileged position to limit competition. The average MENA manufacturing firm faces close to six times fewer competitors in its domestic market compared to the average firm in Eastern Europe.

Private sector performance has been subdued due to a variety of factors, critical among which are issues surrounding the quality of reforms in the region. This is captured by the low private sector investment response to past reform in the region. As shown in figure 22.2, private investment across MENA increased by a modest 2 percentage points in response to the reforms. Compare this to a private investment response to similar reforms in other regions of more than 10 percentage points in East Asia, 7 in South Asia, and 5 in Latin American economies.

Evidence shows that investment response has been dampened by weak and uneven implementation of reforms and lack of enforcement by institutions whose transformation lags behind policy change. Too many would-be entrepreneurs across the region still believe that the key to success is how connected or how privileged they are—instead of how creative, persistent, and competitive. World Bank enterprise surveys show that 60 percent of business managers do not think that the rules

Figure 22.2 Reform Episodes and Private Investment Response, Middle East and North Africa

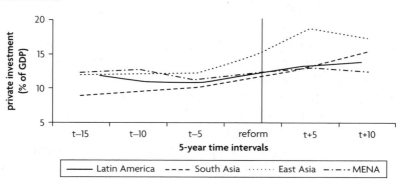

Source: World Bank 2009a.

and regulations, as they appear "on paper," are applied consistently and predictably in MENA. The same surveys also show that regulatory policy uncertainty, unfair competition practices, and corruption often appear as top constraints to businesses.

The challenge is to enable a new generation of entrepreneurs to emerge, to create dynamic firms that can compete on the basis of productivity and that are efficient enough to export even advanced products to the rest of the world. It is important that this new generation sees evidence that business-friendly policy reforms will benefit them as well—and not just a minority of privileged or connected individuals. Institutions need to be reformed to implement private sector policies equitably and consistently. For a real improvement in the business environment in the region, transparency, accountability, and quality of service in public agencies interacting with firms should be at the core of reform.

There are some regional examples where this has begun to occur, such as customs reform in Morocco and Tunisia and the one-stop-shop for investors in Egypt's General Authority for Investment (GAFI). More transparent and computerized processes, strong incentives for agency staff members to improve the quality of service to investors, and limiting of the points of interactions with public servants (thus limiting opportunities for discretion) have allowed GAFI to reduce delays for business registration at its Cairo offices from 34 days to 3. Streamlining also eliminated some 40 procedures. Business registration increased dramatically thereafter. To be sure, such institutional reforms will need to expand to other agencies for their impact to be felt.

The private sector also has a responsibility—and an important role to play—within this agenda. Too often, its voice has been dominated by proponents of the status quo in order to maintain their privileges. But the world is changing. Already, a new generation of entrepreneurs is emerging in MENA. Their ability to influence the future direction of reform will be crucial. For this, the private sector needs to be better organized and more inclusive. It needs to be a stronger partner with governments in developing, implementing, and evaluating reforms.

Skeptics voicing doubt that the private sector will succeed in generating needed jobs and growth are legion in the region and elsewhere, and the global financial crisis may have added to this skepticism. However, the lessons of past crises as well as the current one support the core message: sustained job creation can only come from a competitive private sector, which in turn requires governments to build efficient regulatory capacity and a supportive, nondiscriminatory environment. This is doubly important because more and more educated women will join the labor market in the future.

Women's Labor Force Participation

The MENA region has made significant progress in reducing gender gaps in human development. The ratio of girls to boys in primary and secondary education is 0.96, which compares favorably with that in low- and middle-income countries worldwide. Women in the MENA region are more likely than men to attend university, and fertility rates have decreased in the past decade. However, as figure 22.3 reveals, this progress has not translated into improvements in economic and political inclusion. The region's female labor force participation rate of 26 percent is well below the developing country average of 39 percent. Women are severely underrepresented in politics, holding only 9 percent of the seats in parliament.

Among those participating in the labor force, women face greater challenges than men in accessing employment opportunities. In most MENA countries, women experience higher unemployment rates than

Figure 22.3 The Gender Gap in Middle East and North Africa

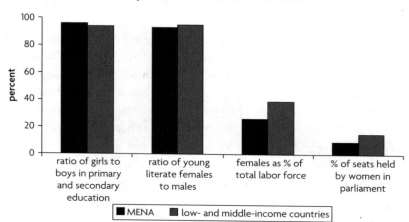

Source: World Bank Central Database/Edstats (August 2009).

men. Also, the World Bank's Enterprise Surveys show that women's entrepreneurship in MENA remains low compared to other regions and that while there are no significant differences in the types of firms owned by women and men, women face a more hostile business environment. In one finding, for example, female-owned firms in Egypt report needing 86 weeks on average to resolve a conflict through the legal system compared to 54 weeks for male-owned firms.

The data suggest that even highly educated young women are increasingly vulnerable. To illustrate, between 1998 and 2006, the percentage of young Egyptian women having a university degree rose from 6 to 12. Strikingly, the female labor force participation rate in this age group remained near stagnant, while their rate of unemployment increased from 19 percent to 27 percent. In Jordan, 27 percent of women compared to 9 percent of men with a bachelor's degree or above are unemployed.

Social and cultural factors remain pertinent to understanding female participation in the labor force. But given such barriers, decisive reforms to create job opportunities through an improved policy environment—especially to propel private sector employment—have the potential to make a big difference. Moreover, cultural norms are slow to change, but change they do. A compelling case in point is the United States, where views about women's work outside the home were fairly conservative even as late as the 1940s, but were transformed as women's economic participation rose (from about 20 percent in 1940 to 60 percent in 1980) due to a combination of factors such as rising education levels, campaigns to attract women to the workplace during World War II, new work opportunities for women in clerical and other "women-friendly" jobs, and the introduction of scheduling flexibility in the workplace.

Conclusion

MENA is a region endowed with considerable human capital, creativity, and resources, and its growth potential is high. Meeting that potential will require a credible commitment to reduce discretion and ensure a more equal enforcement of the rules, so that more entrepreneurs can invest in and create jobs.

Job creation is indeed a burning challenge in MENA, especially because many more educated young women are entering the labor market. Deep analytic work and policy experimentation are called for to identify the scope for policy reforms that would positively contribute to an increase in female labor force participation in the region.

Note

1. For ease of analysis and exposition, the MENA region is divided into three main groups: the GCC oil exporters, developing oil exporters, and oil importers. The first group contains the GCC countries, namely, Bahrain, Kuwait, Oman, Qatar, Saudi Arabia, and United Arab Emirates. The second group comprises the developing oil exporters such as Algeria, the Islamic Republic of Iran, Iraq, Libya, the Syrian Arab Republic, and the Republic of Yemen. Oil importers include countries with strong GCC links (Djibouti, Jordan, and Lebanon) and those with strong European Union links (the Arab Republic of Egypt, Morocco, and Tunisia).

References

Samba Financial Group. 2010. "Oil Market Outlook and Implications for GCC Economies." Samba Financial Group, Saudi Arabia.

World Bank. 2009a. *From Privilege to Competition: Unlocking Private-Led Growth in the Middle East and North Africa.* MENA Development Report. Washington, DC: World Bank.

———. 2009b. *Strengthening China's and India's Trade and Investment Ties to the Middle East and North Africa.* Orientations in Development Series. Washington, DC: World Bank.

———. 2010. *Recovering from the Crisis.* Middle East and North Africa Economic Update. Washington, DC: World Bank.

Yemtsov, R., and F. Iqbal. 2009. "The Impact of the Global Economic Crisis on Poverty in MENA." Washington, DC, World Bank.

23

Economic Policy Challenges for South Asia

Dipak Dasgupta, Ejaz Ghani, and
Ernesto May

The restoration of high growth should not be taken for granted.
— Dr. Manmohan Singh, Prime Minister of India, March 2010

South Asia has weathered the 2008–09 global financial crisis much better than expected. The slowdown in regional gross domestic product (GDP) growth of 3 percentage points—from the peak of 8.8 percent in 2007 to 6.2 percent in 2009—was the least pronounced among all developing regions, compared with the decline of 13 percentage points for emerging Europe, 8 percentage points for Latin America, and 5 percentage points for East Asia. South Asia is now rebounding and is expected to grow around 7 percent in 2010 and nearly 8 percent in 2011, close to precrisis levels—only slightly behind East Asia and better than its own historical average (6.5 percent annually between 2000 and 2007). However, as the prime minister of India cautioned in his comments on the problems facing the Eleventh Five-Year Plan, "the restoration of high growth should not be taken for granted" (*Business Standard* 2010).

Economic growth is not enough to make significant gains in poverty reduction. South Asia has the largest concentration of poor people—home to 1.5 billion people with over 1 billion living on less than US$2 a day. In the region, growth has not been fast enough and inclusive enough to reduce the total number of people living on less than US$1.25 a day, which has increased and stands at around 600 million people. The challenge ahead for South Asia is to make the recovery stronger, inclusive, and sustainable. Policy makers need to start reshaping tomorrow today and position the region in what will be the "new normal."

There is significant consensus that what will come after the global financial crisis will not look like the normal of recent years. To position the region in this "new normal," policy makers need to draw lessons from the crisis and reassess the policy reforms that can best position South Asian countries to take advantage of the restructuring of the economic order. While ensuring that the exit from fiscal and monetary stimulus is gradual and in tune with the recovery of private demand, policy makers in the region will need to establish the basis for the future. They need to do the following:

- Create fiscal space to improve macroeconomic stability, avoid crowding out the private sector, and permit financing of infrastructure and social safety nets.
- Manage inflationary pressures, particularly food prices, with renewed attention to agricultural productivity growth.
- Revisit South Asia's trade and investment integration strategy to take advantage of the global rebalancing underway, including supporting faster manufacturing growth.

The aim of these policies is to achieve faster, inclusive growth with more and better jobs. To succeed, policy makers in South Asia will need to focus their attention on four areas of transformational change in the region: governance, conflict, demographic transition, and urbanization and spatial transformation. The future of the region depends on the positive outcome of these changes.

Learning from the Global Crisis and Positioning the South Asia Region in the New Normal

To ensure future growth and realize its potential, South Asia needs to address the following nine areas.

Creating Fiscal Space. One of the urgent tasks facing South Asia after the 2008–09 global crisis is to create fiscal space to provide governments room to address three objectives:

- Improving macroeconomic stability—including building more room to run countercyclical policies to deal with unexpected future shocks
- Not crowding out the private sector and growth as economies recover, by reducing their deficits and borrowing needs
- Permitting governments to increase the financing of crucial expenditures for public goods, especially infrastructure and social safety nets.

Entering the global financial crisis, South Asia's economies were a large outlier in having inadequate fiscal space to accommodate countercyclical policies to support the fall in aggregate demand. In this crisis, South Asia showed the least ability to inject additional countercyclical demand to counteract the global shock (although some did, such as India and Bangladesh). Indeed, Pakistan, the Maldives, and Sri Lanka bound themselves to conservative fiscal stances to control expenditures. The reasons were structural: high initial fiscal deficits (figure 23.1) and high public debt (figure 23.2)—the highest in the developing world. How might South Asian countries create more fiscal

Figure 23.1 Government Fiscal Balance

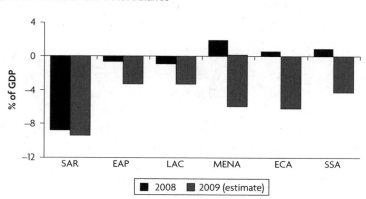

Source: World Bank 2010a.
Note: EAP = East Asia and Pacific; ECA = Europe and Central Asia; LAC = Latin America and the Caribbean; MENA = Middle East and North Africa; SAR = South Asia; SSA = Sub-Saharan Africa.

Figure 23.2 Public Debt Dynamic

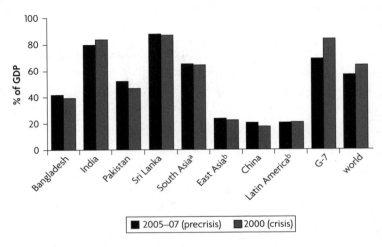

Source: Economic Intelligence Unit and the World Bank's Unified Survey.
a. South Asia is a simple weighted average of Bangladesh, India, Pakistan, and Sri Lanka.
b. The data include only developing countries in the region.

space? Lessons from other countries suggest some options—including faster growth itself.

Raising Revenue. The tax-to-GDP ratios of South Asia's economies are low compared to many similarly placed developing and emerging market economies (figure 23.3) and relative to its development needs, and thus, a key focus of attention should be on efforts to increase domestic resource mobilization. The evidence seems to indicate that relative to income, tax efforts in South Asia are below expected levels—averaging around 8 to 14 percent of GDP in countries other than India and about 19 percent in India (figure 23.4). Structural constraints to raising revenues in South Asia are nevertheless significant—in particular, the high share of agriculture and the informal sector in the region.

Reprioritizing Expenditure. Focusing on more productive spending is also important. While considerable gains in prioritizing spending on primary health and education are being made, there still remains large and escalating budget and off-budget spending on petroleum, electricity, fertilizer, and food subsidies, which can drain as much as 4 to 6 percent of GDP by

Figure 23.3 Ratio of Tax Revenues to GDP and GDP (PPP Per Capita) from 1975 to 2000

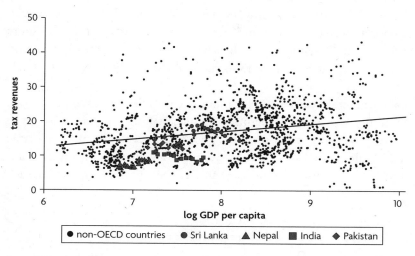

Source: Authors' calculations.
Note: OECD = Organisation for Economic Co-operation and Development.

Figure 23.4 Tax Revenue

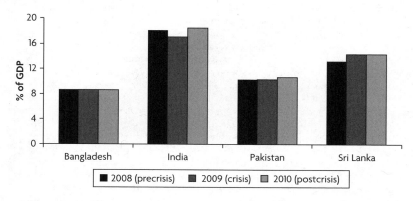

Source: World Bank unified survey.
Note: India's revenues reflect the central government only.

some estimates—with large leakages to the better off. More carefully targeted and designed schemes would save resources, better protect the poor, and raise growth. Agricultural subsidies, for example, now exceed capital investment in agriculture in many South Asian countries. Rising civil service salaries, which distort recruitment without gains in service delivery, are another issue, as are escalating military and security expenditures. These are political-economy-sensitive areas, especially for influential electorates used to a pattern of receiving public largess in lieu of more effective public services. The challenge will be to turn the logic around and convince citizens of the rationale and desirability of better services.

Infrastructure Financing. A key binding constraint to economic growth in South Asia is infrastructure. The biggest infrastructure gaps are in energy, transport, ports, airports, and urban development. Given large fiscal deficits, it is essential to crowd in private investment. South Asia is already well on its way (box 23.1) and will benefit from supporting such

---

Box 23.1 Private Participation in Infrastructure (PPI) Is Bouncing Back

South Asia accounted for around 40 percent of total developing country PPI investment commitments (hereafter investment) in the first three quarters of 2009, a record for the region. Investment in new PPI projects in the region has grown every year since 2005, reaching a record US$26.2 billion in the first three quarters of 2009. South Asia has had the most resilient investment during the financial crisis. In the first three quarters of 2009, investment was 72 percent higher than in the same period in 2008, and there were 41 new projects, 28 percent more than in the same period in 2008.

The growing activity in private infrastructure, however, is not a regionwide trend—India accounted for almost all the PPI activity in the region in the first three quarters of 2009, registering US$25 billion of investment and 33 new projects in this period. Larger projects have been implemented in India since 2006. The average size of new projects tripled from US$211 million in 2006 to US$638 million in 2009. The growth of private infrastructure activity was facilitated by national and state government policies to encourage private sector investment in infrastructure and by the depth and liquidity in India's local capital market. In 2009, the top four initial Mandated Lead Arrangers (MLAs) for project loans in the Asia-Pacific region were Indian banks.

Excluding India, investment in new PPI projects in the rest of South Asia amounted to US$1.4 billion in 2008 and US$1.1 billion in the first three quarters of 2009. The latter activity was confined to eight power plant projects in three countries—Pakistan (3 projects; US$852 million), Bhutan (1 project; US$205 million), and Bangladesh (4 projects; US$52 million).

The energy sector has driven investment in PPI projects, growing from US$1.3 billion in 2005 to US$19.4 billion in the first three quarters of 2009. Investment in transport projects has remained in the range of US$4.6 billion to US$5.8 billion annually since 2007. Investment in telecommunications remained in the range of US$12 billion to US$14 billion between 2005 and 2008, while there has been minimal investment in new water projects in the region. There is also a large pipeline of new projects coming to the market. As of September 2009, 96 projects with associated investment totaling US$48.5 billion were at one of the following stages: "awarded," "looking for financing," or "advanced stage of tender." Of those projects, India accounted for 55, with associated investment of US$44.5 billion.

Source: Authors.

private provision of an even larger set of investments—with transparent and appropriately managed institutional frameworks as essential and including intraregional coordination and cross-border investments.

Social Safety Nets. The availability of effective safety nets to respond to shocks is critical to ensure an adequate toolkit for policy makers. Indeed, social safety nets should be established during good times. Designing effective social protection systems can be particularly important for the poor, women, and disadvantaged social groups, which are disproportionately represented among the unemployed and have riskier jobs and fewer tools to manage their risks. It is important to ensure that programs do not discourage the ability to move from place to place, which is central to facilitating labor market transitions.

Inflation and Food Prices. The upsurge in global commodity prices immediately before the global financial crisis posed a significant challenge to the region and clearly indicated one of its key vulnerabilities. While global commodity prices have since declined and the rest of the world is still facing very low rates of inflation, prices are rising much faster in South Asia. The price rises have been led by food items, raising additional concerns given large numbers of the population at or near caloric deficiency levels. Farmers are benefiting, but poor households, even in rural areas, are net buyers of food, and this puts a strong political economy premium on managing food price inflation in South Asia, unlike elsewhere (for example, where land is more abundant and surplus-producing farming households dominate in rural areas, as in Latin America).

Core inflation in South Asia is now converging to a distinctly higher level of 7 to 10 percent, surpassing the previous decade's precrisis average of 4 to 6 percent. India's increase is correlated not just with the food price shocks, but also with fuel prices. Pakistan's core inflation fell from high levels during a contractionary phase and is now rising, and in Bangladesh, it is rising steadily upward (independently of commodity price shocks). The issue that monetary authorities now face in South Asia as economies recover is whether more aggressive steps are needed to moderate demand-side pressures on core inflation. The Reserve Bank of India has already started tightening the capital account and raising policy rates and reserve ratios from very low levels. Others face similar choices. In Nepal, liquidity management pressures were growing even earlier, and overheating land and real estate markets were notable, as a result of very large remittance inflows (and fixed exchange rates).

Revitalizing Agriculture. Food prices are expected to remain high, providing an opportunity to focus on policies in agriculture, with a second "green revolution" aimed to increase productivity in the sector. In particular, productivity-enhancing investments (improvements in input supply, extension services, irrigation, and so forth) can facilitate the supply response. Part of that will be a shift to the lagging states and regions of South Asia, where yield potentials remain large. Another part will benefit from the increasing adoption of better seeds and fertilizers. Although still controversial, the adoption of genetically modified seeds is rising rapidly in South Asia, with large gains (as in cotton production and exports). The private sector is also turning its focus to the possibilities for agricultural and rural areas.

Global Rebalancing. South Asia needs to shift its market integration strategy with the global rebalancing underway, as developed countries start to save more and spend less and grow more slowly in North America and Europe and as the East, especially Asia and emerging markets overall, looks to become a bigger driver of global growth. As can be seen in figure 23.5, bilateral trade between India and China has been on the rise since 2008 and has overtaken the bilateral trade between India and the United States. Furthermore, trade between India and China remained constant during the crisis, while trade between India and the United States declined. This provides initial evidence that South-South trade is becoming more important and has recovered much faster than South-North trade.

There is similar evidence from other South Asian countries. The share of exports from Pakistan to the United Arab Emirates and Afghanistan has surpassed the corresponding share from Pakistan to the United States. It is also worth noting that the top four importing countries from Pakistan are developing or Middle Eastern countries. Similarly for Bangladesh and Sri Lanka, China and India are the two most important trading partners, accounting for 30 percent of total imports for both countries.

Figure 23.5 Share of India's Bilateral Trade with China and the United States

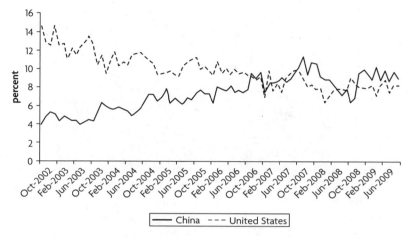

Source: CEIC Data Ltd. http://www.ceicdata.com/.

In revisiting its integration strategy, the South Asia region needs to enhance its Look East Strategy, looking to integrate more quickly with East Asia (the gains being potentially large—some US$450 billion of increased trade), and find opportunities to integrate more closely with each other in the region (the gains are also potentially large—some US$50 billion of additional trade).

Supporting Faster Manufacturing Growth. A critical area to reposition South Asia in the ongoing global rebalancing is the faster development of an outward-oriented manufacturing sector, especially the "missing middle" of medium-size firms. During the past decade, services growth has been the biggest driver of overall growth and employment in South Asia (figure 23.6, panel a), in contrast to East Asia, where manufacturing and industry have been the main drivers (figure 23.6, panel b).

The biggest reason for the rapid shift away from agriculture in both regions has been the highly constrained land-labor ratios in Asia, relative to elsewhere (see figure 23.7, which shows the relative endowments of education and land-labor ratios). But given much lower human capital endowments (as proxied by expected years of schooling), especially compared to East Asia, and the paucity of physical capital accumulation, South Asia was forced to shift to services at a much faster speed. Over

Figure 23.6 Structural Change of South Asia's GDP Compared to East Asia's GDP

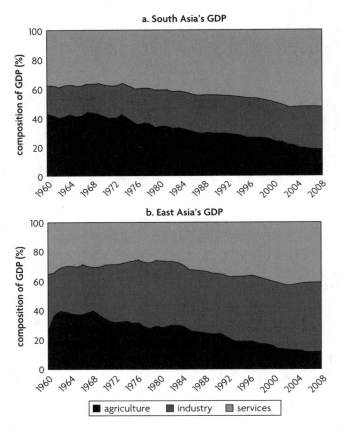

Source: World Bank 2010c.

time, with increased openness in South Asia, its services are increasingly driven by modern services and exports, including information technology, business process services, trade, transport, tourism, and finance. The result has been faster productivity growth.

The opportunity now exists to transform the manufacturing sector in South Asia—with East Asia transitioning to more skill-intensive manufactures, rising wages there, and faster accumulation of human and physical capital in South Asia. South Asia's manufacturing will remain more labor intensive, with differences among countries depending on their endowments: Bangladesh is more labor intensive, Pakistan is more

Figure 23.7 Comparative Advantage Driven by Land and Human Capital Endowments

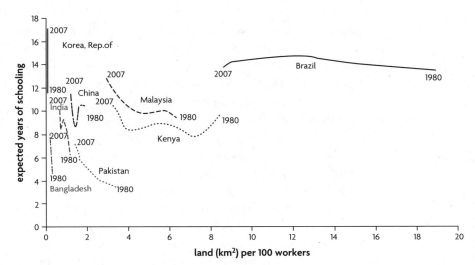

Source: World Bank 2010c.
Note: km² = square kilometer.

natural-resource oriented, and India is starting to move into higher skills and to be oriented to larger-scale domestic markets, while the smaller countries find more specialized niches. This process is beginning. In garments and textiles, Bangladesh is emerging as a competitive supply alternative to China in lower-cost segments, Sri Lanka is emerging in higher-end niches, and India is scaling up with larger factories. India is also emerging as a competitive producer of small cars (over 230,000 units exported in the first six months of 2009, overtaking China), with the relocation of scale production to Chennai from the Republic of Korea. Faster trade and investment integration is thus an important element to realize this potential.

Key Areas of Transformational Change

This section discusses the four key areas of transformational change.

Governance

For the first time since their independence, all countries in South Asia have democratically elected governments. However, governance remains a key development challenge in the region. Political instability and corruption are cited most frequently in investment climate surveys as major or severe constraints to business. Weak property rights and corruption permeate the business environment in South Asia. Indeed, the region's growth has been affected by weak governance. The rule of law (especially property rights enforcement and law and order) and judicial systems are weak, and some parts of public administration appear to be worsening due to politicization, distorted incentives, and limited accountability. The costs of poor governance—whether unenforceable property rights and contracts, deteriorating law and order, or widespread teacher and doctor absenteeism—are largely borne by the poor.

Rising standards of living are increasing demands by citizens for better results from governments in areas such as service delivery, law and order, the courts, the right to information, budgeting and implementation of government programs, corruption, and the cost of doing business. New initiatives in South Asia, including India's Freedom of Information Act, Bhutan's Anti-Corruption Commission, and Bangladesh's strengthening of public expenditure programs, suggest that governments in the region are listening. Indeed, if policy makers in South Asia continue to respond to these growing citizen demands for greater accountability, building on successes and learning from failures, they will help accelerate and sustain the growth and inclusion that the region needs.

Conflict. South Asia has the world's largest conflict-affected population and has become the most violent region in the world, including war, insurgency, terrorism, and other forms of organized violence. Afghanistan is in the midst of conflict. Pakistan faces serious localized insurgency. Nepal and Sri Lanka are facing the challenges of reintegration in the aftermath of conflict and insurgency. India has been affected by serious terrorist attacks. Insurgencies are rooted in long-standing regional and cross-border tensions and rivalries, creating politicization of regional issues. The development paths of most of the countries in the region will be determined by their ability to transition out of conflict to peace and security.

Figure 23.8 plots the trend in conflict rates and real per capita income for a large group of developing and developed countries. The vertical

Figure 23.8 Conflict and Development, 1998–2004

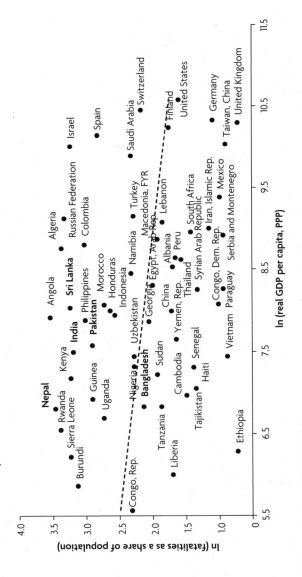

Source: Global Terrorism Database II, 1998–2004 (2008).

Note: The figure takes the arithmetic mean for fatalities and income per capita during 1998–2004. Fatality is the number of total confirmed fatalities for the incident. The number includes all victims and attackers who died as a direct result of the incident. PPP = purchasing power parity.

axis reports the number of people killed in terrorist incidents (normalized by population) as a measure of conflict rate. The horizontal axis plots real GDP per capita. The downward sloping line suggests that countries that have lower per capita incomes also have higher conflict rates. Most South Asian countries (except for Bangladesh) are huge outliers on conflict, that is, they have much higher conflict rates given their income levels.

What are the costs of conflict for the region? Or in a positive sense, what might reduced insecurity and conflict deliver? First, the "peace dividend," or bounce-back potential, is large, and recent faster regional growth could accelerate. For example, countries in past or current heightened conflict (Nepal, Pakistan, and Sri Lanka) have tended to show slower growth—with a differential of 2 to 3 percentage points of annual GDP growth.[1] Second, countries would integrate faster and trade more. When differentiated by two groups—conflict affected compared to others—the former showed sharply slowing trade-to-GDP ratios throughout the past decade, becoming markedly less open, while the opposite was the case for the others. The transition was especially marked after 2003, when the average trade-to-GDP ratio climbs to over 70 percent for the nonconflict countries (unweighted average), while the ratio for the conflict-affected group falls to about 50 percent by 2008—a 20 percentage point gap. The reasons that conflict reduced trade are rising risk-aversion of trade partners; higher transaction costs, such as higher insurance risk premiums on international shipping; and reduced trade financing.

This is consistent with broader findings in the literature that suggest that conflict has a powerful negative effect on trade (using a gravity model for a large set of countries for trade in 1999–2000 and an internationally comparable Heidelberg conflict-intensity index) (Pasteels, Fontagné, and Brauer 2003) (figure 23.9, panel a). The effect of conflict in that study was calculated as equivalent to a 33 percent tariff barrier and additive to other factors. There is also evidence of the opposite— that increased trade between partners reduces the probability of conflict (O'Neal and Russett 1999) (figure 23.9, panel b). But the worst is when partners do not trade. One study, for example, finds that contiguity enhances conflict when contiguous states conduct little trade (Chang, Polachek, and Robst 2004).

Figure 23.9 Conflict Reduces GDP Growth

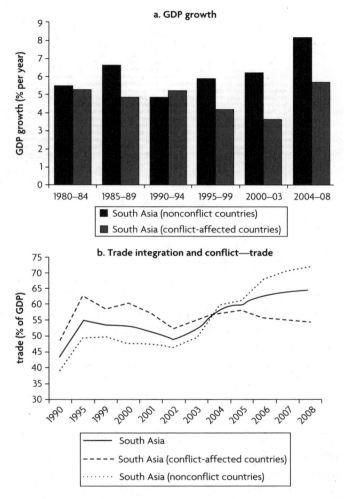

Source: World Bank 2010c.
Note: Conflict-affected countries include Nepal, Pakistan, and Sri Lanka but not Afghanistan. Maldives' weight is adjusted by a factor of 0.4. Simple unweighted averages are used.

Reaping the Demographic Dividend. As figure 23.10 shows, South Asia's changing population pyramid will bring about a growing young labor force, which for the region could turn out to be a blessing or a curse. Without urgent action, the potential demographic dividend from about 150 million entrants into the labor force over the next decade could

Figure 23.10 The Changing Population Pyramid in South Asia

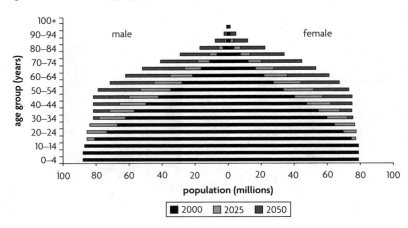

Source: U.S. Census Bureau International Database, Population Projections. http://www.census.gov/ipc/www/idb/informationGateway.php.

become a liability. For assurance that South Asia reaps the demographic dividend, attention needs to be given to labor demand (creating more and better jobs), labor supply (improving the technical skills and education of the labor force), and labor market functioning (providing for efficient matching of labor supply and demand through regulations and mobility).

Despite high growth in South Asia, workers are often trapped in low-wage, low-productivity jobs. In the addressing of this issue, a key challenge will be to increase the productivity of the large number of workers in the agricultural sector and facilitate the transition of surplus labor from agriculture to more productive sectors. Policy makers will also have to address the economic factors that are keeping firms small and informal. In terms of labor supply, it is important to understand that half of the population in South Asia is illiterate. Except for the Maldives and Sri Lanka, less than 20 percent have reached twelfth grade, and the average schooling is only four to five years. Skills bottlenecks are emerging, as revealed by increasing returns to secondary and tertiary education relative to lower levels. Returns to education in South Asia are high, but there are low enrollment levels at the secondary and tertiary levels and low levels of vocational training. South Asia therefore needs to improve the quality and accessibility of education and training systems so that new entrants are able to respond to the demand for higher skills.

At the same time, informality is rampant (estimated at over 80 percent of employment in India), and the problems with formal-market regulations affect both the formal and the informal sectors. Within countries, the persistence of productivity differentials across sectors and locations (rural and urban) indicates significant constraints to both professional and geographic mobility. Policy makers therefore need to first identify the obstacles to mobility across jobs, sectors, and locations, and then take action to remove them.

Accelerating Spatial Transformation. It is a paradox that South Asia, which is among the most densely populated regions in the world, is also among the least urbanized. Figure 23.11 compares urbanization rates with income in more than 100 countries. It shows that urbanization rates (as measured by the share of the urban population in the total population) are positively associated with real per capita income. Spatial transformations that give rise to urbanization accelerate growth because households and firms benefit from economies of scale, mobility, and specialization. Increased urbanization contributes to productivity, which in turn is associated with higher growth and poverty reduction. This can indeed become a virtuous circle.

The paradox of India is that the urbanization rate is low—less than 30 percent of the total population lives in urban areas compared to 40 percent in China. In 2005, only 11 percent of the total Indian population lived in cities with a population of more than 1 million compared to nearly twice that percentage in China. China has many more cities than India, which is significantly underurbanized given its level of income. Nepal and Sri Lanka are among the least urbanized countries in the world; in fact, all South Asian countries are well below the urbanization line that is expected for each level of GDP per capita.

The urban population of South Asia will double over the next 20 years, so the region will need to devote more resources and leadership to develop the infrastructure necessary for urbanization. Jobs, education,

Figure 23.11 Much Lower Urbanization Rates in South Asia, 2005

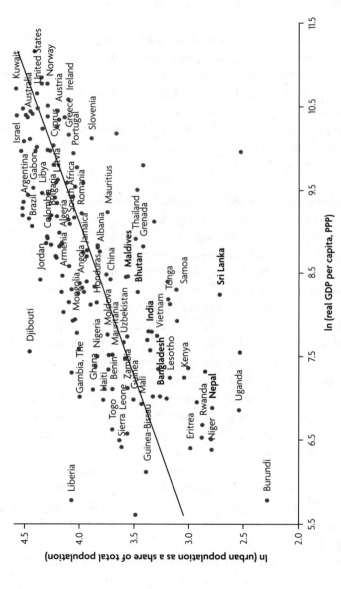

Source: World Bank 2010c.

health, and infrastructure are all strategic objectives closely intertwined with cities. If managed well, urbanization can be a key driver of long-term economic growth.

Note

1. Insecurity and conflict affect all countries in the region to varying degrees, and the exact classification is debatable; nevertheless, these growth differentials emerge within countries as well as in the lagging states in India.

Bibliography

Adam, C., and D. Bevan. 2002. "Fiscal Deficits and Growth in Developing Countries." University of Oxford Discussion Papers, Cambridge, United Kingdom.

Blanchard, O., G. Dell'Ariccia, and P. Mauro. 2010. "Rethinking Macroeconomic Policy." IMF Staff Position Note SPN/10/03, International Monetary Fund, Washington, DC.

Business Standard. 2010. "PM's Plainspeaking," March 27. New Delhi.

Chang, Y.-C., S. W. Polachek, and J. Robst. 2004. "Conflict and Trade: The Relationship between Geographic Distance and International Interactions." *Journal of Socio-Economics* 33 (4): 491–509.

Easterly, W., and K. Schmidt-Hebbel. 1993. "Fiscal Deficits and Macroeconomic Performance in Developing Countries." *World Bank Research Observer* 8 (2): 211–37.

Engen, E., and R. G. Hubbard. 2004. "Federal Government Debt and Interest Rates." NBER Working Paper 10681, National Bureau of Economic Research, Cambridge, MA.

Ghani, E., and R. Anand. 2009. "How Will Changes in Globalization Impact South Asia?" Policy Research Working Paper 5079, World Bank, Washington, DC.

Global Terrorism Database II, 1998–2004. 2008. http://www.icpsr.umich.edu/icpsr-web/TPDRC/studies/22600.

Laubach, T. 2007. "New Evidence on the Interest Rate Effects of Budget Deficits and Debt." Staff Working Paper 2003-12, Finance and Economics Discussion Series, National Federal Reserve Board, Washington, DC.

O'Neal, J., and R. Russett. 1999. "Assessing the Liberal Peace with Alternative Specifications: Trade Still Reduces Conflict." *Journal of Peace Research* 36 (3): 423–42.

Pasteels, J.-M., L. Fontagné, and J. Brauer. 2003. "Conflict and Trade." Paper for the 7th Annual Conference on Economics and Security, University of Bristol, United Kingdom, June 26–28.

Reinhart, C., and K. Rogoff. 2010. "Growth in a Time of Debt." NBER Working Paper 15639, National Bureau of Economic Research, Cambridge, MA.

World Bank. 2010a. *Global Economic Prospects 2010: Crisis, Finance, and Growth.* Washington, DC: World Bank.

———. 2010b. "South Asia Economic Update 2010: Moving Up, Looking East." World Bank, Washington, DC.

———. 2010c. "Six Monthly Growth Outlook for South Asia." World Bank, Washington, DC.

About the Editors and Authors

Luca Barbone is Director of the Poverty Reduction and Economic Management (PREM) Department of the Europe and Central Asia (ECA) Region of the World Bank. Mr. Barbone joined the World Bank in 1988 as an Economist in the Latin America and the Caribbean Region, and has held a number of positions in the Europe and Central Asia and the Africa Regions of the Bank. During 2000–04, he was World Bank Director for Ukraine, Moldova, and Belarus; during 2004–07, he was the Director for Poverty Reduction, PREM Network. Prior to the World Bank, Mr. Barbone worked for the Organisation for Economic Co-operation and Development (Paris), the International Monetary Fund, the Planning Institute of Jamaica, and the Bank of Italy. He holds a bachelor's degree in economics from the Milan Bocconi University and a Ph.D. in economics from the Massachusetts Institute of Technology. Mr. Barbone has published a number of books and articles in professional journals. He speaks Italian, English, French, Spanish, and Russian.

Milan Brahmbhatt is Senior Adviser in the World Bank's Poverty Reduction and Economic Management (PREM) Network. In this capacity, he advises and leads work on a wide range of issues, including policy responses to the global financial crisis, fiscal policy for growth and development, and economic policy aspects of climate change and other environmental issues. In previous positions at the Bank, Mr. Brahmbhatt has been adviser to the Chief Economist of the World Bank's East Asia and Pacific Region and was leader of the global economic prospects and forecasting team in the Bank's Development Economics Department. Before joining the Bank, he was a research manager at DRI/McGraw-Hill, where he consulted on international economic, trade, and environmental issues with corporate and government clients. In addition he, was the director for DRI's Asian Economic Service, where he focused on macroeconomic prospects for Asian economies. Mr. Brahmbhatt holds an M.Sc. from the London School of Economics and Political Science and is a former member of the Institute of Chartered Accountants in England and Wales.

Jim Brumby is Sector Manager, Public Sector and Governance, at the World Bank. He has been engaged in public management reform at the state, national, and international levels for 27 years. Prior to joining the Bank in 2007, Mr. Brumby spent three years as head of the internal Budget Reform Division of the International Monetary Fund (IMF) and five years in the IMF's Fiscal Affairs Department while working on public expenditure management and providing technical assistance to many countries, including Bulgaria, China, Ghana, Indonesia, Malawi, Nigeria, the Slovak Republic, and Slovenia. He has also contributed to fiscal transparency reports on Italy, Malawi, and the United States and has played a leading role in assessing public expenditure management systems in heavily indebted poor countries. Prior to joining the IMF, he was in charge of the Organisation for Economic Co-operation and Development's program on budgeting and management in member countries. Mr. Brumby also worked in the New Zealand Treasury for four years as head of its unit that provides advice on public service reform. Before that time, he worked at the central finance ministry of the State of Victoria in Australia. He has a master's degree in public administration from Harvard University.

Mayra Buvinic is Sector Director for gender and development at the Poverty Reduction and Economic Management (PREM) Network of the World Bank. Between 1996 and 2004, she was division chief for social development at the Inter-American Development Bank (IDB), where she oversaw work on the social sectors, including health, urban development, labor markets, early childhood development, social inclusion, and violence prevention, as well as on both the Women in Development Unit and the Indigenous Peoples Unit. Prior to working at the IDB, Ms. Buvinic was a founding member and president of the International Center for Research on Women. She is past president of the Association for Women's Rights in Development (AWID) and a member of a number of nonprofit boards, including the International Water Rights Management Institute (Sri Lanka) and the International Institute of Tropical Agriculture (Nigeria). A Chilean national, her published works are in the areas of gender, poverty, and development; health and reproductive health; aggression and violence prevention; social inclusion and cohesion; and project and program evaluations. Ms. Buvinic holds a Ph.D. in social psychology from the University of Wisconsin at Madison.

Otaviano Canuto is Vice President and Head of the Poverty Reduction and Economic Management (PREM) Network of the World Bank, a division of more than 700 economists and other professionals working on economic policy, poverty reduction, and analytic work for the Bank's client countries. He assumed his position in May 2009, after serving as the Vice President for Countries at the Inter-American Development Bank since June 2007. Dr. Canuto provides strategic leadership and direction on economic policy formulation in the area of growth and poverty, debt, trade, gender, and public sector management and governance. He is involved in managing the Bank's overall interactions with key partner institutions, including the International Monetary Fund, the Organisation for Economic Co-operation and Development, and regional development banks. Dr. Canuto has lectured and written widely on economic growth, financial crisis management, and regional development, with recent work on financial crisis and economic growth in Latin America. He speaks Portuguese, English, French, and Spanish.

Jeff Chelsky has served as a Senior Economist in the International Policy and Partnerships Group of the Poverty Reduction and Economic Management (PREM) Network of the World Bank since June 2008, where International Monetary Fund (IMF)–World Bank collaboration is among his main responsibilities. Prior to coming to the Bank, he worked in various capacities at the IMF, including as Senior Adviser to the Executive Director representing Canada, Ireland, and the Caribbean; on staff; and in the Independent Evaluation Office, where he did extensive work on IMF governance. Before coming to Washington, D.C., Mr. Chelsky worked as a senior economist and senior project leader for Industry Canada and for the Canadian Department of Finance. He is a graduate of the University of Toronto and Queen's University.

Stefano Curto is a Senior Economist in the International Policy and Partnerships Group of the Poverty Reduction and Economic Management (PREM)

Network of the World Bank, where he works on international policy issues relevant to a set of external partners and shareholders, including the G-8, the G-20, the G-24, Asia-Pacific Economic Cooperation (APEC), the Organisation for Economic Co-operation and Development, and the United Nations. He previously worked at the European Central Bank (ECB), focusing on macroeconomic and financial issues in emerging markets, and at the Overseas Development Institute, concentrating on regional trade and foreign direct investment to developing countries. Mr. Curto holds degrees from the University of Rome, the University of Glasgow, and the Kiel Institute of World Economics with a special focus on international economics.

Dipak Dasgupta is Lead Economist for the World Bank's South Asia Region. Immediately prior to this position, he was the World Bank's Lead Economist for India, based at the Bank's New Delhi Office from 2006 to 2009. Mr. Dasgupta joined the World Bank in 1981 as a Young Professional. He has worked on a number of other countries, including Bangladesh, Brazil, China, Indonesia, the Islamic Republic of Iran, Jordan, and Thailand; in several regions; and in the Bank's research department. Before joining the South Asia Region, he was Sector Manager for the Middle East and North Africa Region, and before that, he was Lead Economist in the Bank's Development Prospects Group. He is an expert on economic management, financial crises, poverty reduction, agriculture, globalization, trade, and capital flows. Mr. Dasgupta was educated at Delhi and Cambridge universities and has taught and published widely. He is the principal author of five World Bank flagship reports: *China Engaged; Global Economic Prospects and the Devloping Countries 1998/99: Beyond Financial Crises; Global Development Finance 2000*; the flagship MENA Development Report of *Trade, Investment, and Development in the Middle East and North Africa*; and the newly released first *South Asia Update 2010: Moving Up, Looking East*. He is also the author or editor of several books and more than 100 articles and lectures. Mr. Dasgupta won the Adam Smith prize at Cambridge University and is a recipient of the Bronze Award of the AMEX Bank Review essays in international finance.

Augusto de la Torre is the Chief Economist for Latin America and the Caribbean Region at the World Bank. Since joining the Bank in 1997, he has held the positions of Senior Adviser in the Financial Systems Department and Senior Financial Sector Adviser, both in the Latin America and the Caribbean Region. From 1993 to 1997, Mr. de la Torre was the head of the Central Bank of Ecuador, and in November 1996, he was chosen by *Euromoney Magazine* as the year's "Best Latin Central Banker." From 1986 to 1992, he worked at the International Monetary Fund (IMF), where, among other positions, he was the IMF's Resident Representative in Venezuela (1991–92). Mr. de la Torre has published extensively on a broad range of macroeconomic and financial development topics. He is a member of the Carnegie Network of Economic Reformers. He earned his M.A. and Ph.D. in economics at the University of Notre Dame and holds a bachelor's degree in philosophy from the Catholic University of Ecuador.

Shantayanan Devarajan is the Chief Economist of the World Bank's Africa Region. Since joining the World Bank in 1991, he has been a Principal Economist and Research Manager for Public Economics in the Development Research Group and the Chief Economist of the Human Development Network and of the South Asia Region. He was the director of the *World Development Report 2004: Making Services Work for Poor People*. Before 1991, he was on the faculty of Harvard University's John F. Kennedy School of Government. He is coauthor of more than 100 publications. His research covers public economics, trade policy, natural resources and the environment, and general equilibrium modeling of developing countries. Born in Sri Lanka, Mr. Devarajan received his B.A. in mathematics from Princeton University and his Ph.D. in economics from the University of California, Berkeley.

Mark A. Dutz is leading the work program on innovation and inclusive growth in the Economic Policy and Debt Department of the World Bank's Poverty Reduction and Economic Management (PREM) Network. As part of the Bank's recent work on business and government-business relations, he was lead author and editor of *Unleashing India's Innovation: Toward Sustainable and Inclusive Growth,* which has been translated into Chinese, Hindi, and Japanese. Dr. Dutz has worked in all geographic regions of the Bank Group and in the Office of the Chief Economist. His experiences outside the World Bank include Senior Consultant with Compass-Lexecon, a private sector consulting firm, where he focused on intellectual property, innovation, antitrust, and information and communications technology issues; Senior Adviser to the State Minister of Economy, where he concentrated on infrastructure and private sector development issues in Ankara, Turkey; Principal Economist in the Office of the Chief Economist, European Bank for Reconstruction and Development in London, where he had responsibilities for policy and research work on investment climate, competition policy, and regulatory issues for transition economies; and consultant to the Organisation for Economic Co-operation and Development's Competition Division, to the World Trade Organization, and to the World Intellectual Property Organization (WIPO). Dr. Dutz has taught at Princeton University and has published articles in journals and monographs in applied microeconomics, including industrial organization, international trade, competition, intellectual property, and innovation issues, as well as in public policy toward network industries. He holds a Ph.D. in economics from Princeton University and a Master's degree in public affairs from Princeton's Woodrow Wilson School. He speaks German, English, French, Spanish, and Turkish.

Thomas Farole is a Senior Economist in the International Trade Department of the World Bank, where his work focuses on export competitiveness, foreign direct investment, and the relationship between trade and lagging regions within countries. Prior to joining the World Bank, Mr. Farole was Regional Director for the South African consultancy Kaiser Economic Development. He holds a Ph.D. in economic geography from the London School of Economics and Political Science (LSE), an M.Sc. in local economic development, also from LSE, and a B.Sc. in economics from the Wharton School of the University of Pennsylvania.

Ejaz Ghani is Economic Adviser in the South Asia Poverty Reduction and Economic Management (PREM) Unit of the World Bank. He has worked in different units of the World Bank Group, including Corporate Strategy, the Independent Evaluation Unit, the East Asia Region, and the Africa Region. Mr. Ghani provided support to Indonesia, Malaysia, and Thailand during the East Asia financial crisis and was involved with starting the policy dialogue with the Bihar government (India). He has edited several books, including *The Service Revolution in South Asia* (Oxford University Press), *Accelerating Growth and Job Creation in South Asia* (Oxford University Press), *Promoting Regional Cooperation in South Asia: Beyond SAFTA* (Sage), and *South Asia: Growth and Regional Integration* (Macmillan). Before joining the World Bank, he taught Economics at Oxford University (United Kingdom) and Delhi University (India). He has an M.Phil. and a D. Phil. in economics from Oxford University. Mr. Ghani was an Inlaks scholar at Oxford University and President of St. Stephen's College Student's Union Society, Delhi.

Marcelo Giugale is the World Bank's Director of Economic Policy and Poverty Reduction Programs for Latin America. An international development leader, his 20 years of experience span the Middle East, Eastern Europe, Central Asia, and Latin America, where he led senior-level policy dialogue and more than US$15 billion in lending operations across the development spectrum. Mr. Giugale has published widely on economic policy, finance, development economics, business, agriculture, and applied econometrics. Notably, he was the chief editor of collections of policy notes published for the presidential transitions in Mexico (2000), Colombia (2002), Ecuador (2003), Bolivia (2006), and Peru (2006). His opinion editorials are published in the leading newspapers of Latin America and the United States. He received decorations from the governments of Bolivia and Peru and taught at the American University in Cairo, The London School of Economics and Political Science, and the Universidad Católica Argentina. A citizen of both Argentina and Italy, Mr. Giugale holds a Ph.D. and an M.Sc. in economics from The London School of Economics and Political Science and a B.A. in economics, summa cum laude, from the Universidad Católica Argentina.

Sudarshan Gooptu is Acting Director, Economic Policy and Debt Department in the Poverty Reduction and Economic Management (PREM) Network of the World Bank. He joined the Bank in 1988. Mr. Gooptu has since held several positions in the Bank's Africa and East Asia and Pacific Regional Vice Presidencies (including a field assignment in Ethiopia), worked on debt and debt service reduction operations in the Cofinancing and Financial Advisory Services Vice Presidency, and conducted policy research in the Development Economics Vice Presidency. Immediately before becoming the Sector Manager for his current department in PREM in 2008, he was the Bank's Lead Economist for China and Mongolia at its headquarters in Washington, D.C. An open-economy macroeconomist by training, Mr. Gooptu has a Ph.D. in economics from the University of Illinois, Urbana-Champaign.

Mona E. Haddad is Sector Manager, International Trade Department, of the World Bank Group. In that capacity, Ms. Haddad manages the group responsible for supporting the development and implementation of trade-related activities at both the country and the regional levels. These activities include trade policy analysis, competitiveness, trade facilitation, and standards. Prior to joining the Trade Department, Ms. Haddad was the Regional Trade Coordinator for the East Asia Region, where she worked on trade issues in various countries, including China, Indonesia, the Lao People's Democratic Republic, and Vietnam. She has a Ph.D. from The George Washington University, Washington, DC.

Bernard Hoekman is Director of the International Trade Department at the World Bank headquarters in Washington, D.C. His previous positions at the World Bank include Research Manager of the trade and international integration team in the Development Research Group, Manager of the trade capacity-building program of the World Bank Institute, and Trade Economist in the Middle East and North Africa and the Europe and Central Asia departments. Before joining the Bank in 1993, Mr. Hoekman was an economist in the General Agreement on Tariffs and Trade (GATT) Secretariat in Geneva (1988–93), supporting the Uruguay Round negotiations. He has published widely on the GATT–World Trade Organization, trade negotiations, international trade and investment in services, trade preferences, and regional integration. Mr. Hoekman is a graduate of the Erasmus University Rotterdam, holds a Ph.D. in economics from the University of Michigan, and is a Research Fellow of the London-based Centre for Economic Policy Research. His most recent publication is *The Political Economy of the World Trading System,* 3rd edition (Oxford University Press).

Alain Ize retired from the International Monetary Fund (IMF) in 2007 after working there since 1985, first in the Fiscal Affairs Department and then in the Monetary and Financial Systems Department. He now consults for the World Bank and teaches at El Colegio de México, where he was a professor prior to joining the IMF. His main research interests and publications are in the areas of macroeconomic theory and policy, finance, central banking, financial intermediation, and prudential policy. He holds an engineering degree from l'Ecole Centrale de Paris, an M.B.A. from Columbia University, and a Ph.D. from Stanford University.

Lili Liu is Lead Economist at the Department of Economic Policy and Debt of the World Bank Group, where she manages the work program on subnational finance. The program focuses on international experiences in the sustainability of subnational finance and its links to macroeconomic frameworks, intergovernmental fiscal systems, capital market development, and infrastructure finance. The program has provided advisory services and support to the World Bank operations in numerous countries, including Brazil, China, India, Indonesia, Poland, and Turkey. Ms. Liu is the author of numerous publications and is a frequent speaker at international conferences and to visiting government delegations to the World Bank. She co-chairs the Decentralization and Subnational Regional Economics Thematic Group, a Bank-wide network, and is a member of the World Bank Group Urban and Transport Sector Boards. Previously, she led policy dialogue and lending operations in countries in the Bank's Africa and South Asia Regional Vice Presidencies. Ms. Liu holds an M.A. and a Ph.D. in economics from the University of Michigan, Ann Arbor, and a B.A. in economics from Fudan University, Shanghai.

Trine Lunde is an Economist in the Poverty Reduction and Economic Management (PREM) Network in the World Bank, where she coordinates the Bank's *Gender Action Plan: Gender as Smart Economics.* Her work focuses on gender issues in employment and health, poverty dynamics, and ethnic dimensions of poverty. Prior to joining the Bank, she worked as a management consultant in the private sector and as a consultant for the United Nations Children's Fund (UNICEF). Ms. Lunde holds a Ph.D. in international economics and development from The Johns Hopkins University and an M.Sc. in management from the École des Hautes Études Commerciales de Paris (HEC Paris).

Nick Manning is one of the leaders of the Public Sector Performance Global Expert Team of the World Bank and an Adviser in the Public Sector and Governance Group. Until March 2010, Mr. Manning was the Sector Manager for the Public Sector and Governance Unit in the World Bank for the Latin America and the Caribbean Region. Previously, he was the Head of the Public Sector Management and Performance Division at the Organisation for Economic Co-operation and Development, Lead Public Sector Management Specialist for South Asia in the World Bank, Adviser on public management to the Commonwealth Secretariat, and Senior Technical Adviser to the United Nations Development Programme (UNDP) in Lebanon. He began his public sector career in local government in the United Kingdom and, before moving to international advisory work, was Head of Strategic Planning for an inner-London Borough. Mr. Manning is Adviser to the Commonwealth Association for Public Administration and Management; a member of the editorial board of the Public Management Review; and Visiting Professor at the Herbert Simon Institute for Public Policy, Administration, and Management. He authored an extensive range of governance publications that cover developing and developed countries, especially linking public administration with public budgeting and policy management.

Ernesto May is the Director for Poverty Reduction and Economic Management (PREM), Finance and Private Sector Development in the South Asia Region of the World Bank. In this position and since November 1, 2007, he is responsible for providing strategic direction for the Bank's research and policy advice to member countries in South Asia in the areas of poverty reduction, economic policy, governance, public sector reform, finance, and private sector development. Mr. May held the position of Director in the Latin America and the Caribbean Region of the World Bank from July 2000 until September 2007. His work and research covers many areas of economic policy such as fiscal, monetary, and exchange rate policy; public sector reform; trade; financial sector and capital markets; poverty; macroeconomic management; monitoring and evaluation; and results-based public sector management. Prior to joining the World Bank, Mr. May was an Adviser to the Director-General of Income Policies in the Ministry of Finance and Assistant to the Director of Economic Studies at the Latin American Institute of Transnational Studies, both in Mexico. Mr. May holds a Ph.D. in economics from the Massachusetts Institute of Technology and a B.A. in economics from the Instituto Tecnológico Autónomo de México. He is the author of several books, including *Design of an Optimal Fiscal Reform: The Case of Mexico, Poverty in Colombia,* and *Colombia: Paving the Way for a Results-Oriented Public Sector,* and is one of the editors of *Towards the Institutionalization of Monitoring and Evaluation Systems in Latin America and the Caribbean: Proceedings of a World Bank/Inter-American Development Bank Conference.*

Sanket Mohapatra is an Economist in the Development Prospects Group of the World Bank. His research interests include international capital flows; sovereign and subsovereign ratings; poverty, inequality, and growth; and the development impact of remittances and migration. Prior to his current assignment, he worked as an economist with the Africa Region of the International Monetary Fund. He holds a Ph.D. in economics from Columbia University and a master's degree from the Delhi School of Economics.

Vikram Nehru is the Chief Economist and Director for Poverty Reduction, Economic Management, and Private and Financial Sector Development in the East Asia Region of the World Bank. He has worked in several capacities and on a number of countries, including China, Ghana, Indonesia, Malaysia, and Nigeria. His latest papers cover issues such as exogenous shocks, debt sustainability, and the development challenges of China and Indonesia. Mr. Nehru has also had extensive research experience on issues of economic growth, capital stock measurement, financial sector policy, industrial and trade policy, and the implications of global trends and developments on the economic prospects of developing countries. He earned his graduate and postgraduate degrees from Oxford University.

Carlos A. Primo Braga has been the Director, Economic Policy and Debt, in the Poverty Reduction and Economic Management (PREM) Network since January 2008. His main roles in this capacity are to provide integrated support to country programs in the areas of debt, macropolicy, and inclusive growth. During February–August 2010, he was the Acting Vice President and Corporate Secretary of the World Bank Group. He received a degree in mechanical engineering from the Instituto Tecnológico de Aeronautica (Brazil) and an M.Sc. in economics from the University of São Paulo. He holds a Ph.D. in economics from the University of Illinois, Urbana-Champaign. His most recent publications include *Innovation and Growth: Chasing a Moving Frontier* (Organisation for Economic Co-operation and Development), coedited with Vandana Chandra, Deniz Eröcal, and Pier Carlo Padoan; *Debt Relief and Beyond* (World Bank), co-edited with Doerte Doemeland; *The WTO and Accession Countries* (Edward Elgar Publishing), a two-volume work co-edited with Olivier Cattaneo; and *Trade Preference Erosion: Measurement and Policy Response* (World Bank), co-edited with Bernard Hoekman and Will Martin.

Dilip Ratha is a Lead Economist and Manager of the Migration and Remittances Team in the Development Prospects Group of the World Bank. A recognized expert on migration, remittances, and innovative financing, he is the author of the article "Workers' Remittances: An Important and Stable Source of External Development Finance," and a lead author of the World Bank flagship *Global Economic Prospects 2006: Economic Implications of Remittances and Migration*. Mr. Ratha has advised many governments and has played a role in international and intergovernmental forums, including the Global Forum on Migration and Development, the G8 Global Remittances Working Group, and the World Economic Forum Council on migration. Reflecting his deep interest in financing development in poor countries, he edited *Innovative Financing for Development*, featuring his work on shadow sovereign rating, diaspora bonds, and future-flow securitization. Prior to joining the World Bank, Mr. Ratha worked as a regional economist for Asia at Credit Agricole Indosuez; an assistant professor of economics at the Indian Institute of Management, Ahmedabad; and an economist at the Policy Group, New Delhi. He has a Ph.D. in economics from the Indian Statistical Institute, New Delhi.

Ritva Reinikka is director of the Economic Development Group in the Middle East and North Africa Region of the World Bank. Since joining the Bank in 1993 as a Country Economist in the Eastern Africa Department, she has held various positions in the Africa Region and the Development Research Group and was Co-Director of the *World Development Report 2004: Making Services Work for Poor People*. Prior to her current assignment, Ms. Reinikka was the World Bank Country Director in South Africa (including Botswana, Lesotho, Madagascar, Mauritius, Namibia, and Swaziland). Her professional and research interests include public economics, incentives, and service delivery; microfoundations of economic growth; and macroeconomic and trade policy. Prior to joining the Bank, Ms. Reinikka was a researcher at the Centre for the Study of African Economies in the University of Oxford and at the Helsinki School of Economics. She has also held operational positions at the United Nations Children's Fund (UNICEF) and with the Ministry of Foreign Affairs in Finland. She holds a Ph.D. in economics from the University of Oxford, and she has published widely on development in peer-reviewed journals and policy-oriented outlets.

José Guilherme Reis is Lead Economist with the International Trade Department of the World Bank, where he is leading a program on competitiveness. He joined the Bank in 2004, and his work has been focused on the microeconomic agenda for growth in Latin America and topics related to competitiveness. He led several studies on competitiveness and growth in Brazil, Chile, Colombia, and Costa Rica. Past positions include Secretary for Economic Policy with the Ministry of Finance in Brazil (2001–02), Chief of Economic Advisors with the Ministry of Planning and Budget (1999–2001), and Chief Economist at the Brazilian National Confederation of Industry (1992–99). Mr. Reis holds a Master's degree in economics and public finance from the Catholic University of Rio de Janeiro, where he has been Professor of the Department of Economics since 1983.

Ana Revenga is the Director of the Poverty Reduction and Equity group at the World Bank. Between 2005 and 2008, she was Lead Economist for Human Development and Manager, Labor and Social Protection, in the East Asia and Pacific Region. Prior to joining the World Bank, she worked in the Research Department of the Central Bank of Spain and taught labor and international economics at the Centro de Estudios Monetarios y Financieros. Ms. Revenga has published extensively on poverty, labor, and trade issues and has worked across a broad spectrum of low-, middle-, and high-income countries in Asia, Europe, Latin America, and North America. She has a Ph.D. in economics from Harvard University and a degree in human rights from the Law Faculty at the University of Geneva. She was one of the authors of the *World Development Report 1995: Workers in an Integrating World* and contributed to the *World Development Report 2006: Equity and Development.*

Jaime Saavedra-Chanduvi is Acting Director of the Poverty Reduction and Equity Group at the World Bank. Prior to that position, he was Manager of the Poverty and Gender Group, in the Latin America and the Caribbean Vice Presidency at the Bank. His major areas of interest include poverty reduction, inequality, labor markets, and social policies. Dr. Saavedra-Chanduvi was Executive Director and Principal Researcher at Grupo de Análisis para el Desarrollo (GRADE), a nonpartisan think tank based in Lima, and was a Principal Adviser to the Ministry of Labor and Social Promotion in Peru. He has been a consultant and researcher for the World Bank, the Economic Commission for Latin America and the Caribbean (ECLAC), the Inter-American Development Bank (IDB), and the International Labour Organization (ILO). Dr. Saavedra-Chanduvi has been President of the Executive Committee of the Network on Inequality and Poverty of the IDB–World Bank–LACEA (Latin American and Caribbean Economic Association) and a board member at the LACEA, the Nutrition Research Institute, and the National Council of Labor in Peru. He has held teaching positions at Pontificia Universidad Católica del Peru and the Universidad del Pacífico in Peru and has been a visiting researcher at the University of Toronto. Dr. Saavedra-Chanduvi holds a Ph.D. in economics from Columbia University and a B.A. in economics from the Catholic University of Peru.

Luis Servén is Senior Adviser in the World Bank's Research Department, where he manages the research program on macroeconomics and growth. He previously managed the Bank's regional research program for Latin

America and the Caribbean. Prior to joining the World Bank, Mr. Servén worked at the Fundación de Estudios de Economía Aplicada in Spain and taught at the Universidad Complutense de Madrid, the Massachusetts Institute of Technology (MIT), and the Centro de Estudios Monetarios y Financieros (CEMFI) in Madrid. He holds a Ph.D. in economics from MIT. Mr. Servén has published numerous books and journal articles on economic growth, international finance, exchange rates, fiscal policy, saving and investment, and the microeconomic foundations of macroeconomics. His recent research focuses on open economy macroeconomics, international portfolio diversification, and fiscal policy and growth.

Sudhir Shetty is Director of the Poverty Reduction and Economic Management (PREM) Department in the Africa Region of the World Bank. This group plays a key role in implementing the World Bank's Africa Action Plan, with particular emphasis on strengthening country-led efforts to ensure shared growth, on building accountable and effective institutions, and on deepening the results orientation of development strategies. Between 2001 and 2005, Mr. Shetty managed the Poverty Reduction group in the Poverty Reduction and Economic Management Vice Presidency of the Bank. He previously held a number of positions as an economist in both the Africa and the East Asia and Pacific Regions of the Bank. Prior to joining the Bank in 1987, he was an Assistant Professor of Public Policy and Economics at Duke University. Mr. Shetty has a Ph.D. in economics from Cornell University.

Nistha Sinha is an Economist in the Gender and Development division of the Poverty Reduction and Economic Management (PREM) Unit of the World Bank. She was a core team member of the *World Development Report 2007: Development and the Next Generation* and the *Global Monitoring Report 2007: Confronting the Challenges of Gender Equality and Fragile States.* Prior to joining the World Bank, Ms. Sinha worked as a Postdoctoral Research Fellow at the Economic Growth Center, Yale University (2001–03). Her work focuses on health, education, employment, infrastructure, and gender issues in low-income countries. She has a Ph.D. in economics.

Marijn Verhoeven is a Lead Economist in the Public Sector Governance unit of the Poverty Reduction and Economic Management (PREM) Unit of the World Bank. Before joining the Bank, he worked in the Fiscal Affairs Department of the International Monetary Fund (IMF), mostly on public expenditure policy issues. During 2001–04, Mr. Verhoeven also was the IMF's resident representative in Bangladesh. His areas of expertise include fiscal policy, the efficiency of government spending, social protection issues, the economics of pensions, and public-private partnerships.

Ekaterina Vostroknutova is a Senior Economist in the East Asia and Pacific Poverty Reduction and Economic Management (PREM) Unit of the World Bank. Since joining the Bank in 2003, she contributed to the *World Development Report 2005: A Better Investment Climate for Everyone* and to several other analytical products concerned with macroeconomic policy in developing countries. Ms. Vostroknutova spent three years in the field office in Vientiane as a country economist for the Lao People's Democratic Republic, where she gained firsthand experience about the development of low-income countries. Her current work focuses on regional macroeconomic issues, natural resource economics, industrial policy, and innovation. Ms. Vostroknutova holds a Ph.D. in economics from the European University Institute in Florence, Italy, where she specialized in stabilization programs during economic transitions and in time-series econometrics.

Deborah L. Wetzel joined the World Bank in 1986 as a consultant and joined the Young Professionals' Program in 1993. Since then, she has held various positions, including Sector Manager posts for the Economic Policy Group and the Public Sector Group in the Europe and Central Asia Region. Her most recent assignment has been as Lead Economist and Poverty Reduction and Economic Management (PREM) Sector Leader in Brazil for the Latin America and the Caribbean Region. Her country work experience includes Brazil, Ghana, Hungary, Ukraine, Vietnam, the Russian Federation, the Former Soviet Republics, and Zambia, as well as Central and Eastern Europe and Western Africa. As Director for the Governance and Public Sector Anchor, Ms. Wetzel provides leadership to the public economics and public finance work of the Bank, especially given current challenges facing governments. She also works on the reinvigoration of the public sector management practice and maintains institutional momentum on Governance and Anti-Corruption and Stolen Asset Recovery Implementation. Ms. Wetzel has a Ph.D. in economics from Oxford University in England. She has written on fiscal decentralization, public finance, governance, and institutions in transition countries.

Index

Boxes, figures, notes, and tables are indicated by b, f, n, and t following page numbers.